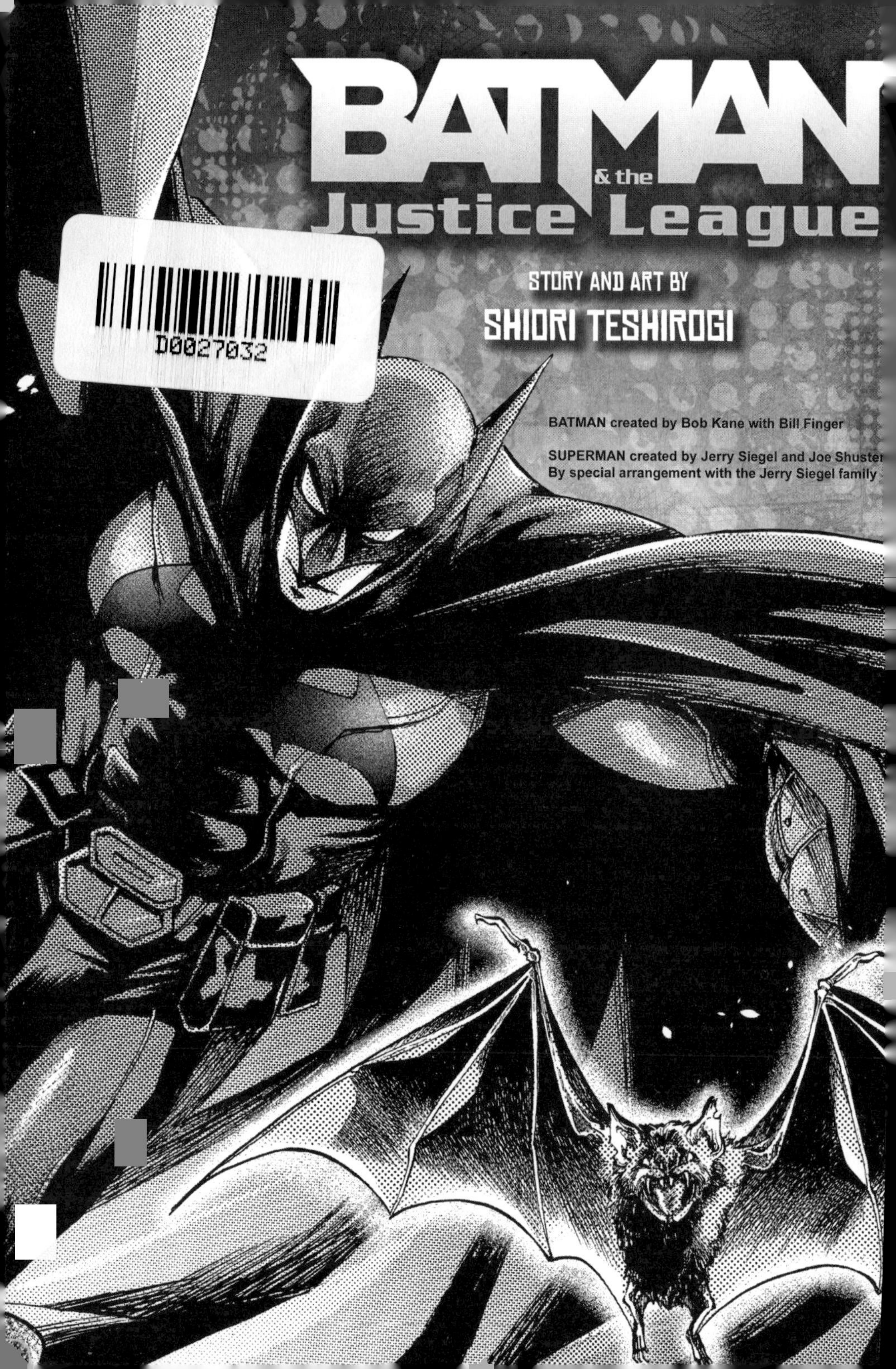
BATMAN
& the
Justice League
STORY AND ART BY
SHIORI TESHIROGI
BATMAN created by Bob Kane with Bill Finger
SUPERMAN created by Jerry Siegel and Joe Shuster
By special arrangement with the Jerry Siegel family

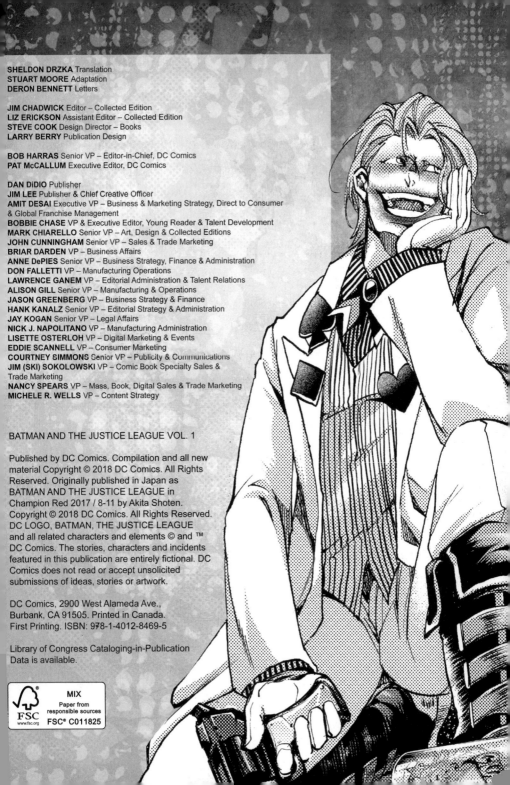

**SHELDON DRZKA** Translation
**STUART MOORE** Adaptation
**DERON BENNETT** Letters

**JIM CHADWICK** Editor – Collected Edition
**LIZ ERICKSON** Assistant Editor – Collected Edition
**STEVE COOK** Design Director – Books
**LARRY BERRY** Publication Design

**BOB HARRAS** Senior VP – Editor-in-Chief, DC Comics
**PAT McCALLUM** Executive Editor, DC Comics

**DAN DiDIO** Publisher
**JIM LEE** Publisher & Chief Creative Officer
**AMIT DESAI** Executive VP – Business & Marketing Strategy, Direct to Consumer
& Global Franchise Management
**BOBBIE CHASE** VP & Executive Editor, Young Reader & Talent Development
**MARK CHIARELLO** Senior VP – Art, Design & Collected Editions
**JOHN CUNNINGHAM** Senior VP – Sales & Trade Marketing
**BRIAR DARDEN** VP – Business Affairs
**ANNE DePIES** Senior VP – Business Strategy, Finance & Administration
**DON FALLETTI** VP – Manufacturing Operations
**LAWRENCE GANEM** VP – Editorial Administration & Talent Relations
**ALISON GILL** Senior VP – Manufacturing & Operations
**JASON GREENBERG** VP – Business Strategy & Finance
**HANK KANALZ** Senior VP – Editorial Strategy & Administration
**JAY KOGAN** Senior VP – Legal Affairs
**NICK J. NAPOLITANO** VP – Manufacturing Administration
**LISETTE OSTERLOH** VP – Digital Marketing & Events
**EDDIE SCANNELL** VP – Consumer Marketing
**COURTNEY SIMMONS** Senior VP – Publicity & Communications
**JIM (SKI) SOKOLOWSKI** VP – Comic Book Specialty Sales &
Trade Marketing
**NANCY SPEARS** VP – Mass, Book, Digital Sales & Trade Marketing
**MICHELE R. WELLS** VP – Content Strategy

BATMAN AND THE JUSTICE LEAGUE VOL. 1

DC Comics, 2900 West Alameda Ave.,
Burbank, CA 91505. Printed in Canada.
First Printing. ISBN: 978-1-4012-8469-5

Library of Congress Cataloging-in-Publication
Data is available.

# CHAPTER 1

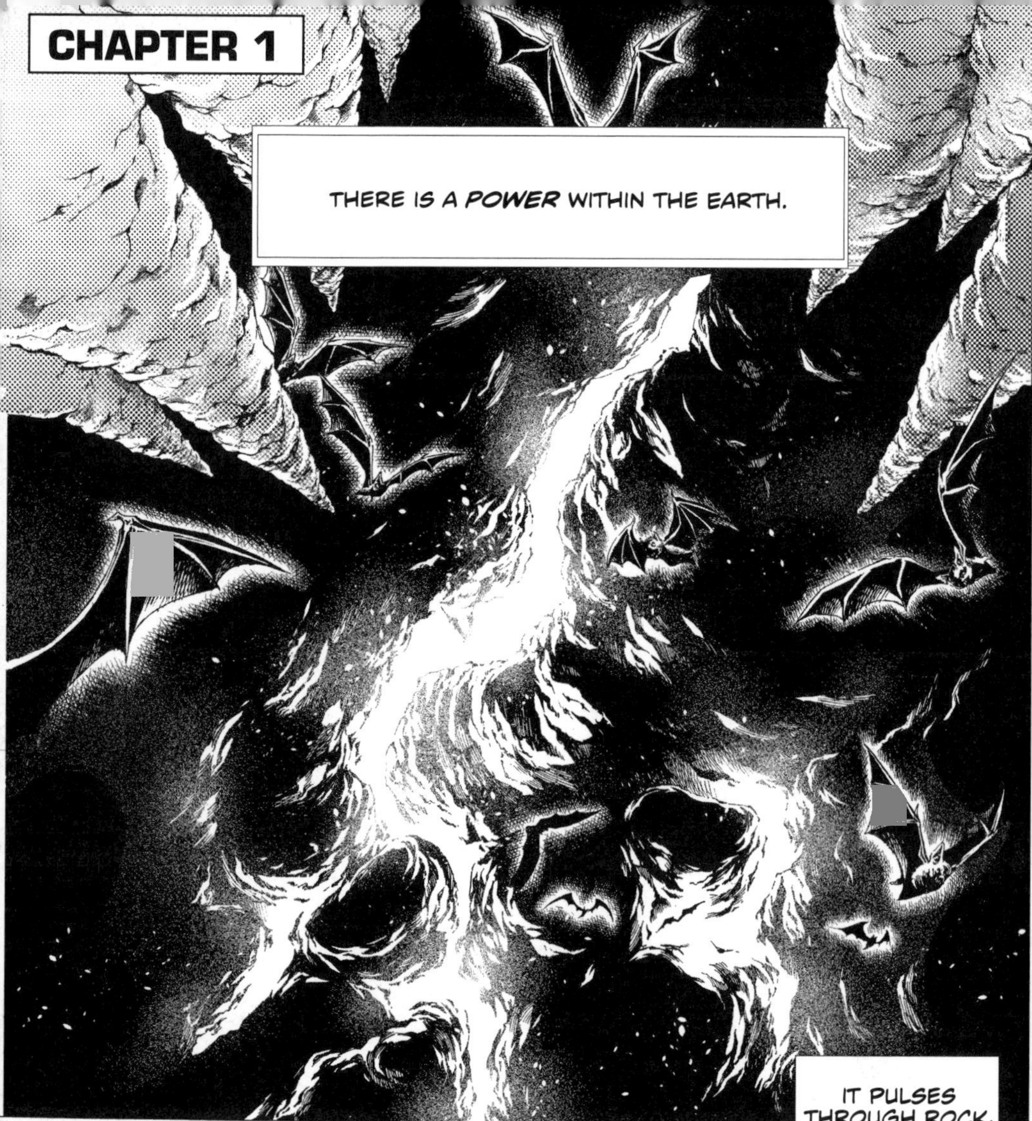
THERE IS A *POWER* WITHIN THE EARTH.

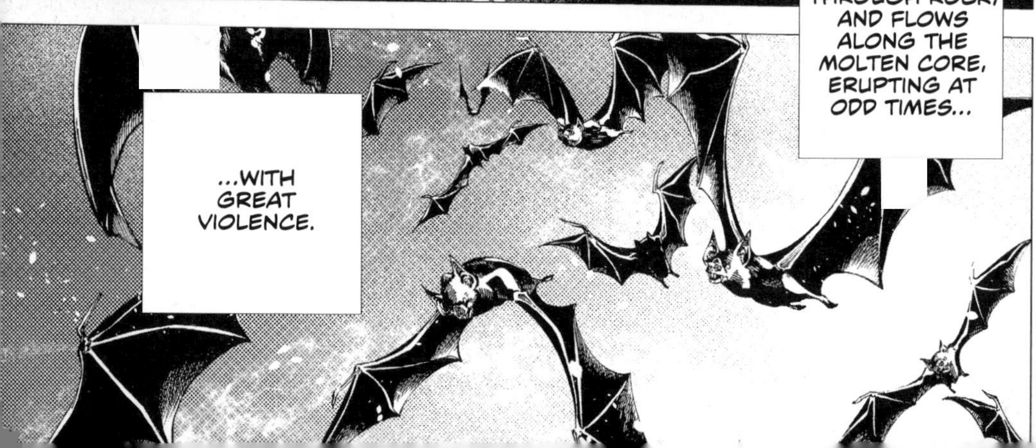
IT PULSES THROUGH ROCK, AND FLOWS ALONG THE MOLTEN CORE, ERUPTING AT ODD TIMES...
...WITH GREAT VIOLENCE.

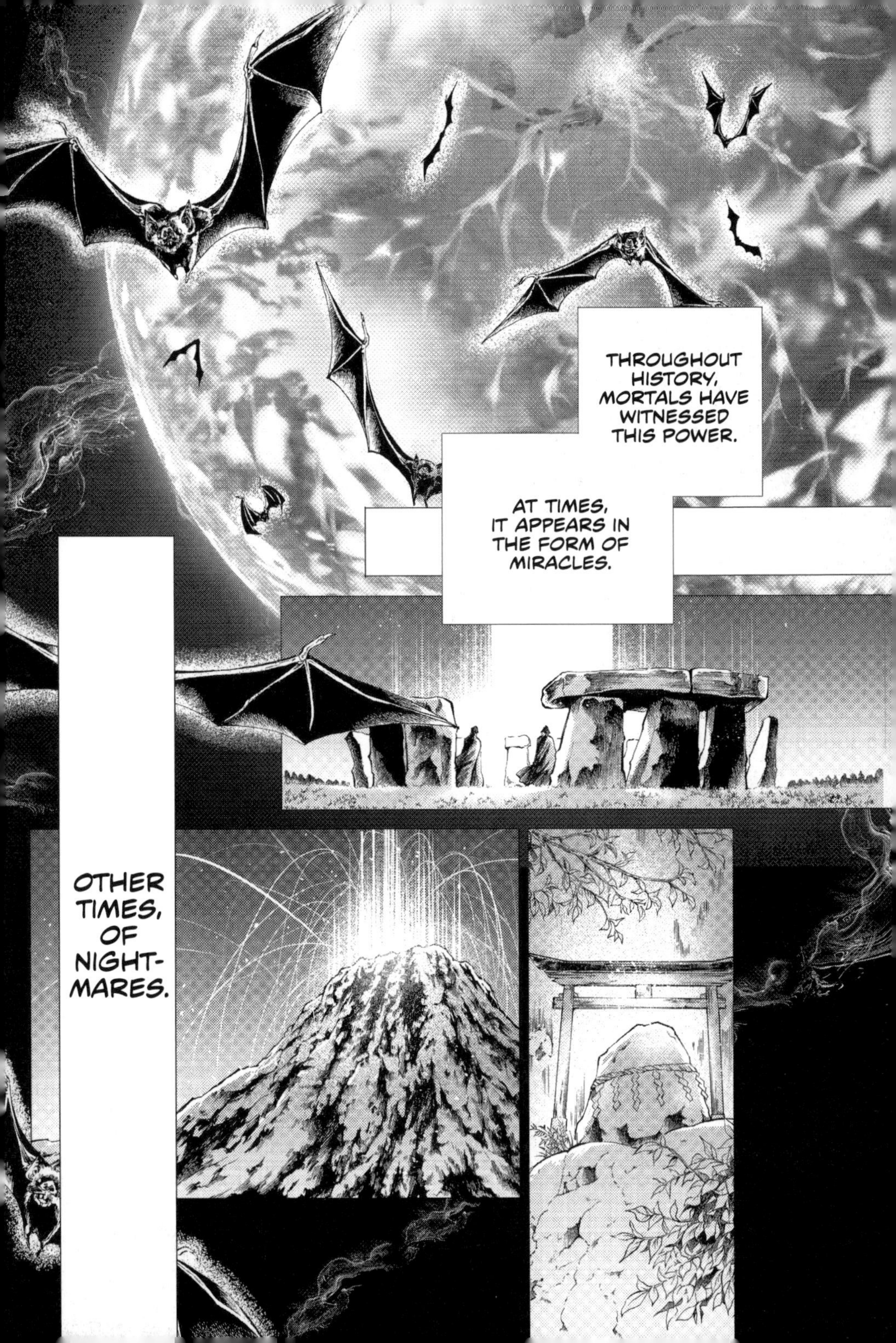
THROUGHOUT HISTORY, MORTALS HAVE WITNESSED THIS POWER.
AT TIMES, IT APPEARS IN THE FORM OF MIRACLES.
OTHER TIMES, OF NIGHT-MARES.

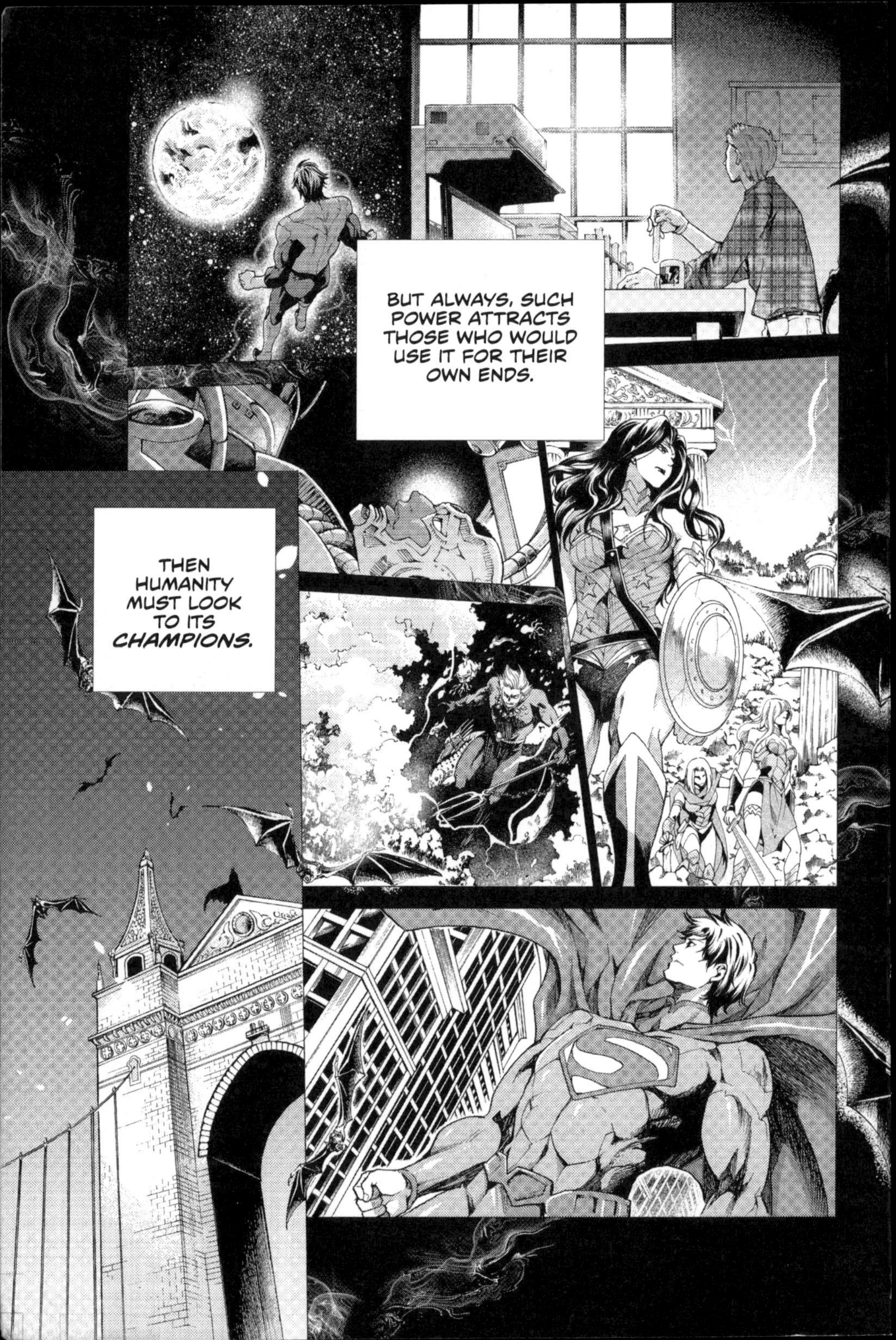

BUT ALWAYS, SUCH POWER ATTRACTS THOSE WHO WOULD USE IT FOR THEIR OWN ENDS.
THEN HUMANITY MUST LOOK TO ITS *CHAMPIONS.*

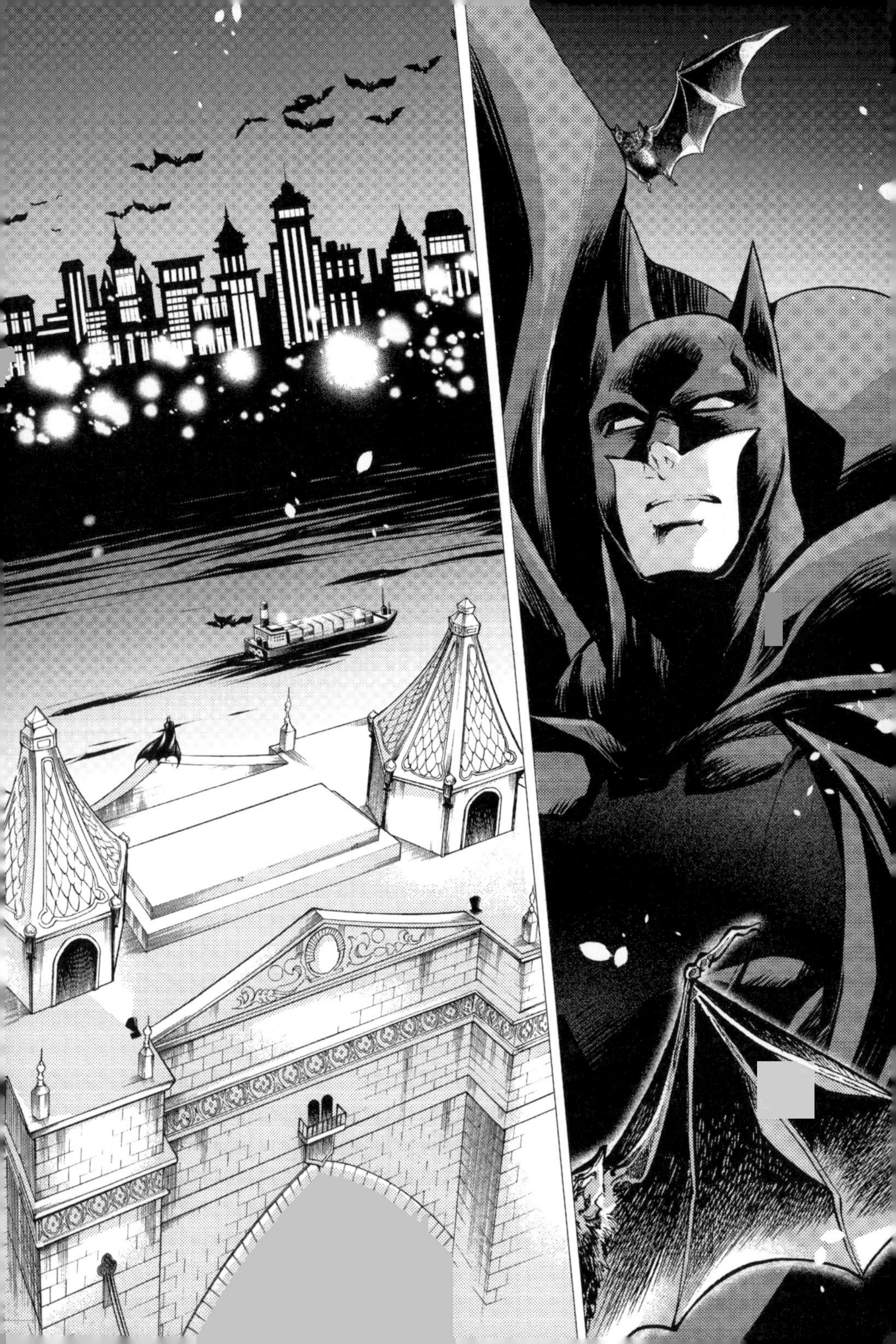

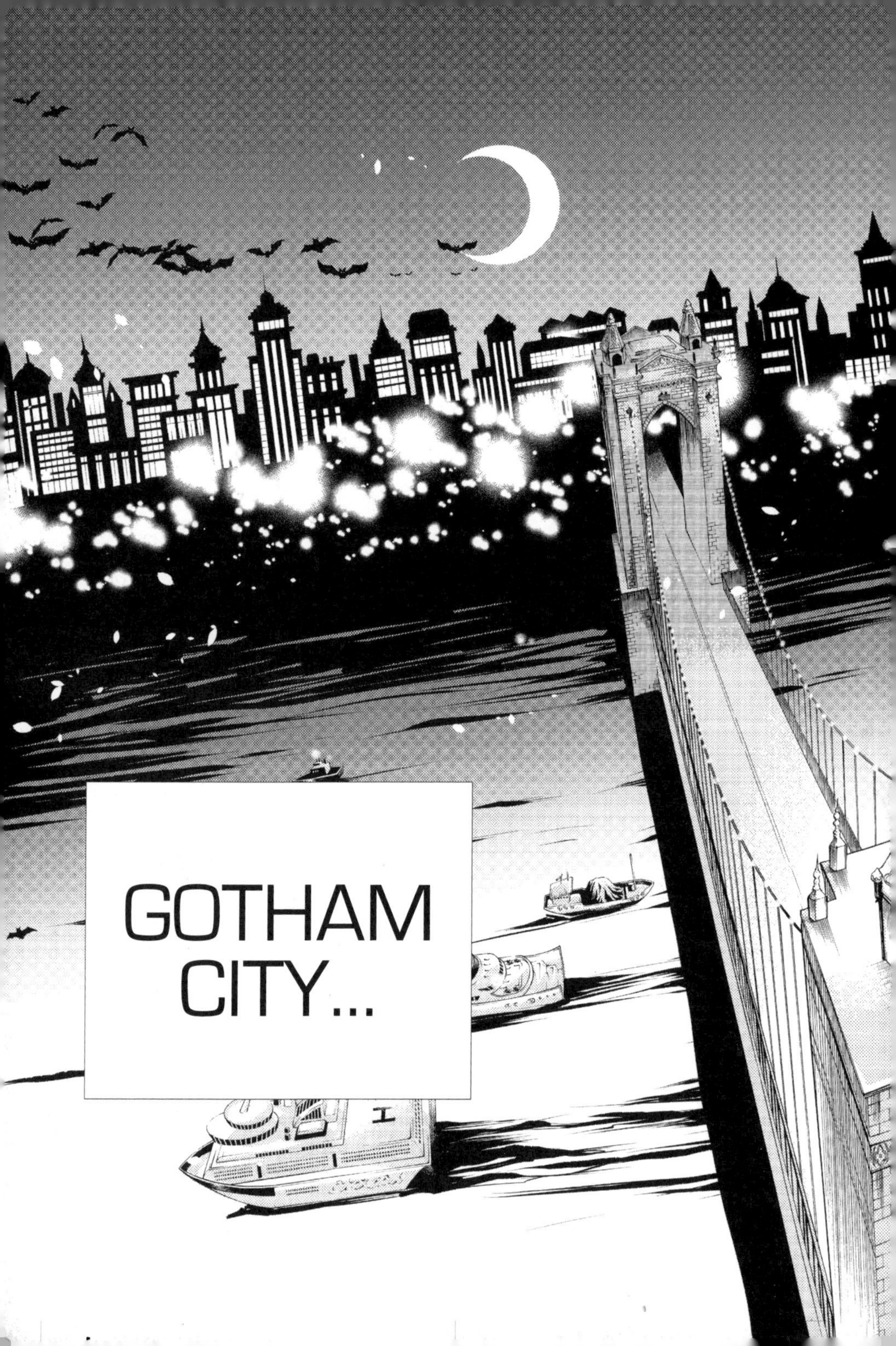
GOTHAM CITY...

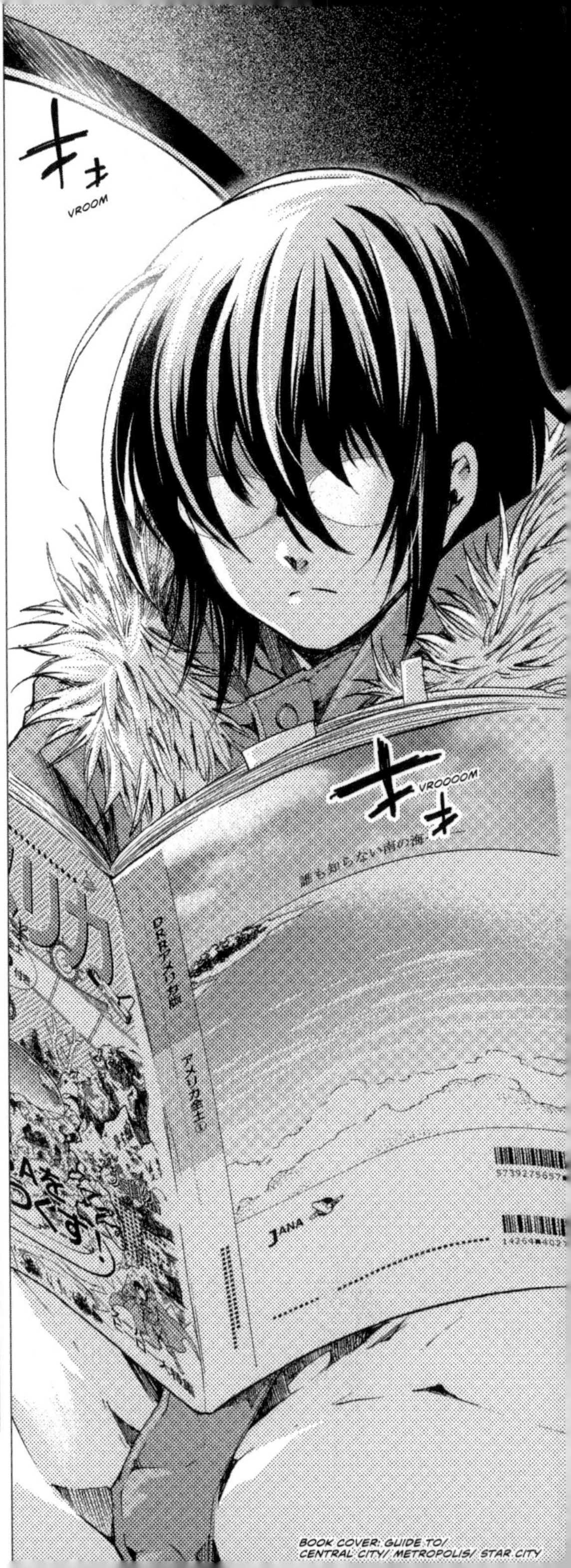
VROOM
VROOOOM
誰も知らない南の海
BOOK COVER: GUIDE TO/ CENTRAL CITY/ METROPOLIS/ STAR CITY

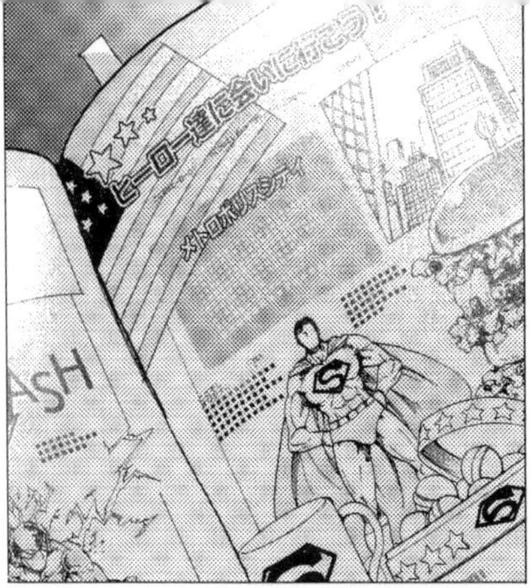
ヒーロー達に会いに行こう!
メトロポリスシティ
BOOK: CITY OF HEROES/ METROPOLIS

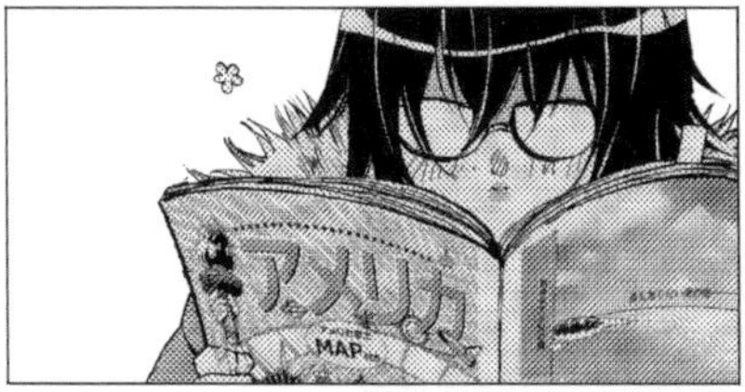
アメリカ
MAP
BOOK: WANDERING TRAVELS MAP

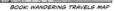

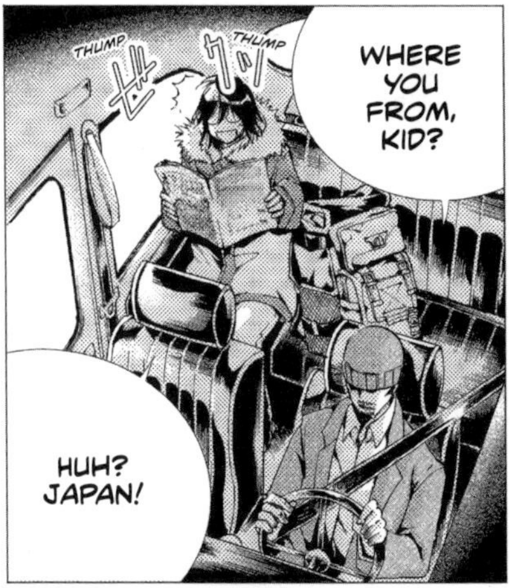
WHERE YOU FROM, KID?
THUMP
THUMP
HUH? JAPAN!

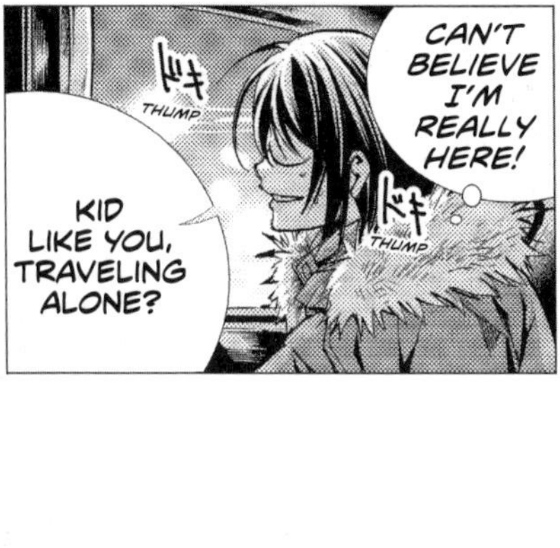
CAN'T BELIEVE I'M REALLY HERE!
ドキ
THUMP
ドキ
THUMP
KID LIKE YOU, TRAVELING ALONE?

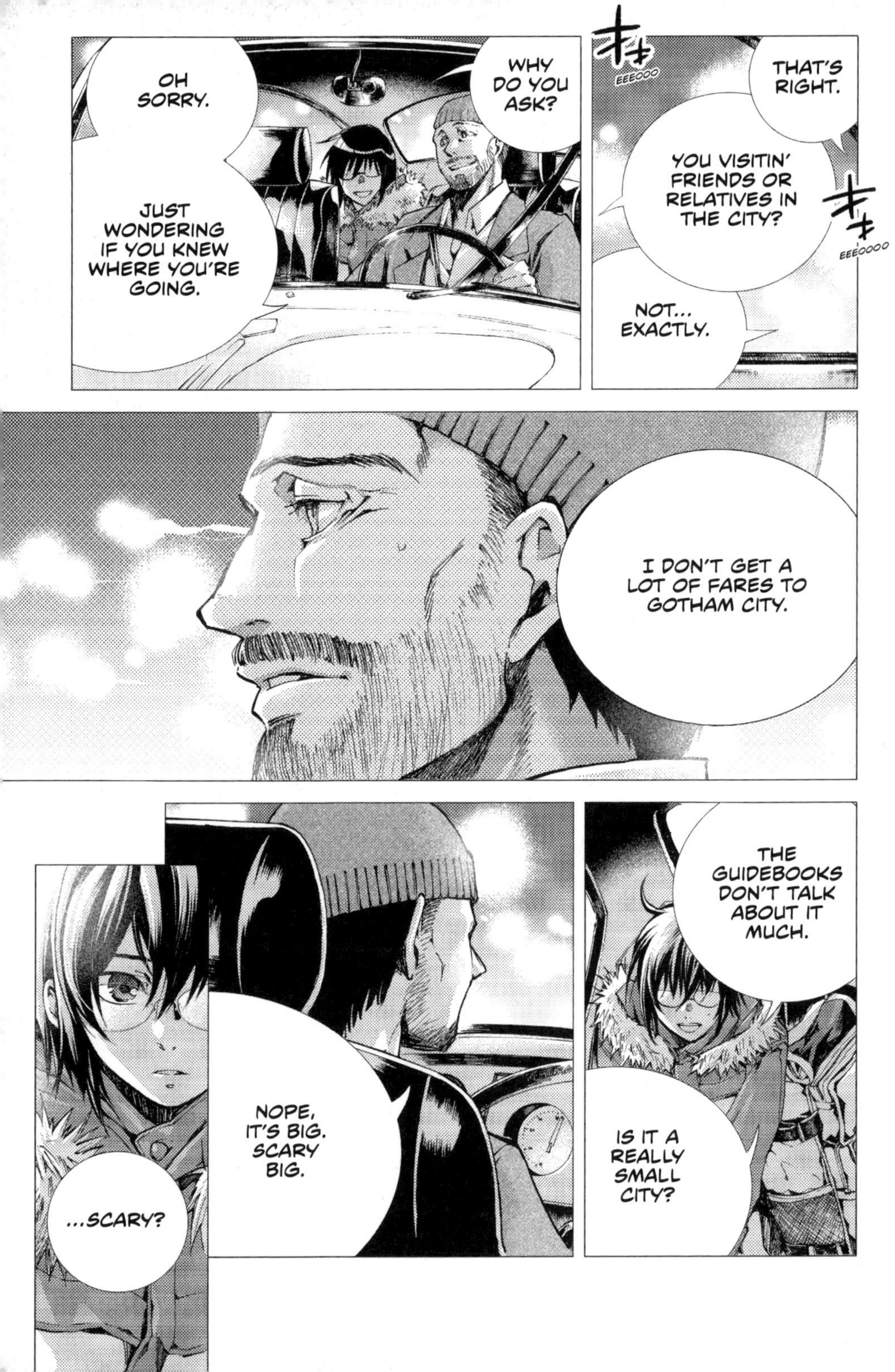
THAT'S RIGHT.
EEEOOO
YOU VISITIN' FRIENDS OR RELATIVES IN THE CITY?
EEEOOOO
NOT... EXACTLY.
WHY DO YOU ASK?
OH SORRY.
JUST WONDERING IF YOU KNEW WHERE YOU'RE GOING.
I DON'T GET A LOT OF FARES TO GOTHAM CITY.
THE GUIDEBOOKS DON'T TALK ABOUT IT MUCH.
IS IT A REALLY SMALL CITY?
NOPE, IT'S BIG. SCARY BIG.
...SCARY?

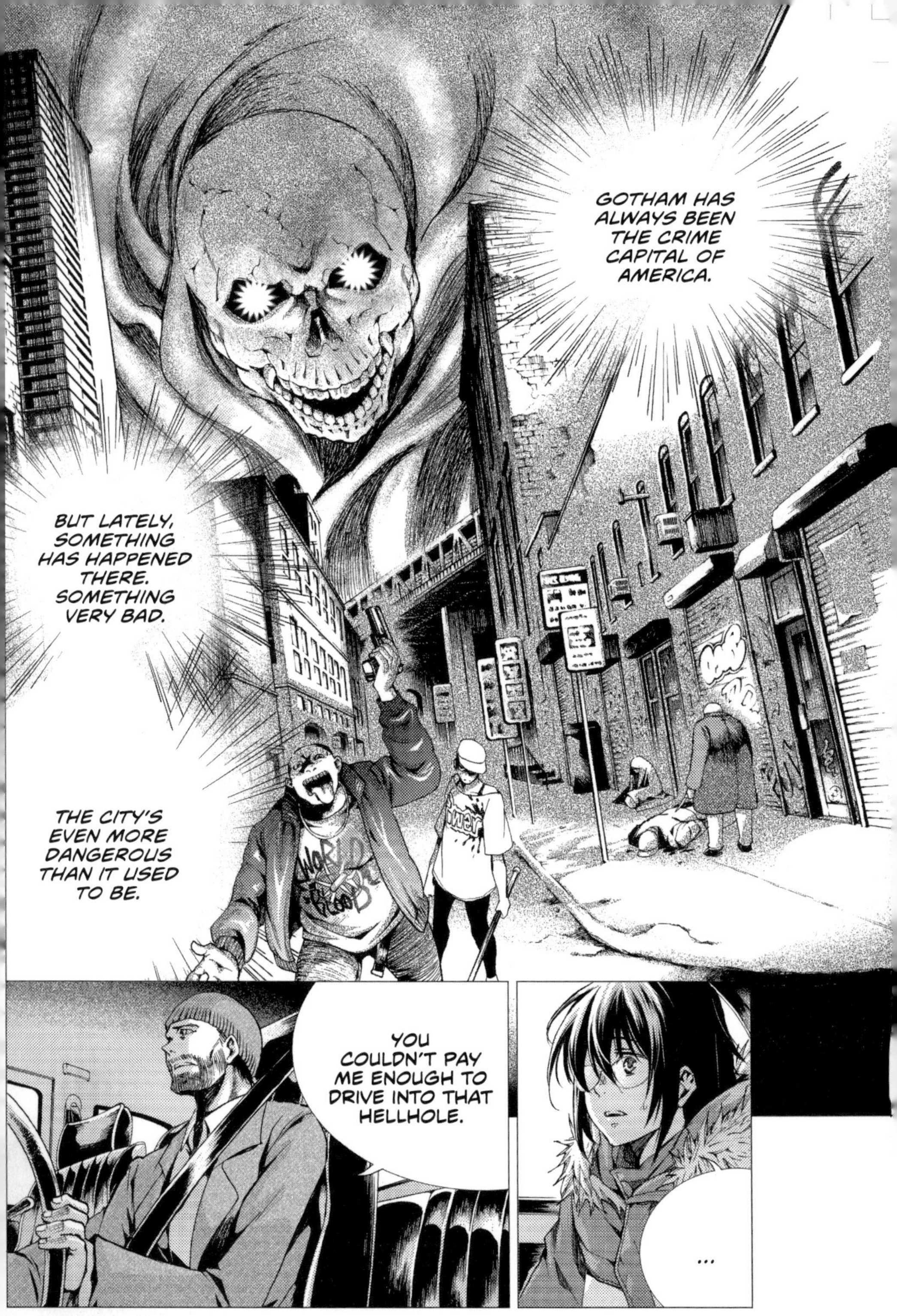
GOTHAM HAS ALWAYS BEEN THE CRIME CAPITAL OF AMERICA.
BUT LATELY, SOMETHING HAS HAPPENED THERE. SOMETHING VERY BAD.
THE CITY'S EVEN MORE DANGEROUS THAN IT USED TO BE.
...
YOU COULDN'T PAY ME ENOUGH TO DRIVE INTO THAT HELLHOLE.

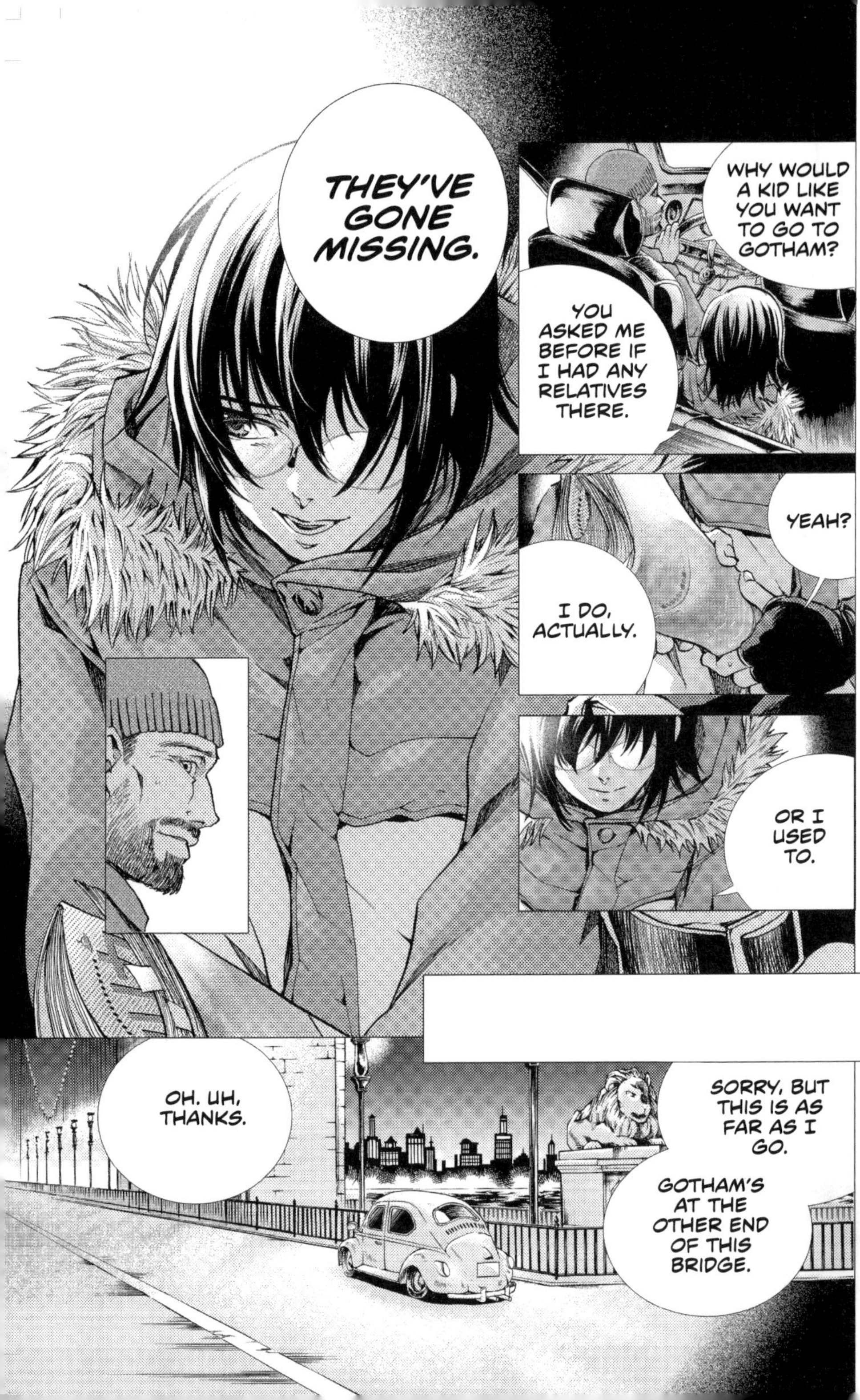

WHY WOULD A KID LIKE YOU WANT TO GO TO GOTHAM?
YOU ASKED ME BEFORE IF I HAD ANY RELATIVES THERE.
YEAH?
I DO, ACTUALLY.
OR I USED TO.
THEY'VE GONE MISSING.
SORRY, BUT THIS IS AS FAR AS I GO.
GOTHAM'S AT THE OTHER END OF THIS BRIDGE.
OH. UH, THANKS.

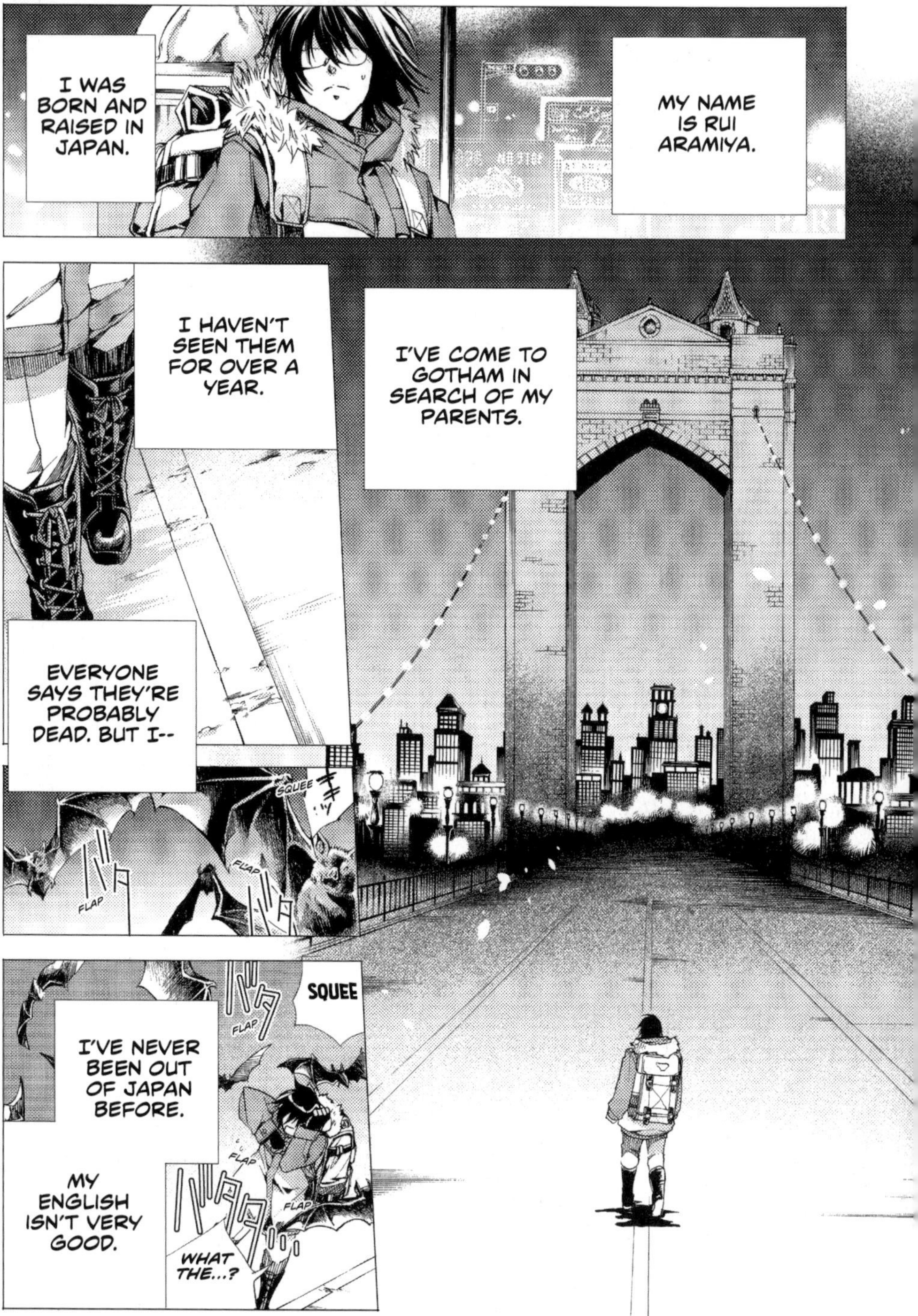
MY NAME IS RUI ARAMIYA.
I WAS BORN AND RAISED IN JAPAN.
I'VE COME TO GOTHAM IN SEARCH OF MY PARENTS.
I HAVEN'T SEEN THEM FOR OVER A YEAR.
EVERYONE SAYS THEY'RE PROBABLY DEAD. BUT I--
SQUEE
FLAP
FLAP
SQUEE
FLAP
I'VE NEVER BEEN OUT OF JAPAN BEFORE.
FLAP
FLAP
MY ENGLISH ISN'T VERY GOOD.
WHAT THE...?

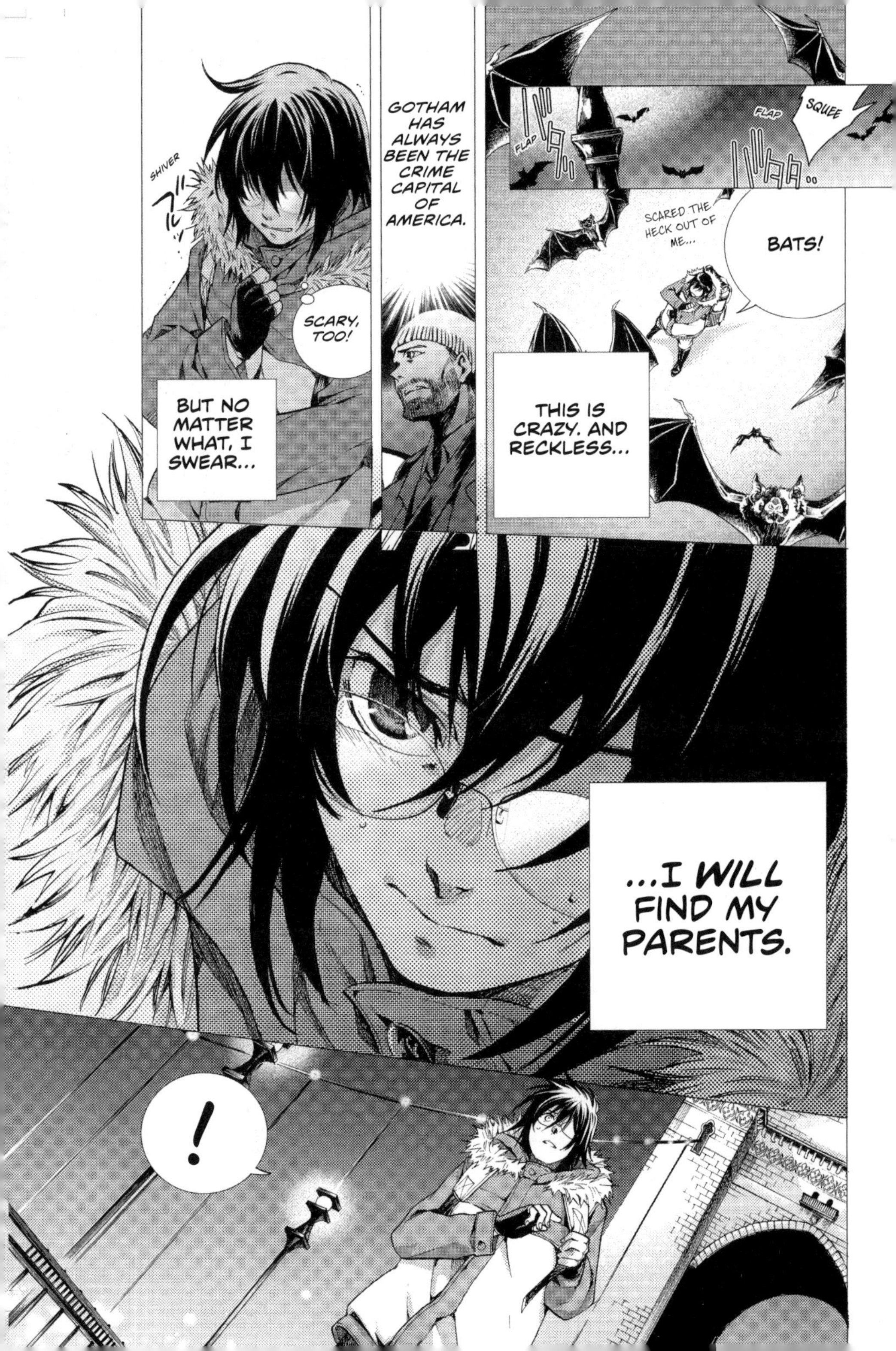
SQUEE
FLAP
FLAP
BATS!
SCARED THE HECK OUT OF ME...
THIS IS CRAZY. AND RECKLESS...
GOTHAM HAS ALWAYS BEEN THE CRIME CAPITAL OF AMERICA.
SHIVER
SCARY, TOO!
BUT NO MATTER WHAT, I SWEAR...
...I *WILL* FIND MY PARENTS.
!

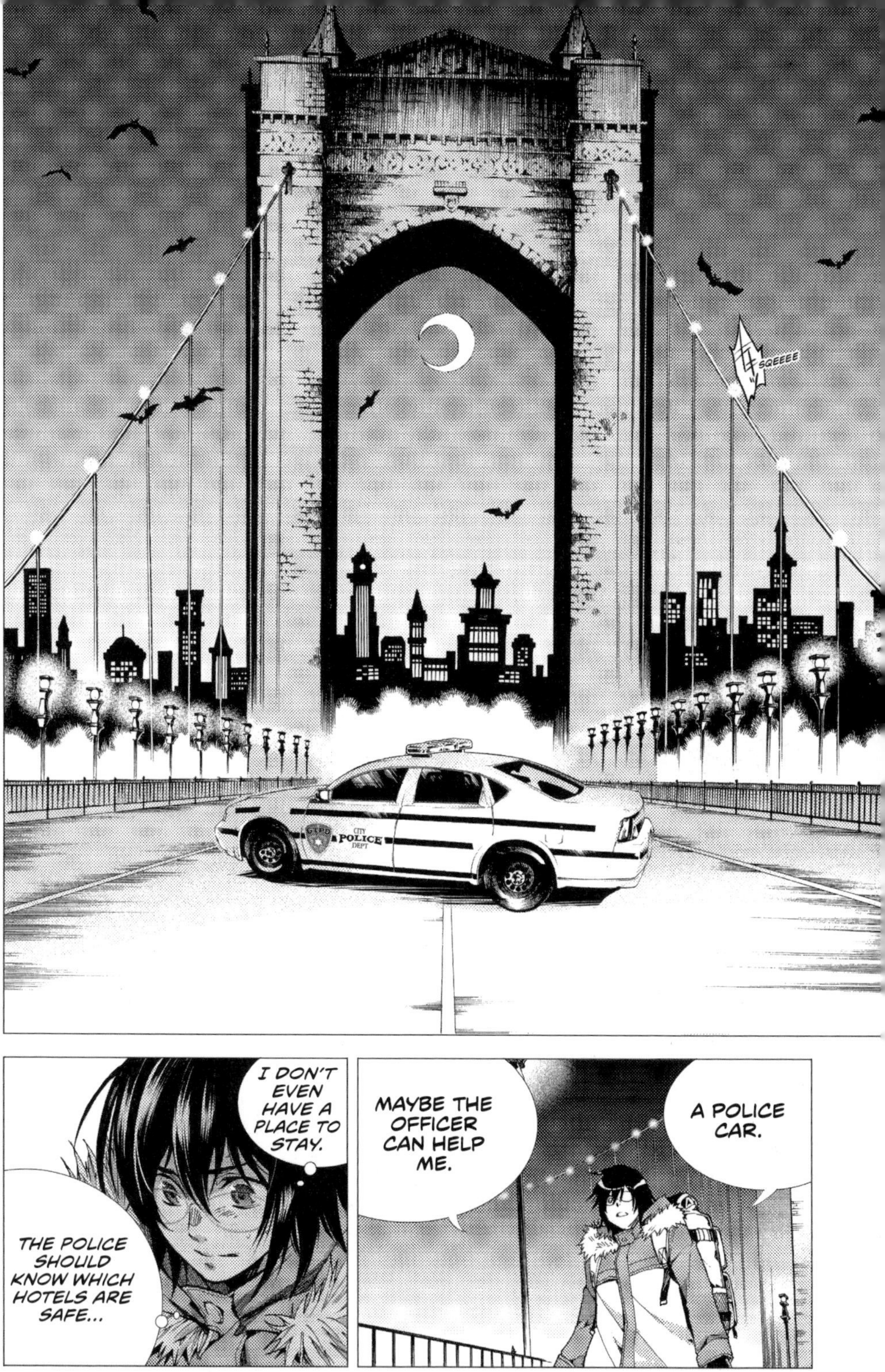
SQEEEE
CITY POLICE DEPT
A POLICE CAR.
MAYBE THE OFFICER CAN HELP ME.
I DON'T EVEN HAVE A PLACE TO STAY.
THE POLICE SHOULD KNOW WHICH HOTELS ARE SAFE...

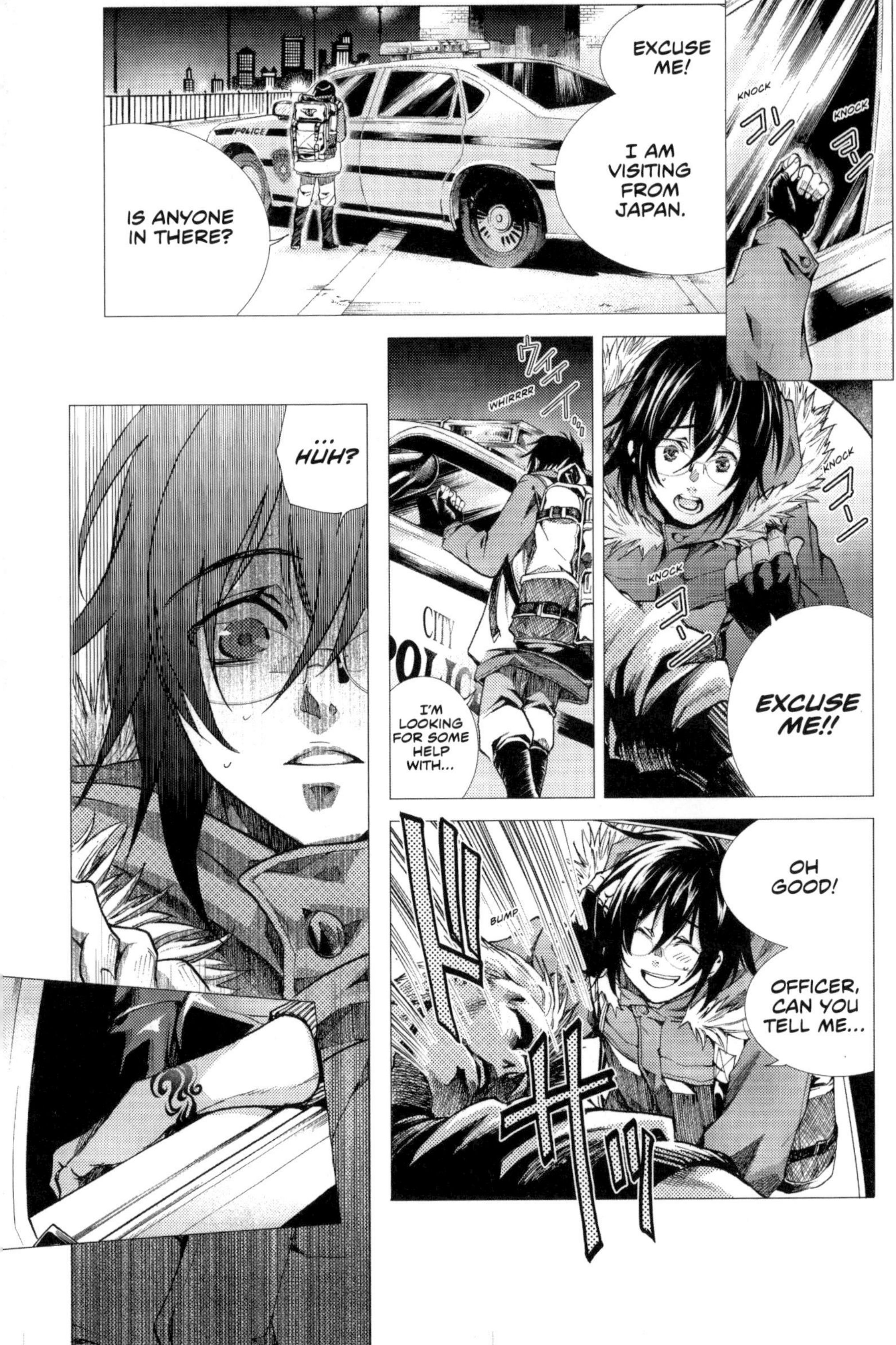
KNOCK
KNOCK
EXCUSE ME!
I AM VISITING FROM JAPAN.
IS ANYONE IN THERE?
KNOCK
KNOCK
EXCUSE ME!!
WHIRRRR
I'M LOOKING FOR SOME HELP WITH...
OH GOOD!
BUMP
OFFICER, CAN YOU TELL ME...
...HUH?

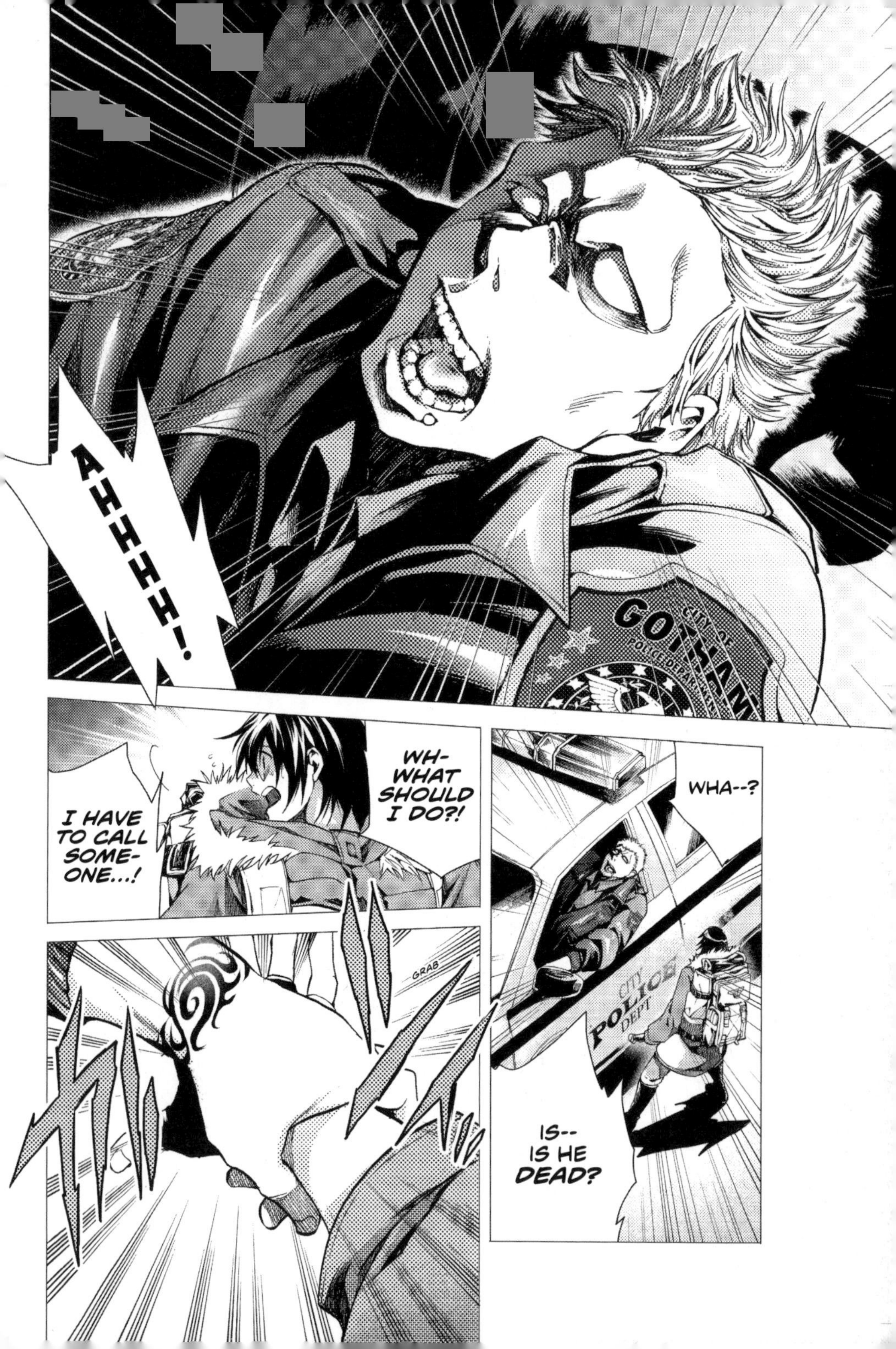
AHHHHH!
GOTHAM
WHA--?
CITY POLICE DEPT
IS-- IS HE DEAD?
WH- WHAT SHOULD I DO?!
I HAVE TO CALL SOME-ONE...!
GRAB

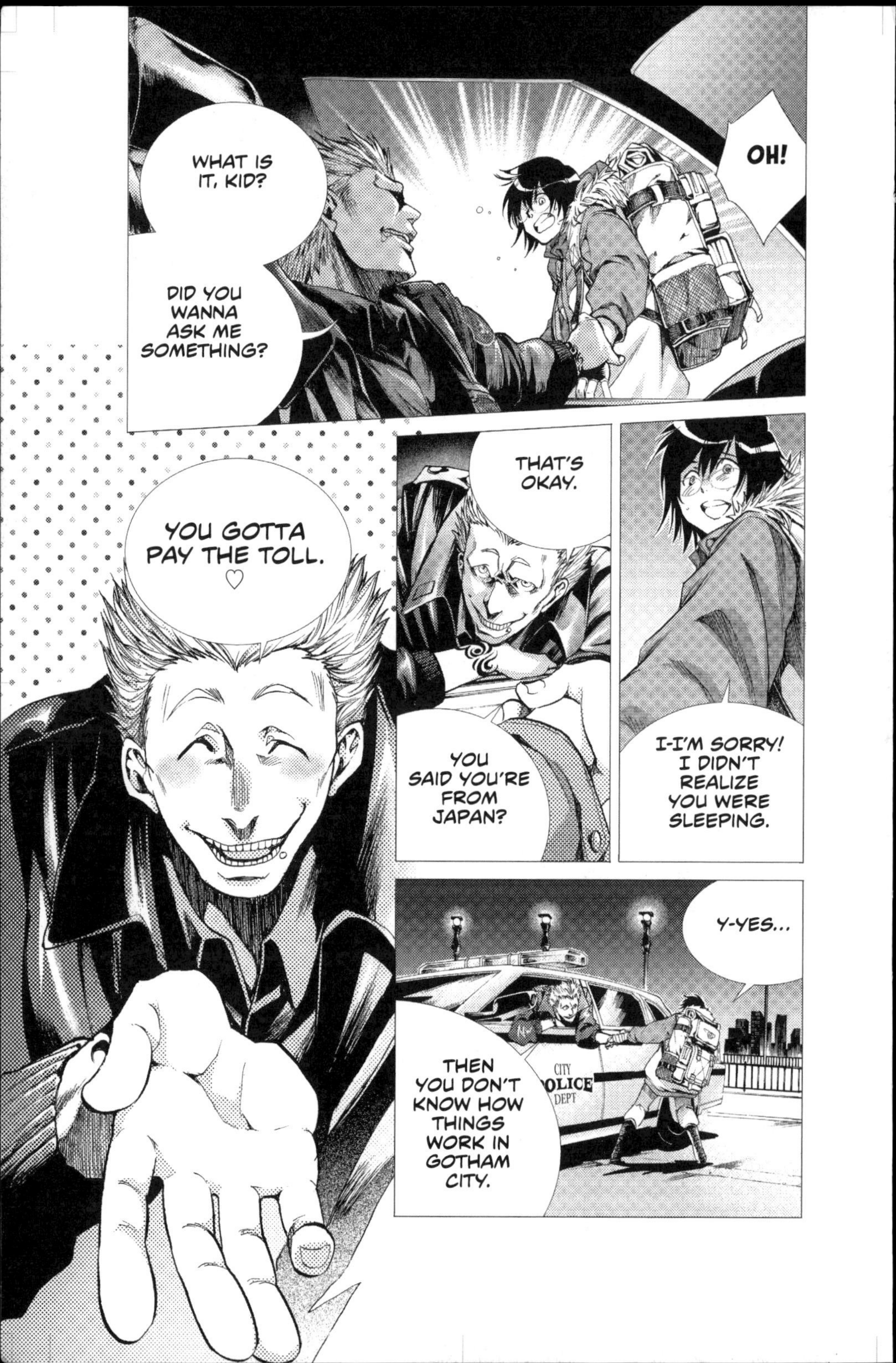
OH!
WHAT IS IT, KID?
DID YOU WANNA ASK ME SOMETHING?
I-I'M SORRY! I DIDN'T REALIZE YOU WERE SLEEPING.
THAT'S OKAY.
YOU SAID YOU'RE FROM JAPAN?
Y-YES...
THEN YOU DON'T KNOW HOW THINGS WORK IN GOTHAM CITY.
YOU GOTTA PAY THE TOLL. ♡

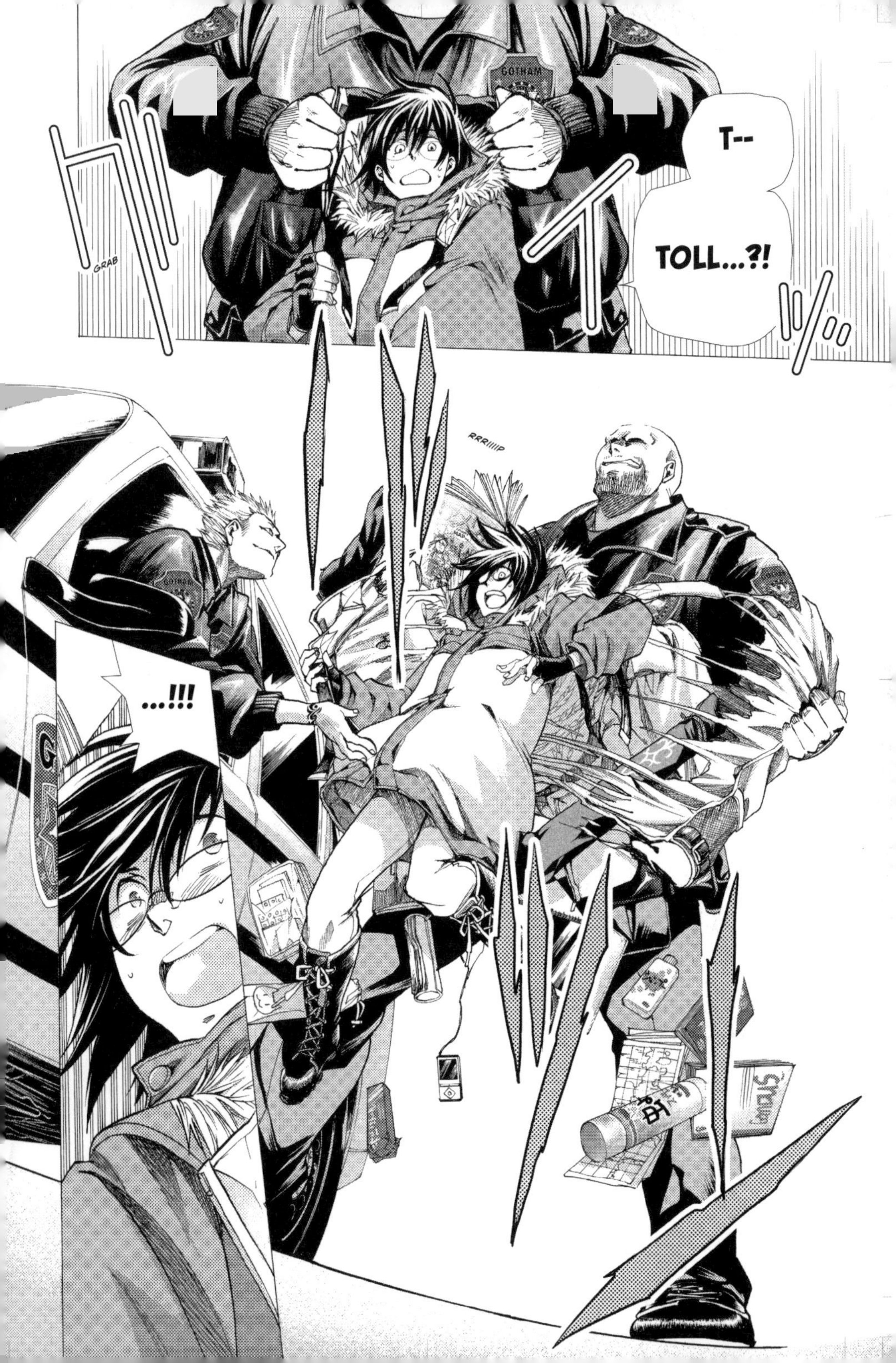
T--
TOLL...?!
GRAB
RRRIIIP
...!!!

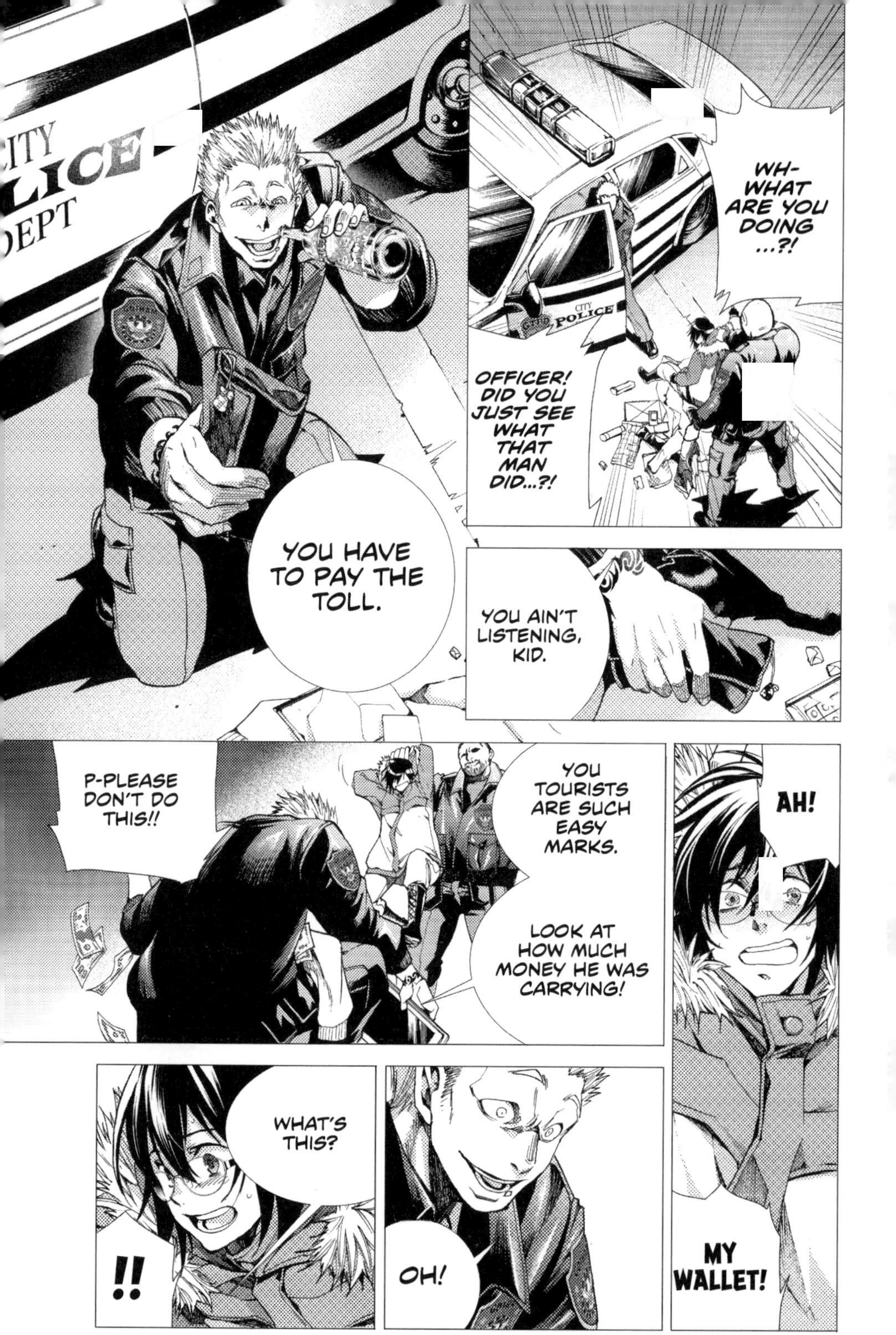
WH- WHAT ARE YOU DOING ...?!
OFFICER! DID YOU JUST SEE WHAT THAT MAN DID...?!
YOU AIN'T LISTENING, KID.
YOU HAVE TO PAY THE TOLL.
AH!
MY WALLET!
YOU TOURISTS ARE SUCH EASY MARKS.
LOOK AT HOW MUCH MONEY HE WAS CARRYING!
P-PLEASE DON'T DO THIS!!
OH!
WHAT'S THIS?
!!

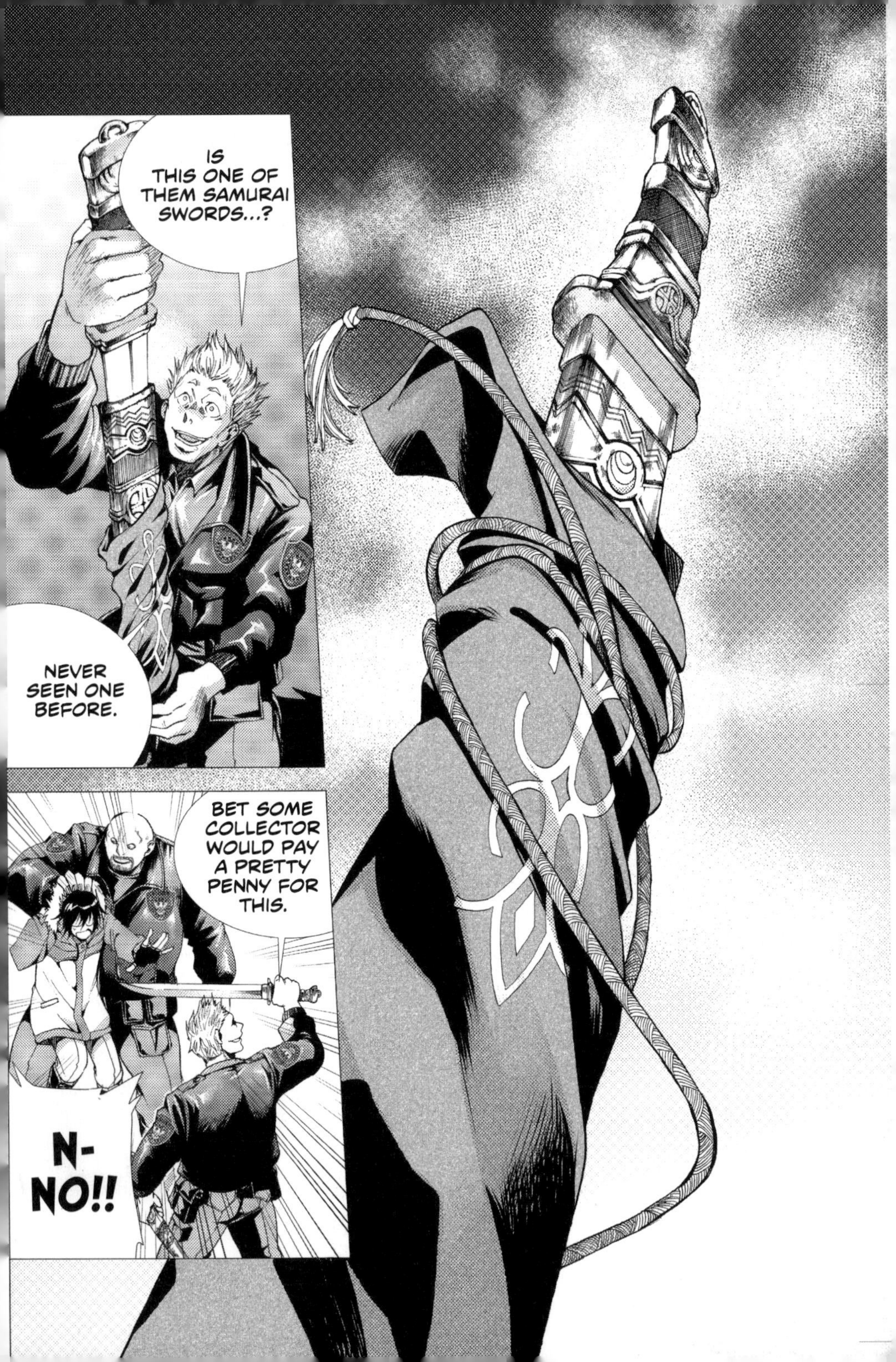
IS THIS ONE OF THEM SAMURAI SWORDS...?
NEVER SEEN ONE BEFORE.
BET SOME COLLECTOR WOULD PAY A PRETTY PENNY FOR THIS.
N- NO!!

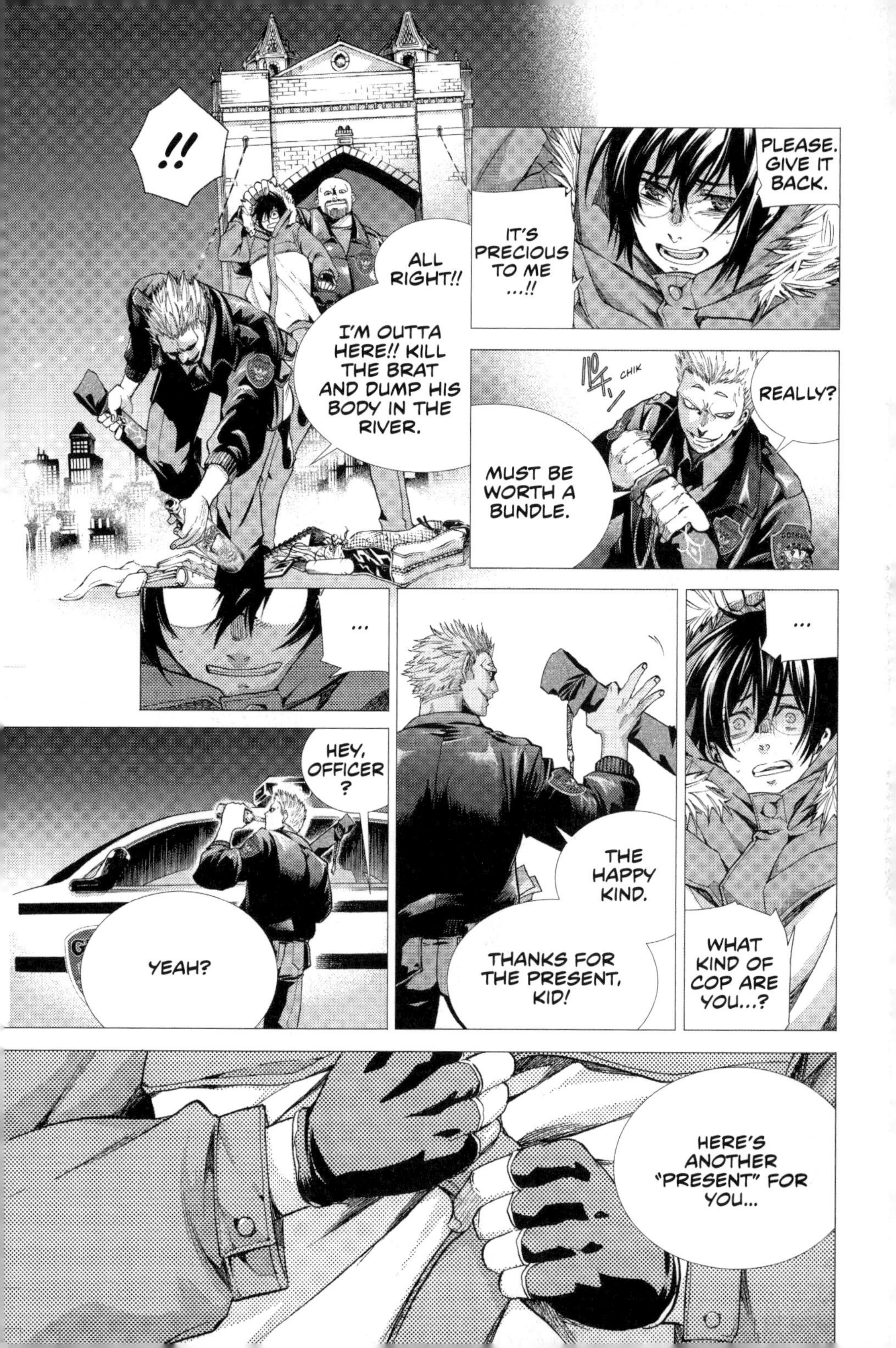
PLEASE. GIVE IT BACK.
IT'S PRECIOUS TO ME ...!!
CHIK
REALLY?
MUST BE WORTH A BUNDLE.
!!
ALL RIGHT!!
I'M OUTTA HERE!! KILL THE BRAT AND DUMP HIS BODY IN THE RIVER.
...
WHAT KIND OF COP ARE YOU...?
THE HAPPY KIND.
THANKS FOR THE PRESENT, KID!
...
HEY, OFFICER?
YEAH?
HERE'S ANOTHER "PRESENT" FOR YOU...

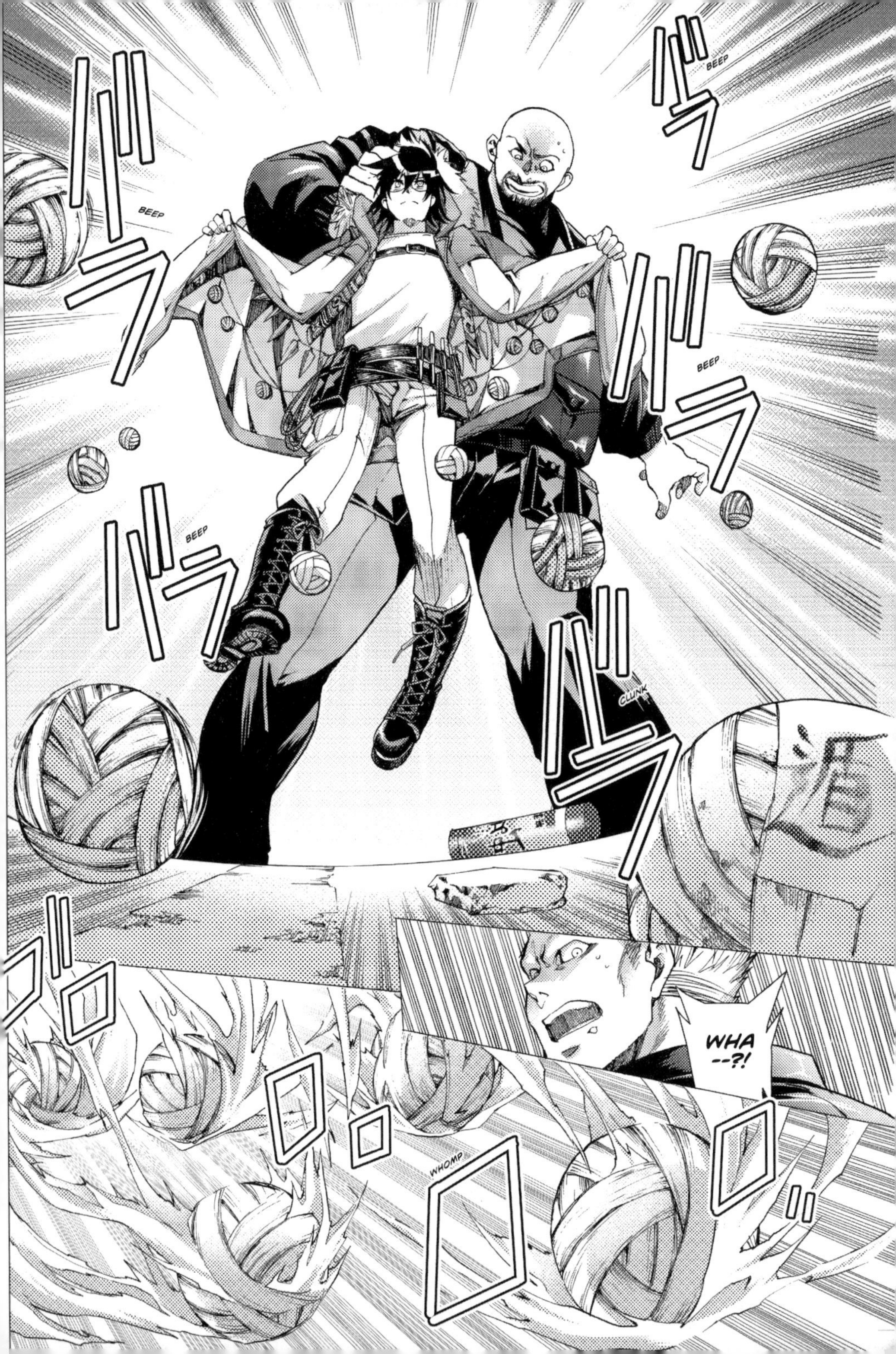
BEEP
BEEP
BEEP
BEEP
CLUNK
WHA --?!
WHOMP

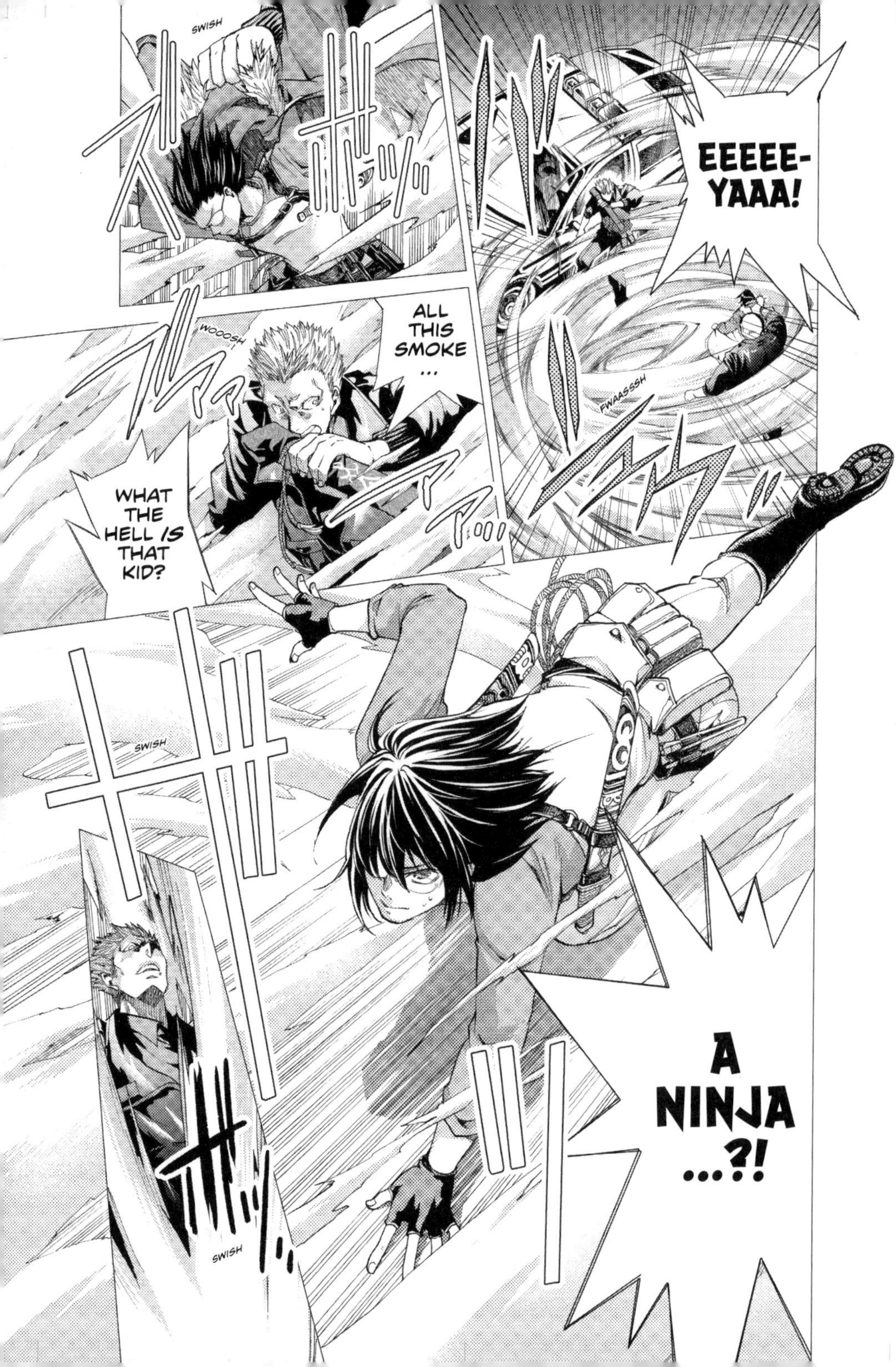
EEEEE-YAAA!
FWAASSSH
SWISH
ALL THIS SMOKE ...
WOOOSH
WHAT THE HELL IS THAT KID?
A NINJA ...?!
SWISH
SWISH

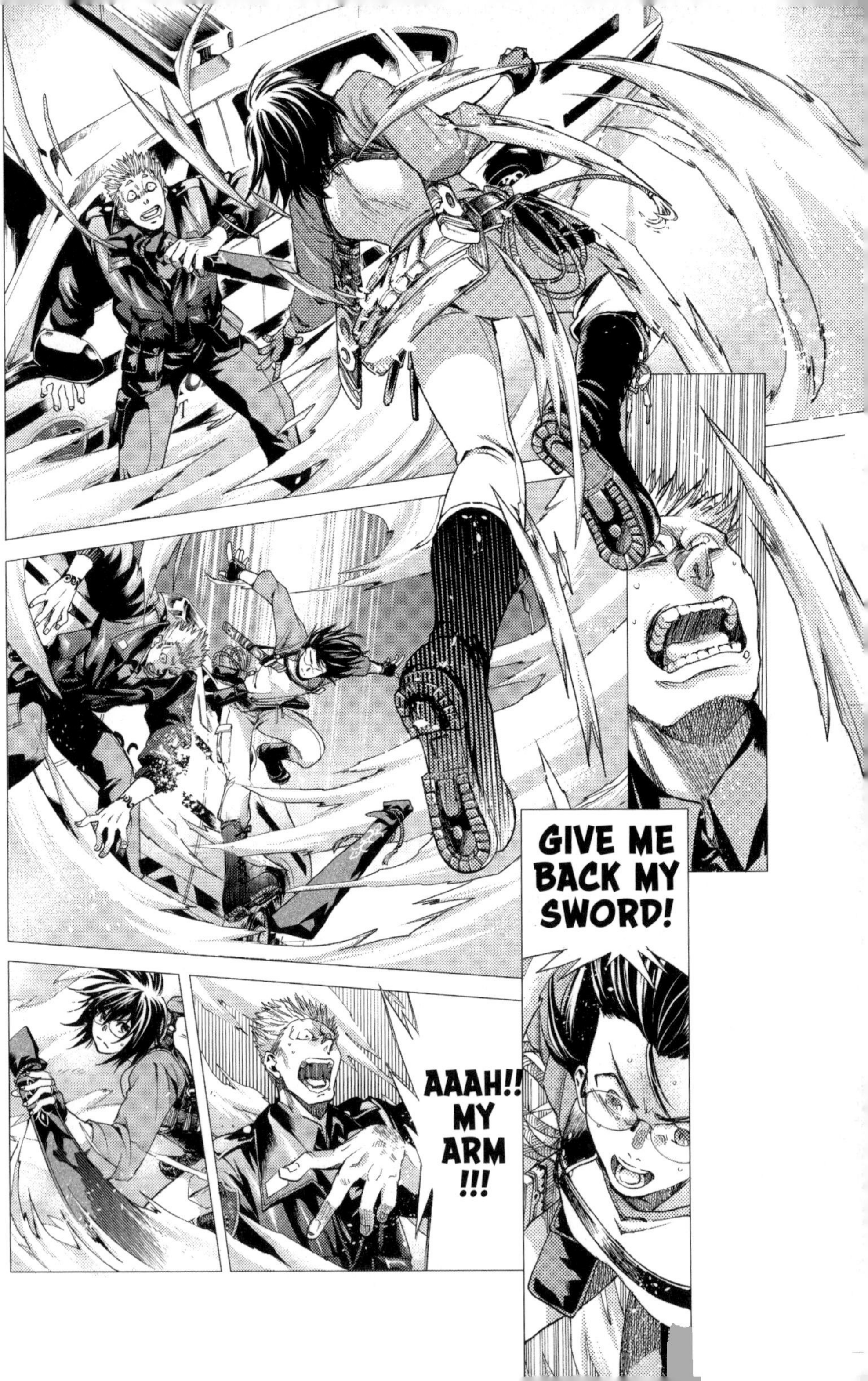
GIVE ME BACK MY SWORD!
AAAH!! MY ARM!!!

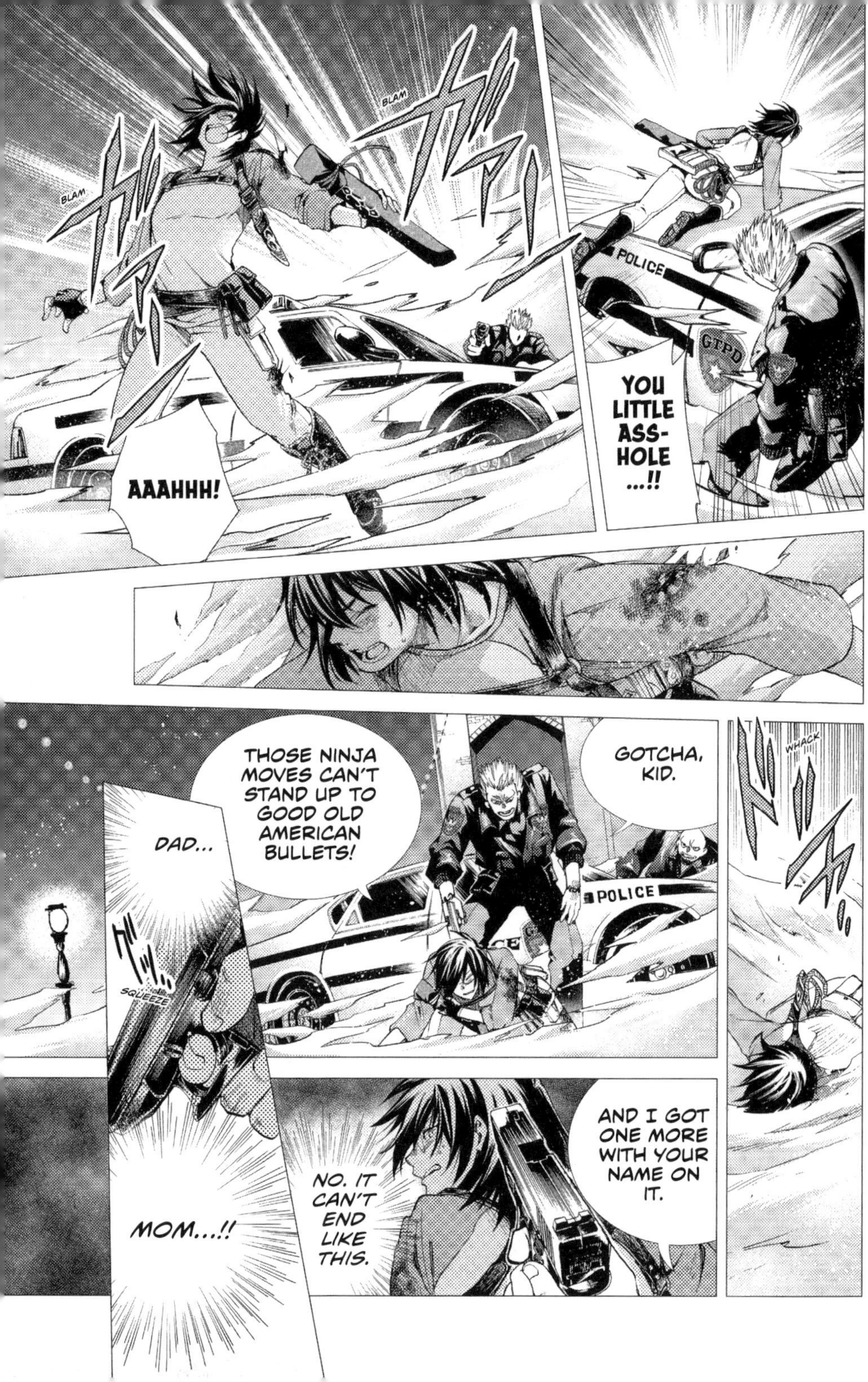
YOU LITTLE ASS-HOLE ...!!
BLAM
BLAM
AAAHHH!
WHACK
GOTCHA, KID.
THOSE NINJA MOVES CAN'T STAND UP TO GOOD OLD AMERICAN BULLETS!
AND I GOT ONE MORE WITH YOUR NAME ON IT.
NO. IT CAN'T END LIKE THIS.
DAD...
SQUEEZE
MOM...!!

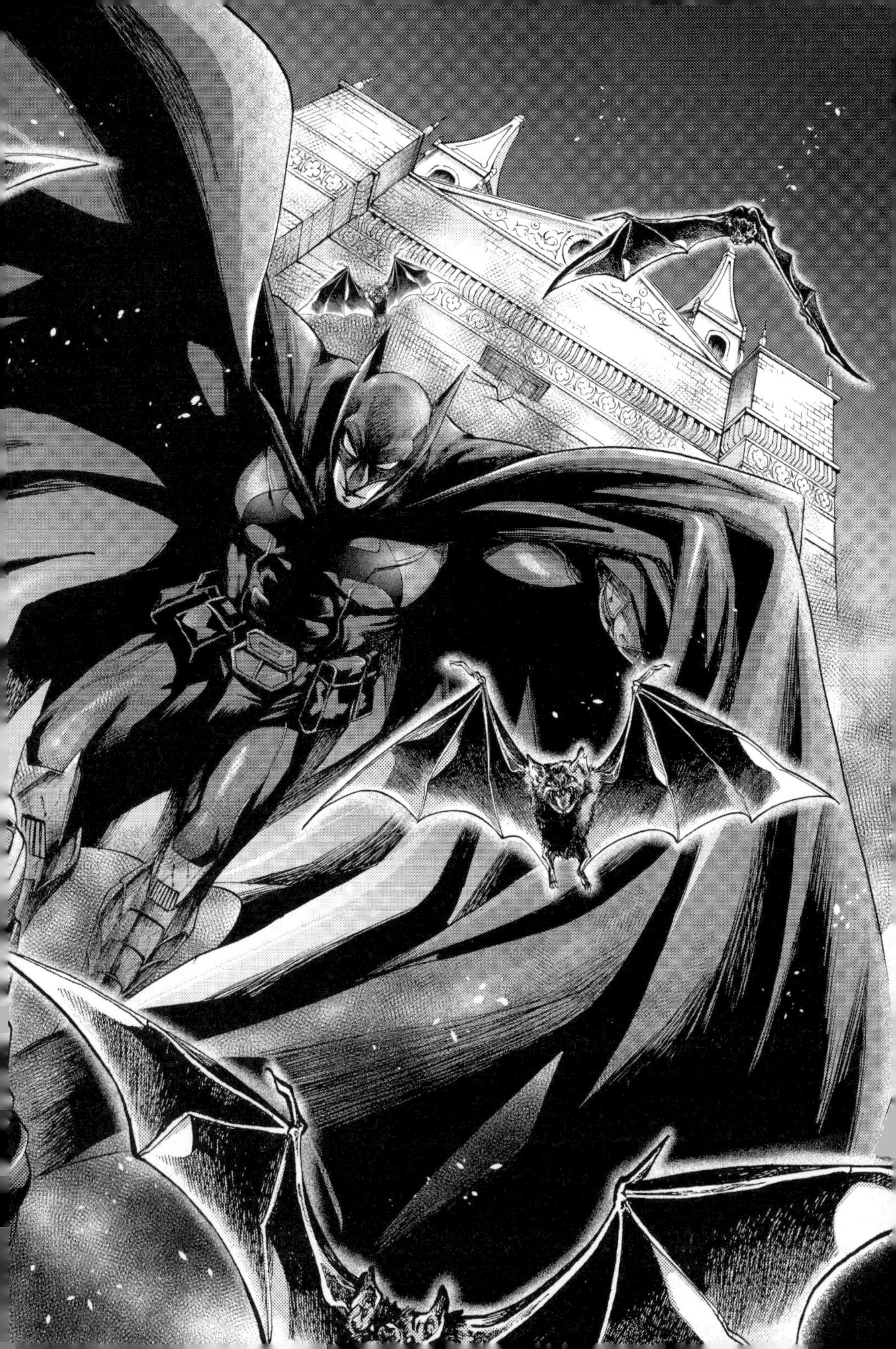

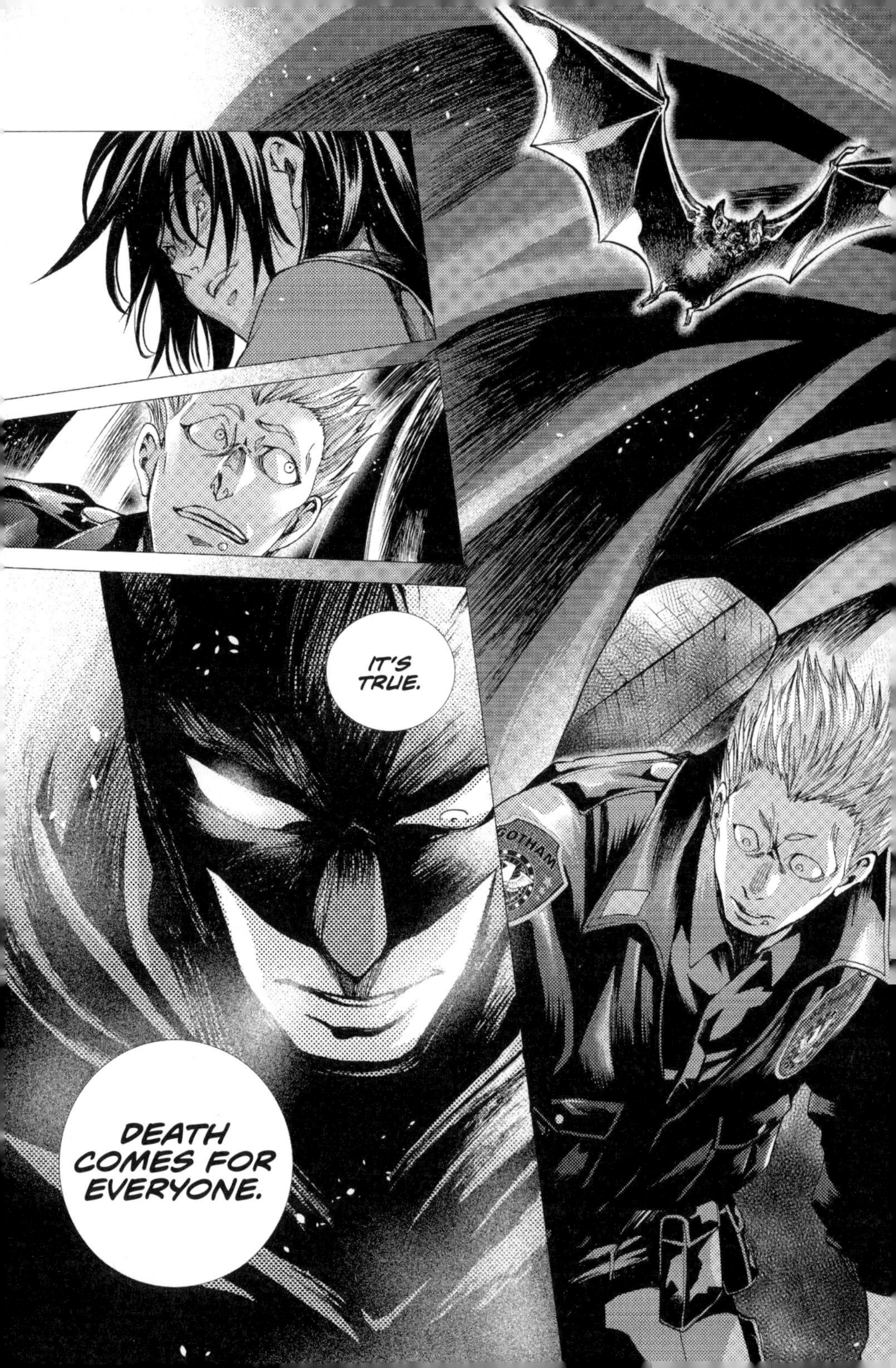
IT'S TRUE.
DEATH COMES FOR EVERYONE.

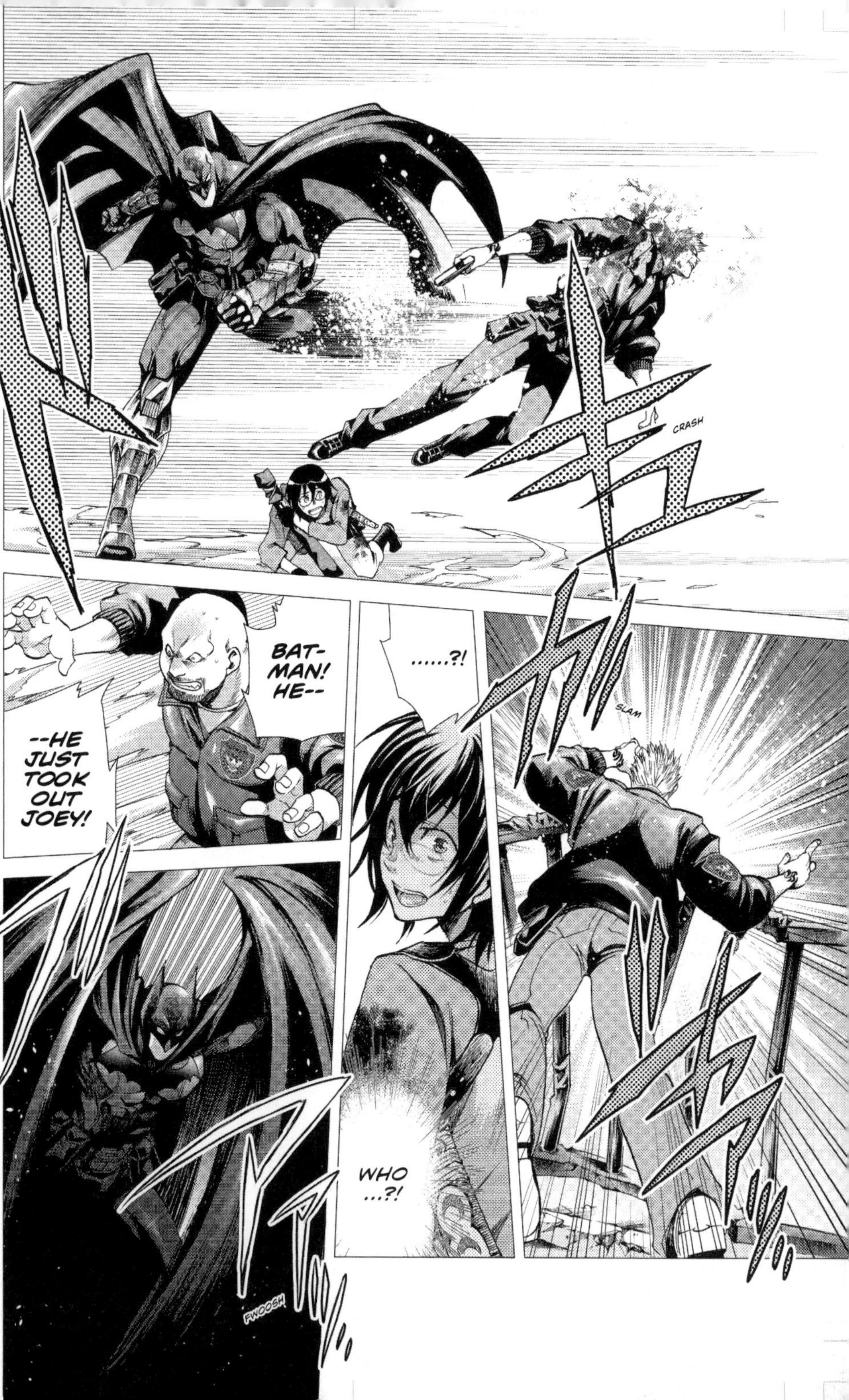
CRASH
SLAM
......?!
WHO
...?!
BAT-
MAN!
HE--
--HE
JUST
TOOK
OUT
JOEY!
FWOOSH

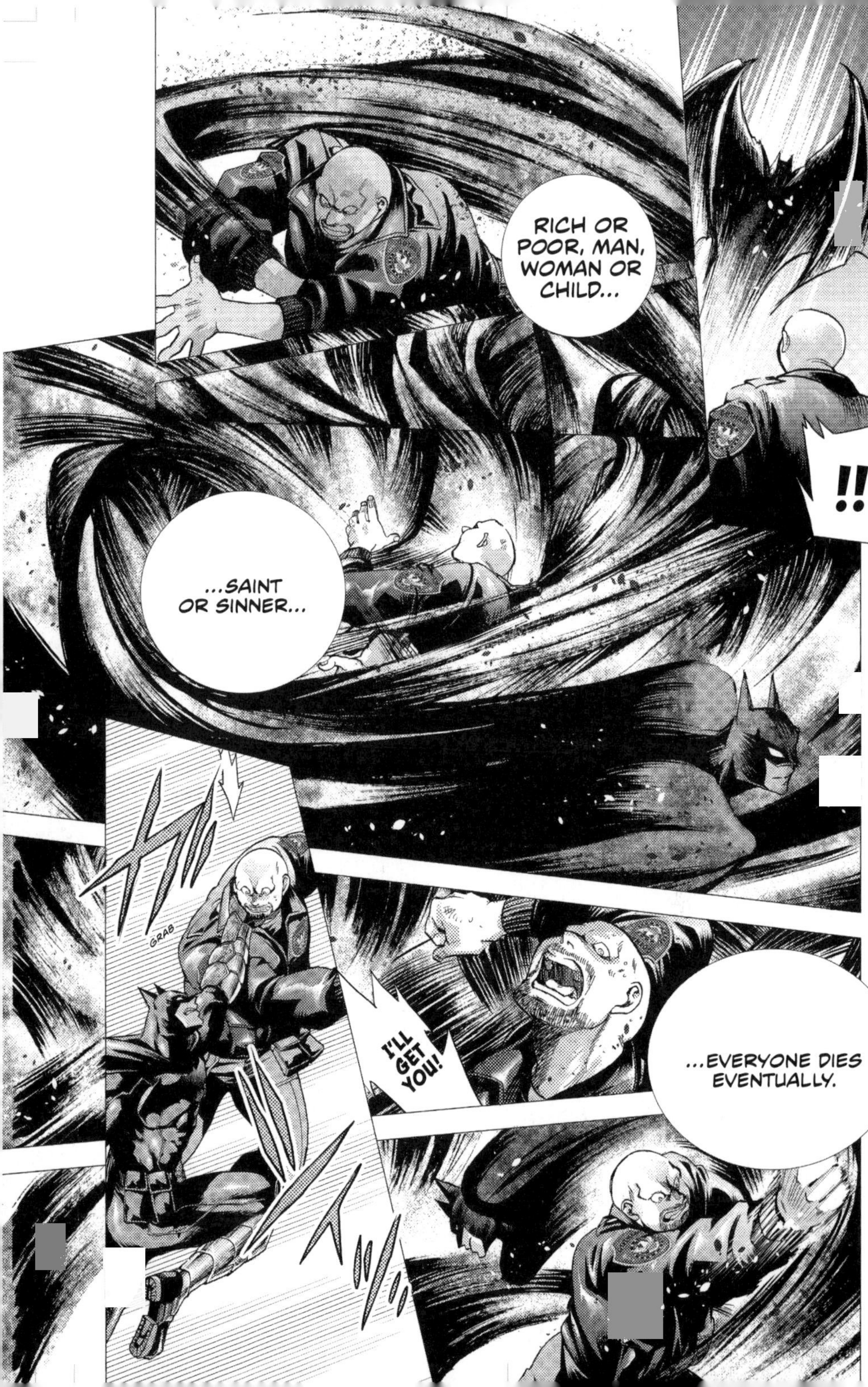
!!
RICH OR POOR, MAN, WOMAN OR CHILD...
...SAINT OR SINNER...
I'LL GET YOU!
...EVERYONE DIES EVENTUALLY.
GRAB

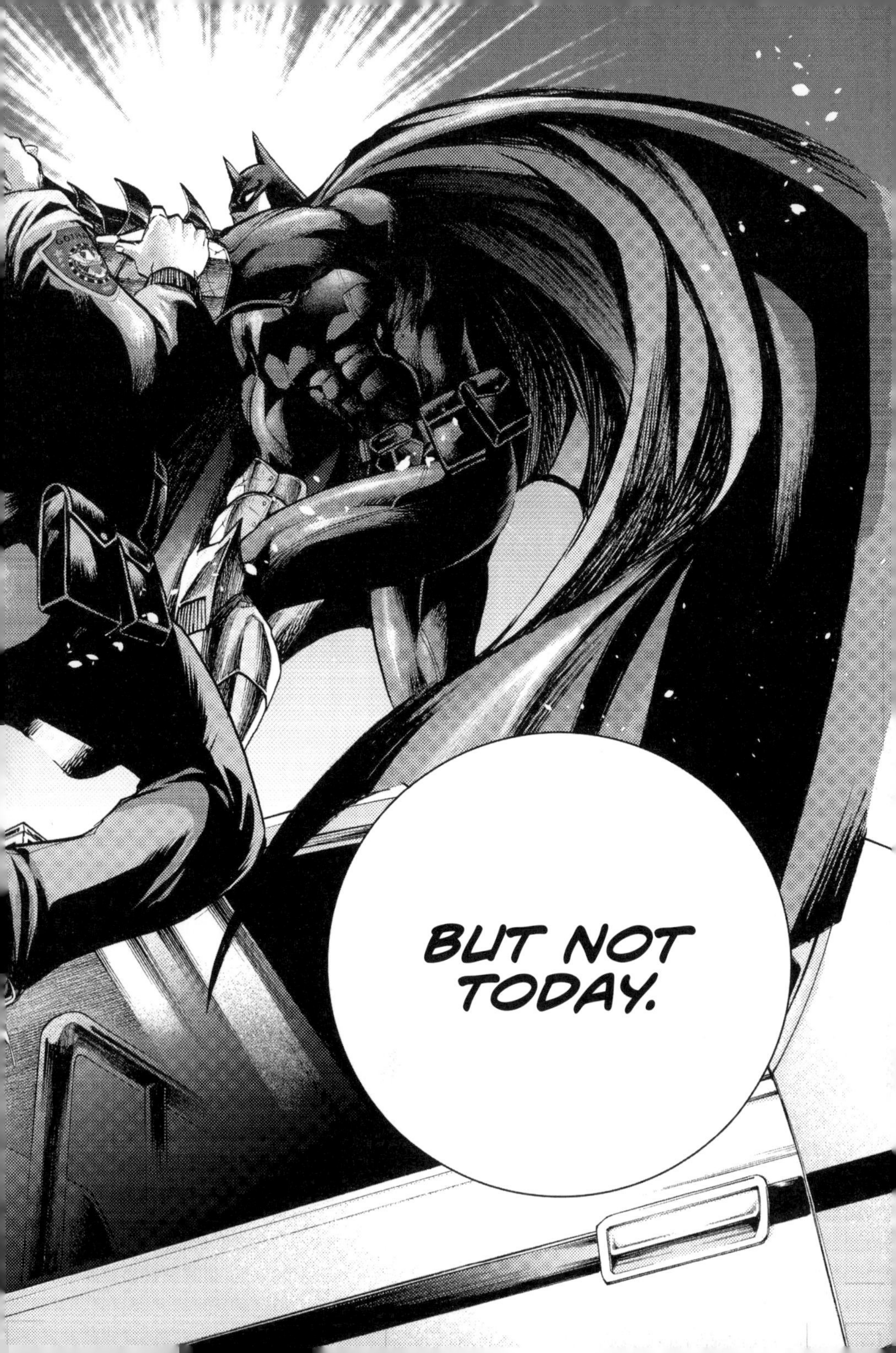
BUT NOT TODAY.

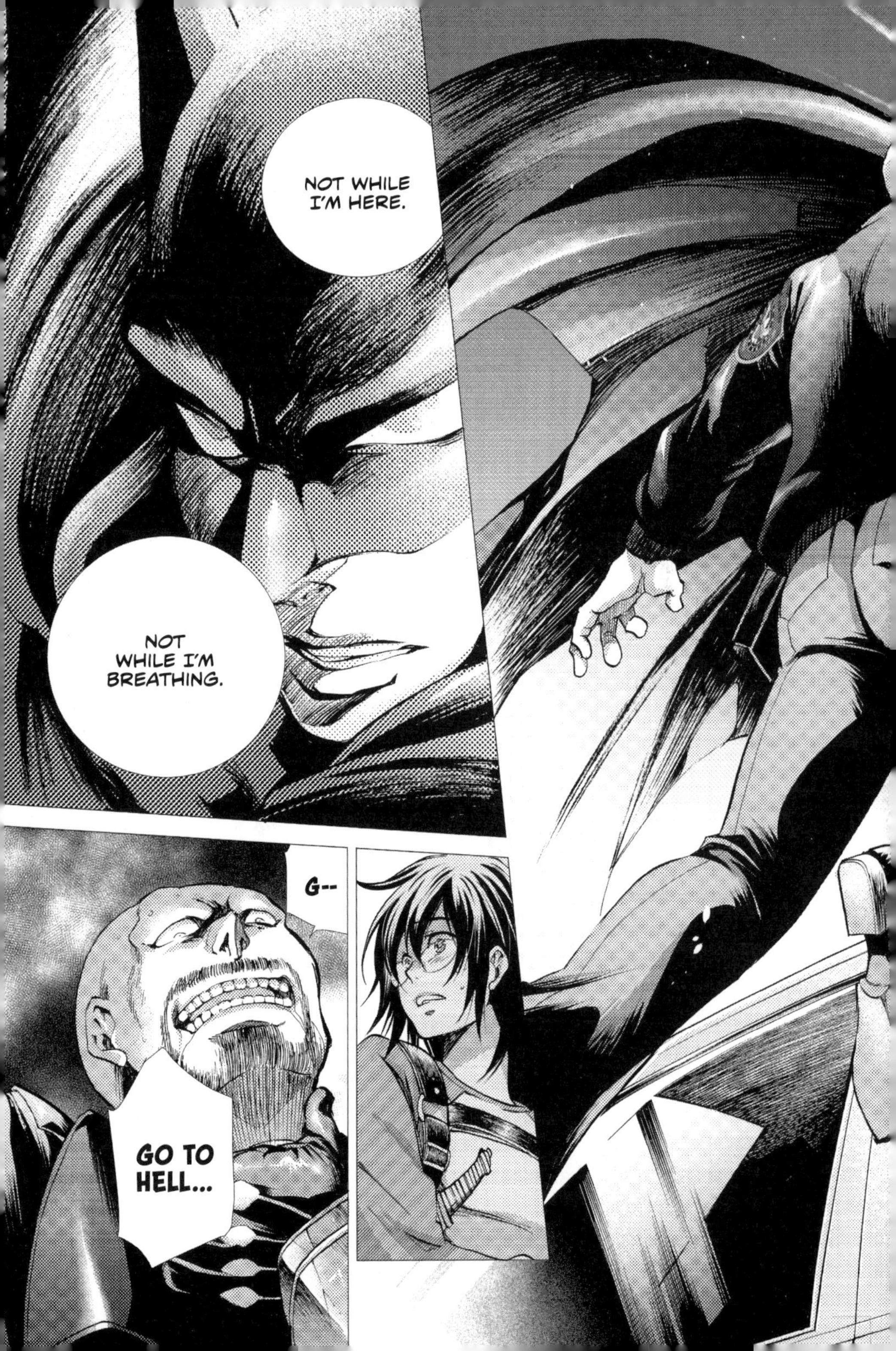
NOT WHILE I'M HERE.
NOT WHILE I'M BREATHING.
G--
GO TO HELL...

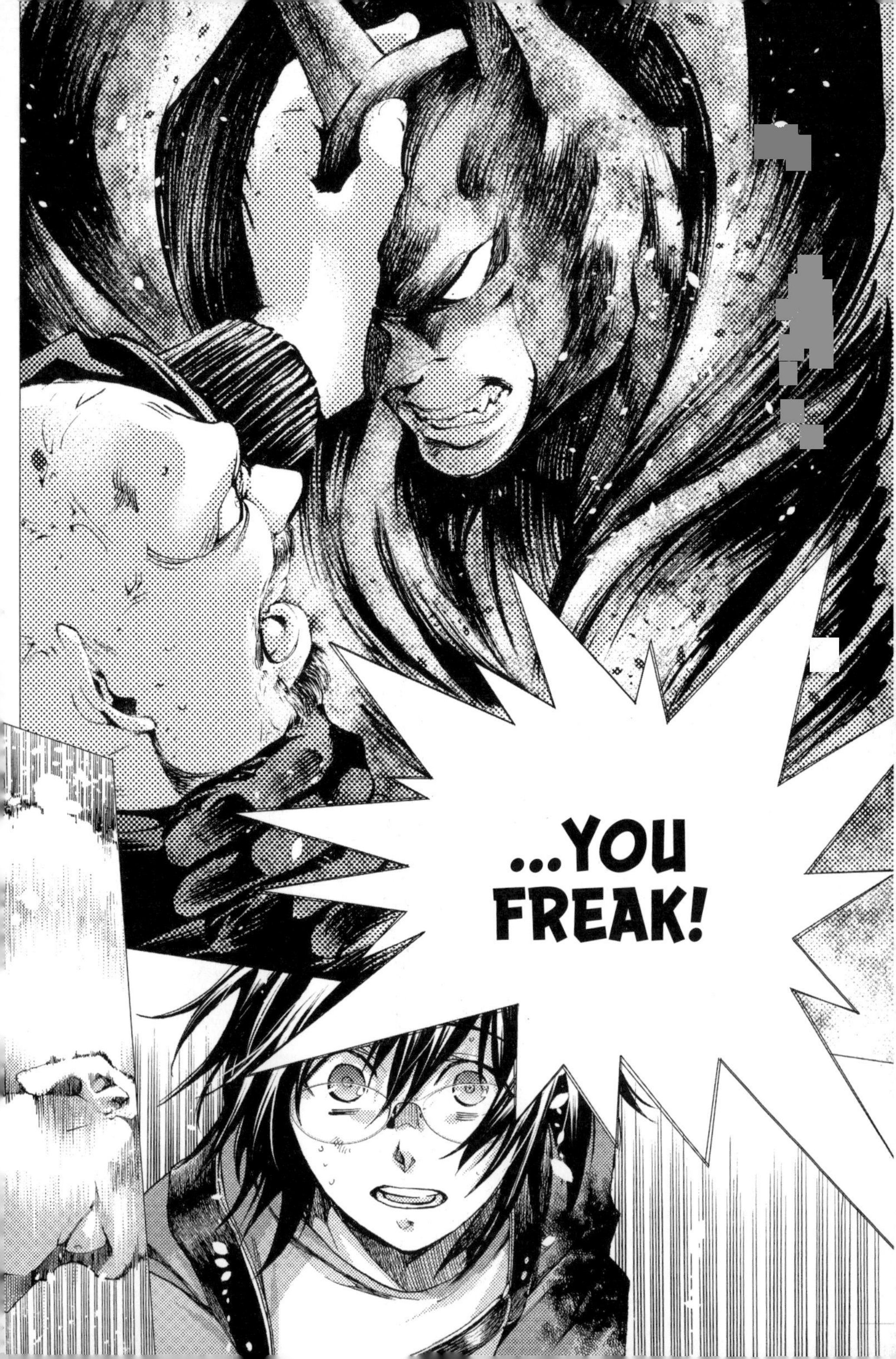
...YOU FREAK!

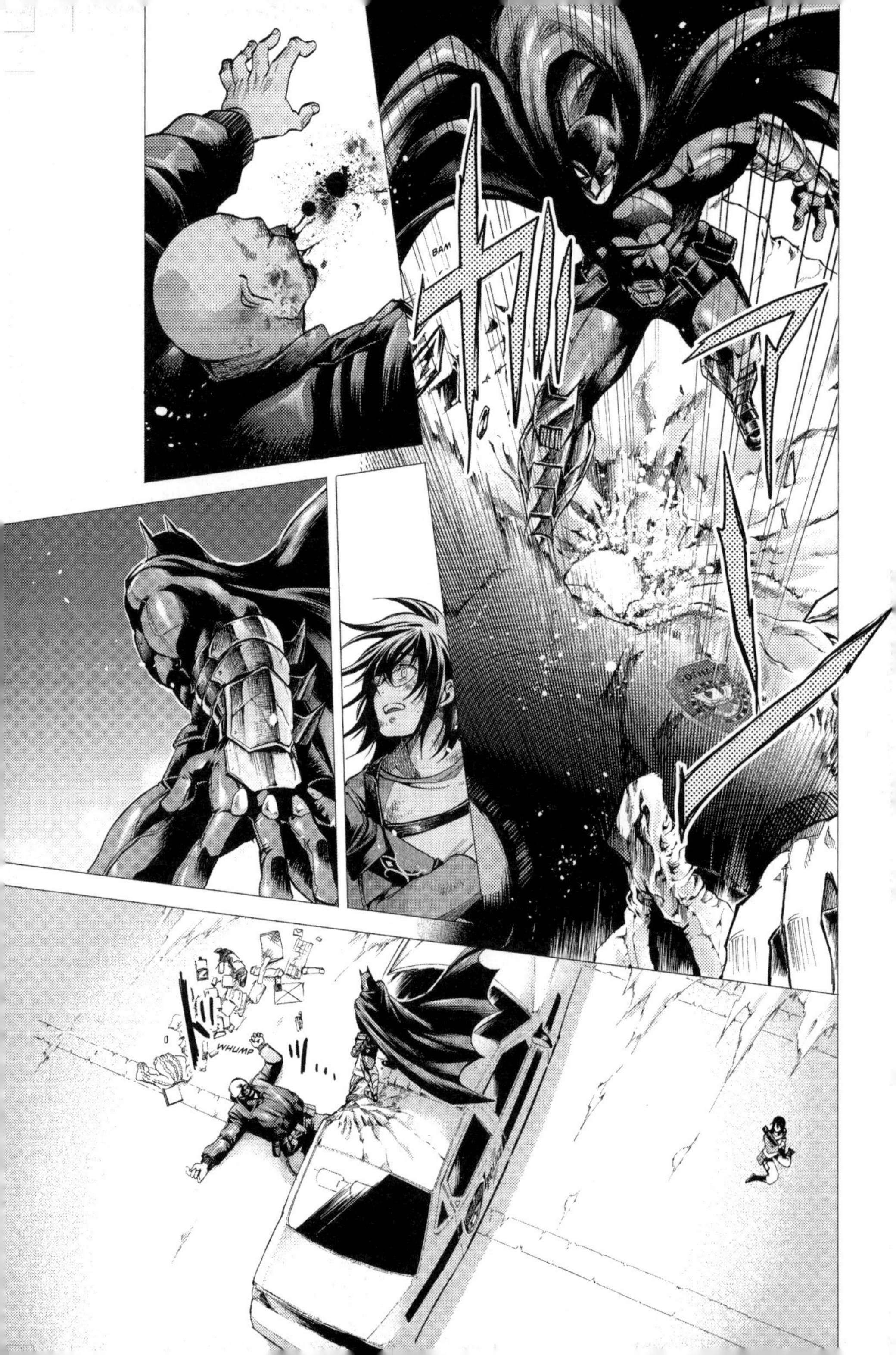
BAM
WHUMP

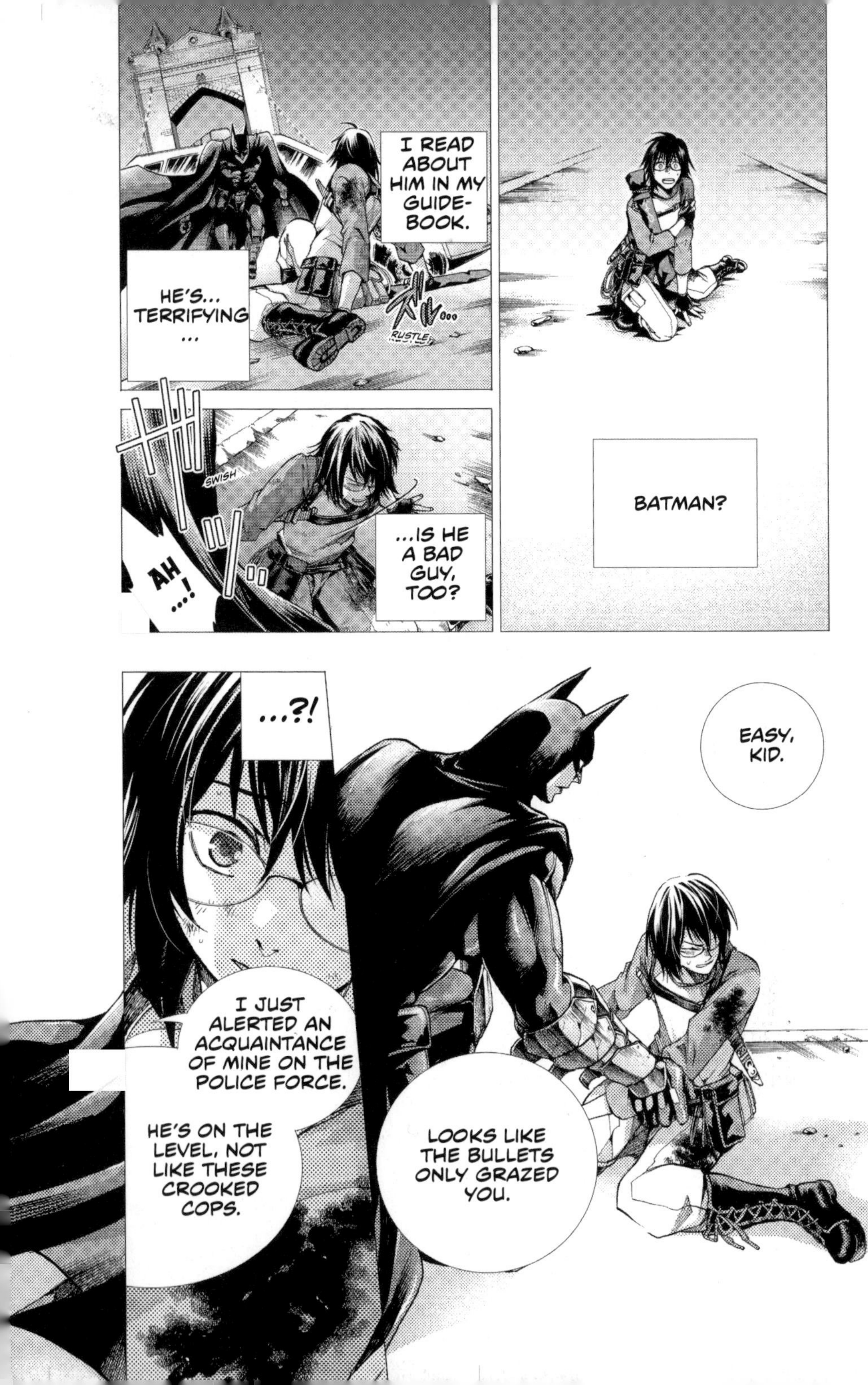
BATMAN?
I READ ABOUT HIM IN MY GUIDE-BOOK.
HE'S... TERRIFYING ...
RUSTLE
SWISH
...IS HE A BAD GUY, TOO?
AH ...!
EASY, KID.
...?!
LOOKS LIKE THE BULLETS ONLY GRAZED YOU.
I JUST ALERTED AN ACQUAINTANCE OF MINE ON THE POLICE FORCE.
HE'S ON THE LEVEL, NOT LIKE THESE CROOKED COPS.

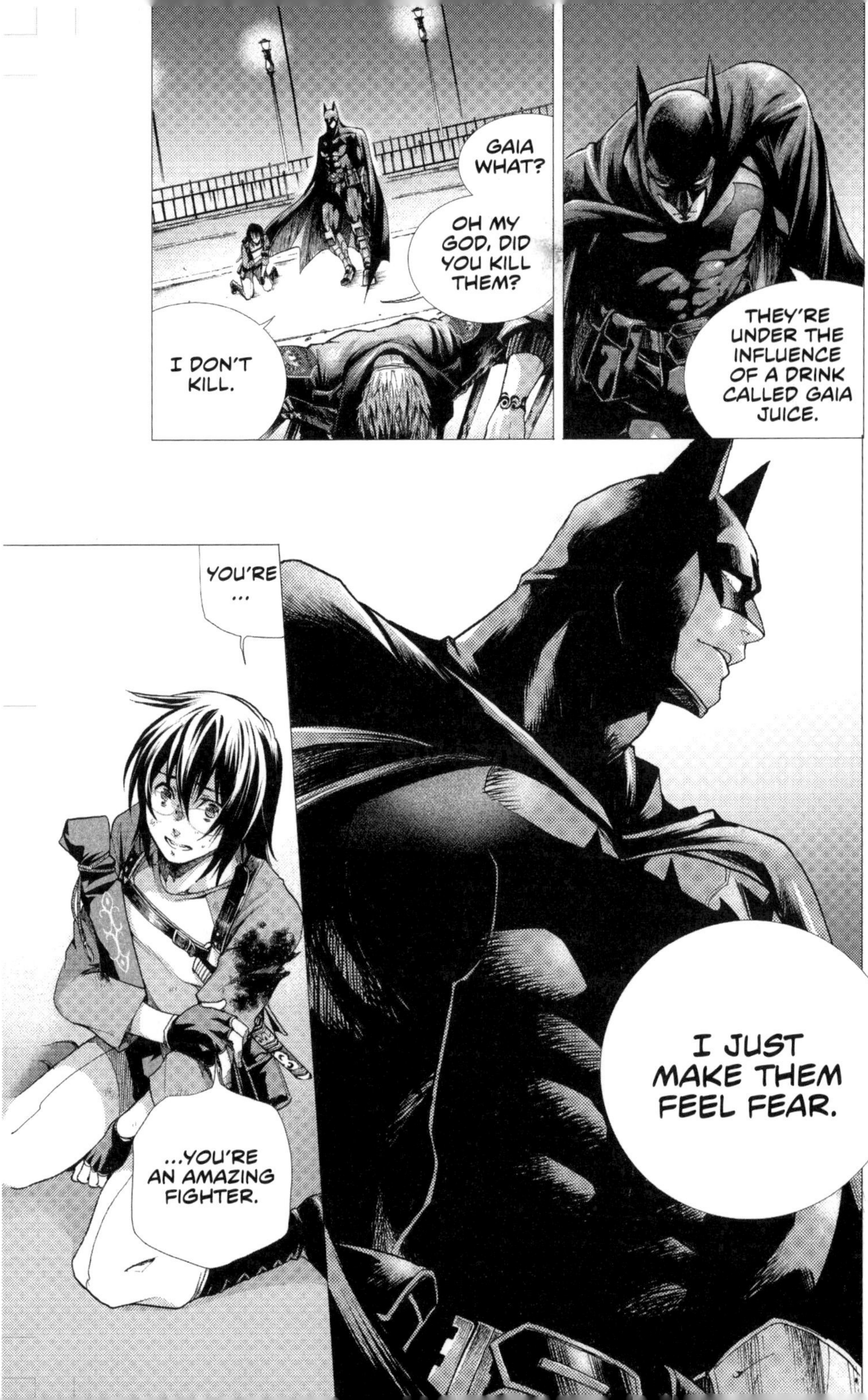
THEY'RE UNDER THE INFLUENCE OF A DRINK CALLED GAIA JUICE.
GAIA WHAT?
OH MY GOD, DID YOU KILL THEM?
I DON'T KILL.
I JUST MAKE THEM FEEL FEAR.
YOU'RE ...
...YOU'RE AN AMAZING FIGHTER.

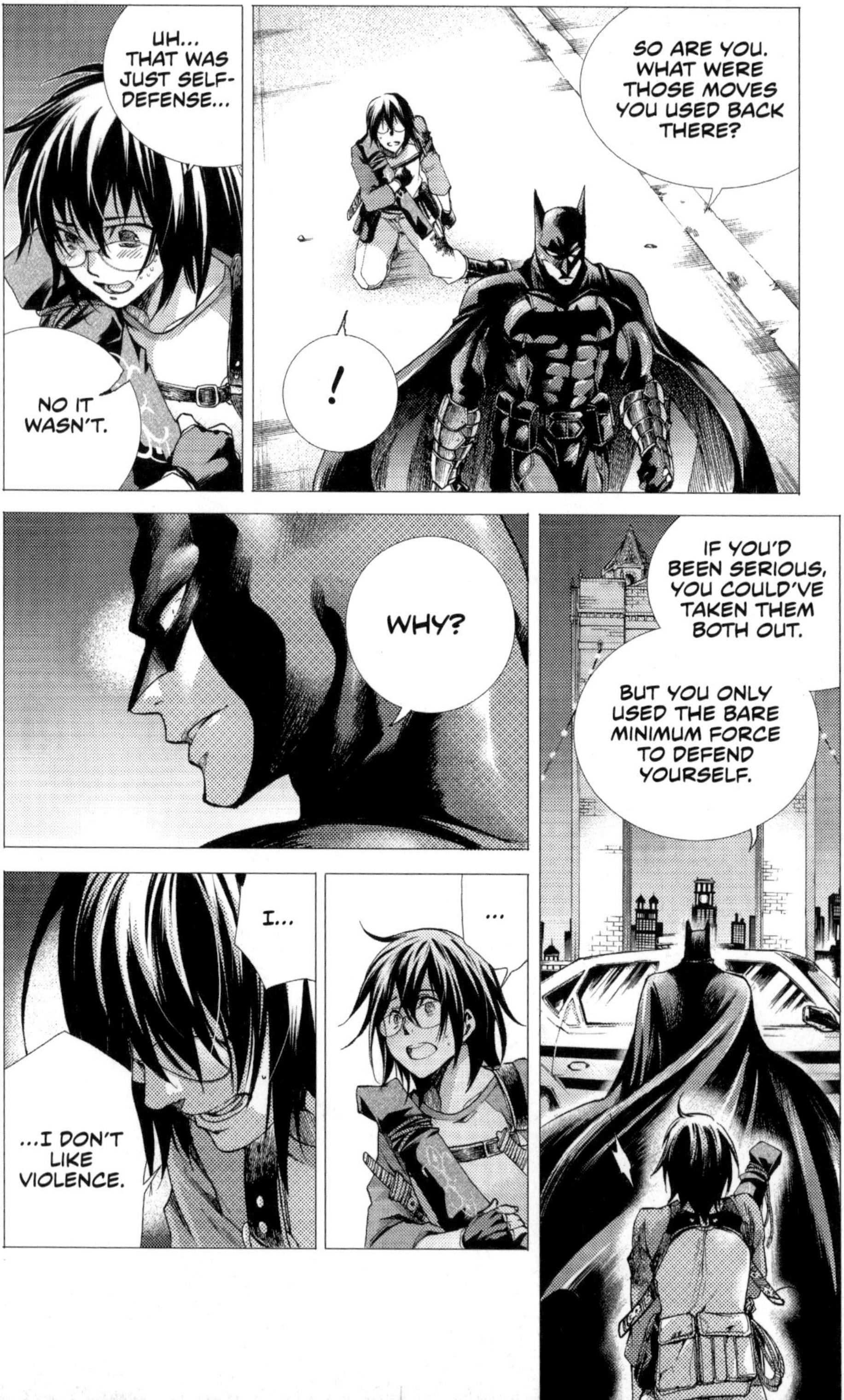
SO ARE YOU. WHAT WERE THOSE MOVES YOU USED BACK THERE?
!
UH... THAT WAS JUST SELF-DEFENSE...
NO IT WASN'T.
IF YOU'D BEEN SERIOUS, YOU COULD'VE TAKEN THEM BOTH OUT.
BUT YOU ONLY USED THE BARE MINIMUM FORCE TO DEFEND YOURSELF.
WHY?
...
I...
...I DON'T LIKE VIOLENCE.

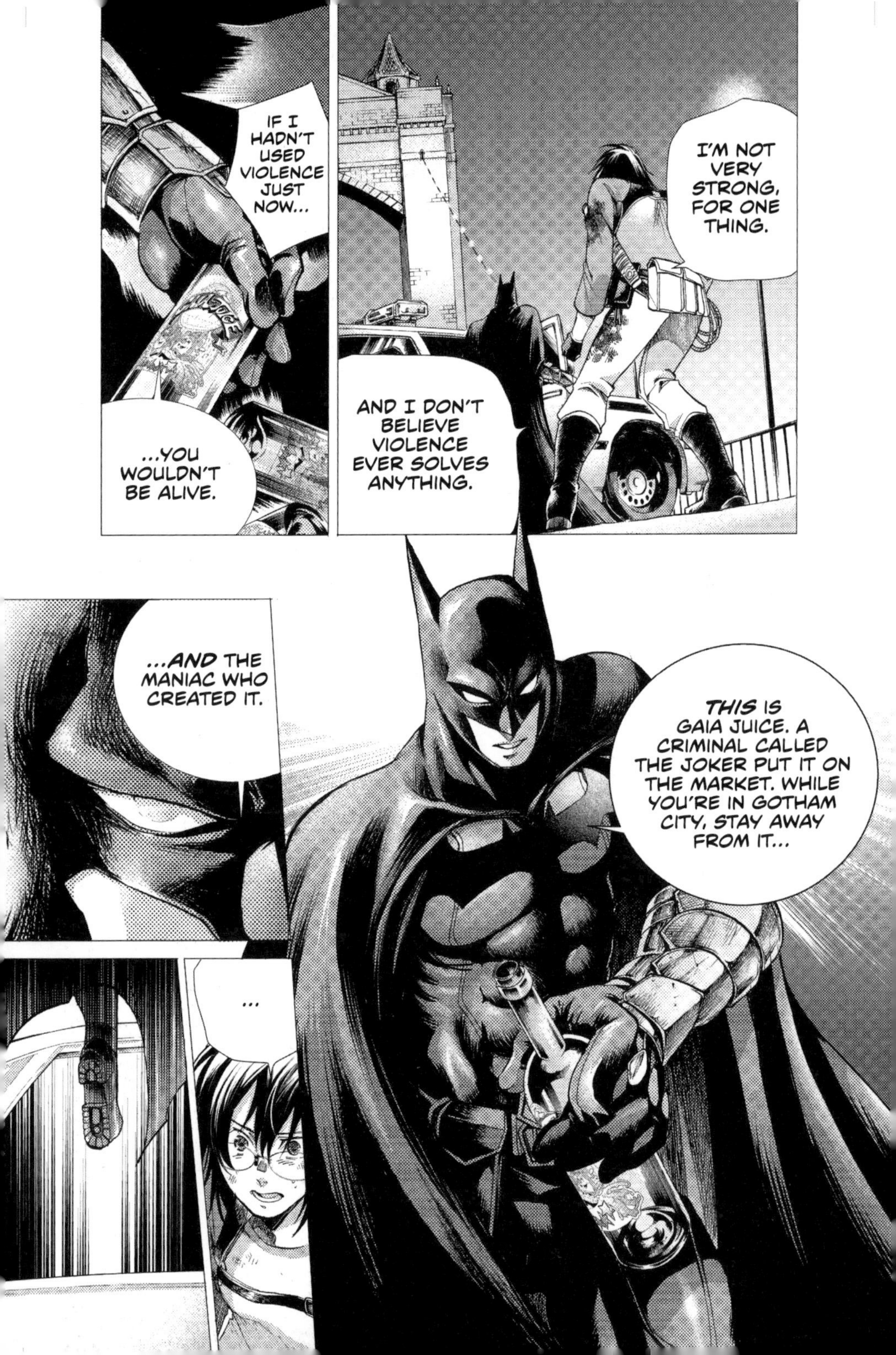
I'M NOT VERY STRONG, FOR ONE THING.
AND I DON'T BELIEVE VIOLENCE EVER SOLVES ANYTHING.
IF I HADN'T USED VIOLENCE JUST NOW...
...YOU WOULDN'T BE ALIVE.
*THIS* IS GAIA JUICE. A CRIMINAL CALLED THE JOKER PUT IT ON THE MARKET. WHILE YOU'RE IN GOTHAM CITY, STAY AWAY FROM IT...
...*AND* THE MANIAC WHO CREATED IT.
...

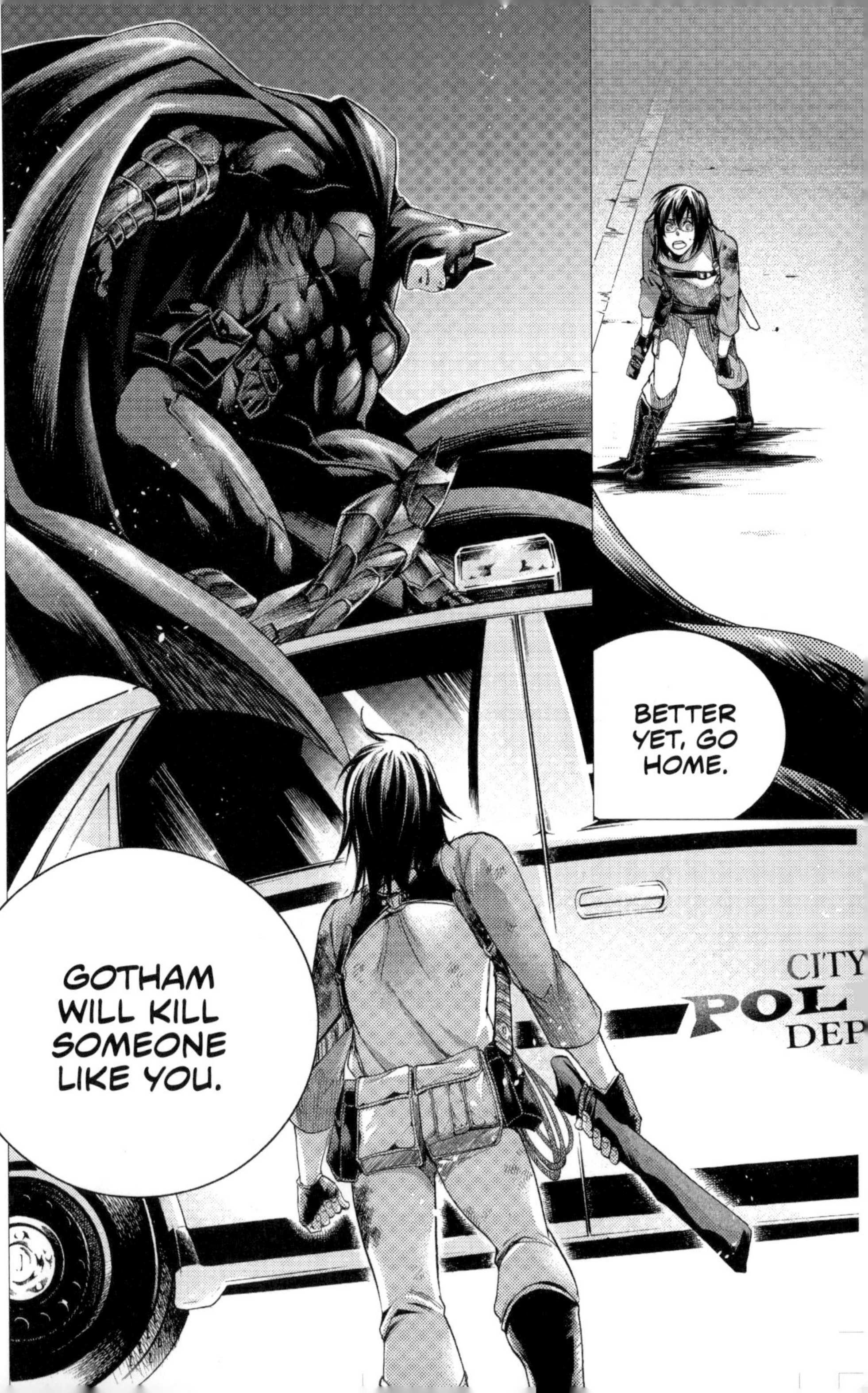
BETTER YET, GO HOME.
CITY
POL
DEP
GOTHAM WILL KILL SOMEONE LIKE YOU.

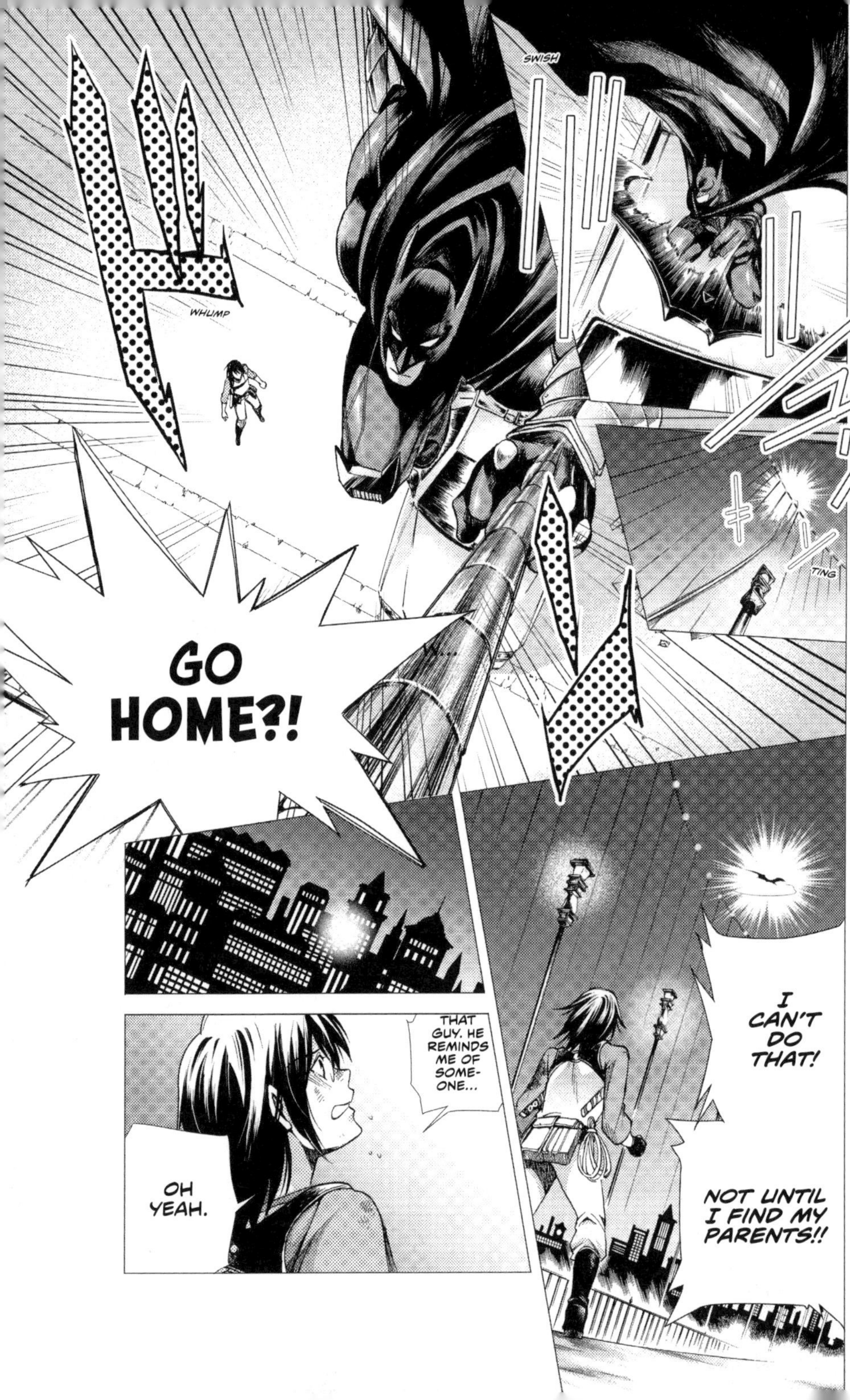
SWISH
WHUMP
TING
GO HOME?!
I CAN'T DO THAT!
NOT UNTIL I FIND MY PARENTS!!
THAT GUY. HE REMINDS ME OF SOME-ONE...
OH YEAH.

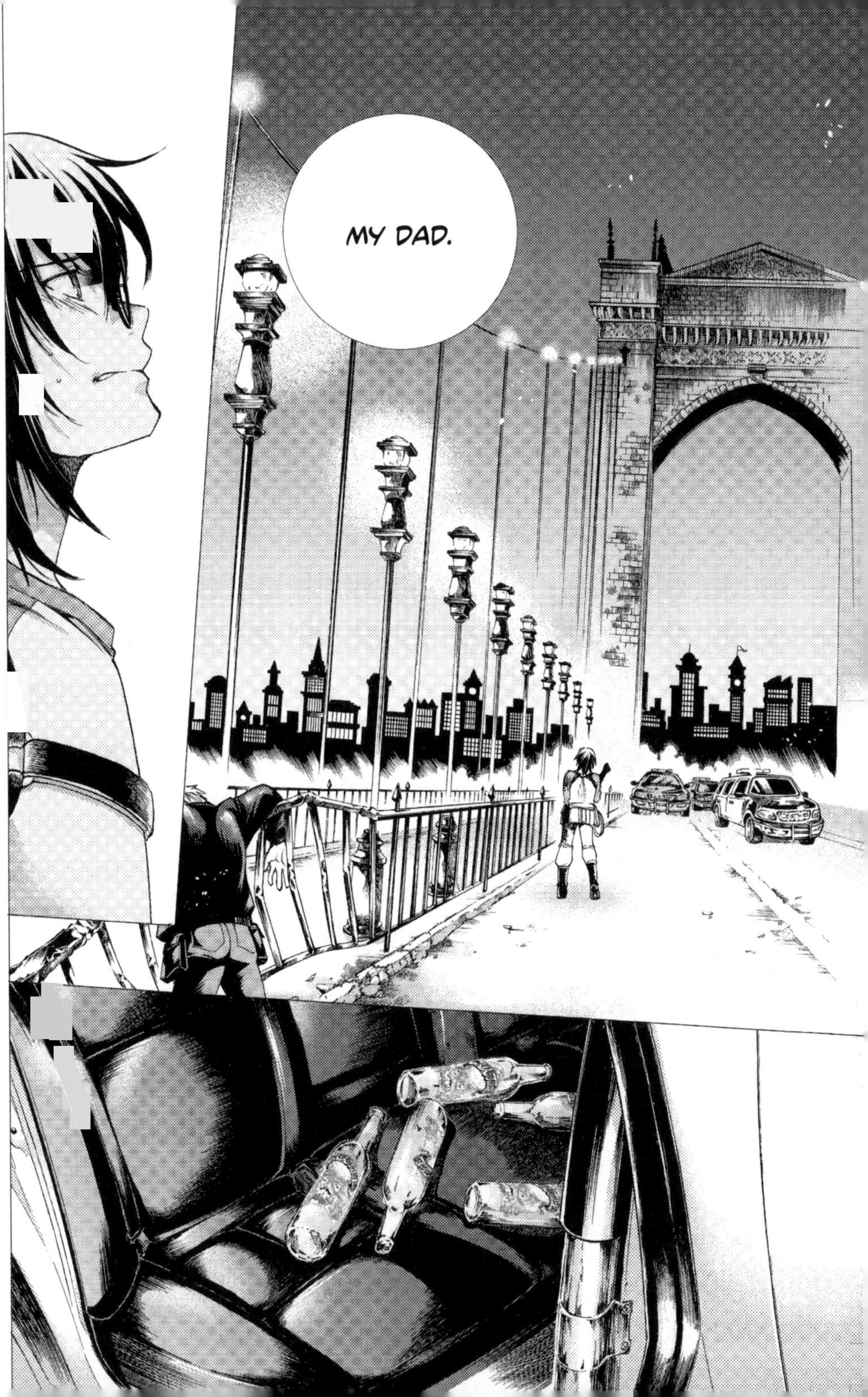
MY DAD.

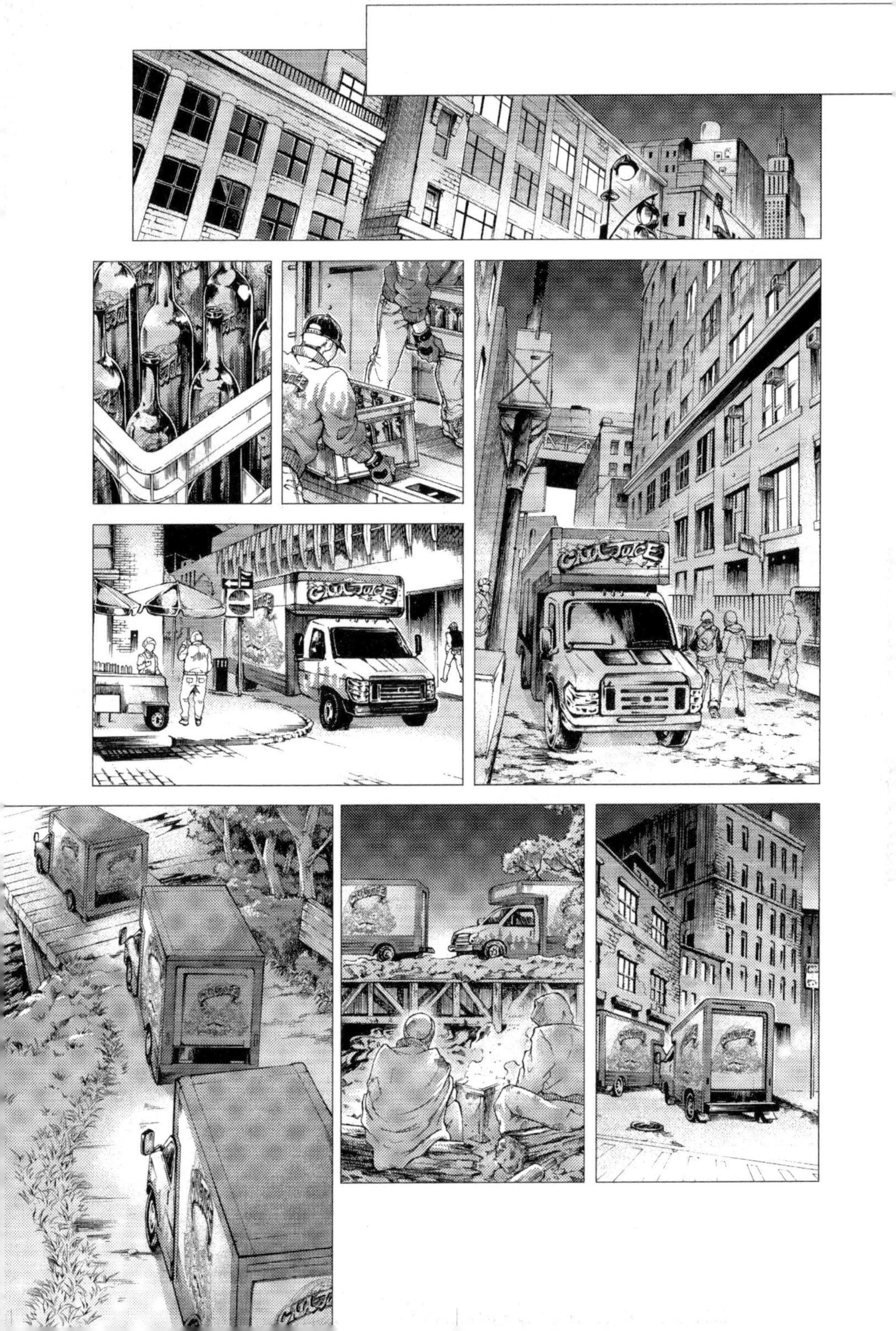

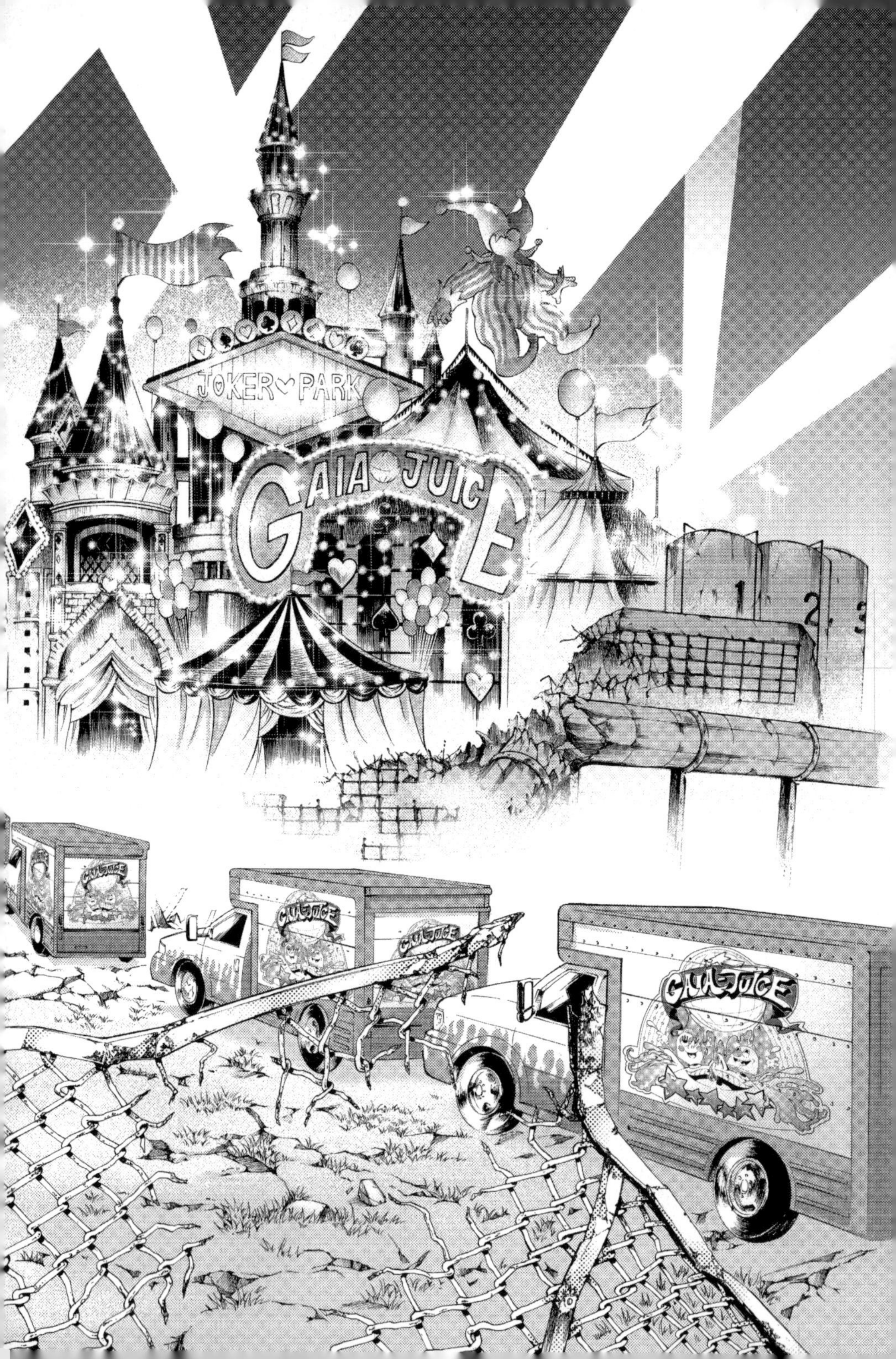
JOKER PARK
GAIA JUICE
GAIA JUICE
GAIA JUICE
GAIA JUICE
GAIA JUICE

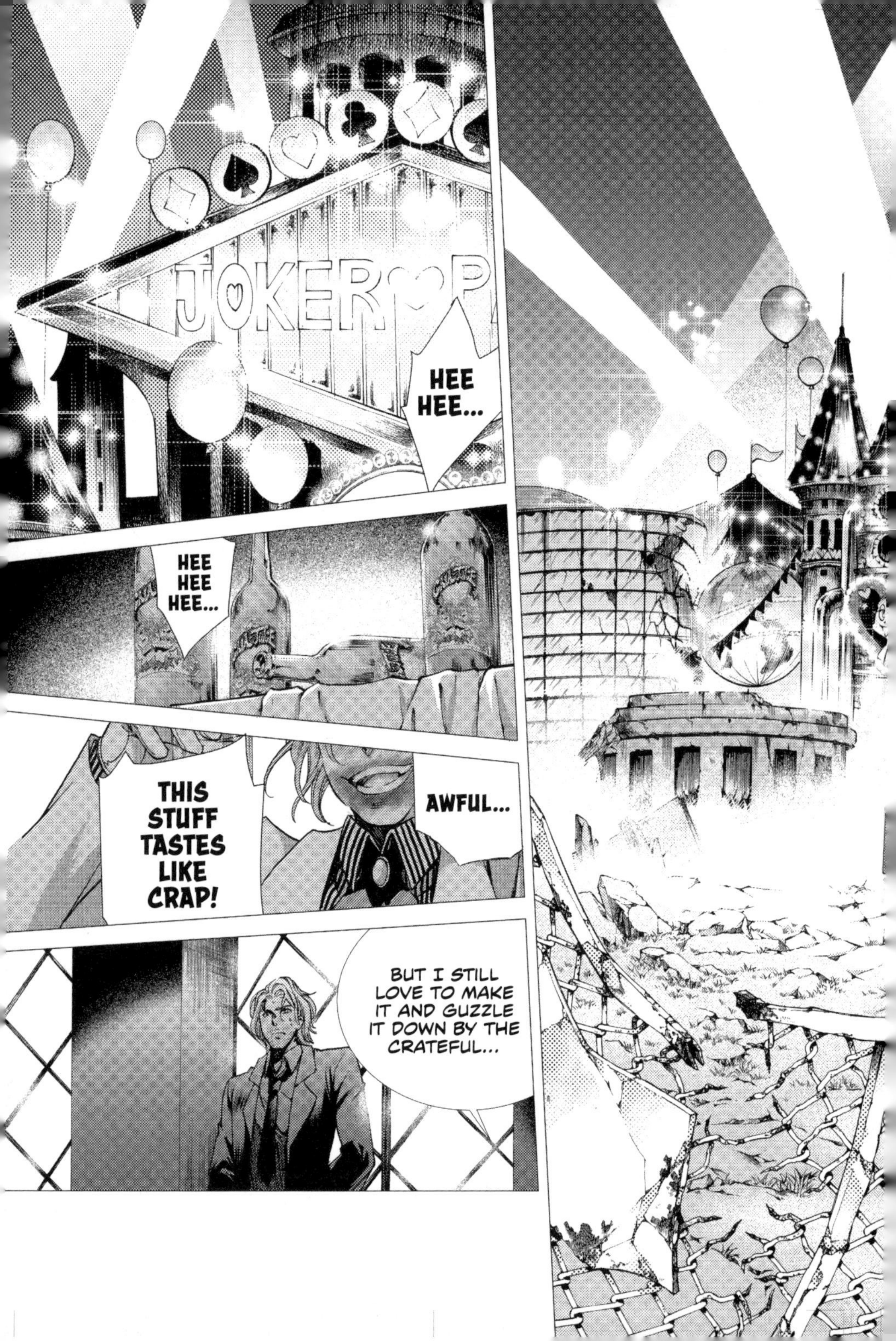
JOKER
HEE HEE...
HEE HEE HEE...
AWFUL...
THIS STUFF TASTES LIKE CRAP!
BUT I STILL LOVE TO MAKE IT AND GUZZLE IT DOWN BY THE CRATEFUL...

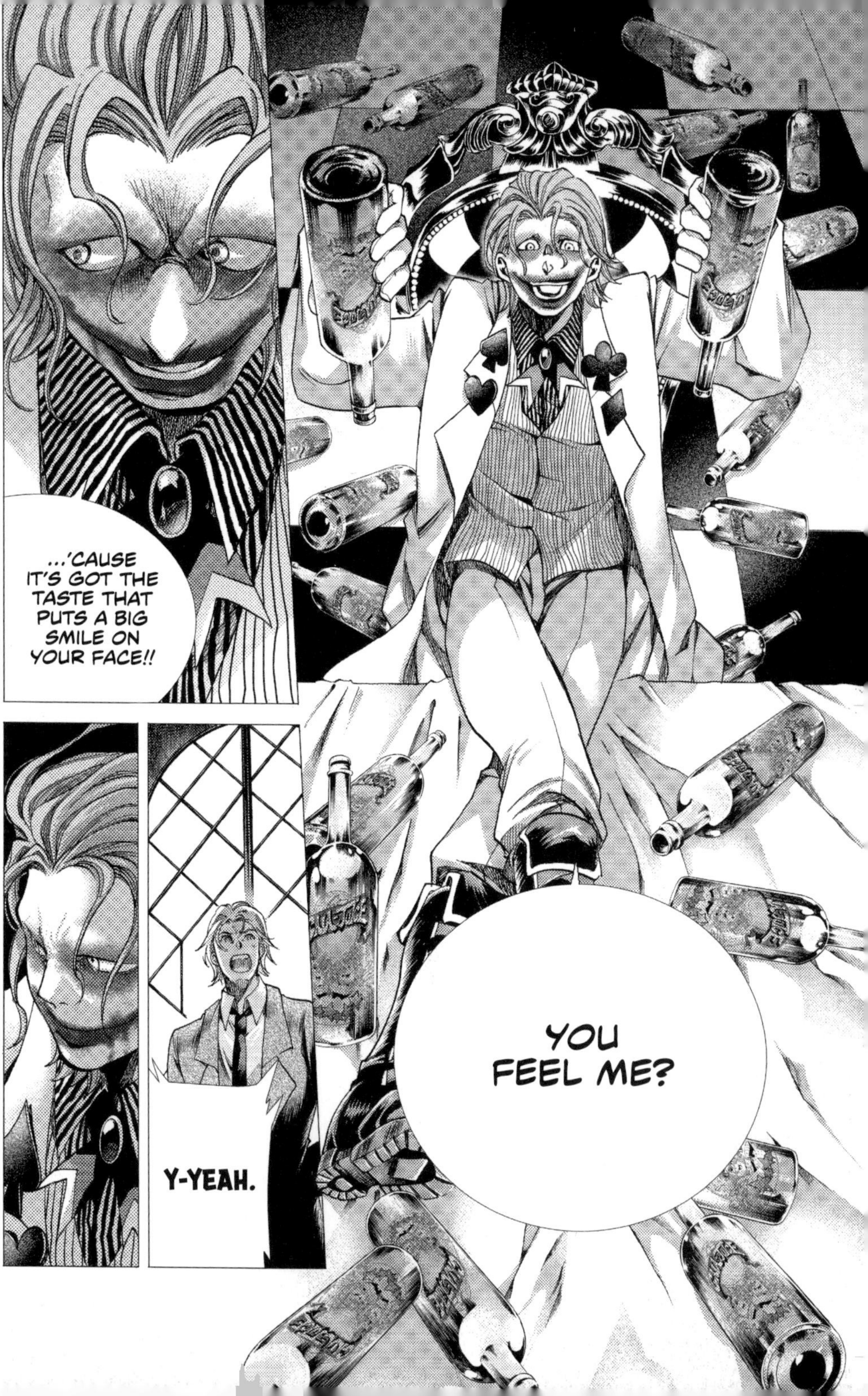
YOU FEEL ME?
...'CAUSE IT'S GOT THE TASTE THAT PUTS A BIG SMILE ON YOUR FACE!!
Y-YEAH.

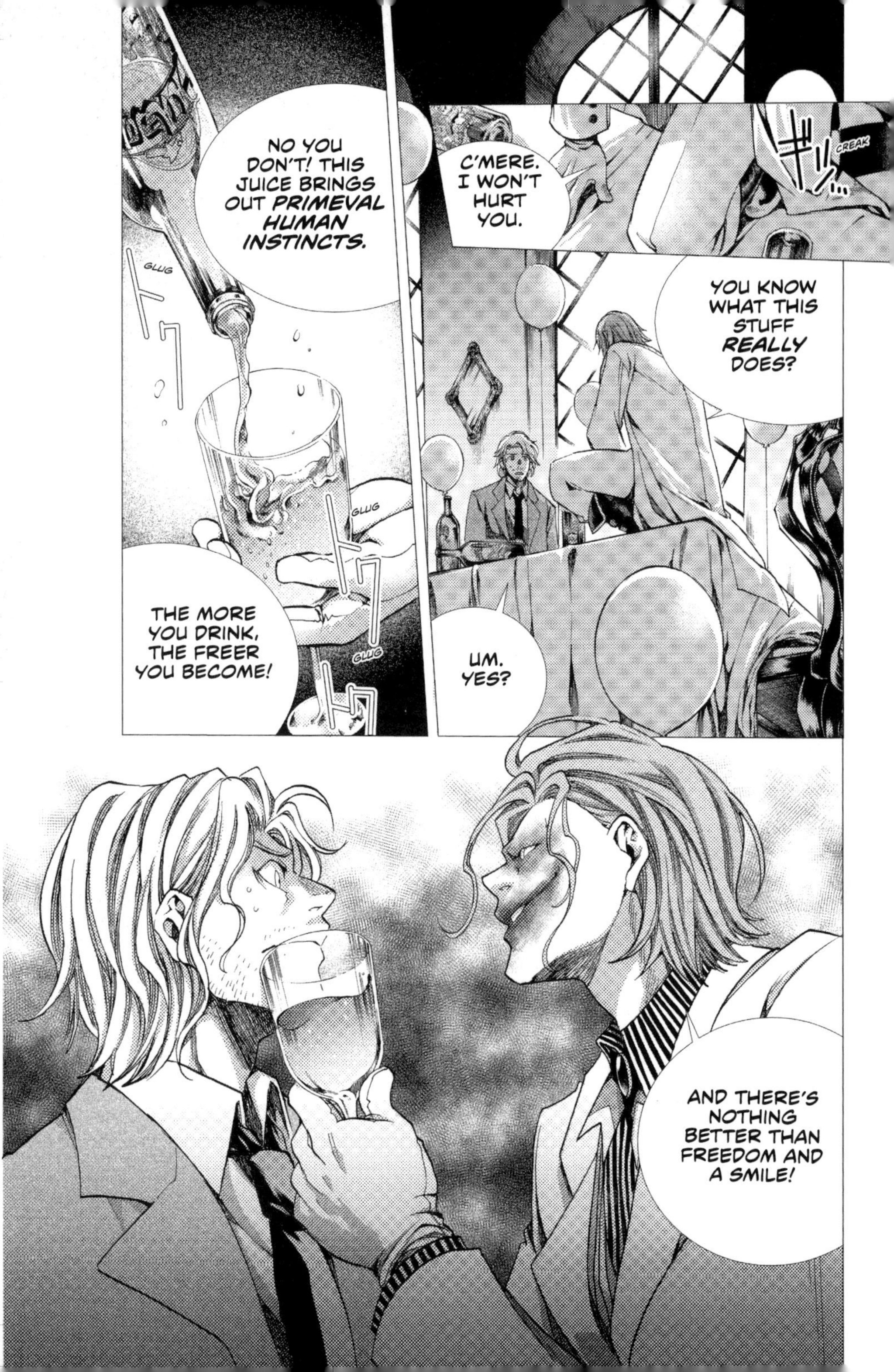
CREAK
C'MERE. I WON'T HURT YOU.
YOU KNOW WHAT THIS STUFF REALLY DOES?
UM. YES?
NO YOU DON'T! THIS JUICE BRINGS OUT PRIMEVAL HUMAN INSTINCTS.
GLUG
GLUG
GLUG
THE MORE YOU DRINK, THE FREER YOU BECOME!
AND THERE'S NOTHING BETTER THAN FREEDOM AND A SMILE!

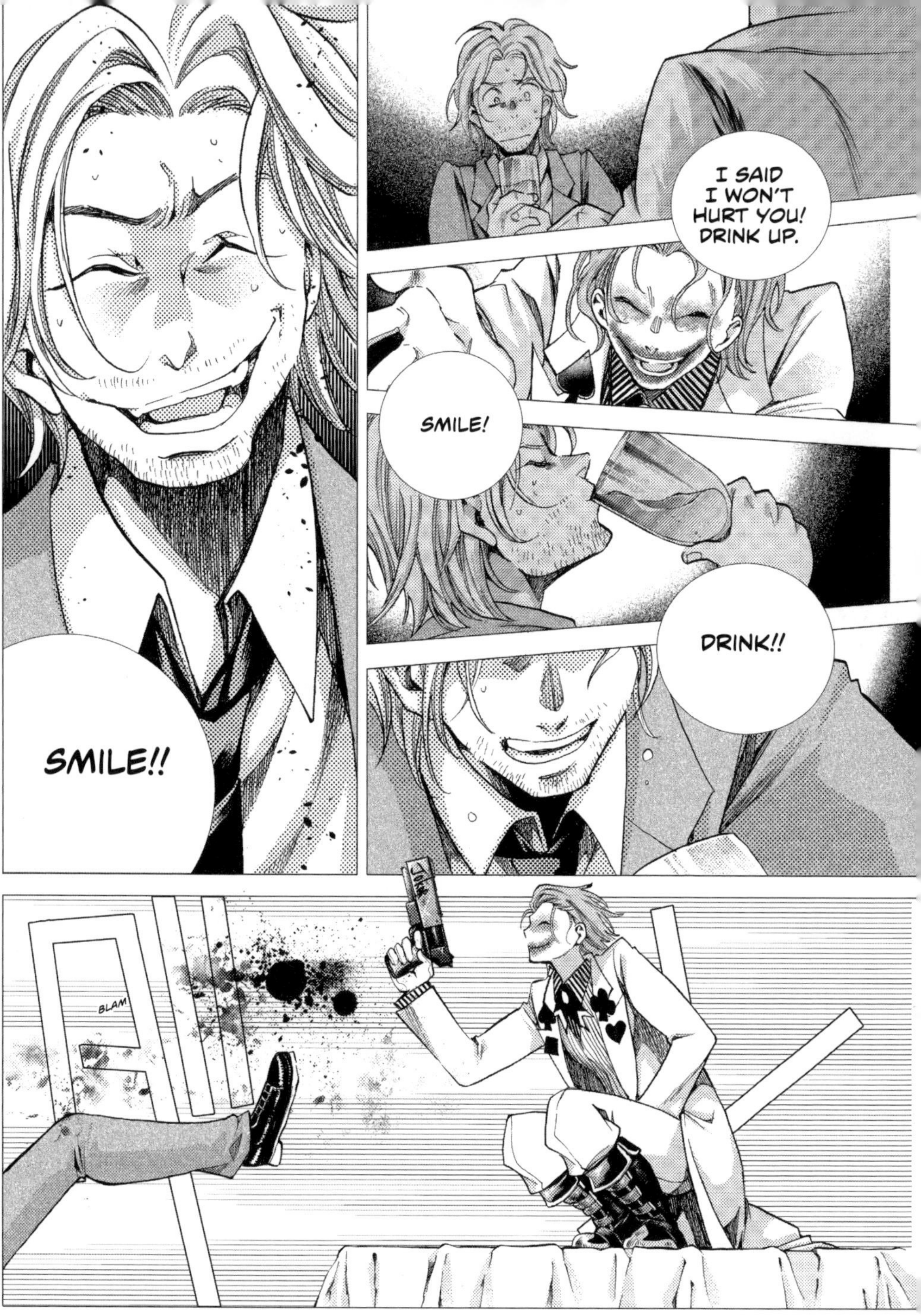
I SAID I WON'T HURT YOU! DRINK UP.
SMILE!
DRINK!!
SMILE!!
BLAM

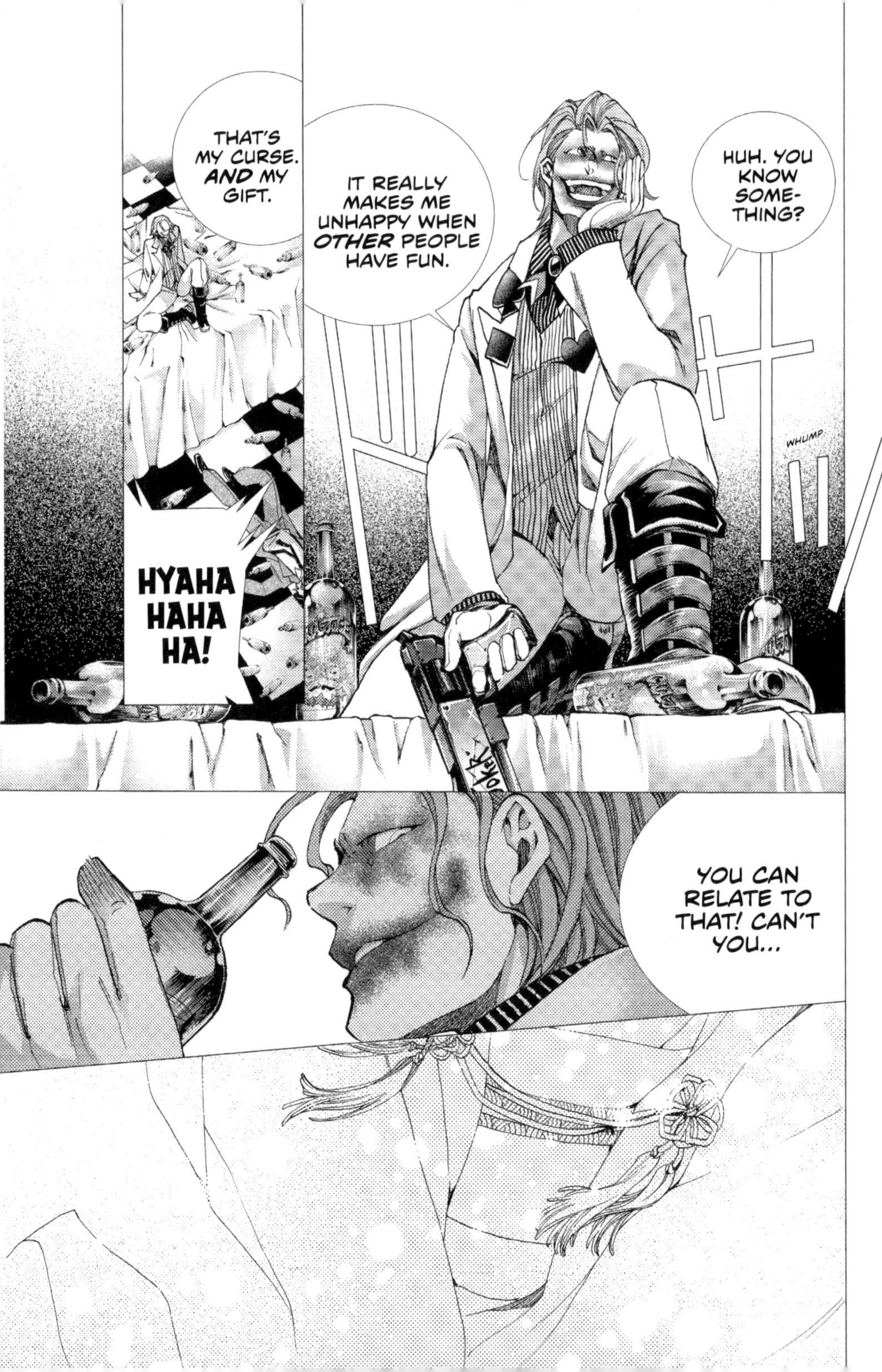
HUH. YOU KNOW SOMETHING?
WHUMP
IT REALLY MAKES ME UNHAPPY WHEN *OTHER* PEOPLE HAVE FUN.
THAT'S MY CURSE. ***AND*** MY GIFT.
HYAHA HAHA HA!
YOU CAN RELATE TO THAT! CAN'T YOU...

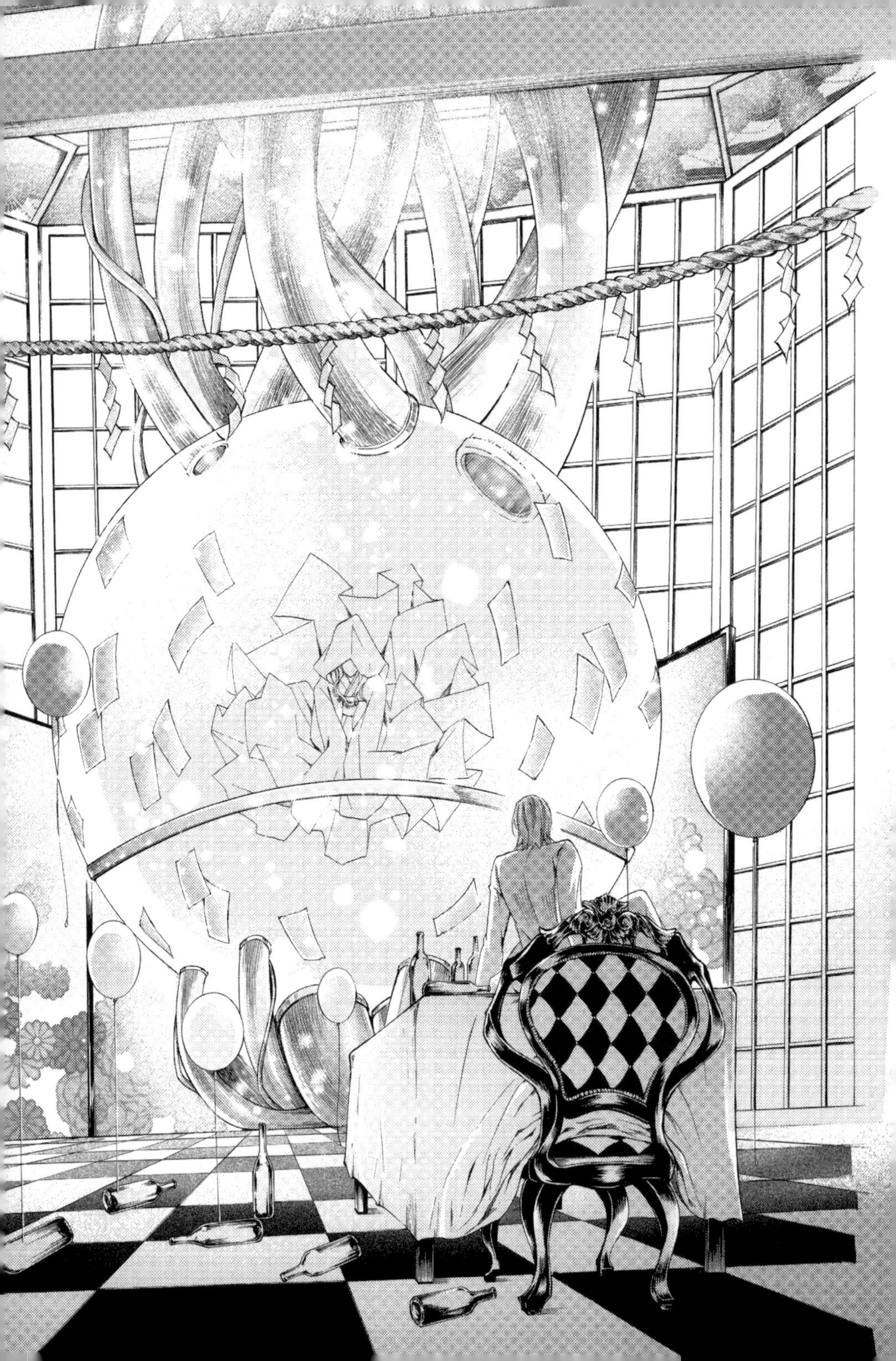

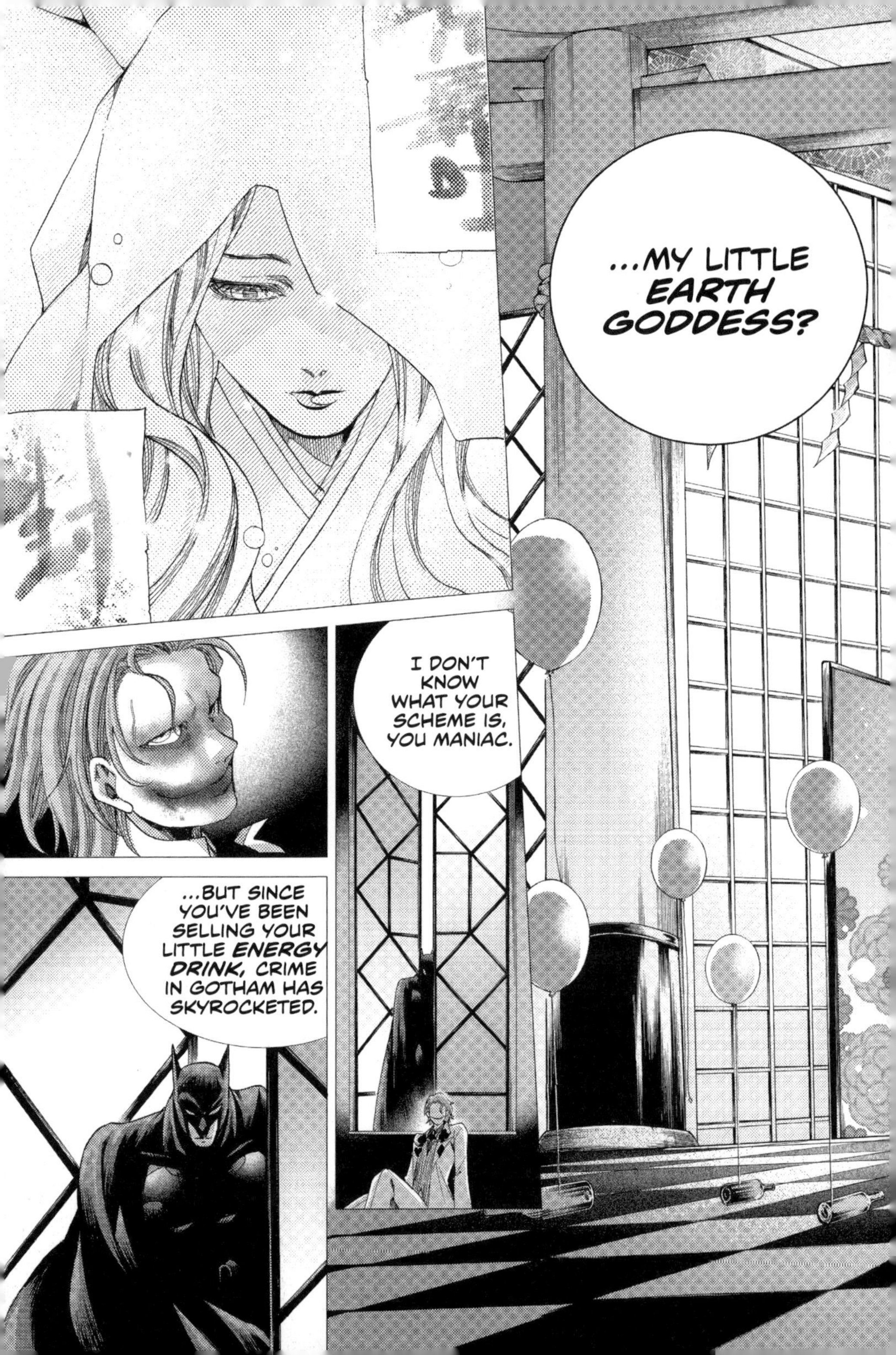
...MY LITTLE EARTH GODDESS?
I DON'T KNOW WHAT YOUR SCHEME IS, YOU MANIAC.
...BUT SINCE YOU'VE BEEN SELLING YOUR LITTLE ENERGY DRINK, CRIME IN GOTHAM HAS SKYROCKETED.

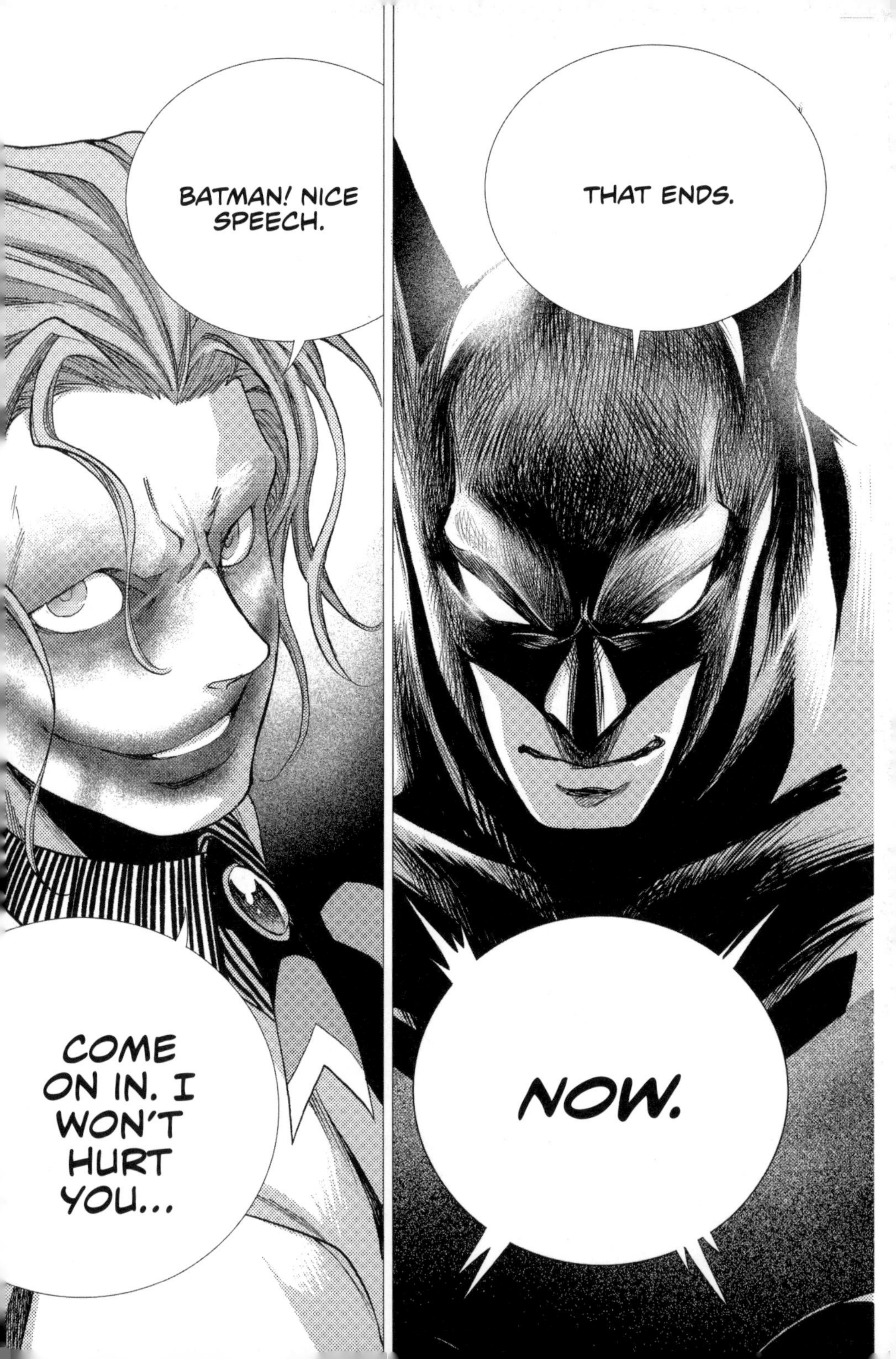
THAT ENDS.
NOW.
BATMAN! NICE SPEECH.
COME ON IN. I WON'T HURT YOU...

# CHAPTER 2

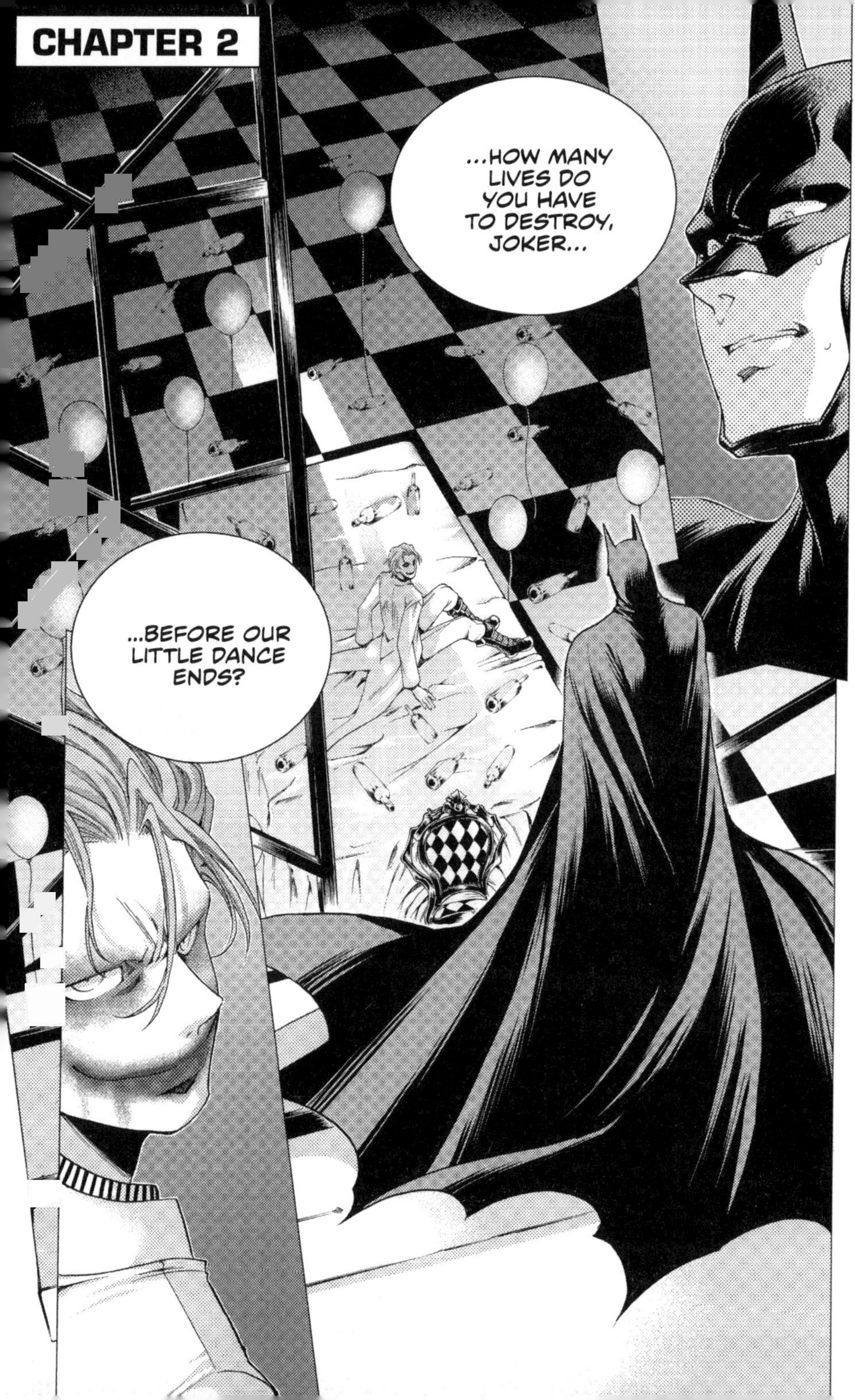
...HOW MANY LIVES DO YOU HAVE TO DESTROY, JOKER...
...BEFORE OUR LITTLE DANCE ENDS?

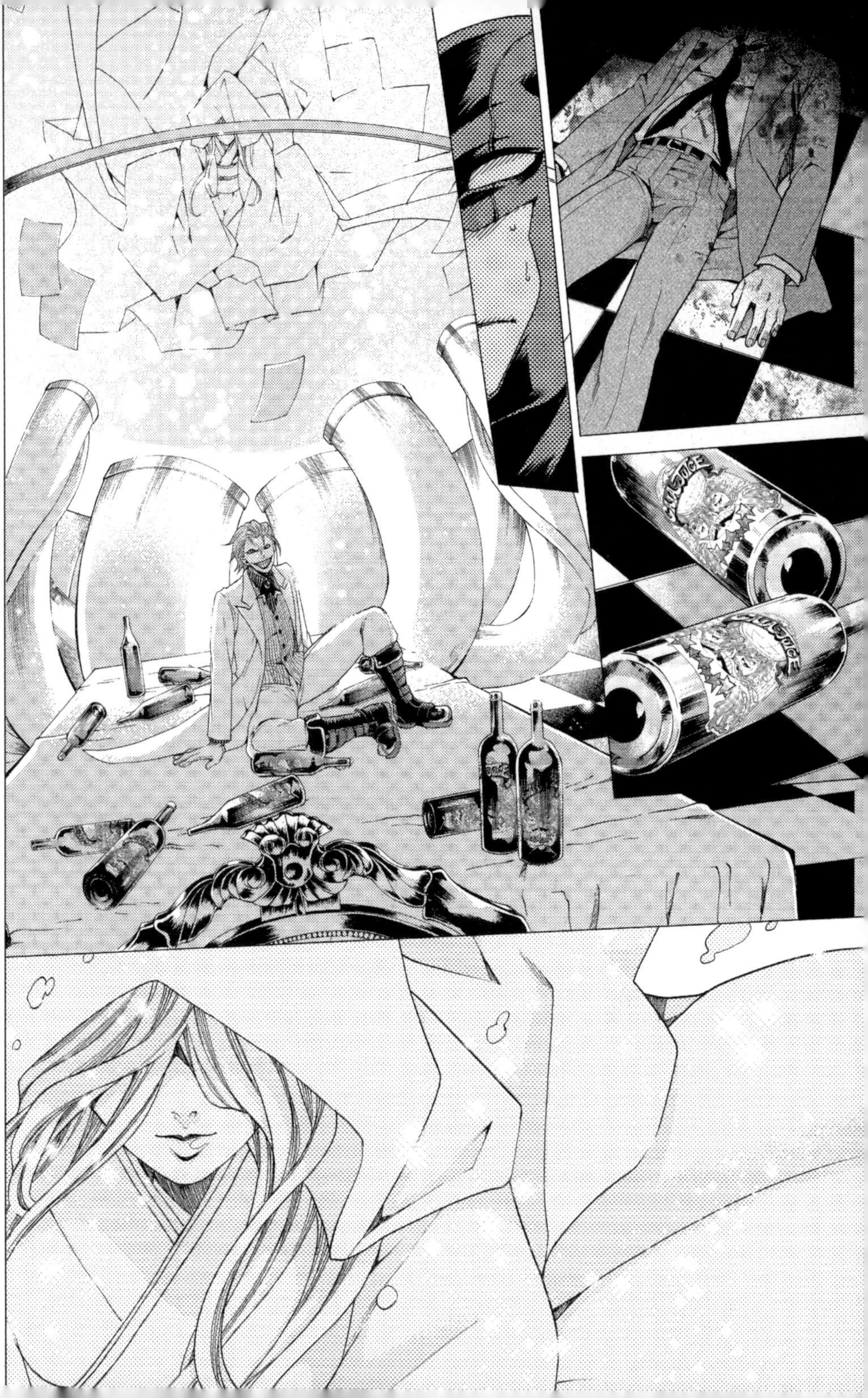

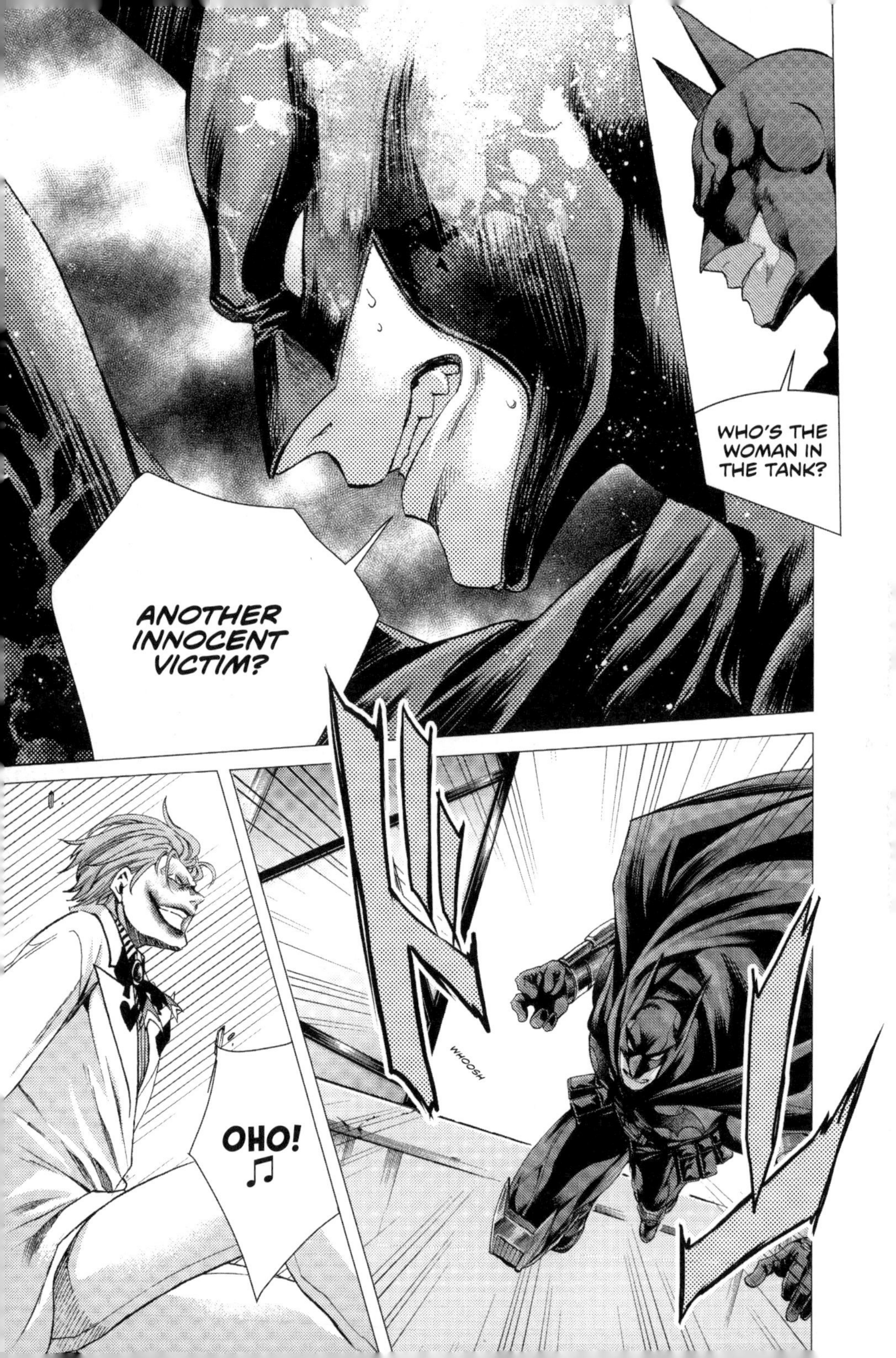
WHO'S THE WOMAN IN THE TANK?
ANOTHER INNOCENT VICTIM?
WHOOSH
OHO! ♫

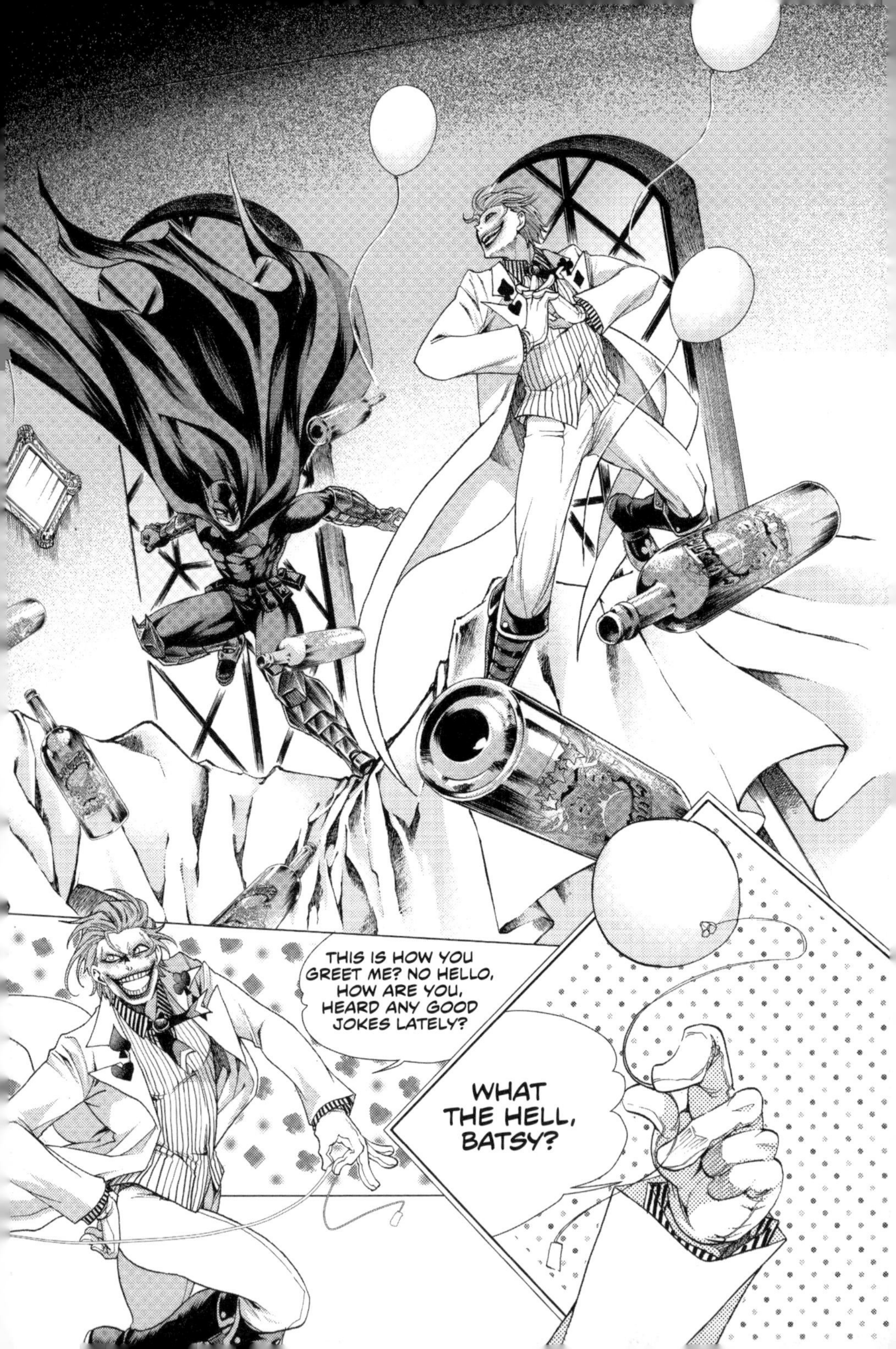
THIS IS HOW YOU GREET ME? NO HELLO, HOW ARE YOU, HEARD ANY GOOD JOKES LATELY?
WHAT THE HELL, BATSY?

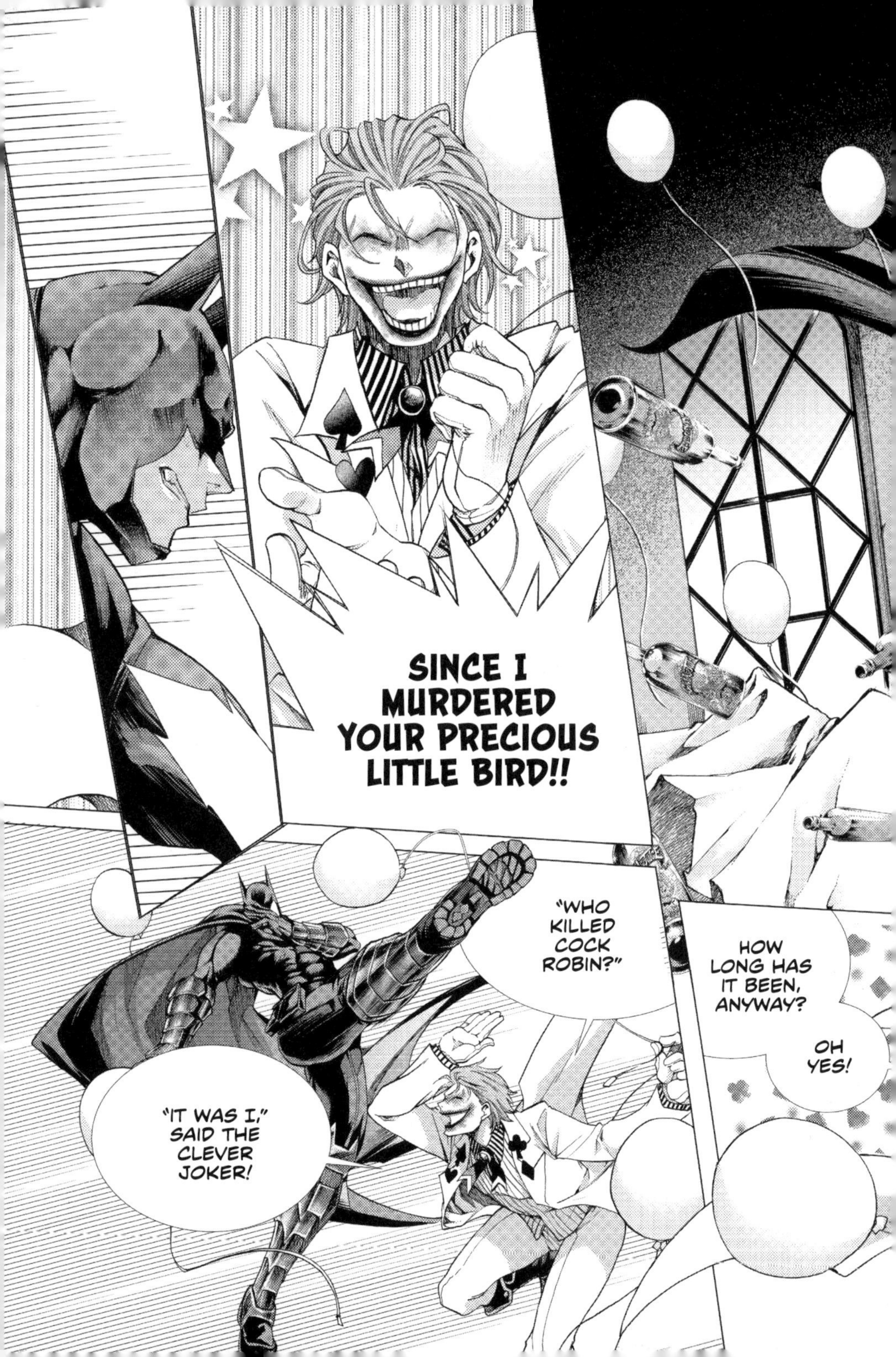
SINCE I MURDERED YOUR PRECIOUS LITTLE BIRD!!
HOW LONG HAS IT BEEN, ANYWAY?
OH YES!
"WHO KILLED COCK ROBIN?"
"IT WAS I," SAID THE CLEVER JOKER!

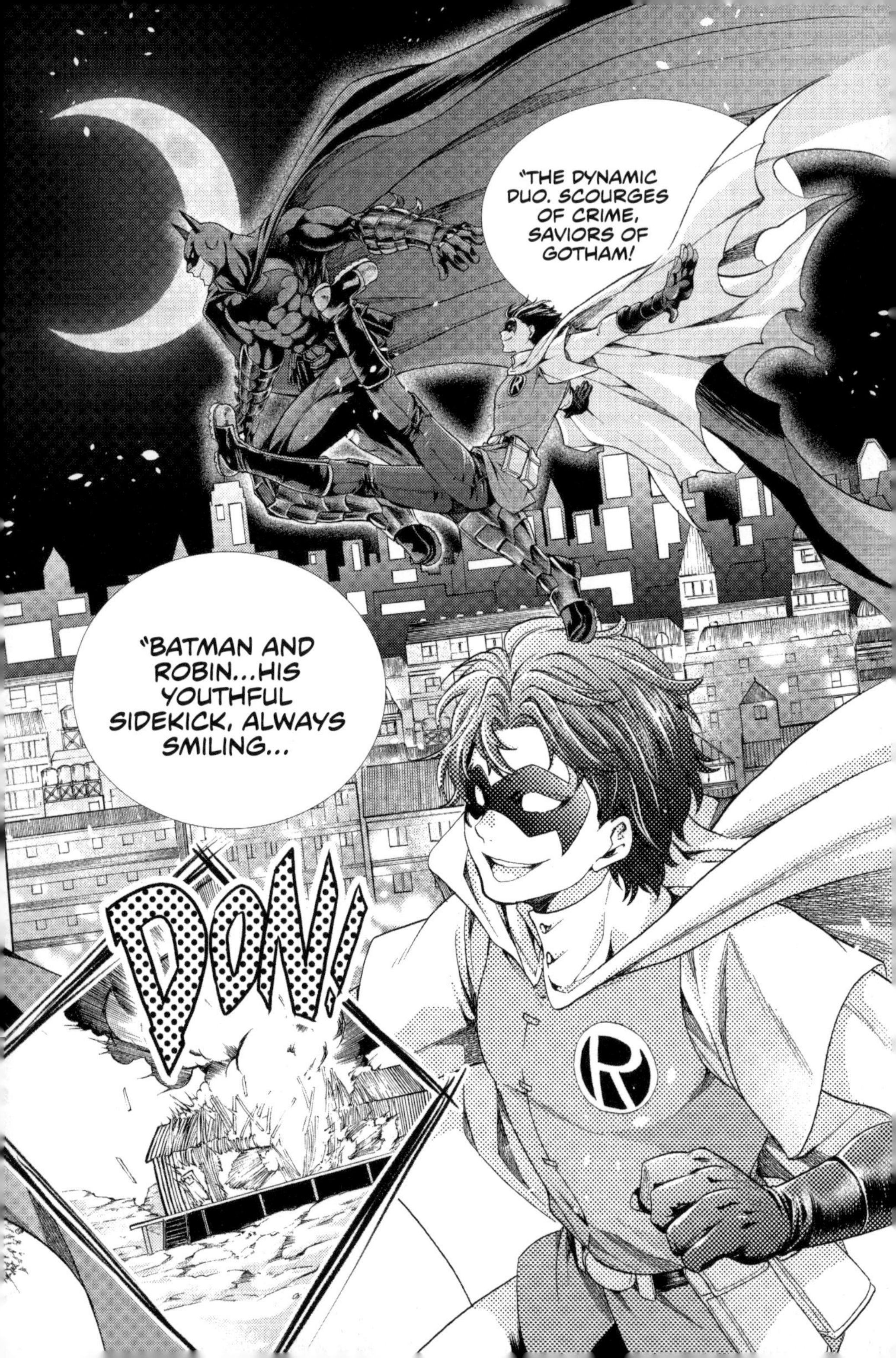
"THE DYNAMIC DUO. SCOURGES OF CRIME, SAVIORS OF GOTHAM!
"BATMAN AND ROBIN...HIS YOUTHFUL SIDEKICK, ALWAYS SMILING...
DOW!

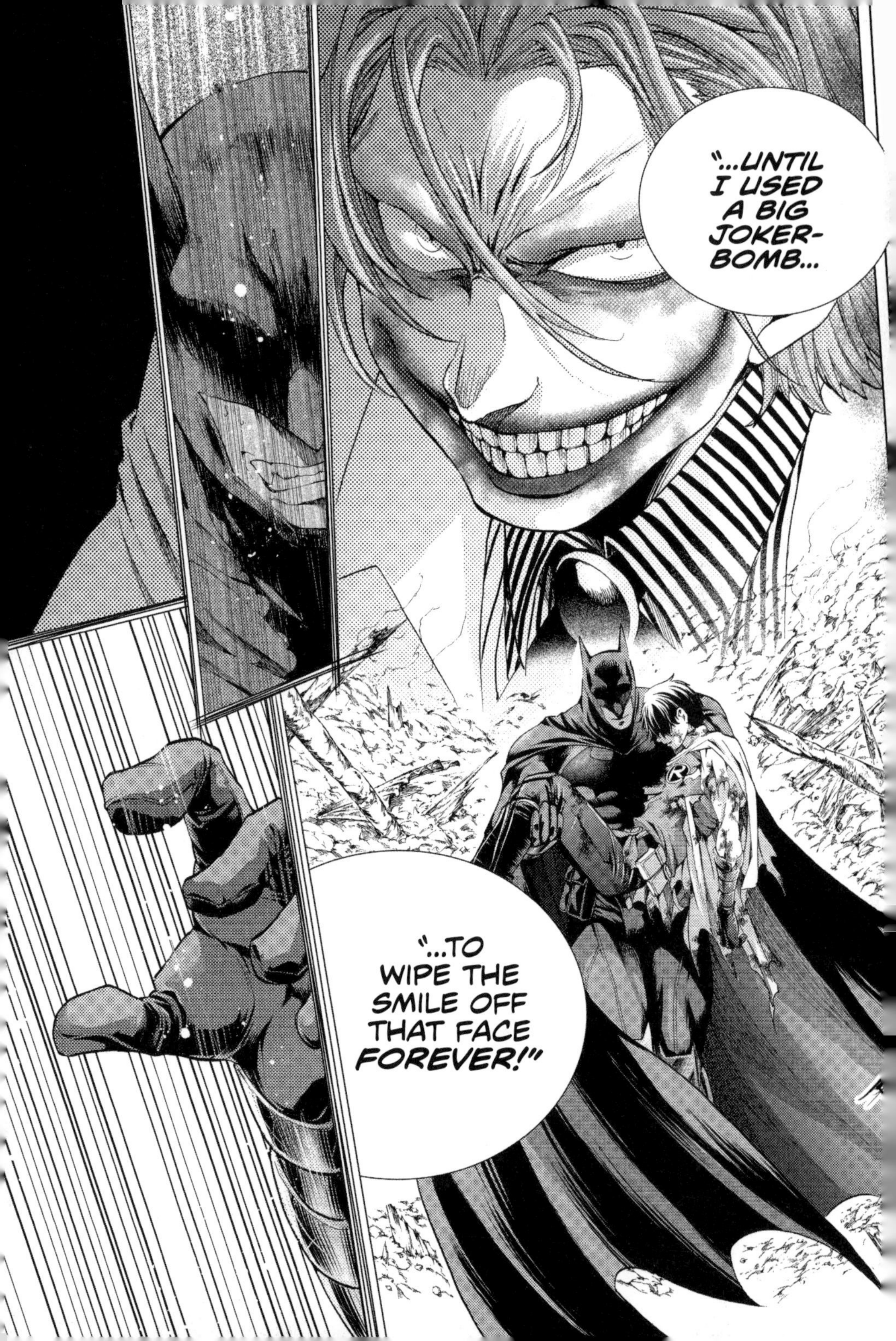
"...UNTIL I USED A BIG JOKER-BOMB...
"...TO WIPE THE SMILE OFF THAT FACE FOREVER!"

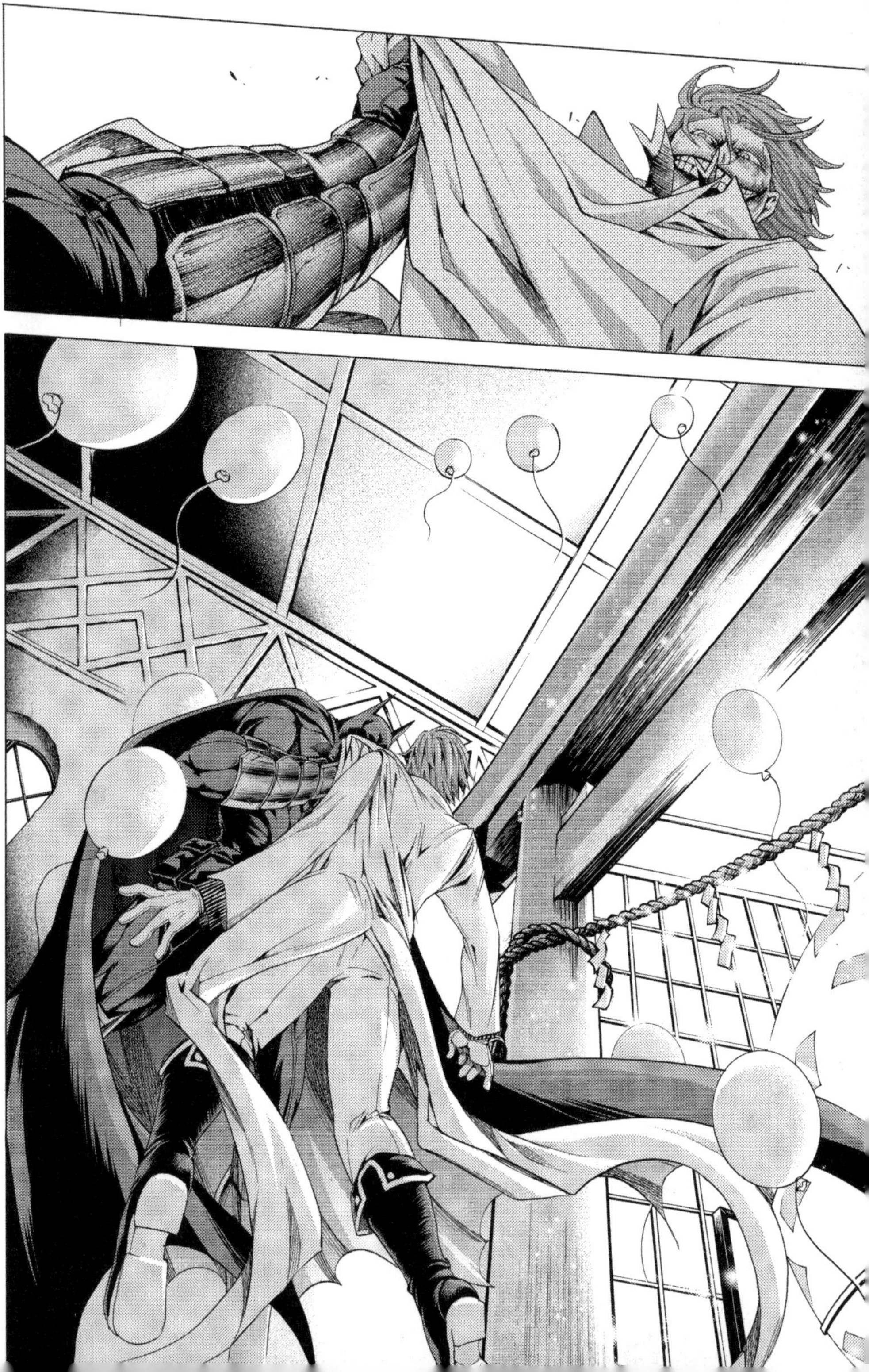

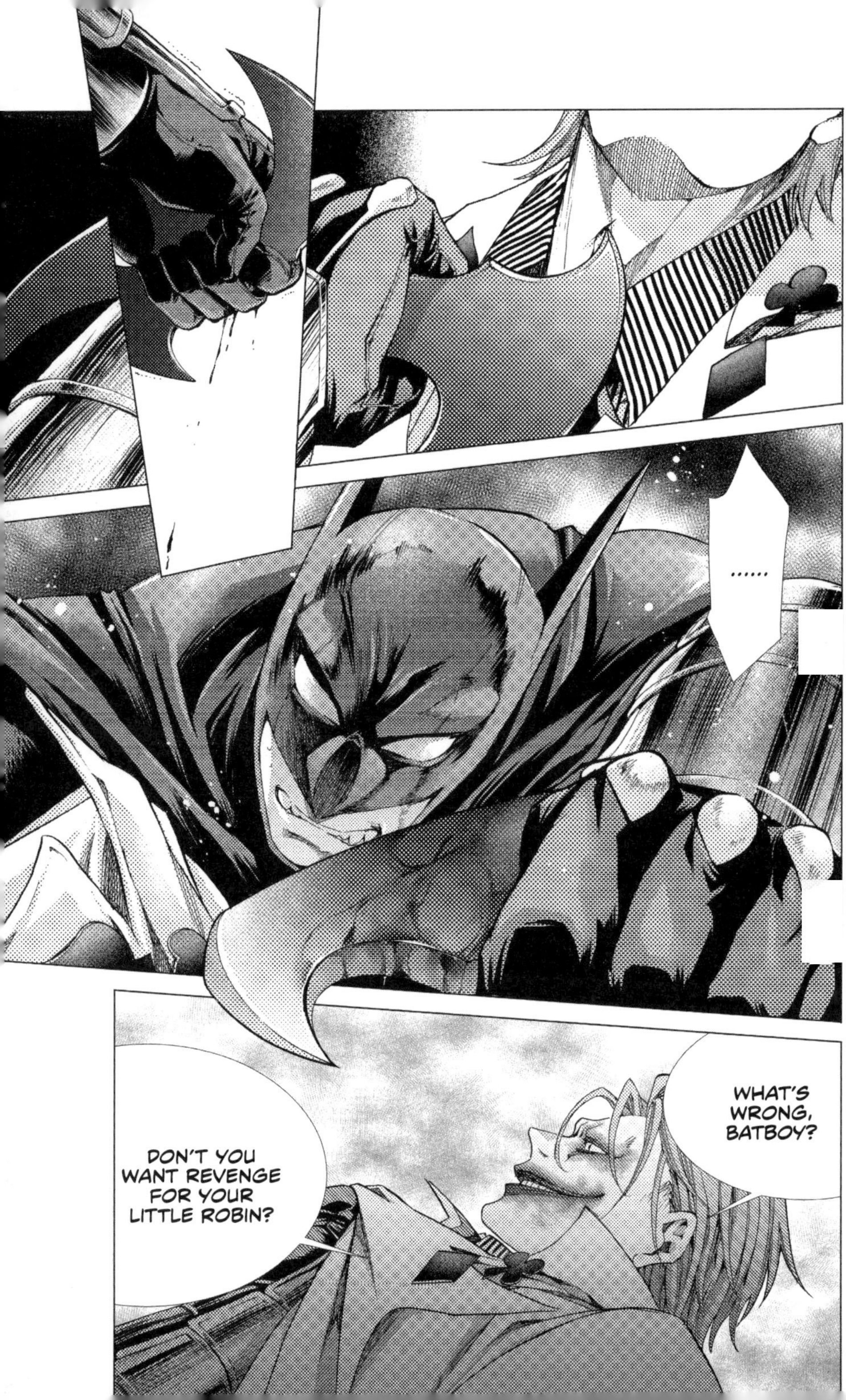
......
WHAT'S WRONG, BATBOY?
DON'T YOU WANT REVENGE FOR YOUR LITTLE ROBIN?

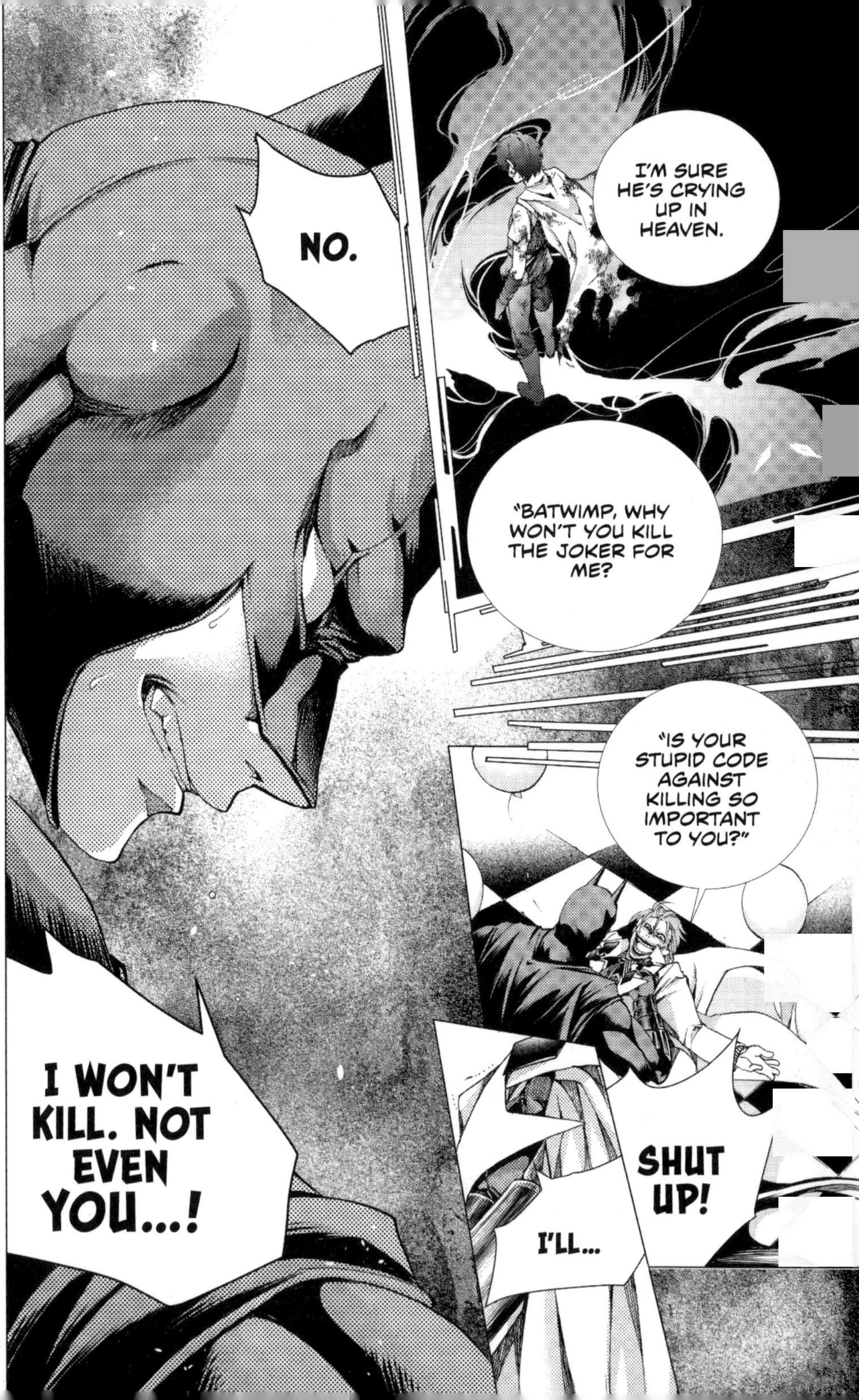
I'M SURE HE'S CRYING UP IN HEAVEN.
"BATWIMP, WHY WON'T YOU KILL THE JOKER FOR ME?
"IS YOUR STUPID CODE AGAINST KILLING SO IMPORTANT TO YOU?"
SHUT UP!
I'LL...
NO.
I WON'T KILL. NOT EVEN YOU...!

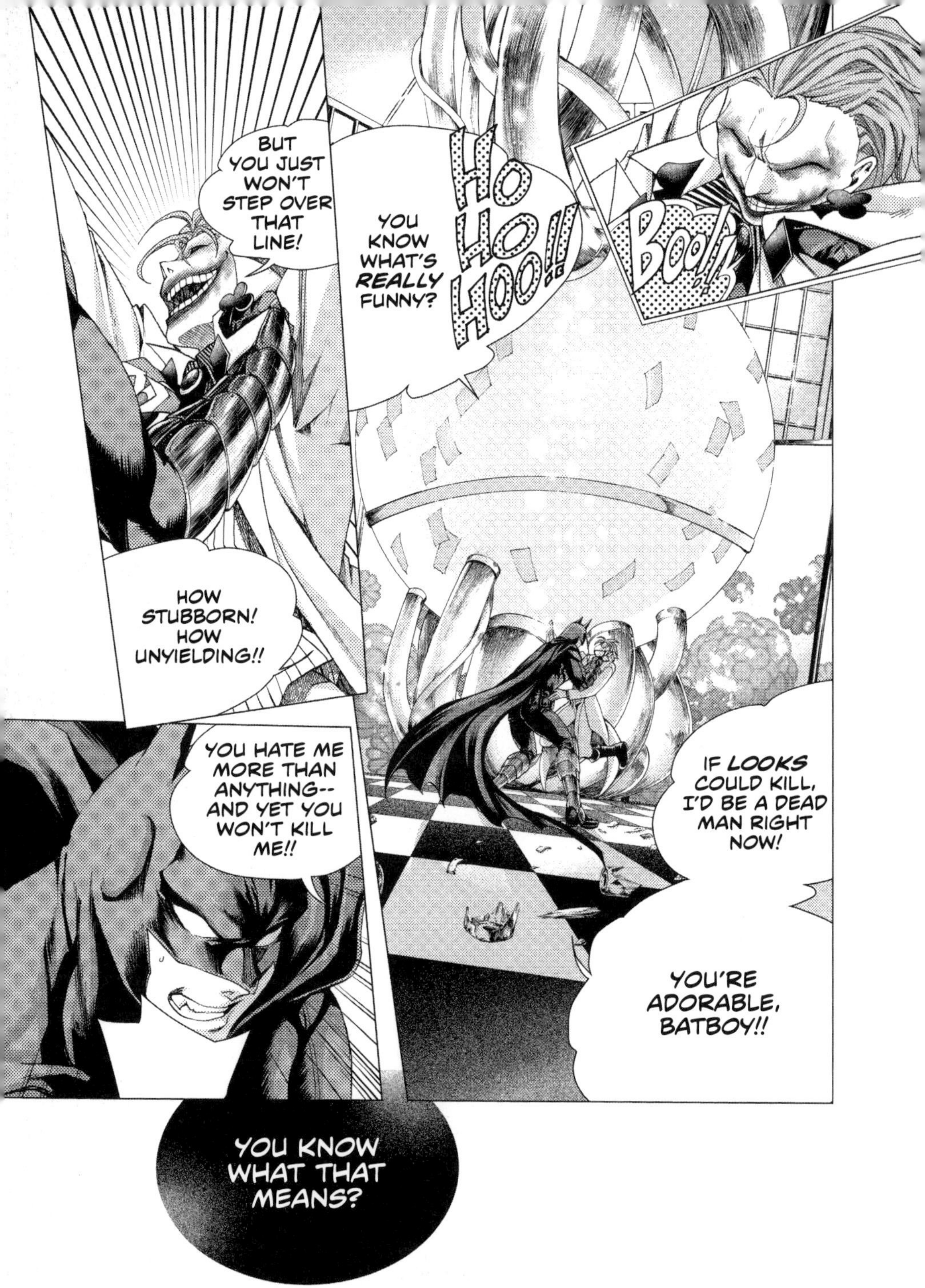
BOO!!
HO HO HOO!!
YOU KNOW WHAT'S *REALLY* FUNNY?
IF *LOOKS* COULD KILL, I'D BE A DEAD MAN RIGHT NOW!
YOU'RE ADORABLE, BATBOY!!
BUT YOU JUST WON'T STEP OVER THAT LINE!
HOW STUBBORN! HOW UNYIELDING!!
YOU HATE ME MORE THAN ANYTHING-- AND YET YOU WON'T KILL ME!!
YOU KNOW WHAT THAT MEANS?

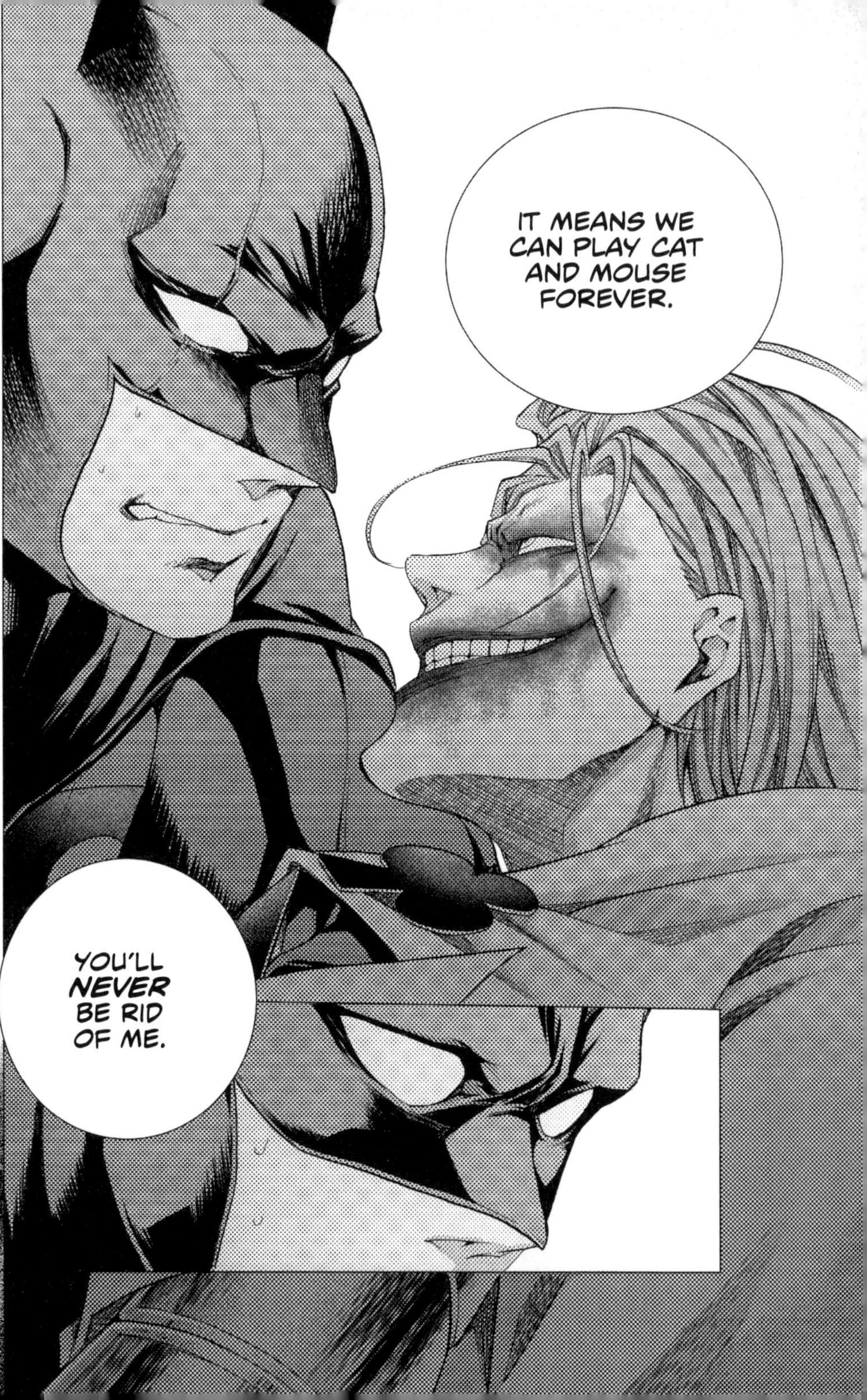
IT MEANS WE CAN PLAY CAT AND MOUSE FOREVER.
YOU'LL *NEVER* BE RID OF ME.

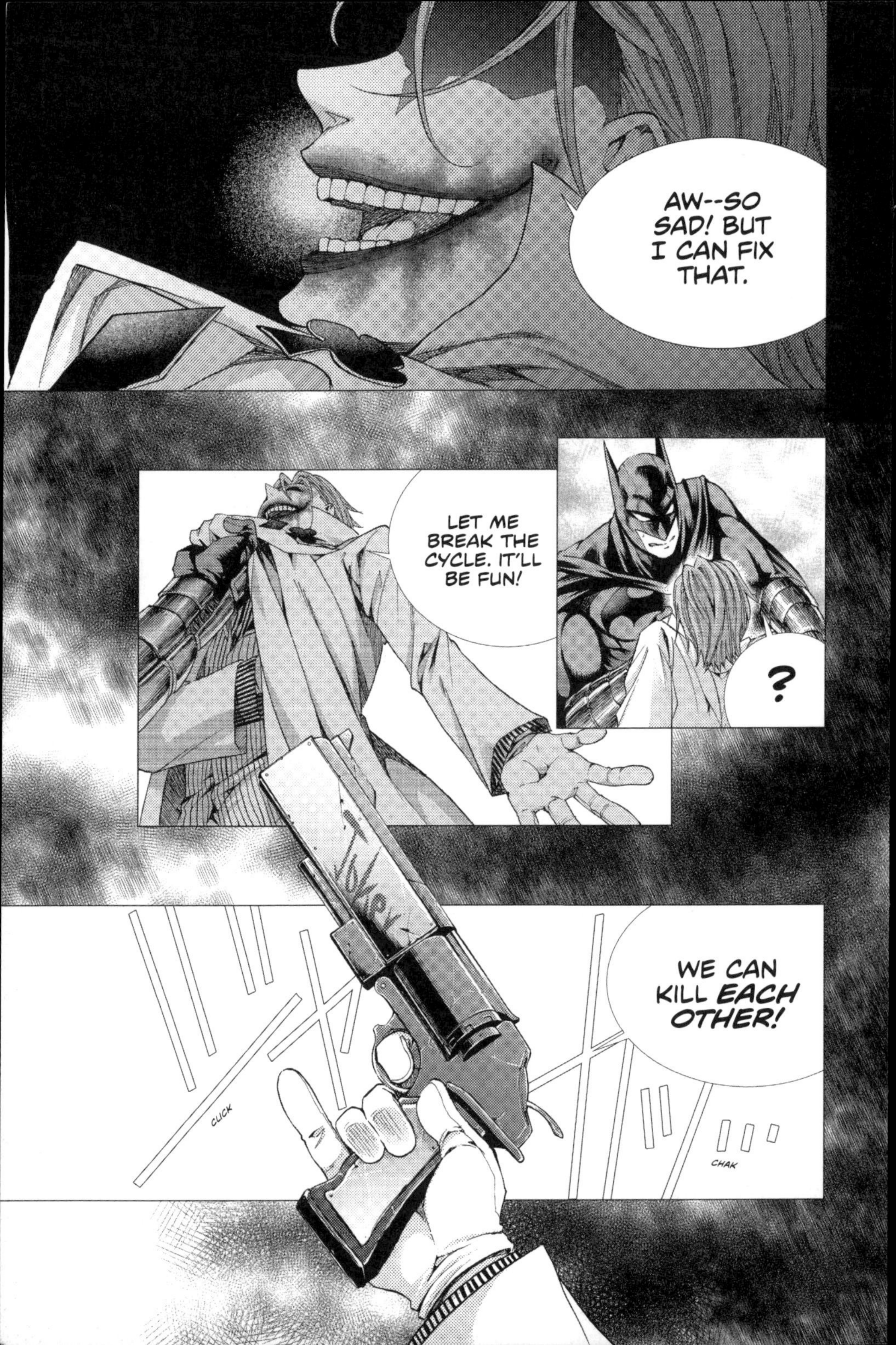
AW--SO SAD! BUT I CAN FIX THAT.
?
LET ME BREAK THE CYCLE. IT'LL BE FUN!
WE CAN KILL EACH OTHER!
CHAK
CLICK

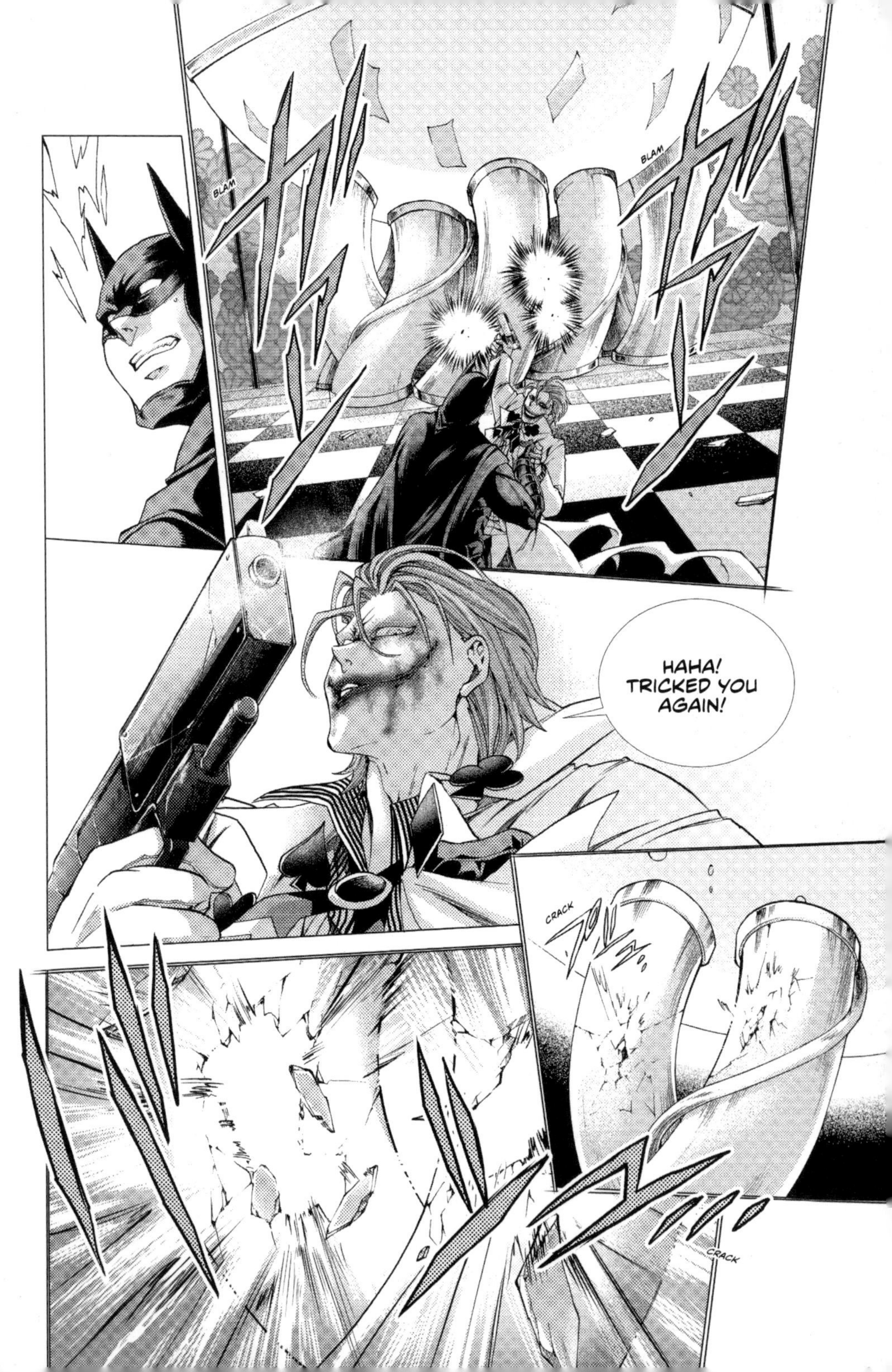
BLAM
BLAM
HAHA! TRICKED YOU AGAIN!
CRACK
CRACK

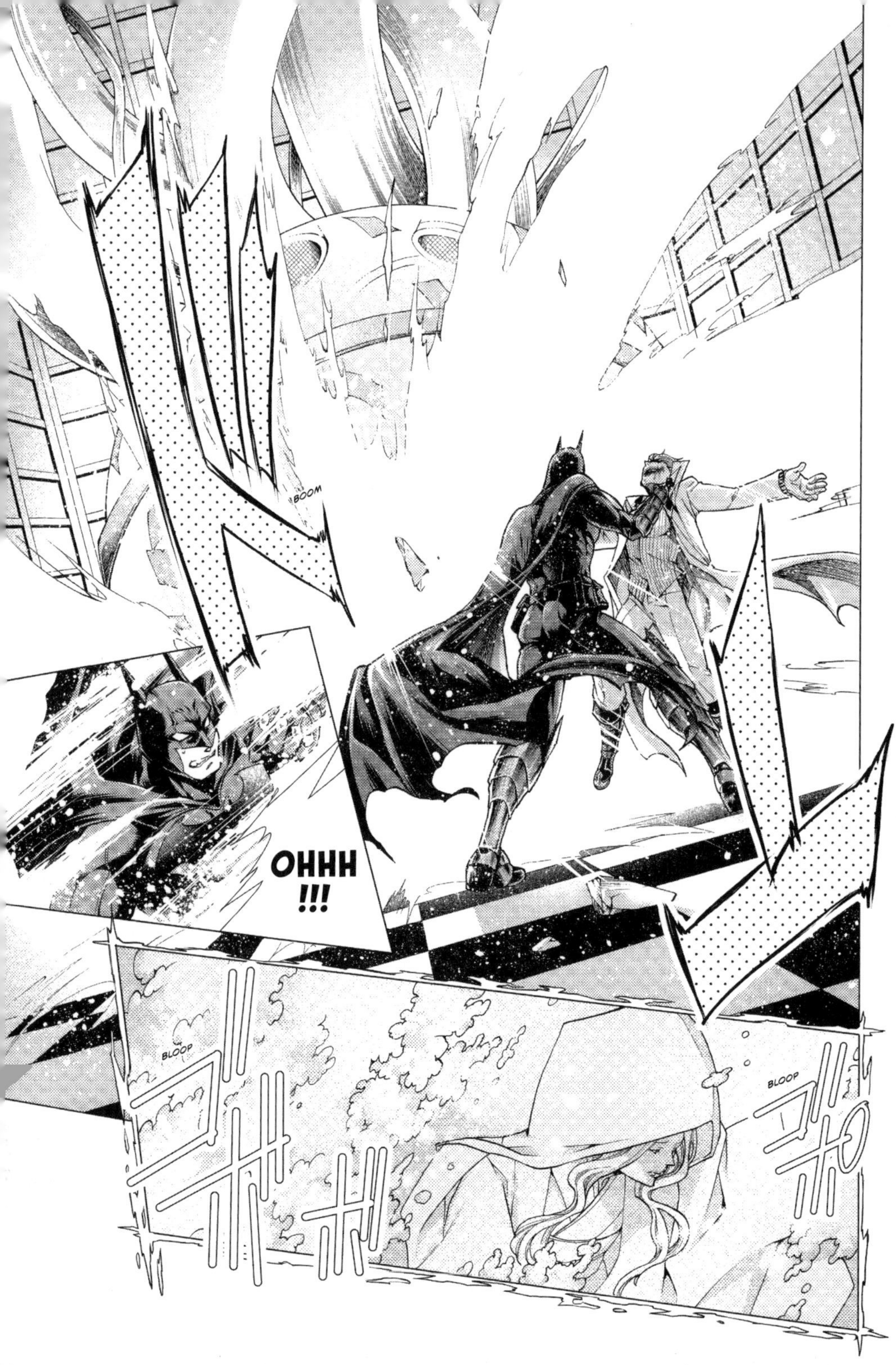
BOOM
OHHH !!!
BLOOP
BLOOP

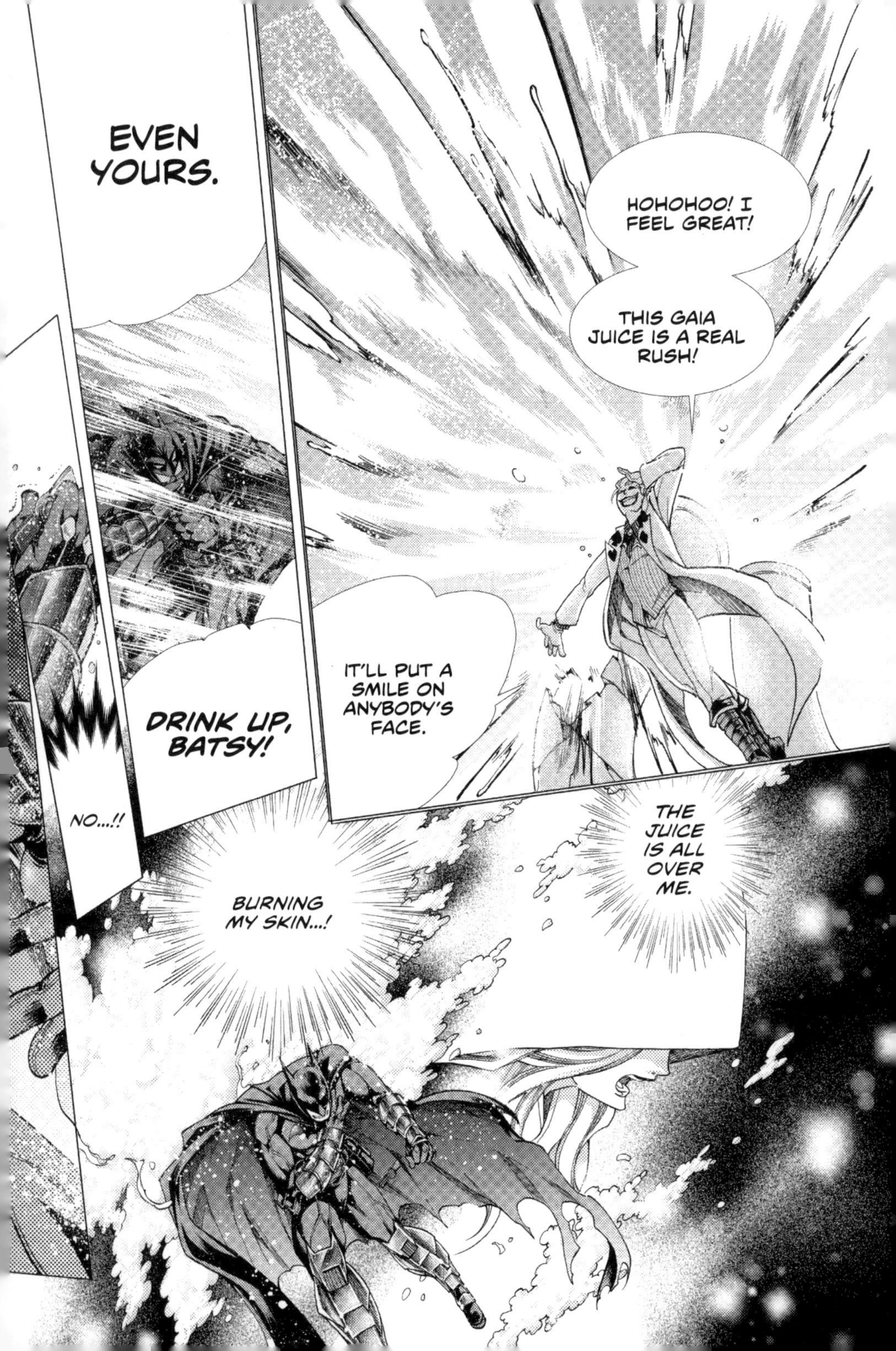
HOHOHOO! I FEEL GREAT!
THIS GAIA JUICE IS A REAL RUSH!
IT'LL PUT A SMILE ON ANYBODY'S FACE.
DRINK UP, BATSY!
EVEN YOURS.
NO...!!
THE JUICE IS ALL OVER ME.
BURNING MY SKIN...!

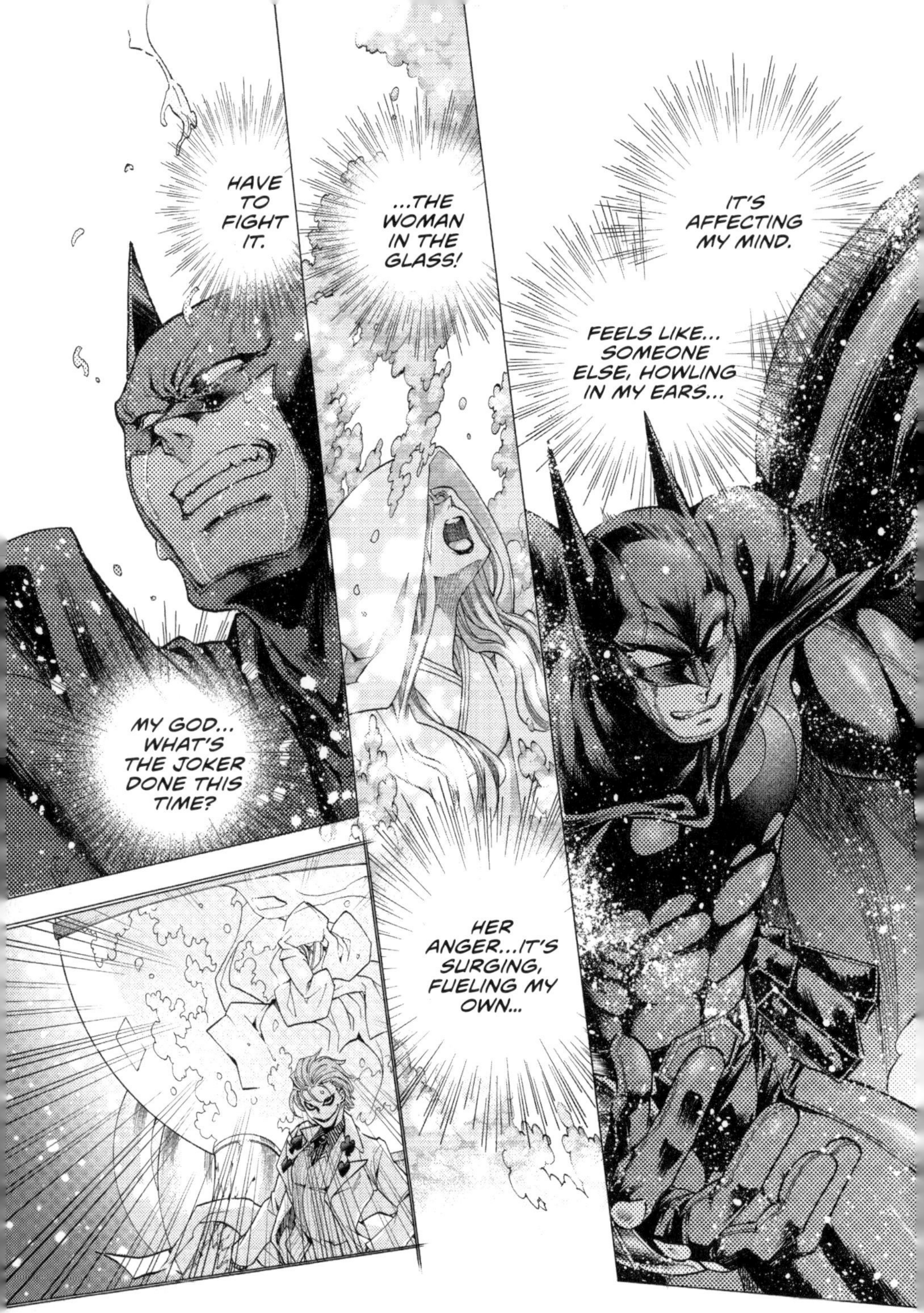
IT'S AFFECTING MY MIND.
FEELS LIKE... SOMEONE ELSE, HOWLING IN MY EARS...
...THE WOMAN IN THE GLASS!
HER ANGER...IT'S SURGING, FUELING MY OWN...
HAVE TO FIGHT IT.
MY GOD... WHAT'S THE JOKER DONE THIS TIME?

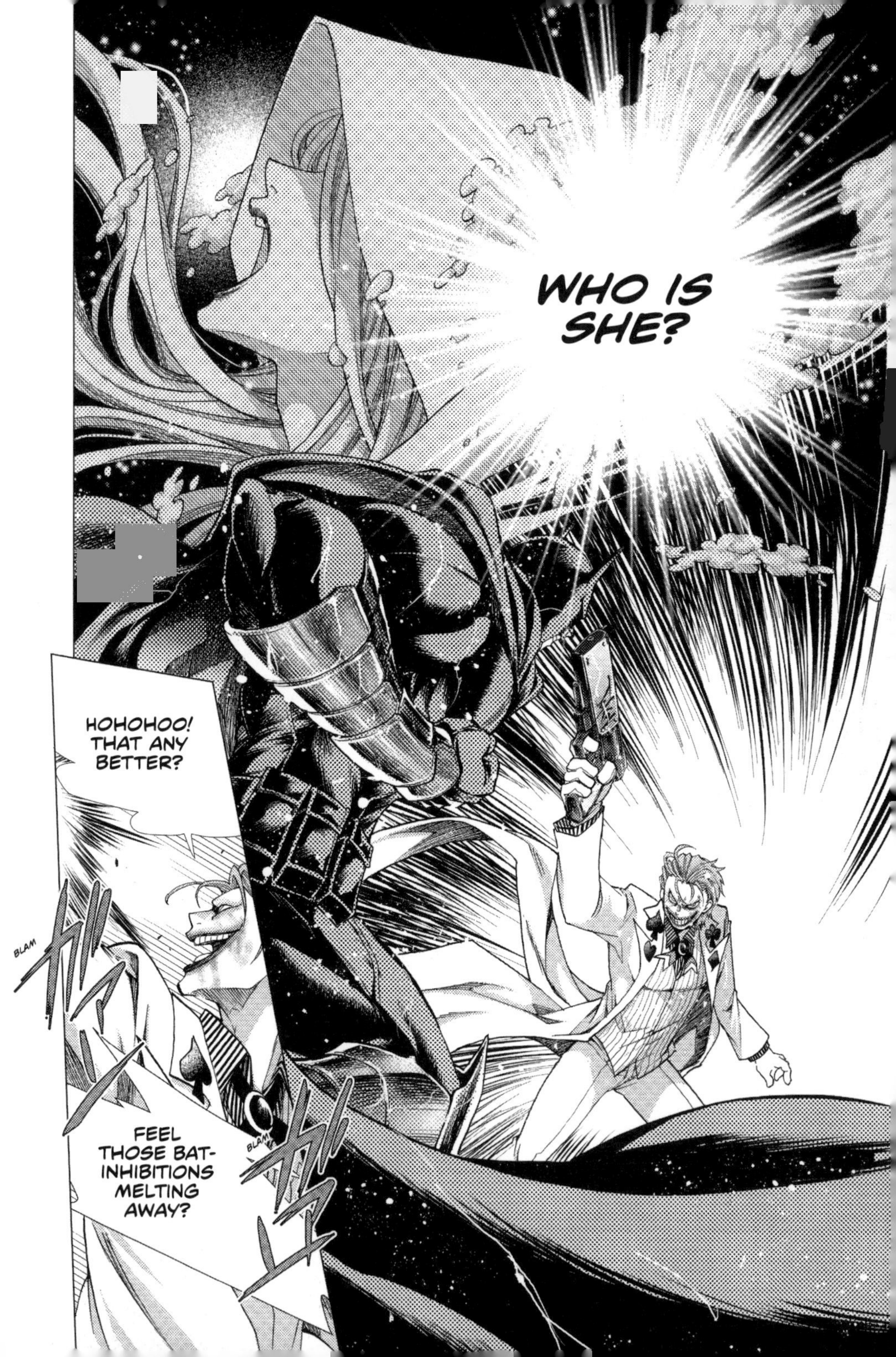
WHO IS SHE?
HOHOHOO! THAT ANY BETTER?
BLAM
FEEL THOSE BAT-INHIBITIONS MELTING AWAY?
BLAM

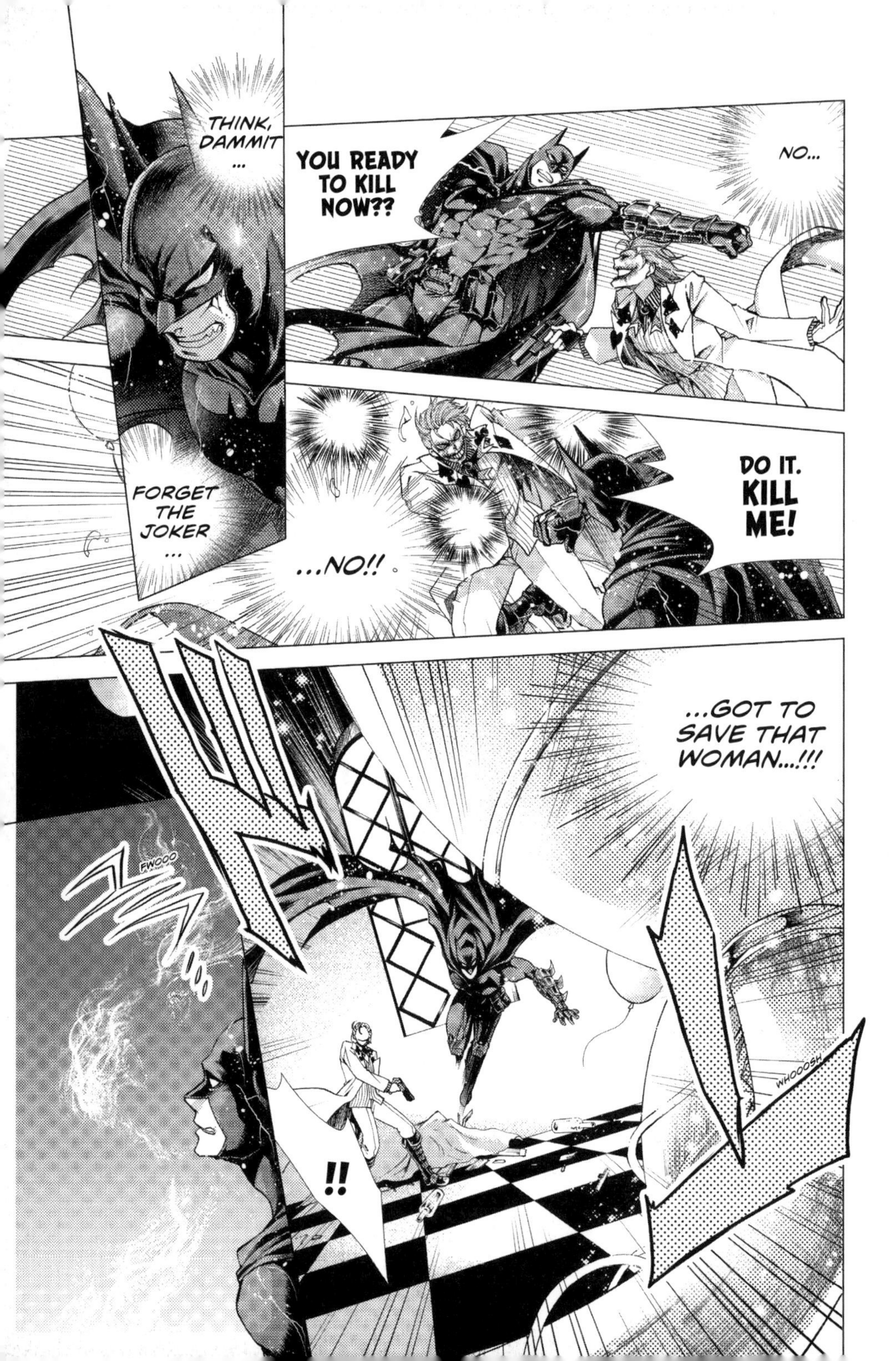

NO...
YOU READY TO KILL NOW??
DO IT. KILL ME!
...NO!!
THINK, DAMMIT ...
FORGET THE JOKER ...
...GOT TO SAVE THAT WOMAN...!!!
WHOOOSH
!!
FWOOO

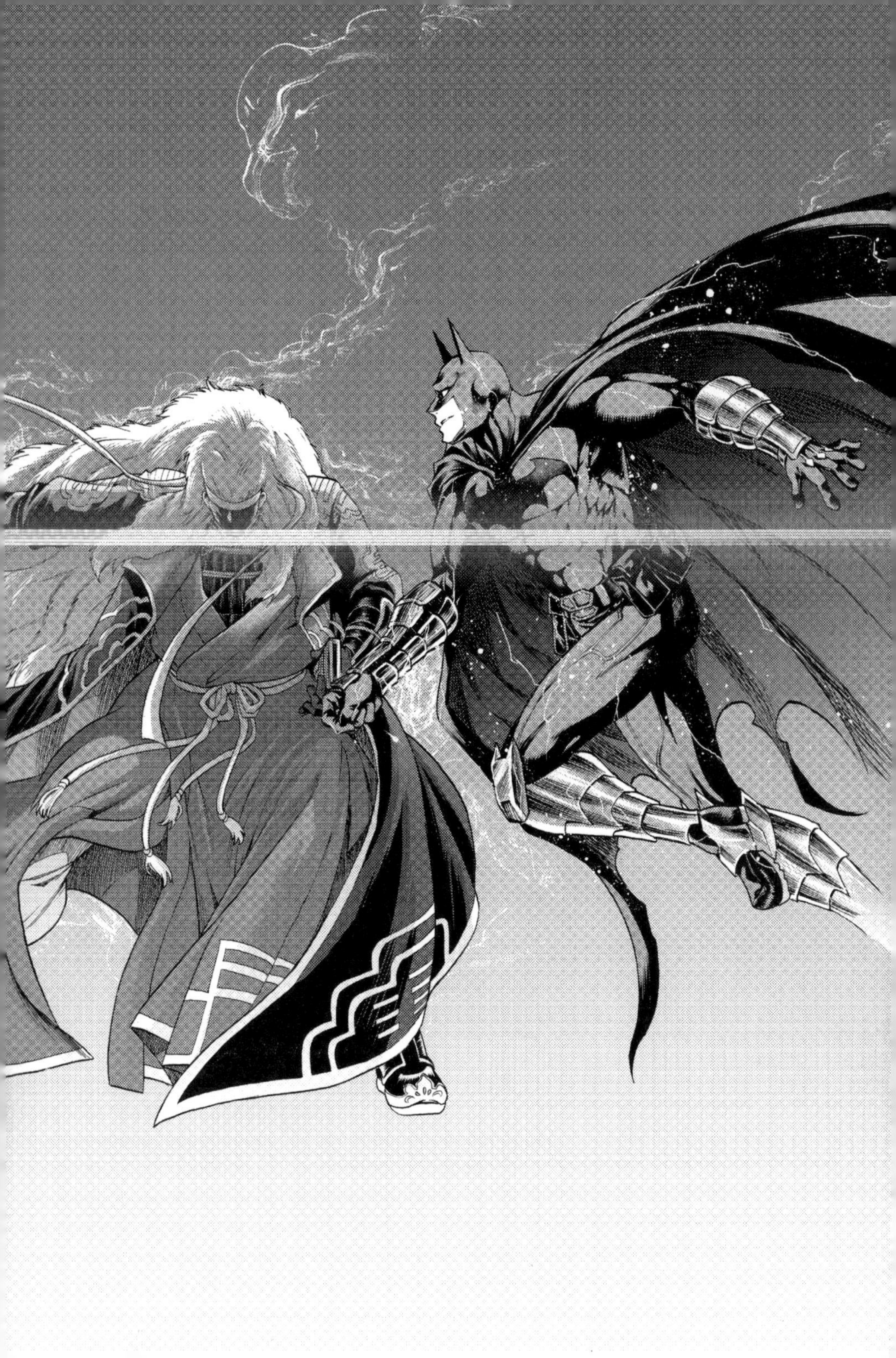

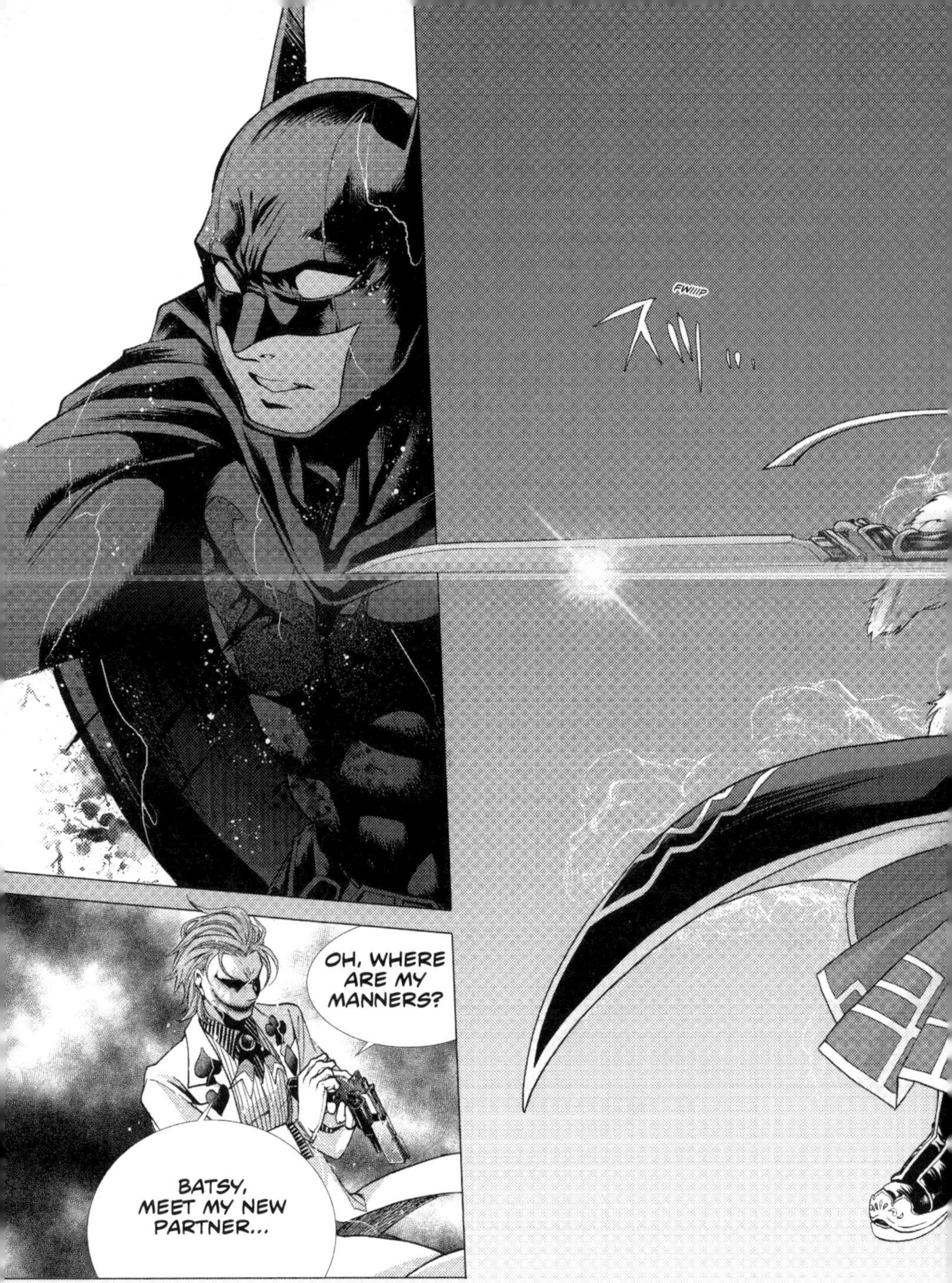
FWIIP
OH, WHERE ARE MY MANNERS?
BATSY, MEET MY NEW PARTNER...

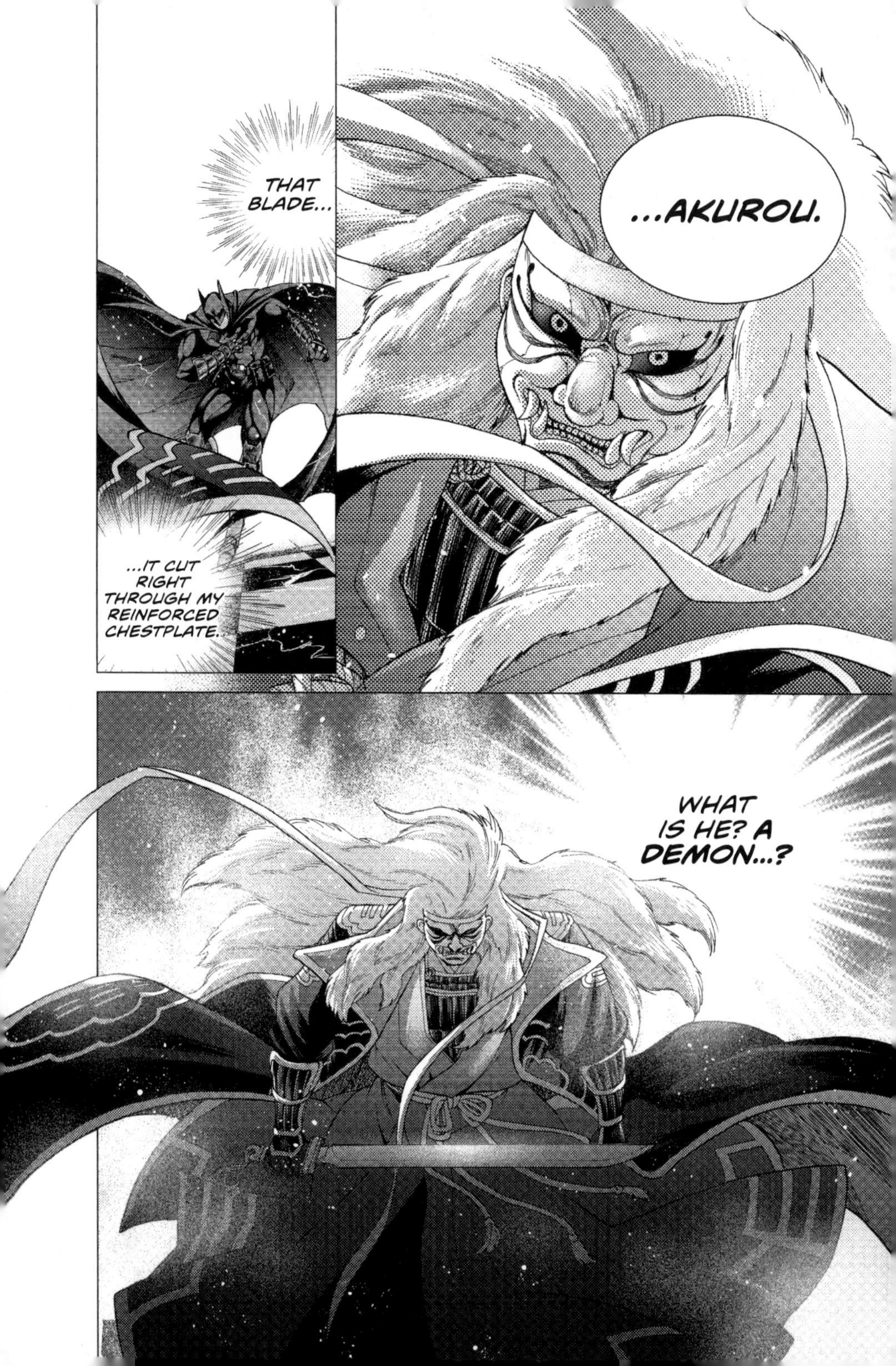
...AKUROU.
THAT BLADE...
...IT CUT RIGHT THROUGH MY REINFORCED CHESTPLATE...
WHAT IS HE? A DEMON...?

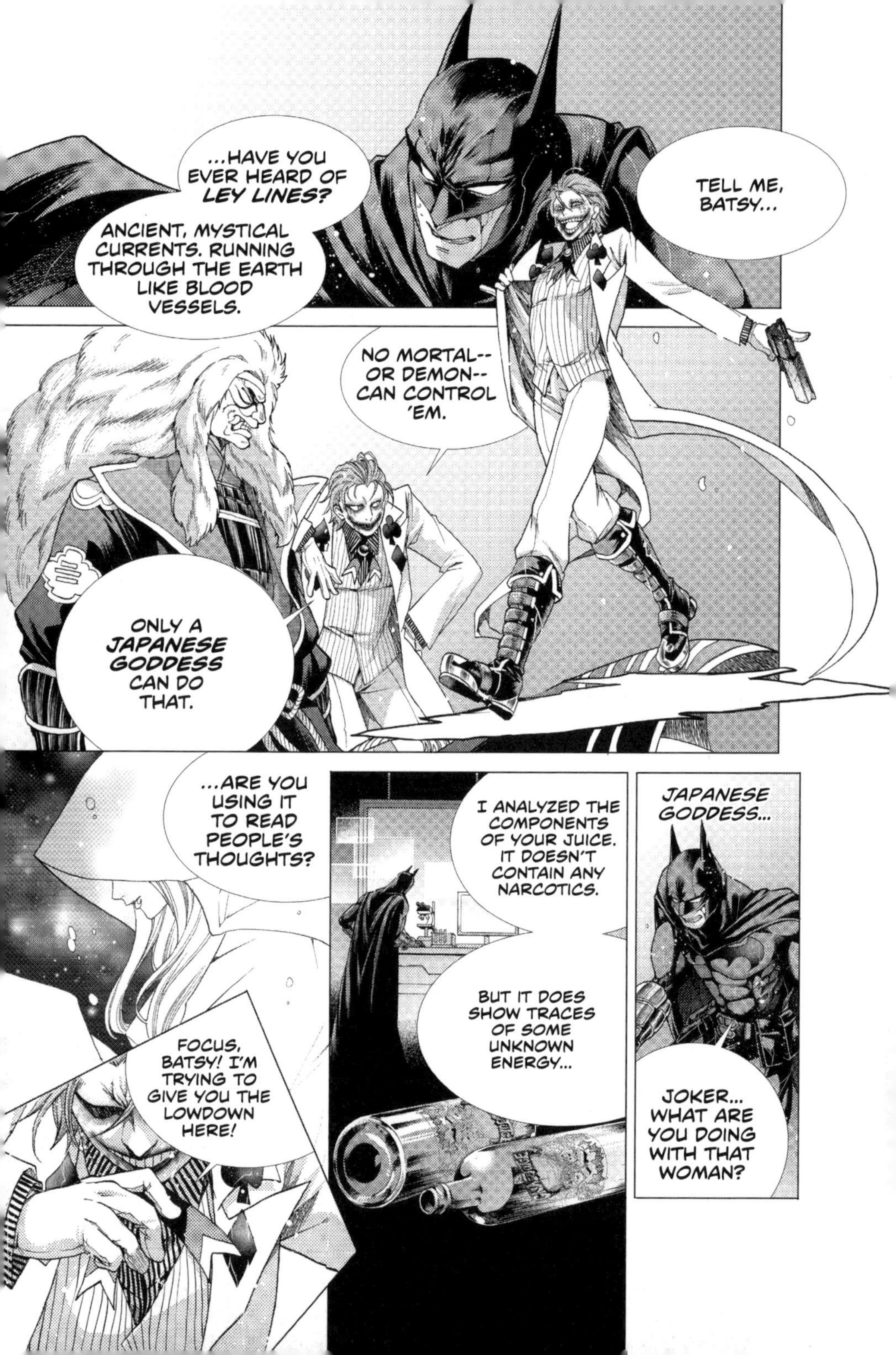
TELL ME, BATSY...
...HAVE YOU EVER HEARD OF *LEY LINES?*
ANCIENT, MYSTICAL CURRENTS. RUNNING THROUGH THE EARTH LIKE BLOOD VESSELS.
NO MORTAL-- OR DEMON-- CAN CONTROL 'EM.
ONLY A ***JAPANESE GODDESS*** CAN DO THAT.
*JAPANESE GODDESS...*
JOKER... WHAT ARE YOU DOING WITH THAT WOMAN?
I ANALYZED THE COMPONENTS OF YOUR JUICE. IT DOESN'T CONTAIN ANY NARCOTICS.
BUT IT DOES SHOW TRACES OF SOME UNKNOWN ENERGY...
...ARE YOU USING IT TO READ PEOPLE'S THOUGHTS?
FOCUS, BATSY! I'M TRYING TO GIVE YOU THE LOWDOWN HERE!

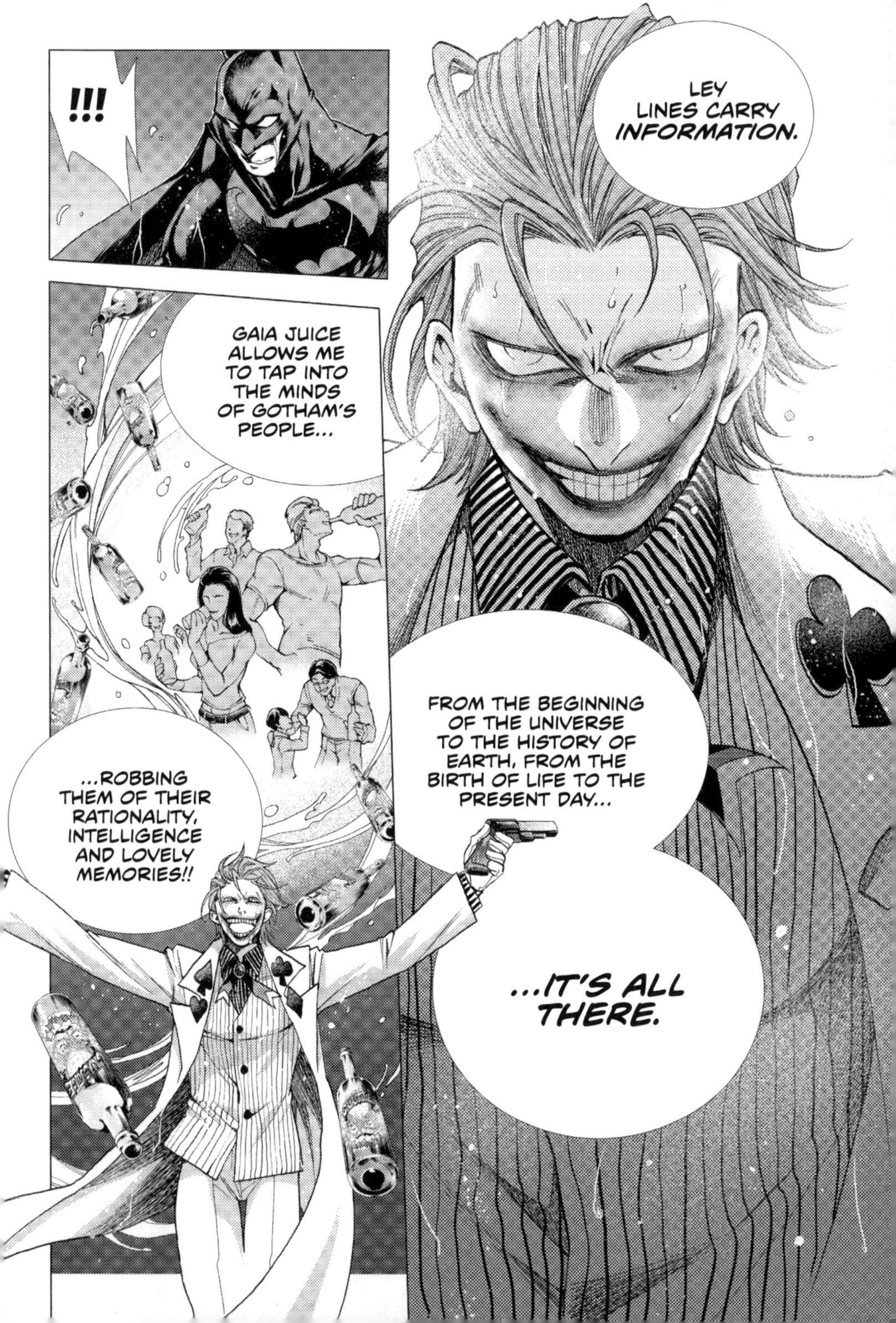
LEY LINES CARRY INFORMATION.
FROM THE BEGINNING OF THE UNIVERSE TO THE HISTORY OF EARTH, FROM THE BIRTH OF LIFE TO THE PRESENT DAY...
...IT'S ALL THERE.
!!!
GAIA JUICE ALLOWS ME TO TAP INTO THE MINDS OF GOTHAM'S PEOPLE...
...ROBBING THEM OF THEIR RATIONALITY, INTELLIGENCE AND LOVELY MEMORIES!!

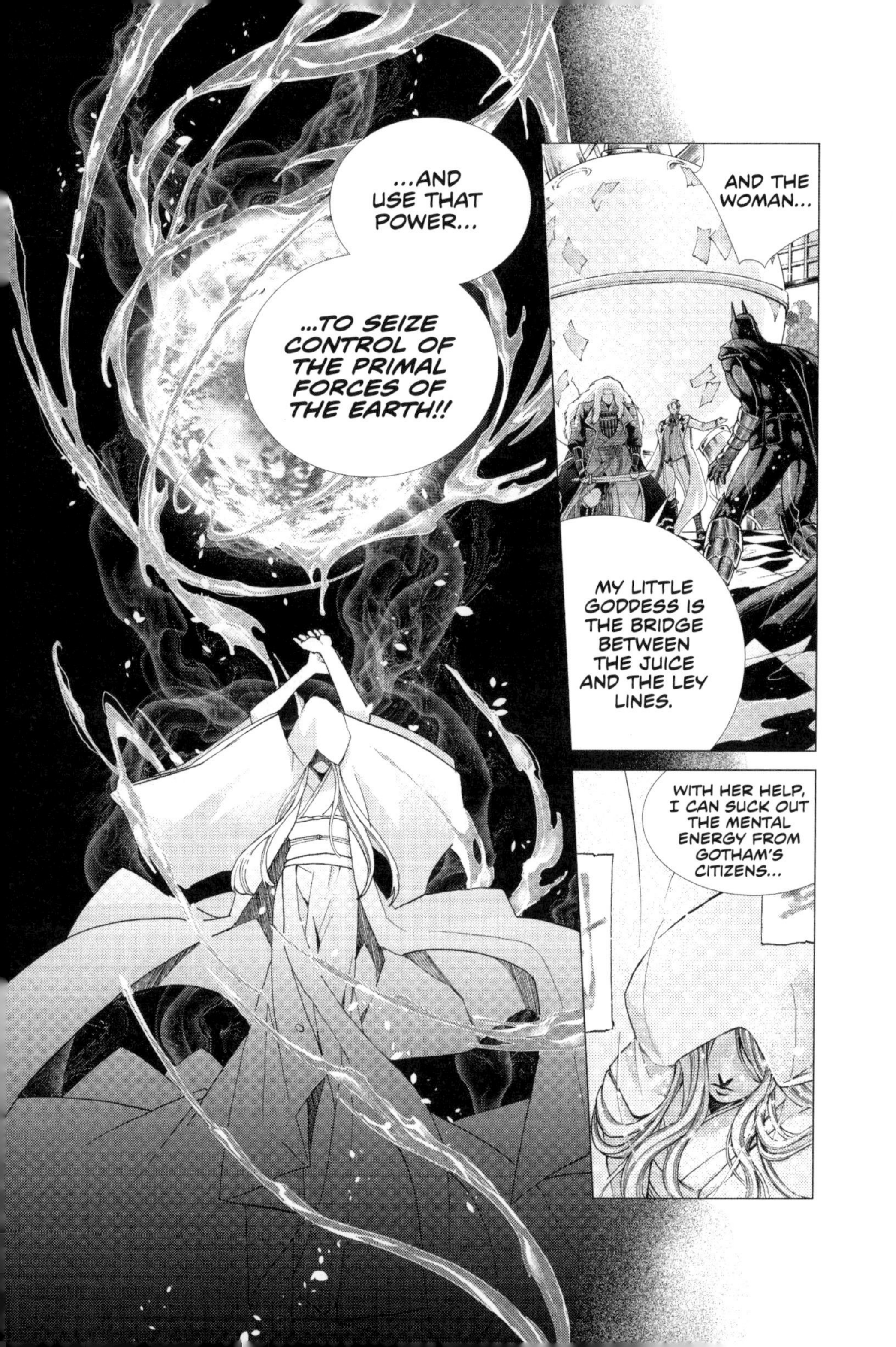
AND THE WOMAN...
MY LITTLE GODDESS IS THE BRIDGE BETWEEN THE JUICE AND THE LEY LINES.
WITH HER HELP, I CAN SUCK OUT THE MENTAL ENERGY FROM GOTHAM'S CITIZENS...
...AND USE THAT POWER...
...TO SEIZE CONTROL OF THE PRIMAL FORCES OF THE EARTH!!

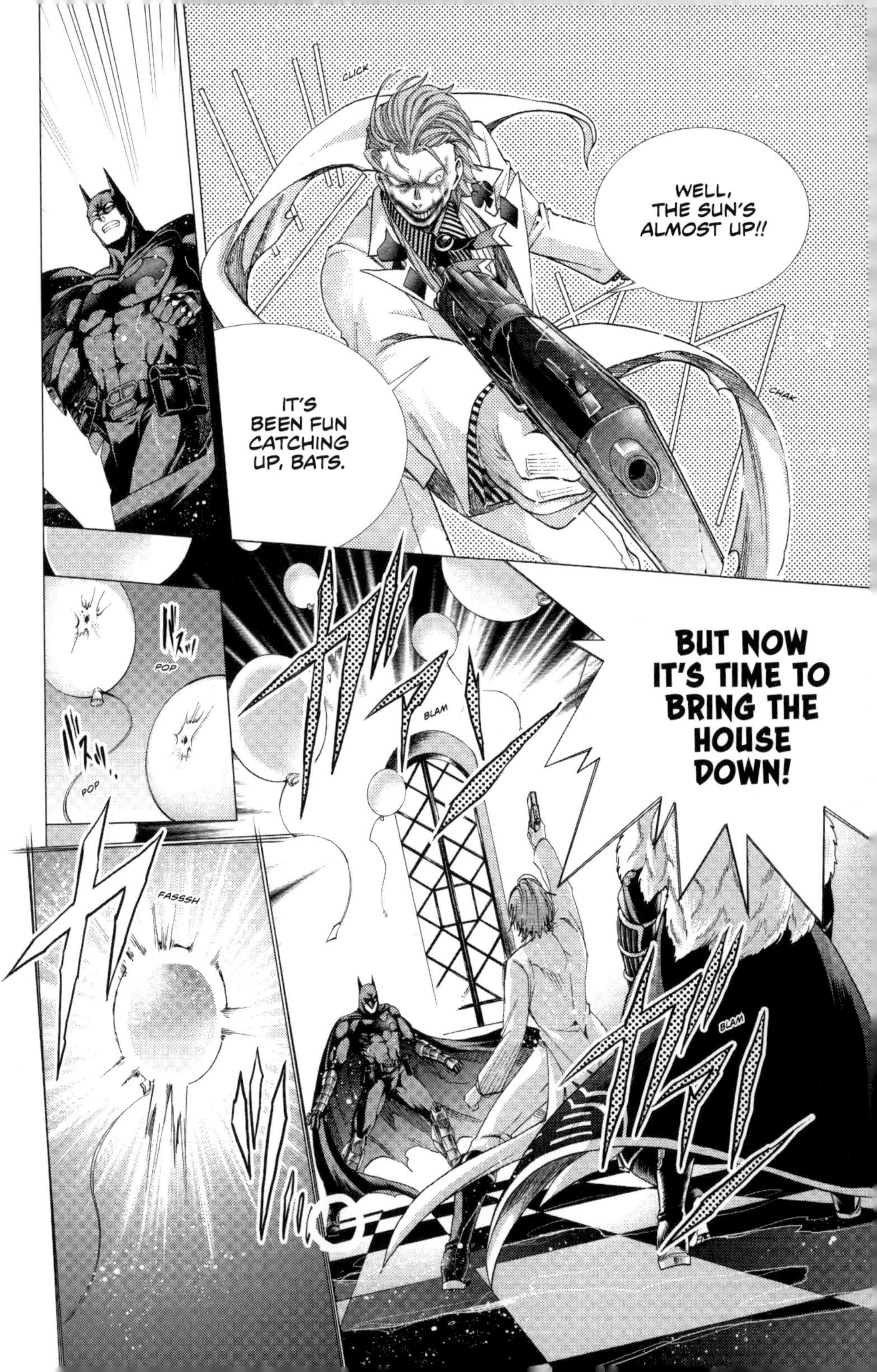
CLICK
WELL, THE SUN'S ALMOST UP!!
CHAK
IT'S BEEN FUN CATCHING UP, BATS.
BUT NOW IT'S TIME TO BRING THE HOUSE DOWN!
BLAM
BLAM
POP
POP
FASSSH

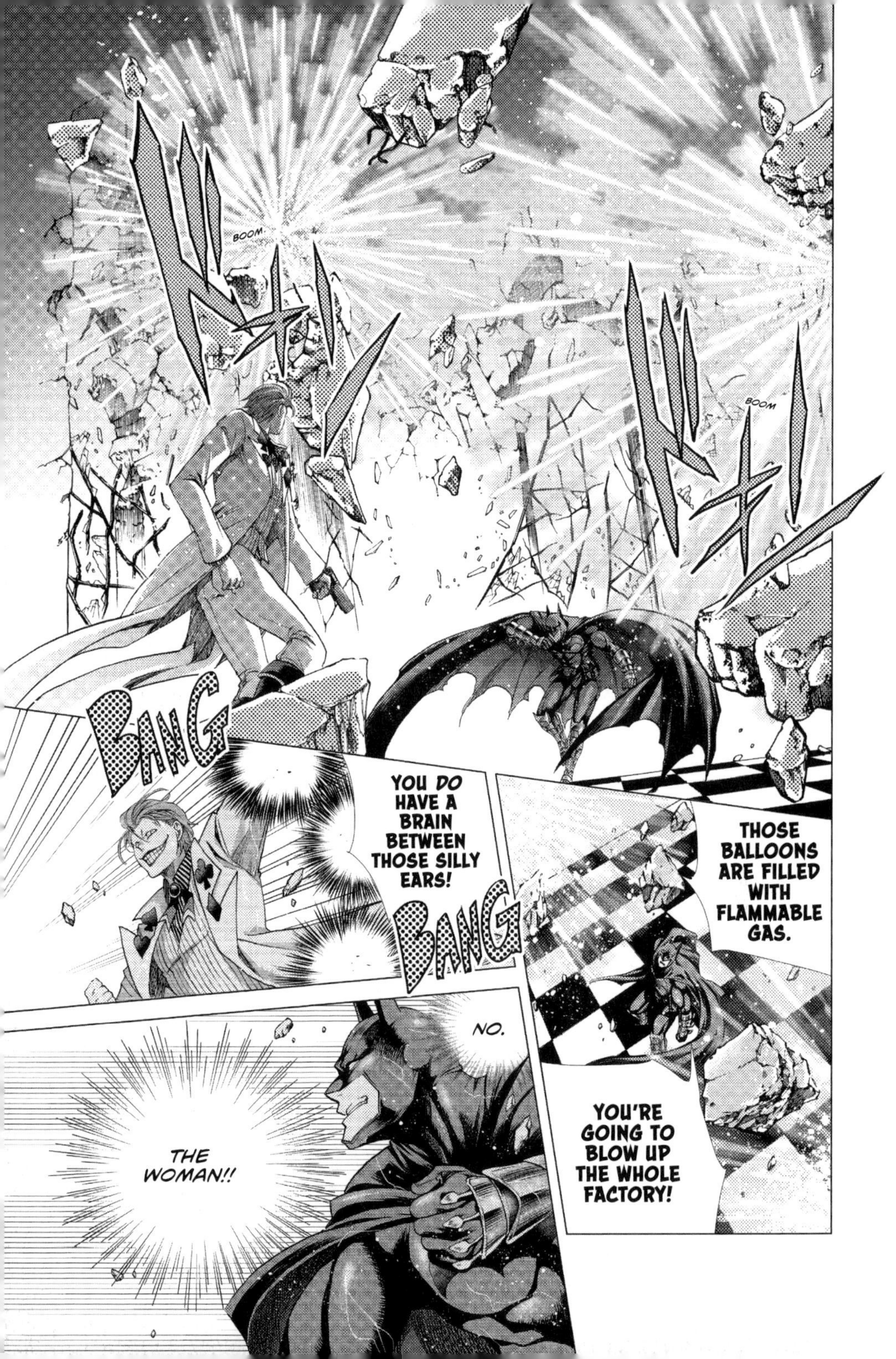
BOOM
BOOM.
THOSE BALLOONS ARE FILLED WITH FLAMMABLE GAS.
YOU'RE GOING TO BLOW UP THE WHOLE FACTORY!
BANG
BANG
YOU DO HAVE A BRAIN BETWEEN THOSE SILLY EARS!
NO.
THE WOMAN!!

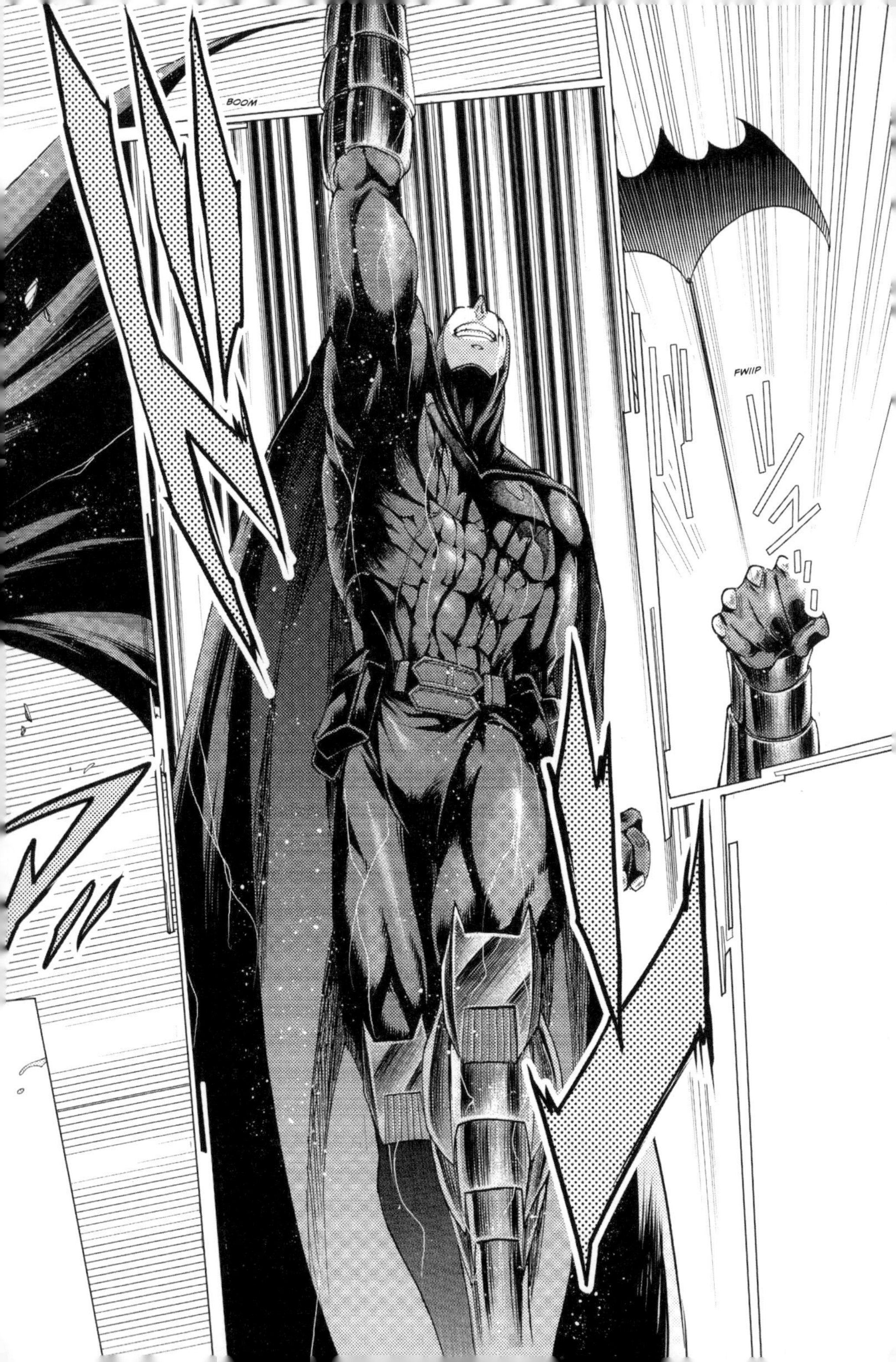
FWIIP
BOOM

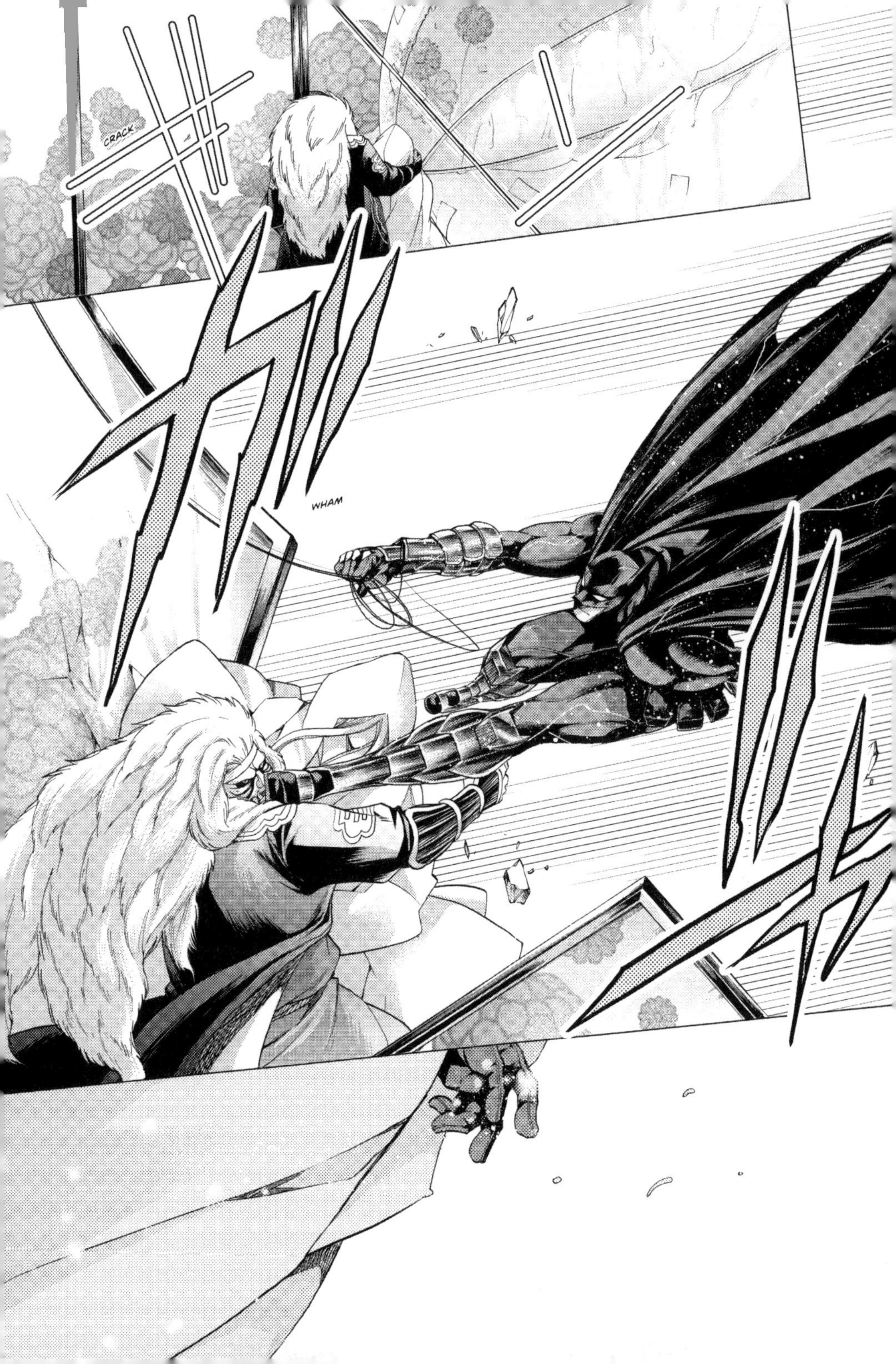
CRACK
WHAM

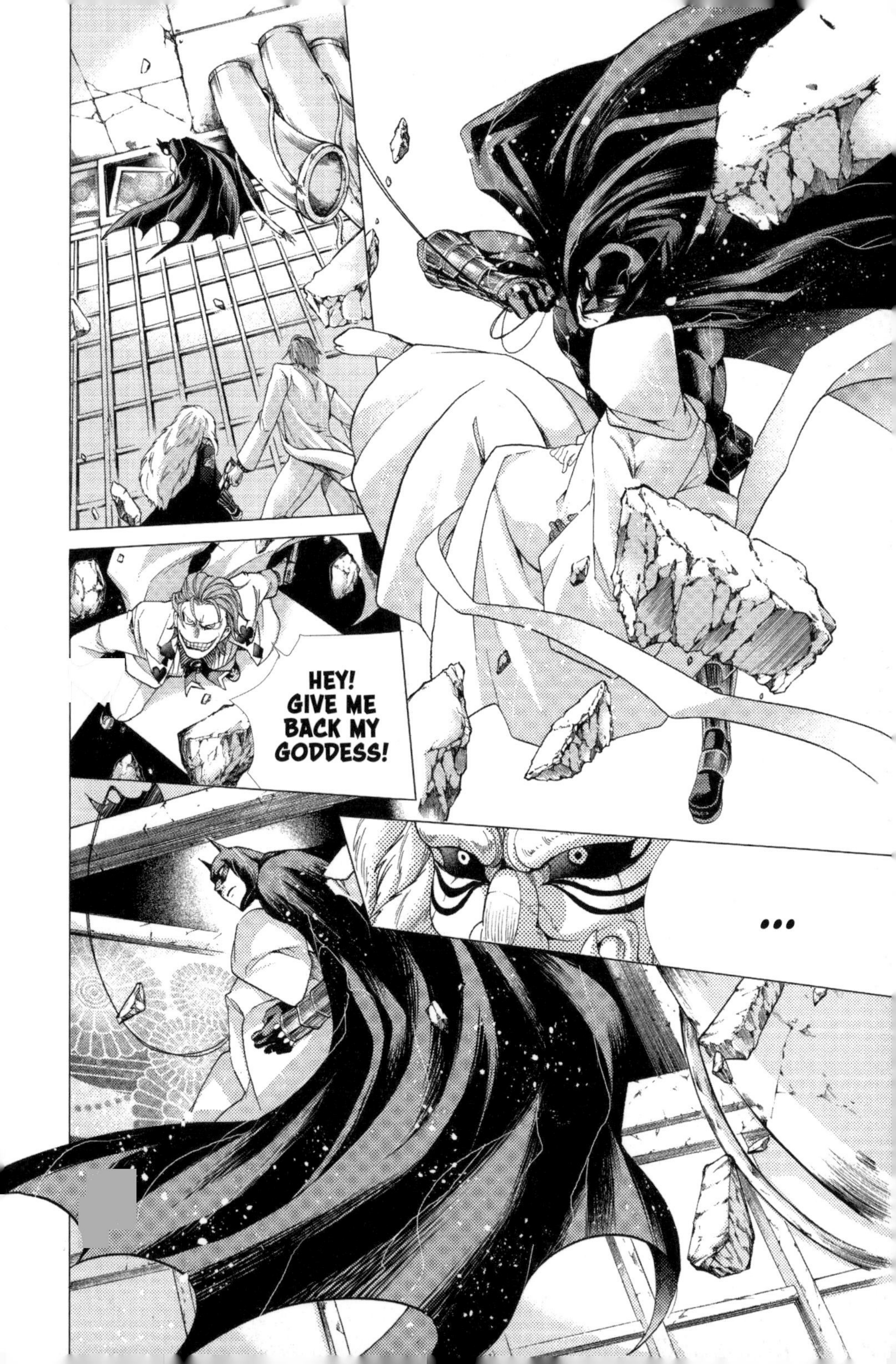
HEY! GIVE ME BACK MY GODDESS!
...

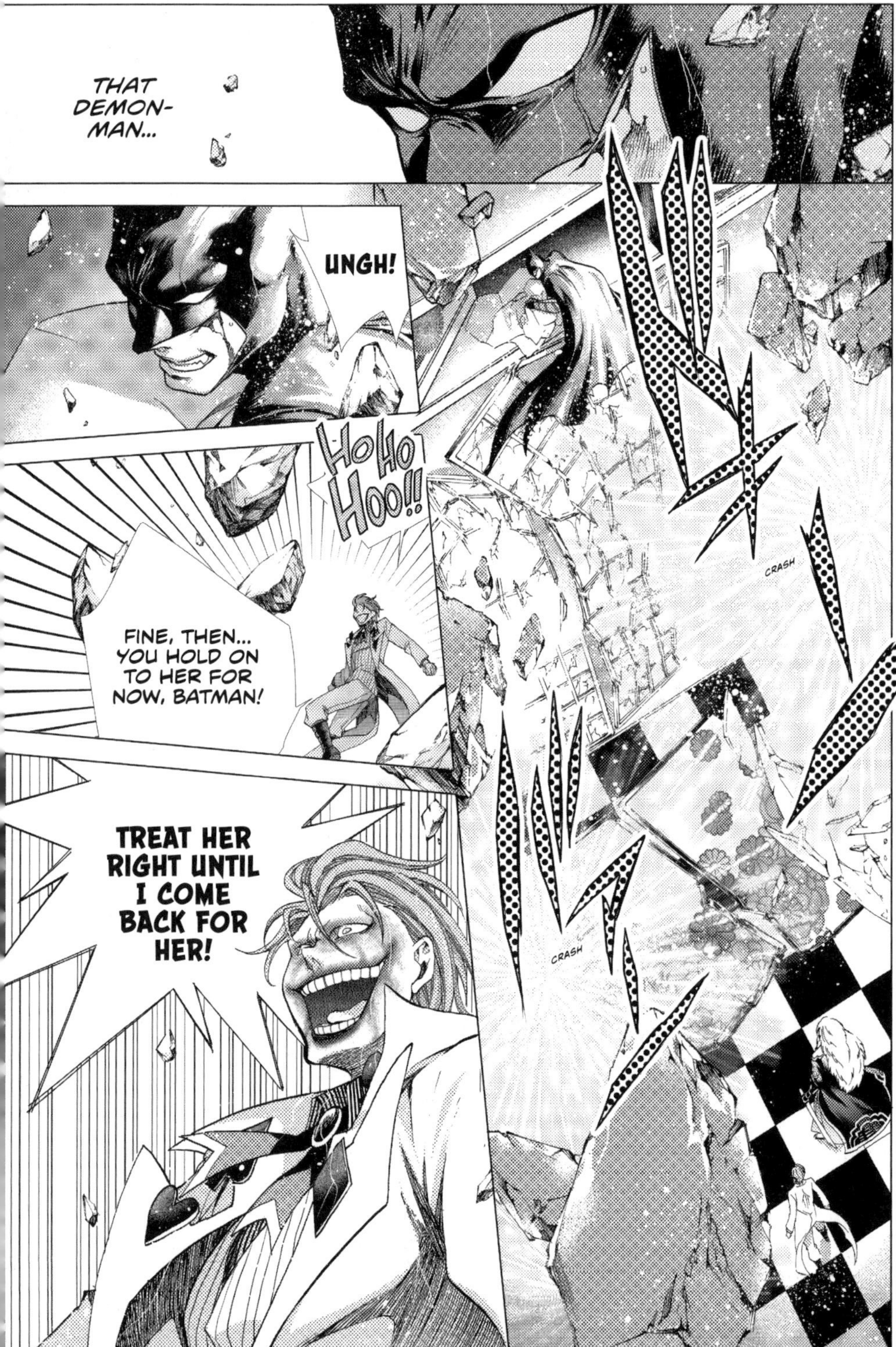

THAT DEMON-MAN...
CRASH
CRASH
UNGH!
HO HO HOO!!
FINE, THEN... YOU HOLD ON TO HER FOR NOW, BATMAN!
TREAT HER RIGHT UNTIL I COME BACK FOR HER!

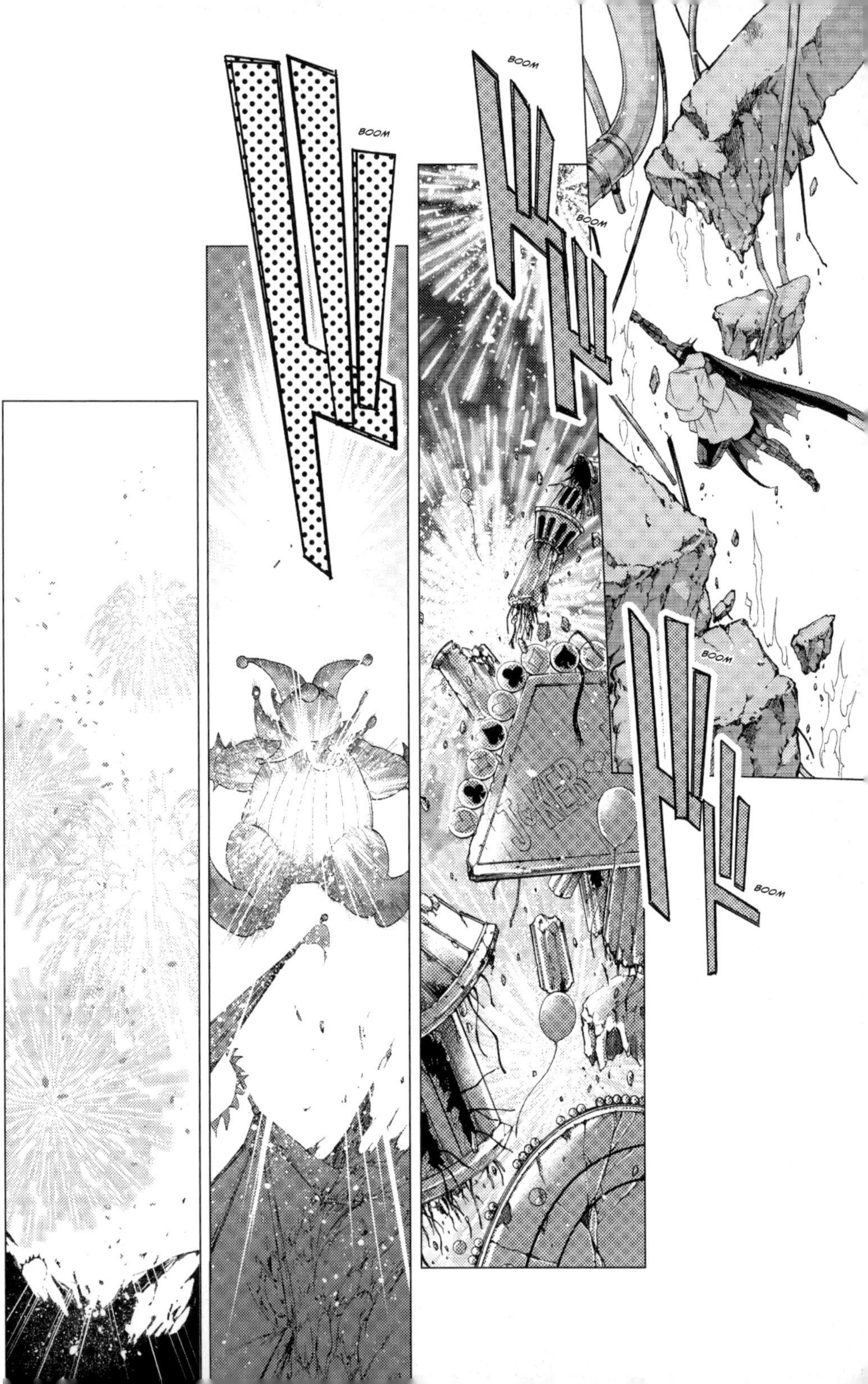
BOOM
BOOM
BOOM
BOOM
BOOM

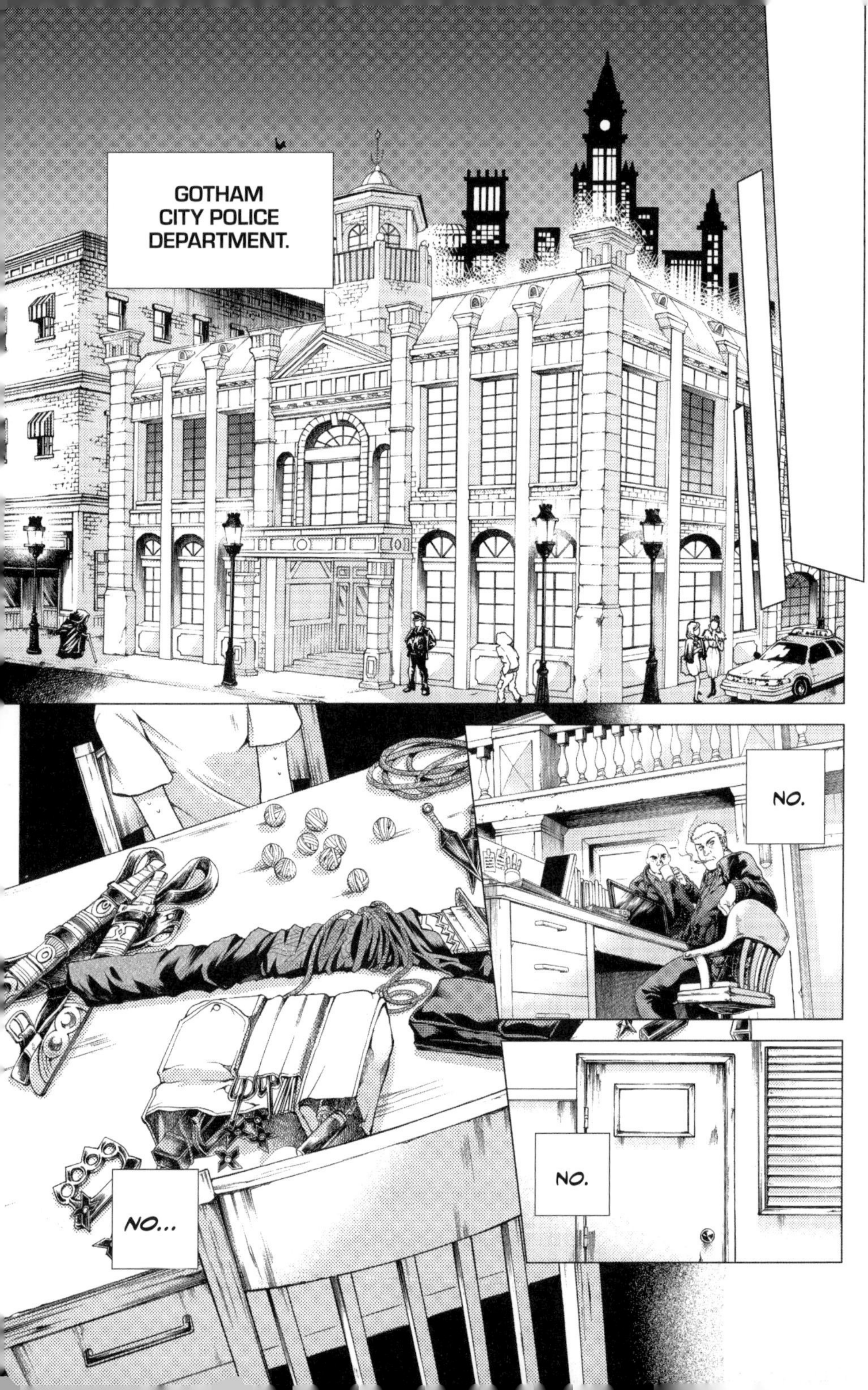
GOTHAM CITY POLICE DEPARTMENT.
NO.
NO.
NO...

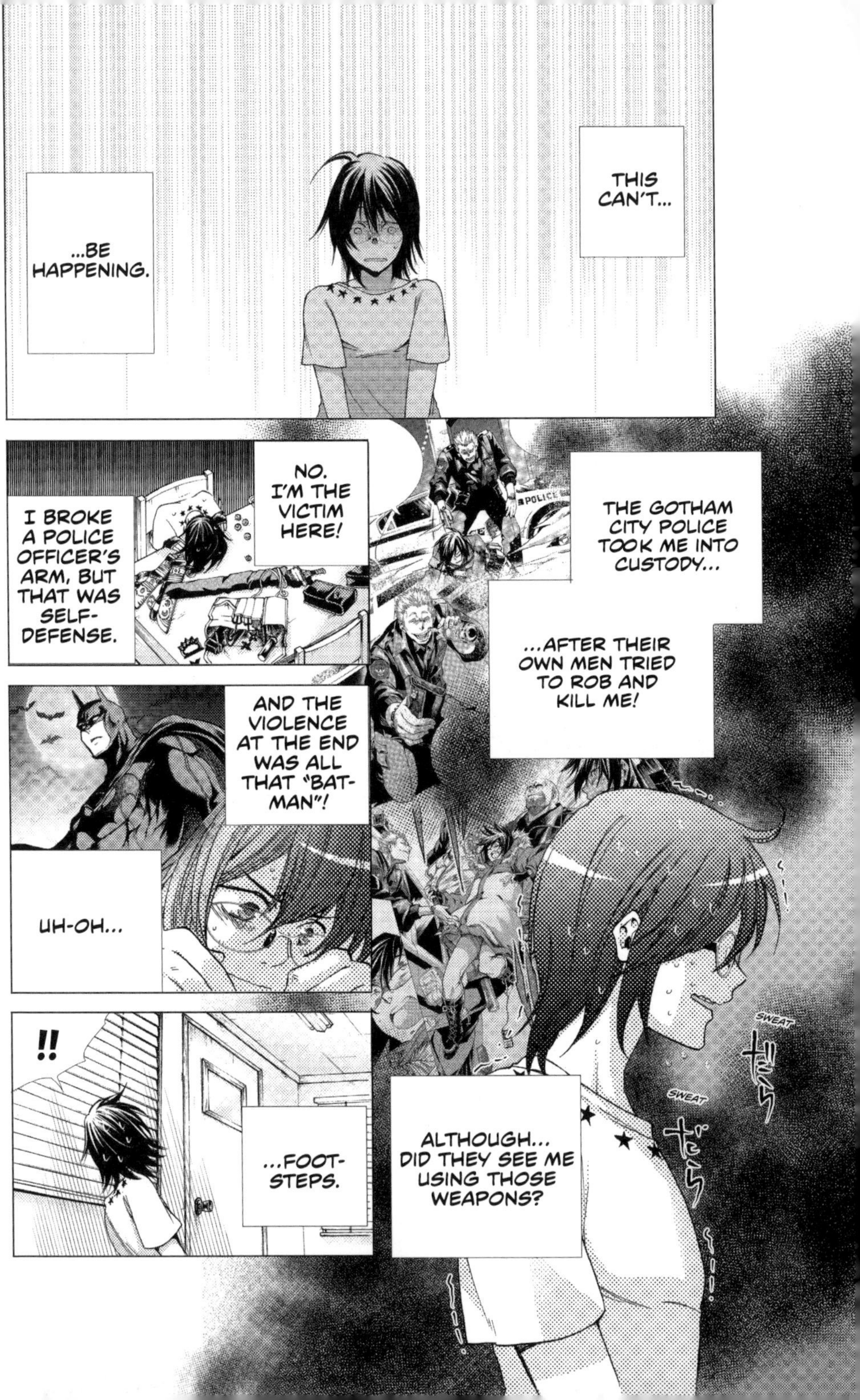
THIS CAN'T...
...BE HAPPENING.
THE GOTHAM CITY POLICE TOOK ME INTO CUSTODY...
...AFTER THEIR OWN MEN TRIED TO ROB AND KILL ME!
NO. I'M THE VICTIM HERE!
I BROKE A POLICE OFFICER'S ARM, BUT THAT WAS SELF-DEFENSE.
AND THE VIOLENCE AT THE END WAS ALL THAT "BAT-MAN"!
SWEAT
SWEAT
ALTHOUGH... DID THEY SEE ME USING THOSE WEAPONS?
UH-OH...
...FOOT-STEPS.
!!

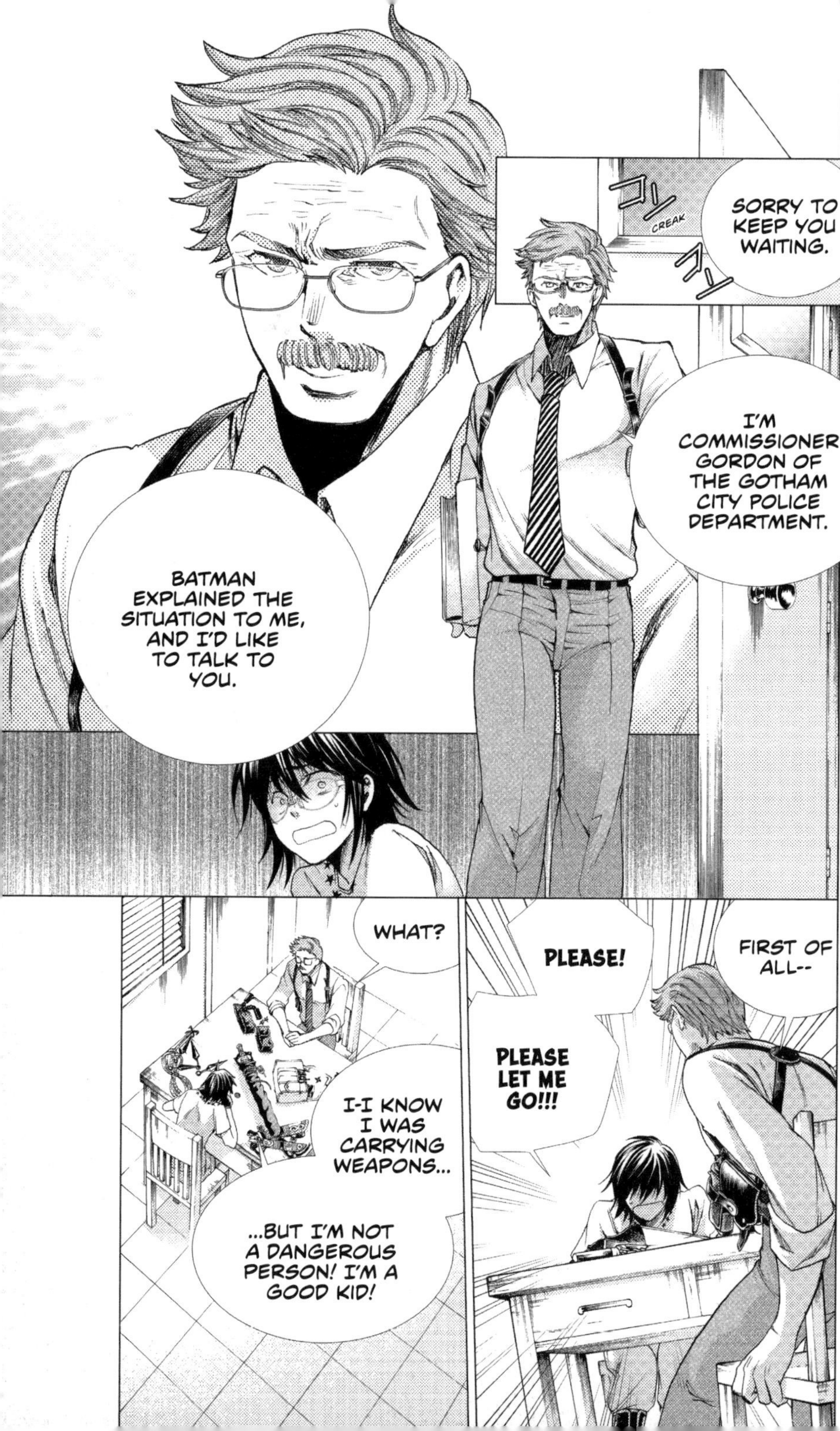
コン コン
CREAK
SORRY TO KEEP YOU WAITING.
I'M COMMISSIONER GORDON OF THE GOTHAM CITY POLICE DEPARTMENT.
BATMAN EXPLAINED THE SITUATION TO ME, AND I'D LIKE TO TALK TO YOU.
FIRST OF ALL--
PLEASE!
PLEASE LET ME GO!!!
WHAT?
I-I KNOW I WAS CARRYING WEAPONS...
...BUT I'M NOT A DANGEROUS PERSON! I'M A GOOD KID!

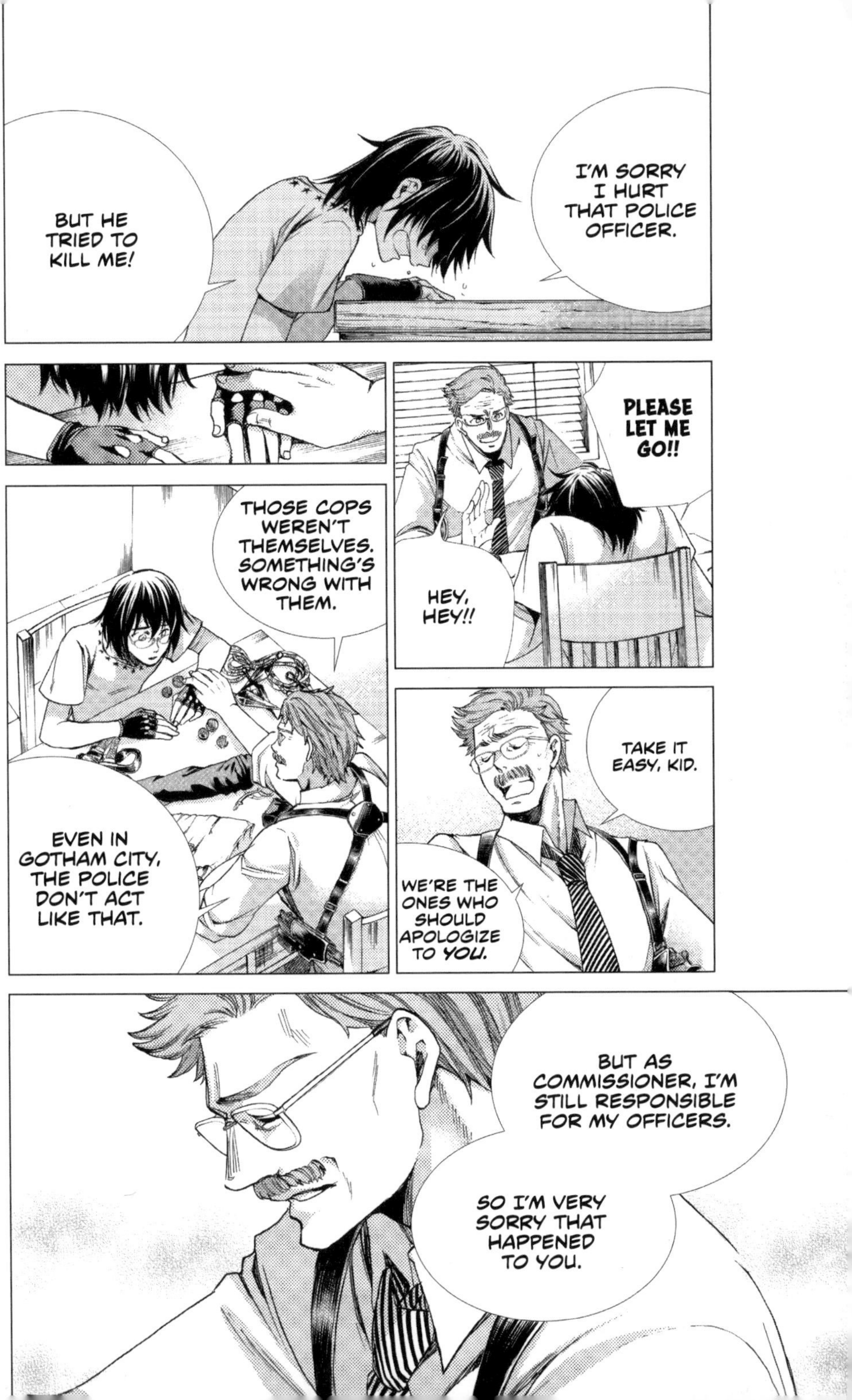
I'M SORRY I HURT THAT POLICE OFFICER.
BUT HE TRIED TO KILL ME!
PLEASE LET ME GO!!
HEY, HEY!!
THOSE COPS WEREN'T THEMSELVES. SOMETHING'S WRONG WITH THEM.
EVEN IN GOTHAM CITY, THE POLICE DON'T ACT LIKE THAT.
TAKE IT EASY, KID.
WE'RE THE ONES WHO SHOULD APOLOGIZE TO *YOU*.
BUT AS COMMISSIONER, I'M STILL RESPONSIBLE FOR MY OFFICERS.
SO I'M VERY SORRY THAT HAPPENED TO YOU.

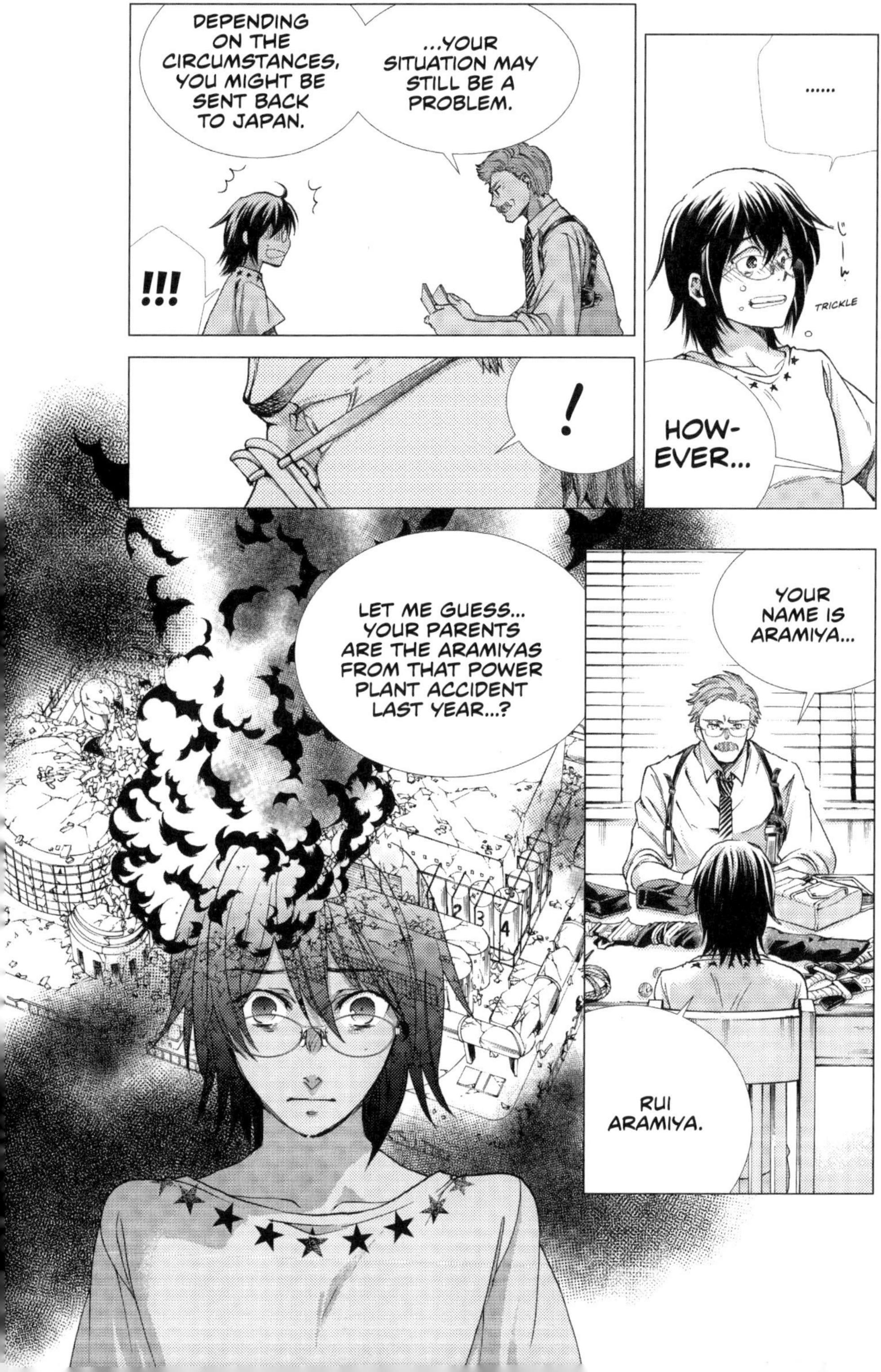
......
じーん
TRICKLE
HOW-EVER...
...YOUR SITUATION MAY STILL BE A PROBLEM.
DEPENDING ON THE CIRCUMSTANCES, YOU MIGHT BE SENT BACK TO JAPAN.
!!!
!
YOUR NAME IS ARAMIYA...
RUI ARAMIYA.
LET ME GUESS... YOUR PARENTS ARE THE ARAMIYAS FROM THAT POWER PLANT ACCIDENT LAST YEAR...?

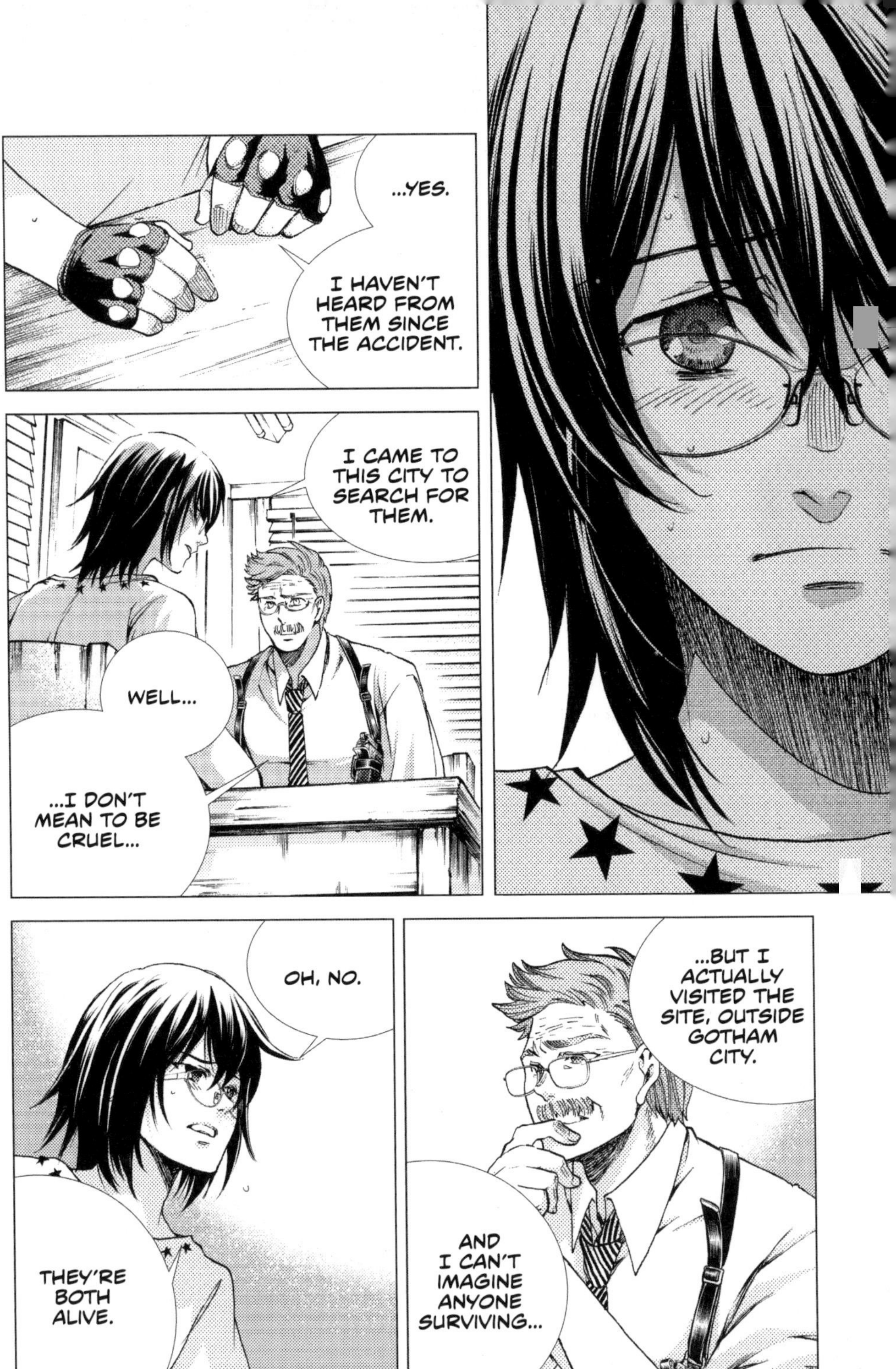
...YES.
I HAVEN'T HEARD FROM THEM SINCE THE ACCIDENT.
I CAME TO THIS CITY TO SEARCH FOR THEM.
WELL...
...I DON'T MEAN TO BE CRUEL...
...BUT I ACTUALLY VISITED THE SITE, OUTSIDE GOTHAM CITY.
AND I CAN'T IMAGINE ANYONE SURVIVING...
OH, NO.
THEY'RE BOTH ALIVE.

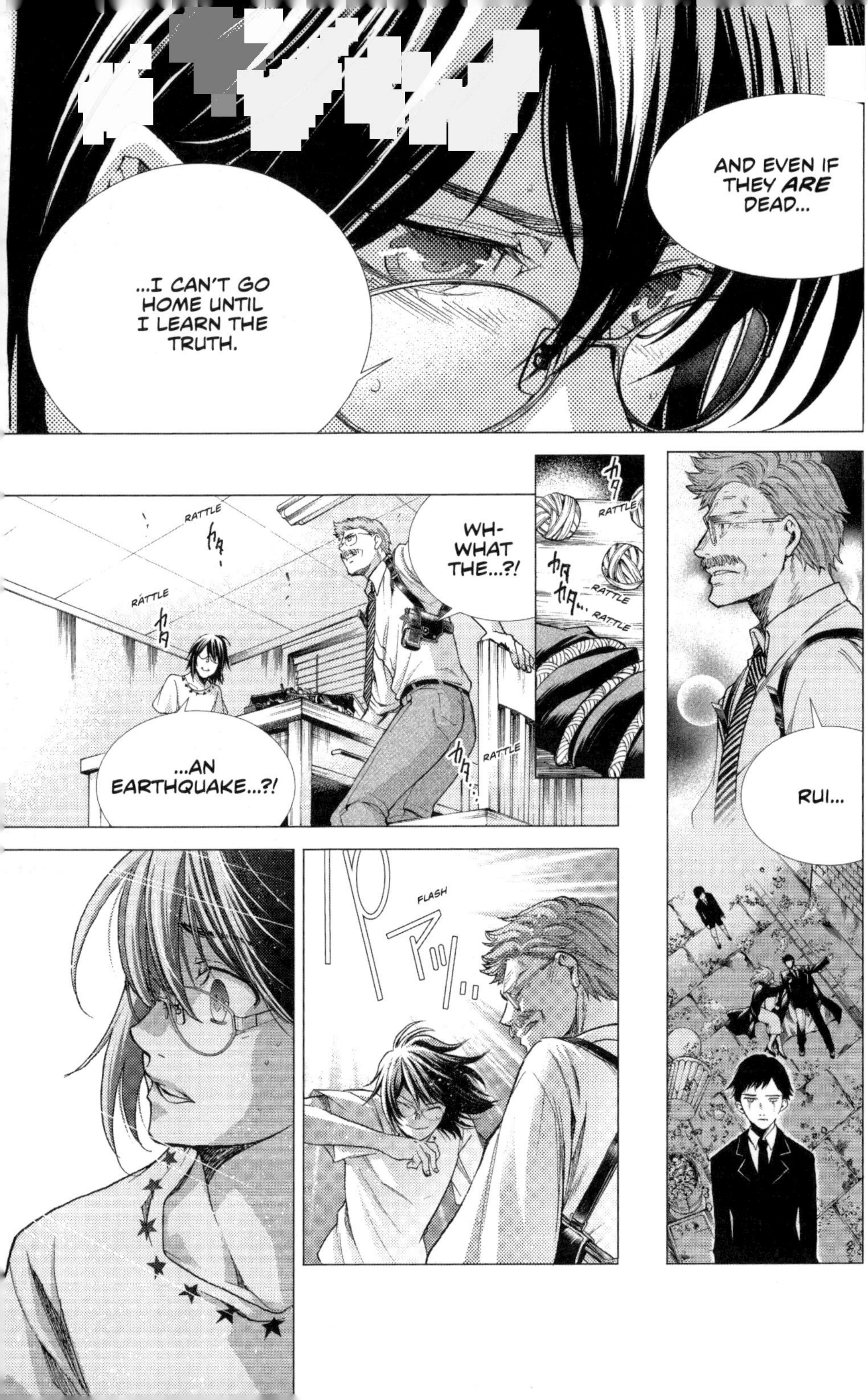
AND EVEN IF THEY *ARE* DEAD...
...I CAN'T GO HOME UNTIL I LEARN THE TRUTH.
RUI...
RATTLE
RATTLE
RATTLE
WH- WHAT THE...?!
RATTLE
RATTLE
RATTLE
...AN EARTHQUAKE...?!
FLASH

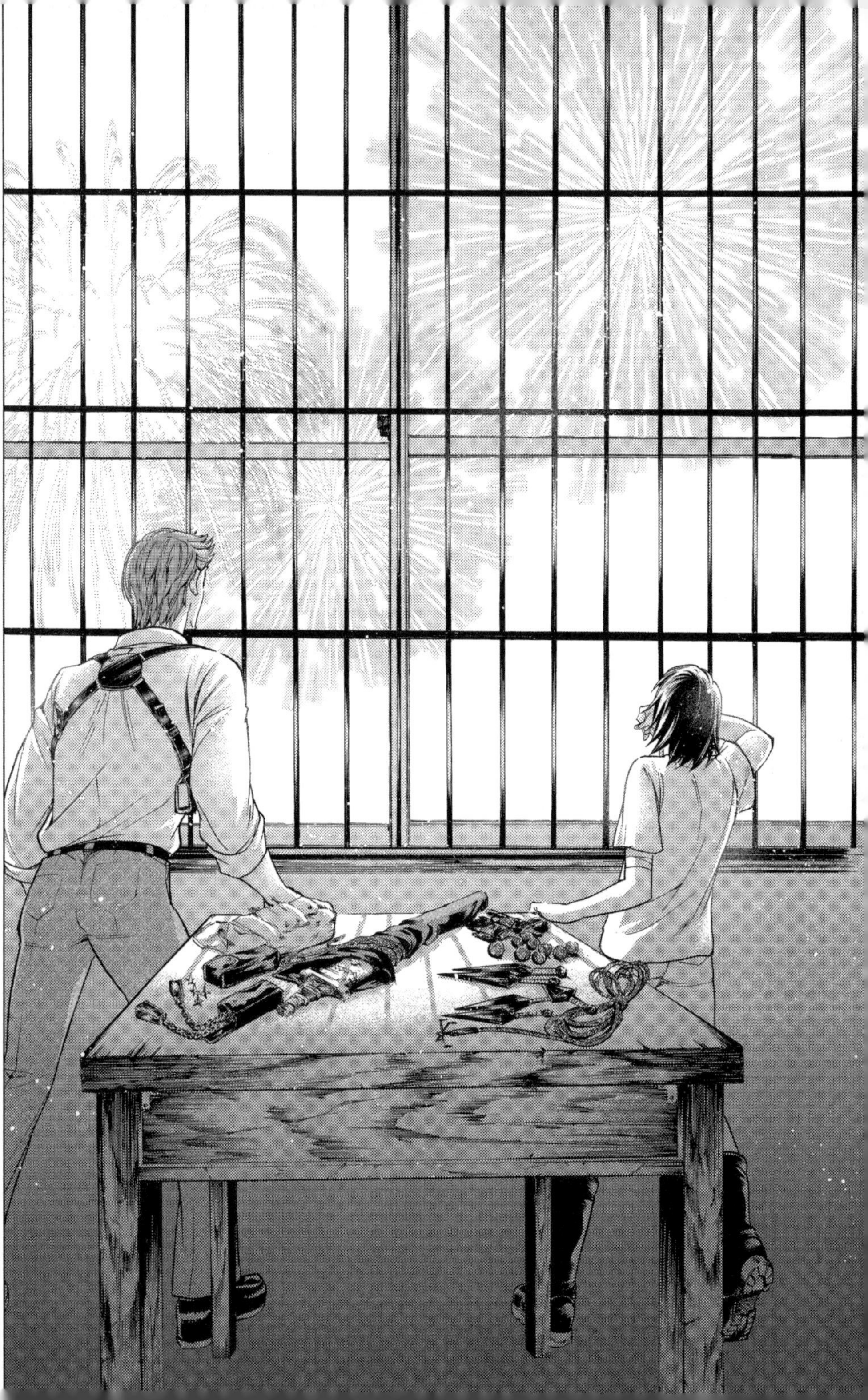

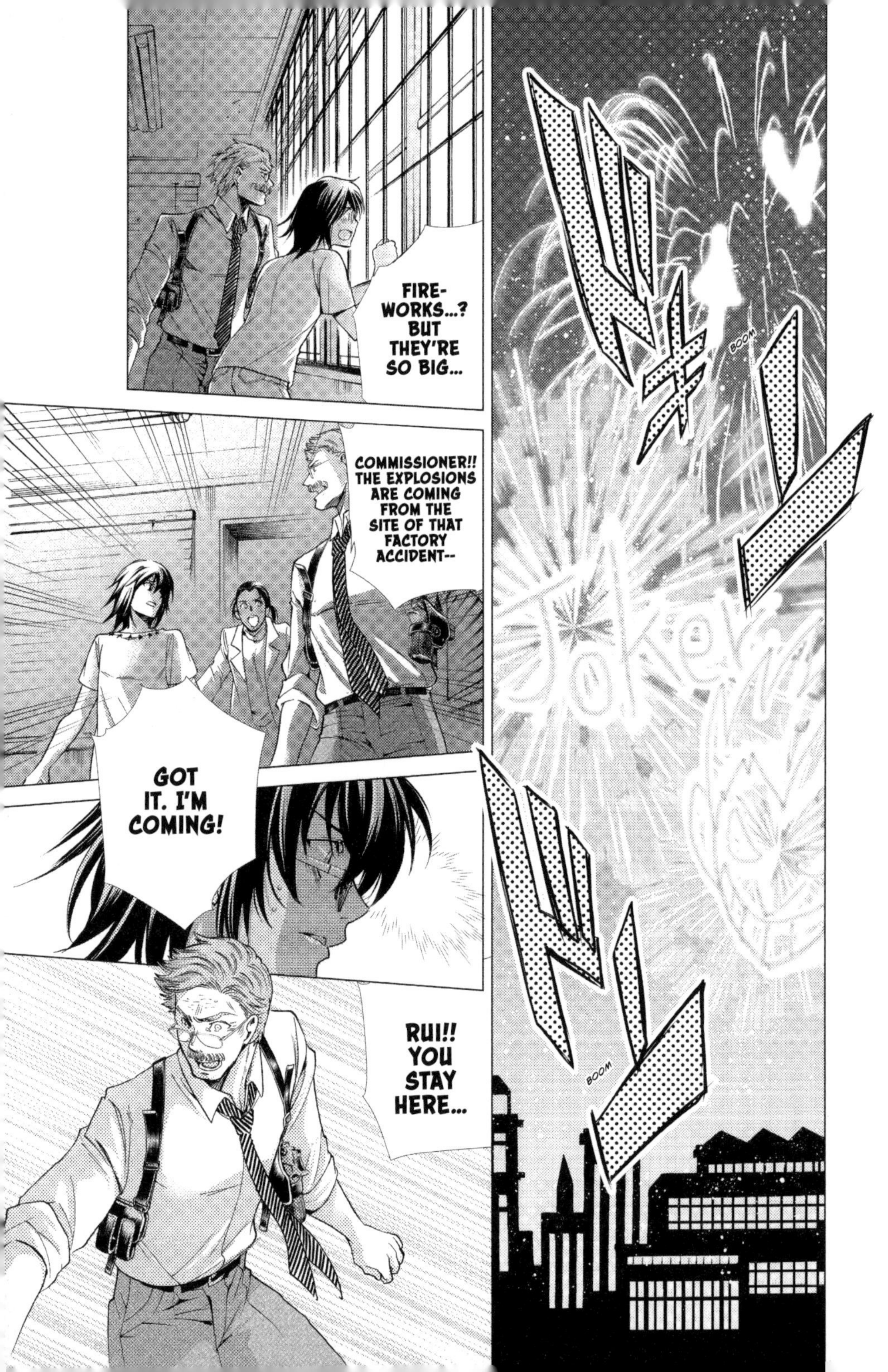
BOOM
BOOM
FIRE-WORKS...? BUT THEY'RE SO BIG...
COMMISSIONER!! THE EXPLOSIONS ARE COMING FROM THE SITE OF THAT FACTORY ACCIDENT--
GOT IT. I'M COMING!
RUI!! YOU STAY HERE...

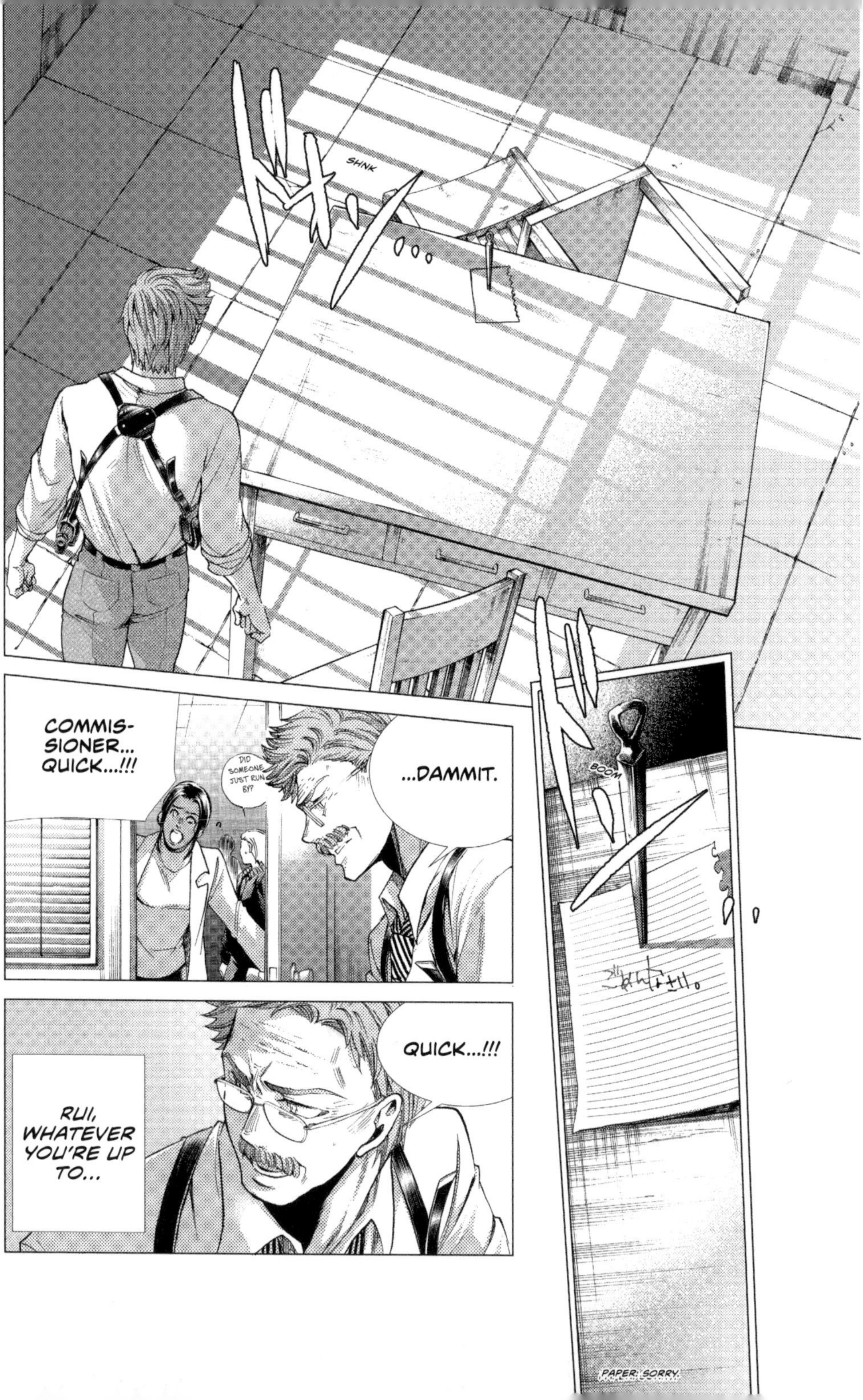
SHNK
BOOM
PAPER: SORRY.
COMMIS-
SIONER...
QUICK...!!!
DID SOMEONE JUST RUN BY?
...DAMMIT.
QUICK...!!!
RUI, WHATEVER YOU'RE UP TO...

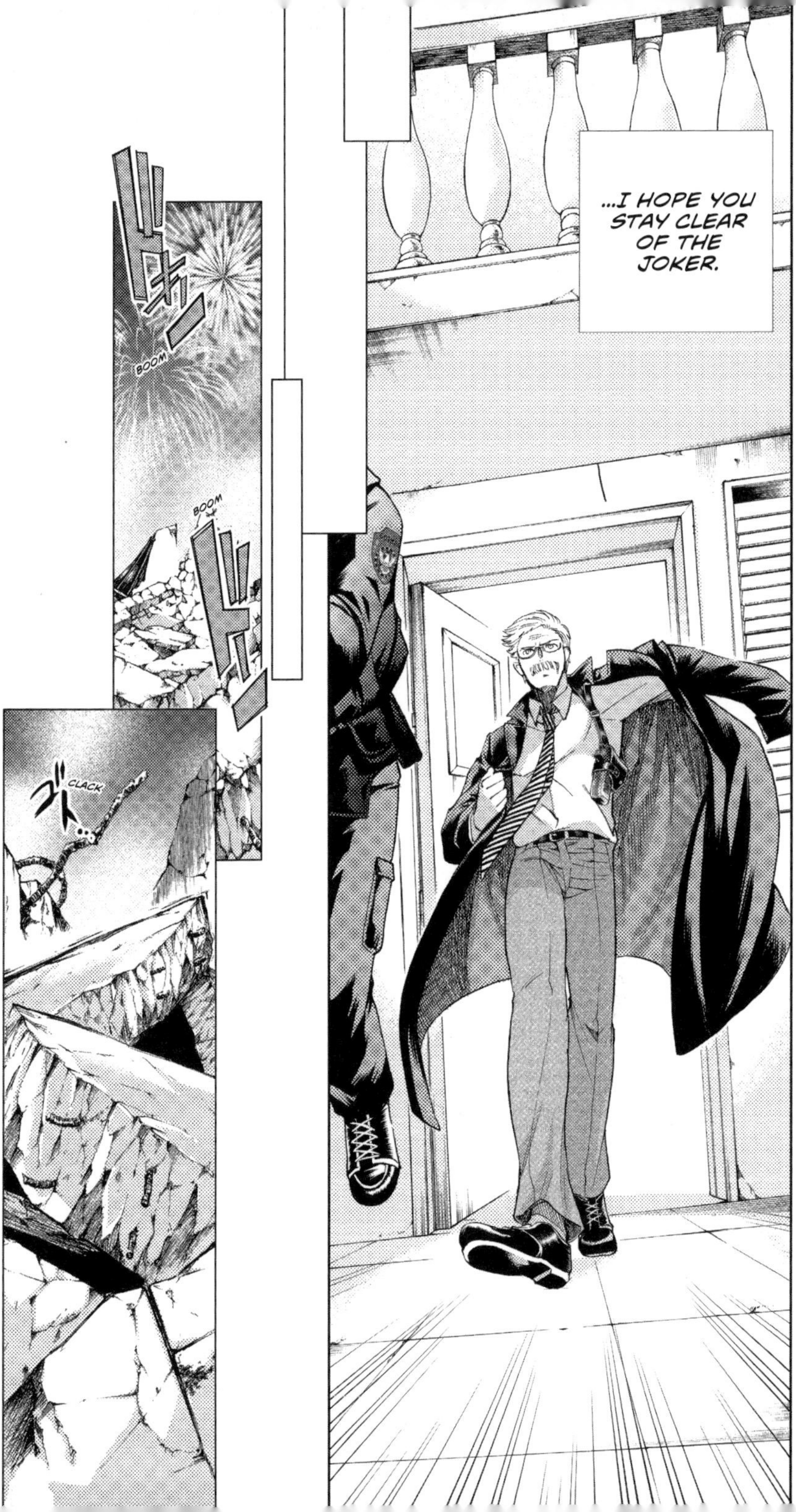
...I HOPE YOU STAY CLEAR OF THE JOKER.
BOOM
BOOM
CLACK

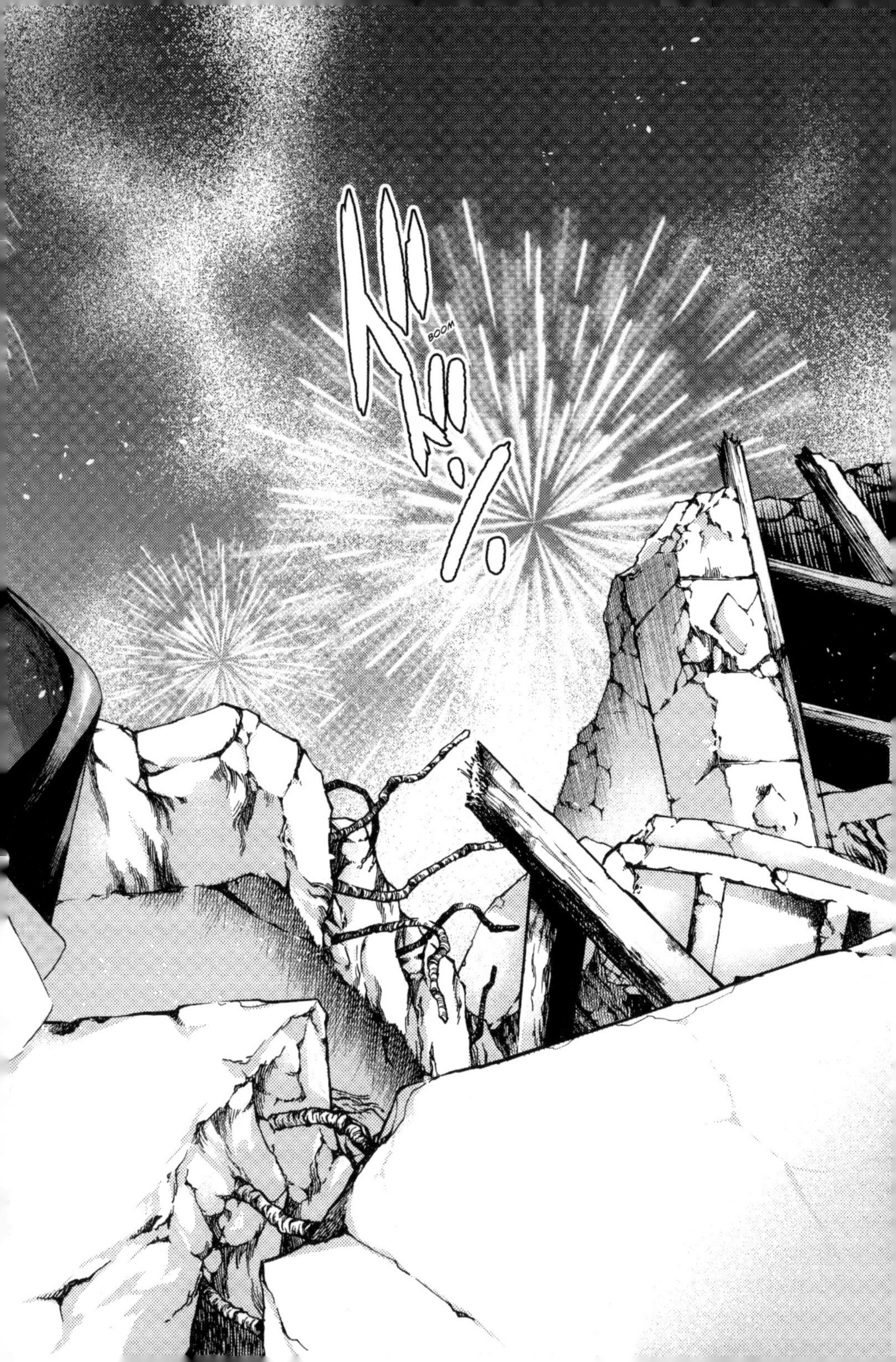
BOOM

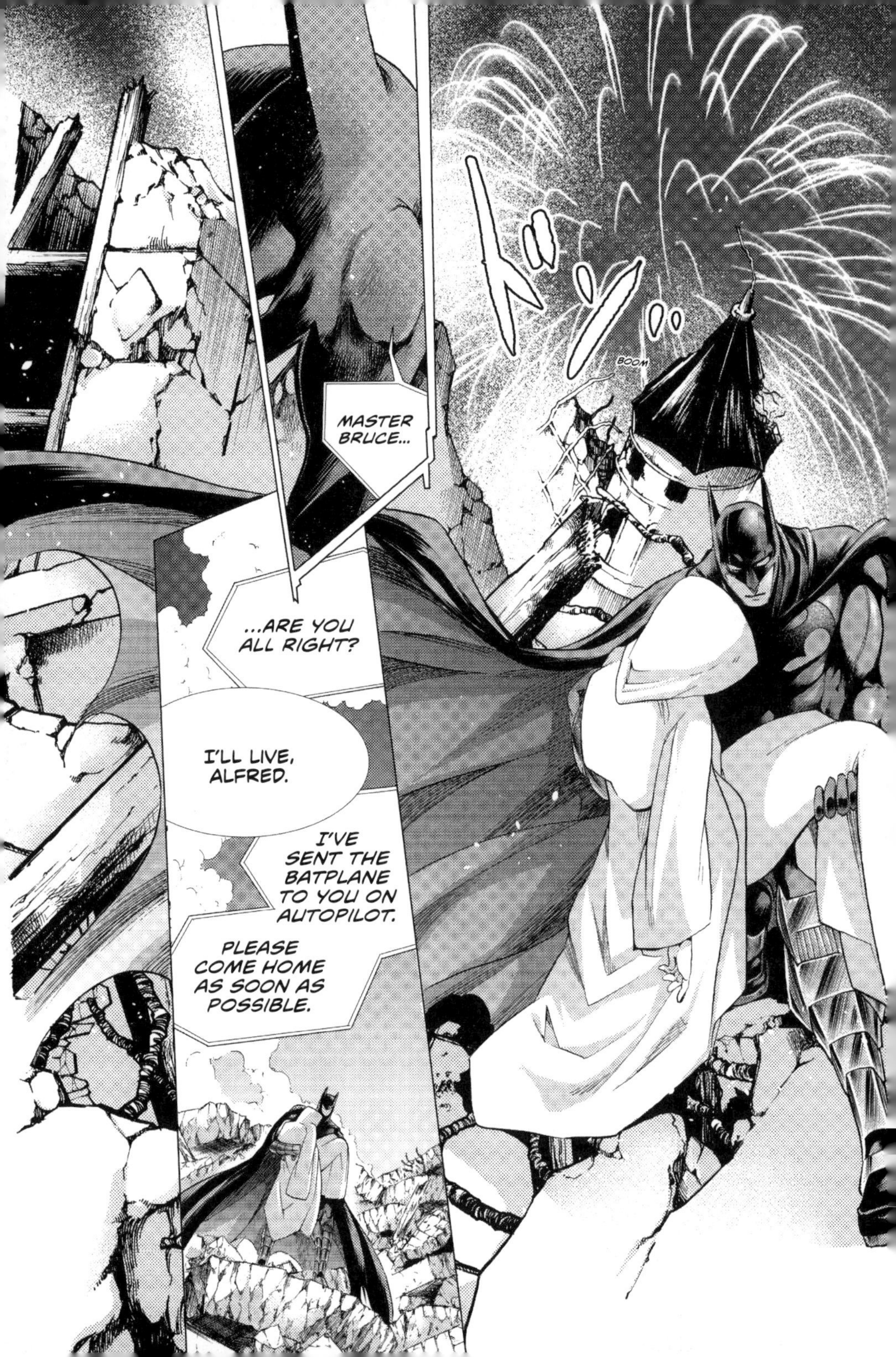
BOOM
MASTER BRUCE...
...ARE YOU ALL RIGHT?
I'LL LIVE, ALFRED.
I'VE SENT THE BATPLANE TO YOU ON AUTOPILOT.
PLEASE COME HOME AS SOON AS POSSIBLE.

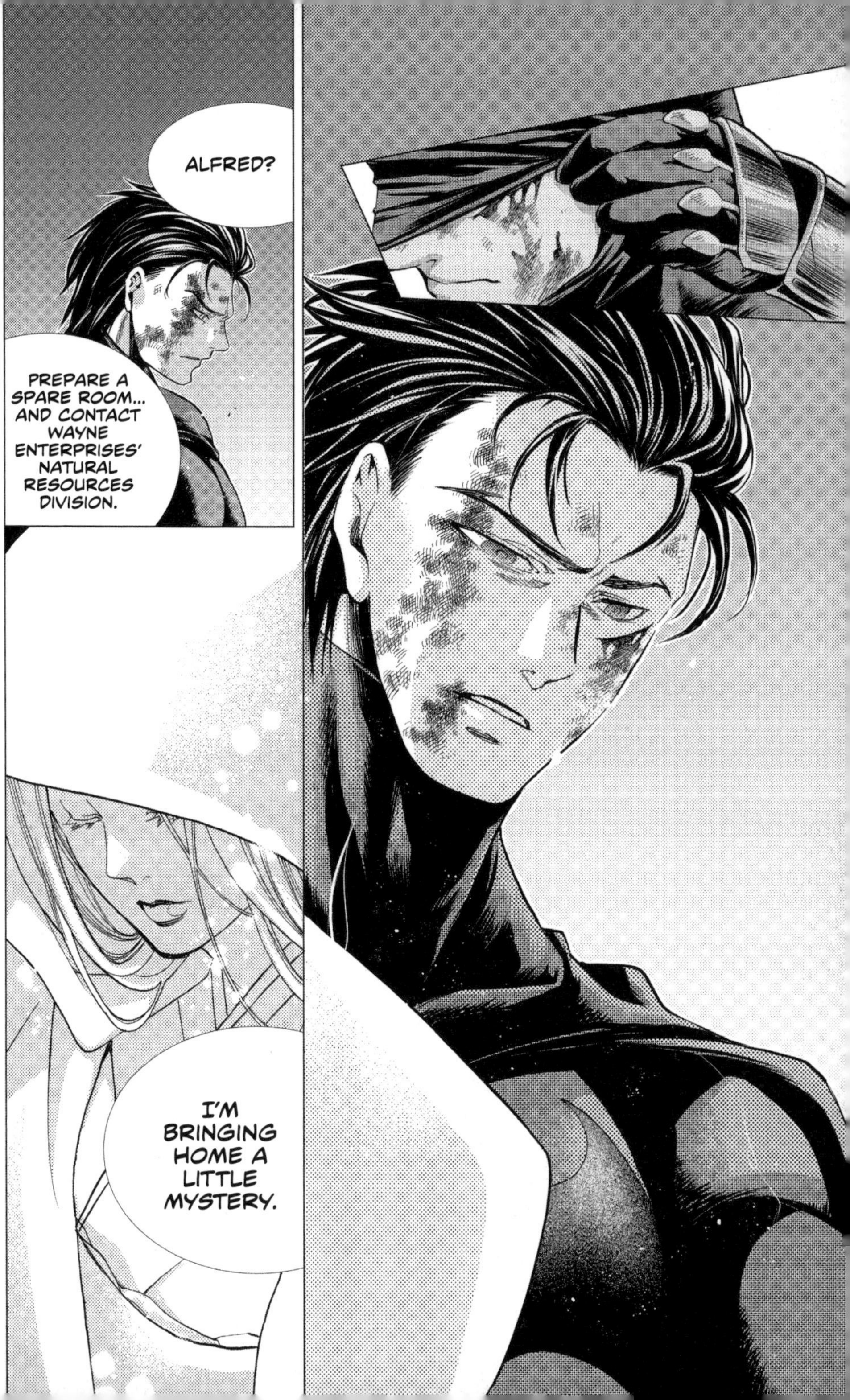
ALFRED?
PREPARE A SPARE ROOM... AND CONTACT WAYNE ENTERPRISES' NATURAL RESOURCES DIVISION.
I'M BRINGING HOME A LITTLE MYSTERY.

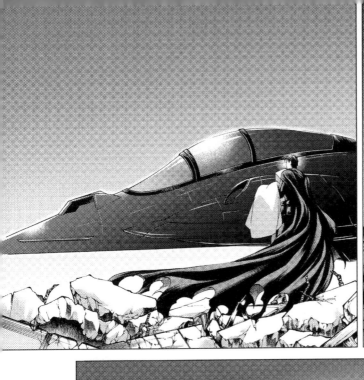

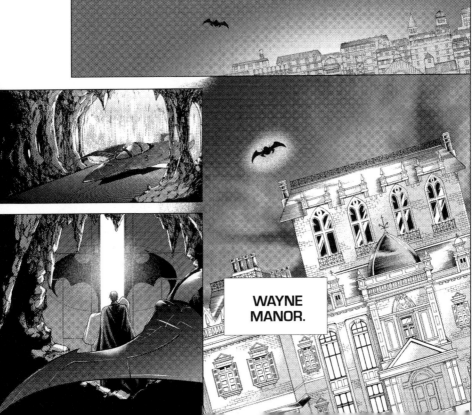

WAYNE
MANOR.

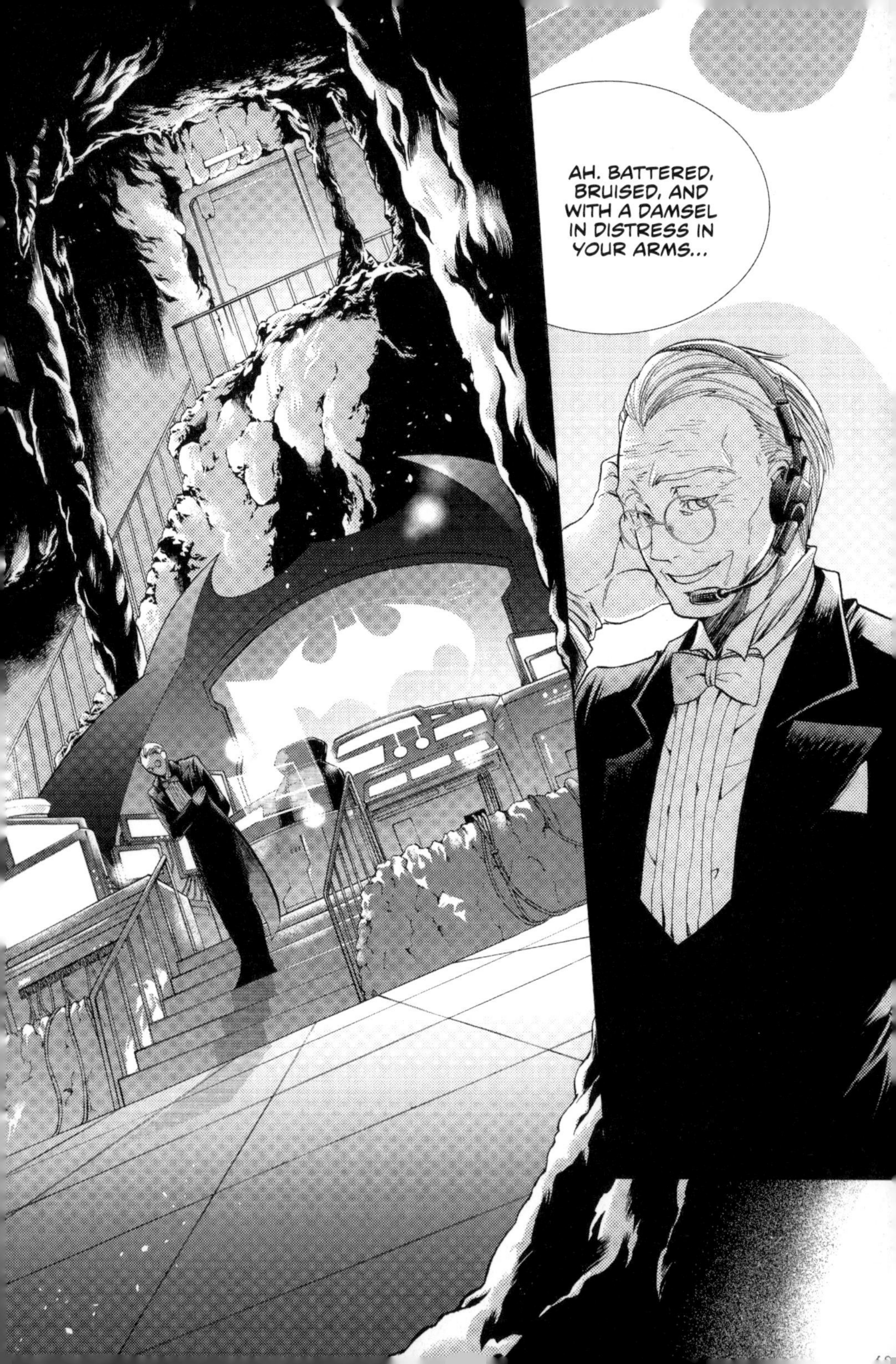
AH. BATTERED, BRUISED, AND WITH A DAMSEL IN DISTRESS IN YOUR ARMS...

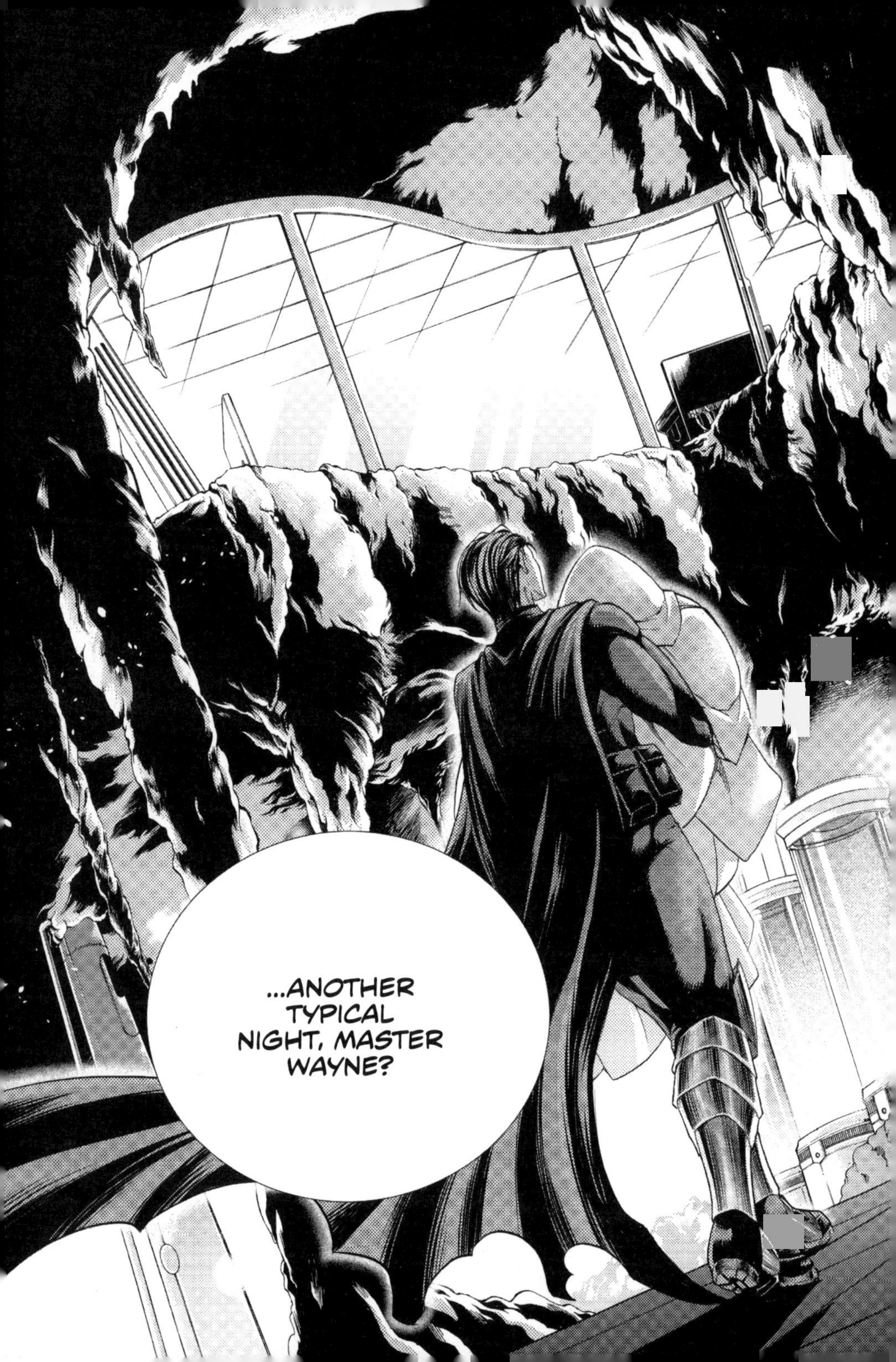
...ANOTHER TYPICAL NIGHT, MASTER WAYNE?

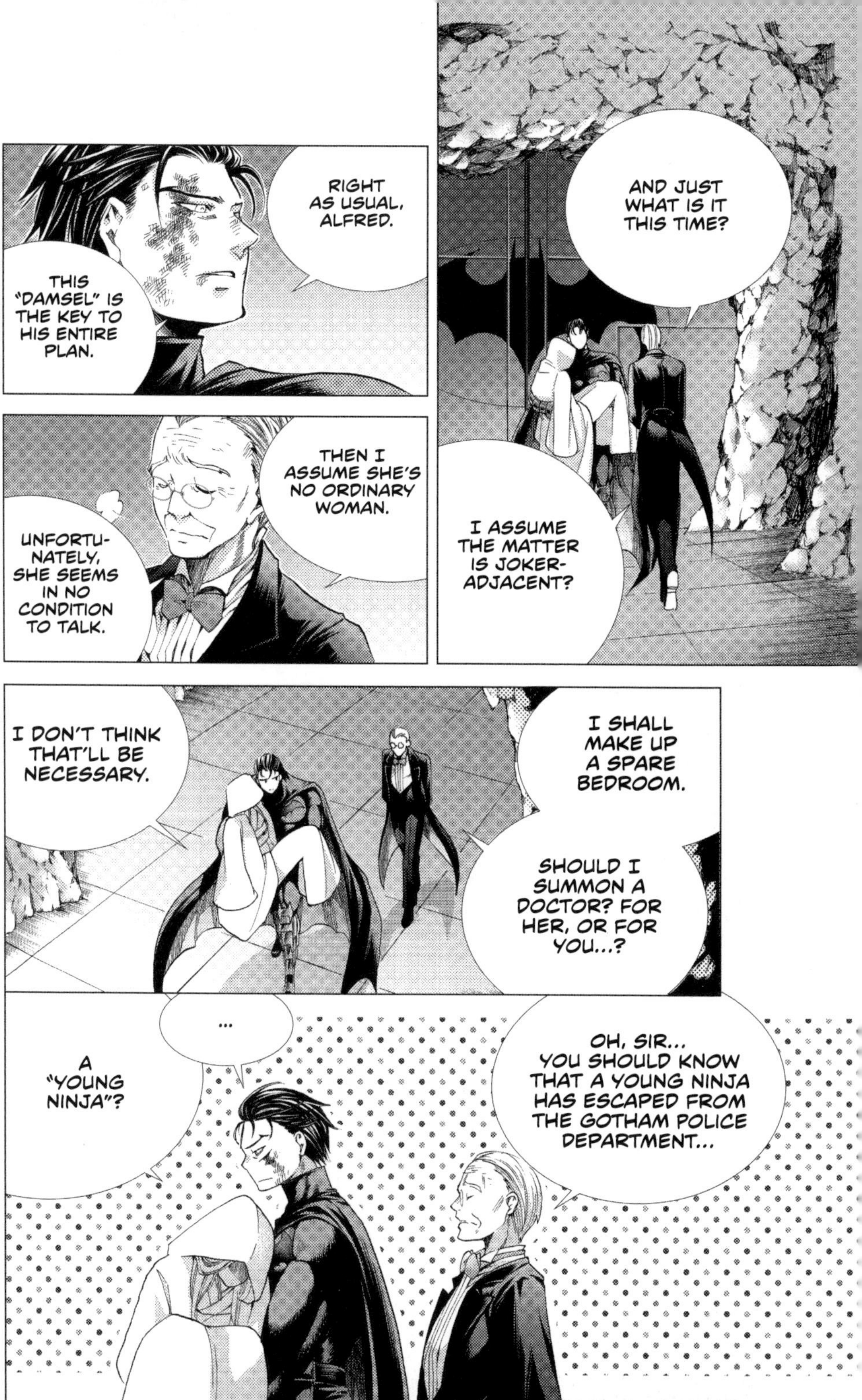
AND JUST WHAT IS IT THIS TIME?
I ASSUME THE MATTER IS JOKER-ADJACENT?
RIGHT AS USUAL, ALFRED.
THIS "DAMSEL" IS THE KEY TO HIS ENTIRE PLAN.
THEN I ASSUME SHE'S NO ORDINARY WOMAN.
UNFORTU-NATELY, SHE SEEMS IN NO CONDITION TO TALK.
I SHALL MAKE UP A SPARE BEDROOM.
SHOULD I SUMMON A DOCTOR? FOR HER, OR FOR YOU...?
I DON'T THINK THAT'LL BE NECESSARY.
OH, SIR... YOU SHOULD KNOW THAT A YOUNG NINJA HAS ESCAPED FROM THE GOTHAM POLICE DEPARTMENT...
...
A "YOUNG NINJA"?

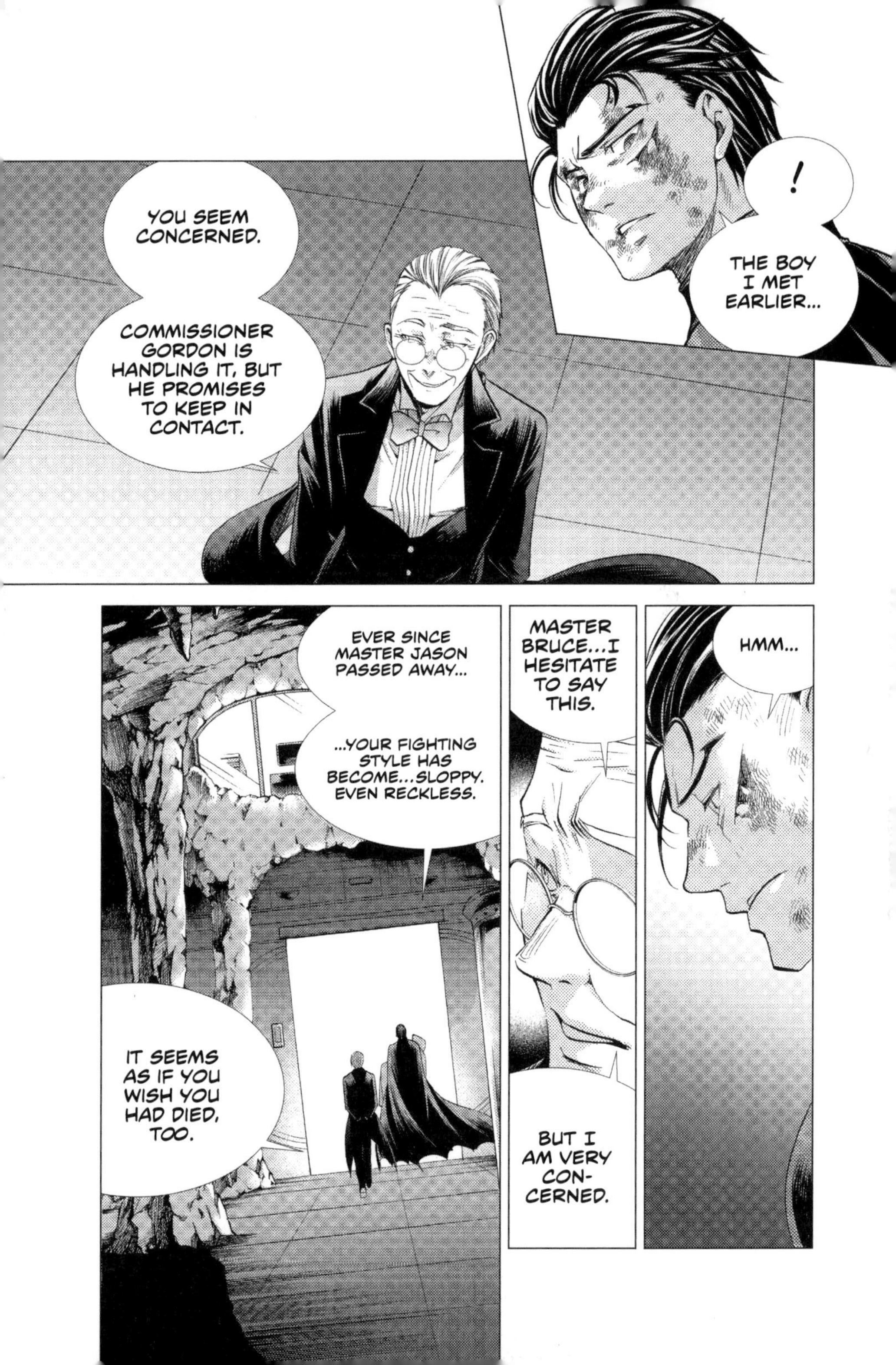
!
THE BOY I MET EARLIER...
YOU SEEM CONCERNED.
COMMISSIONER GORDON IS HANDLING IT, BUT HE PROMISES TO KEEP IN CONTACT.
HMM...
MASTER BRUCE...I HESITATE TO SAY THIS.
BUT I AM VERY CON-CERNED.
EVER SINCE MASTER JASON PASSED AWAY...
...YOUR FIGHTING STYLE HAS BECOME...SLOPPY. EVEN RECKLESS.
IT SEEMS AS IF YOU WISH YOU HAD DIED, TOO.

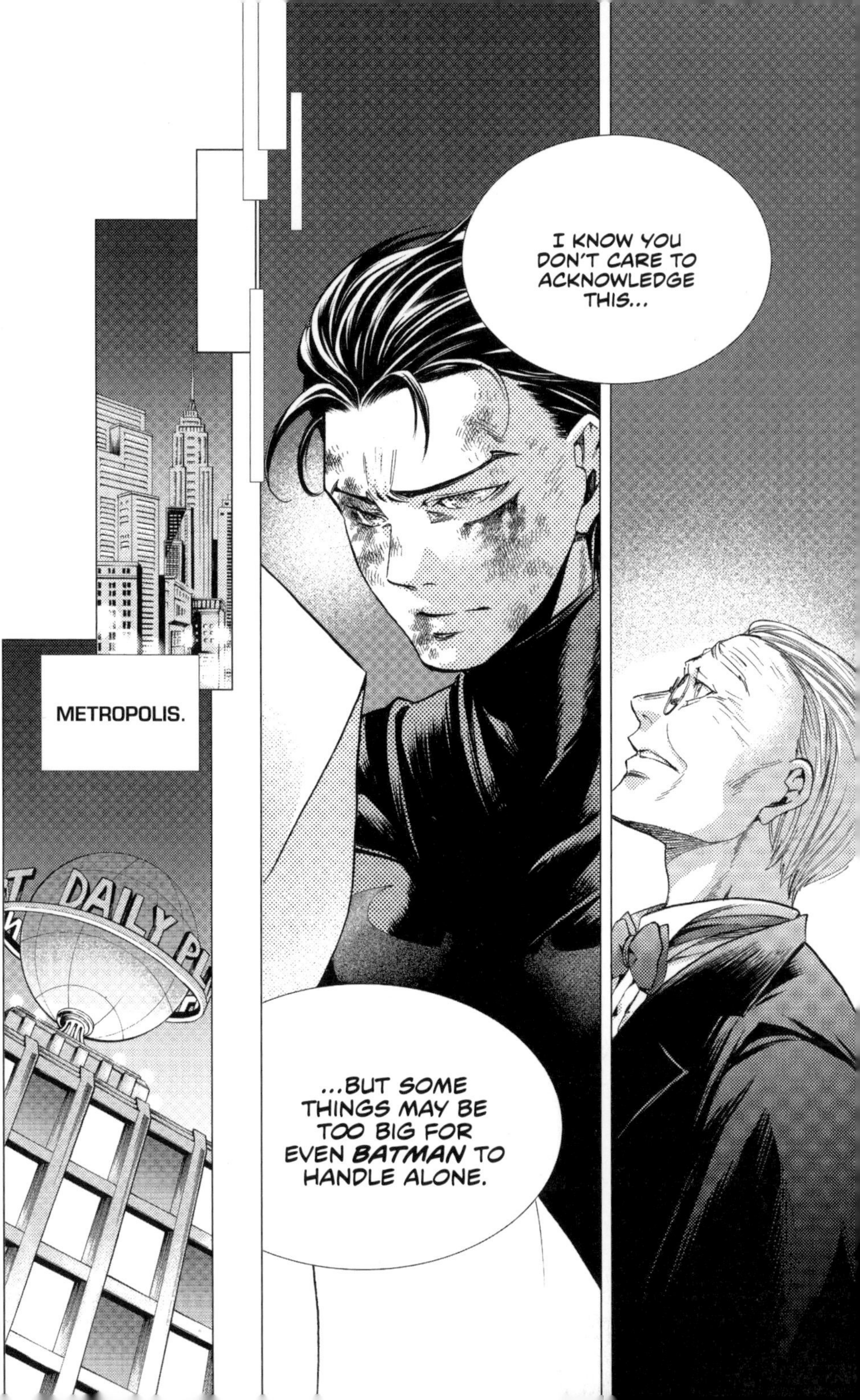
I KNOW YOU DON'T CARE TO ACKNOWLEDGE THIS...
...BUT SOME THINGS MAY BE TOO BIG FOR EVEN *BATMAN* TO HANDLE ALONE.
METROPOLIS.

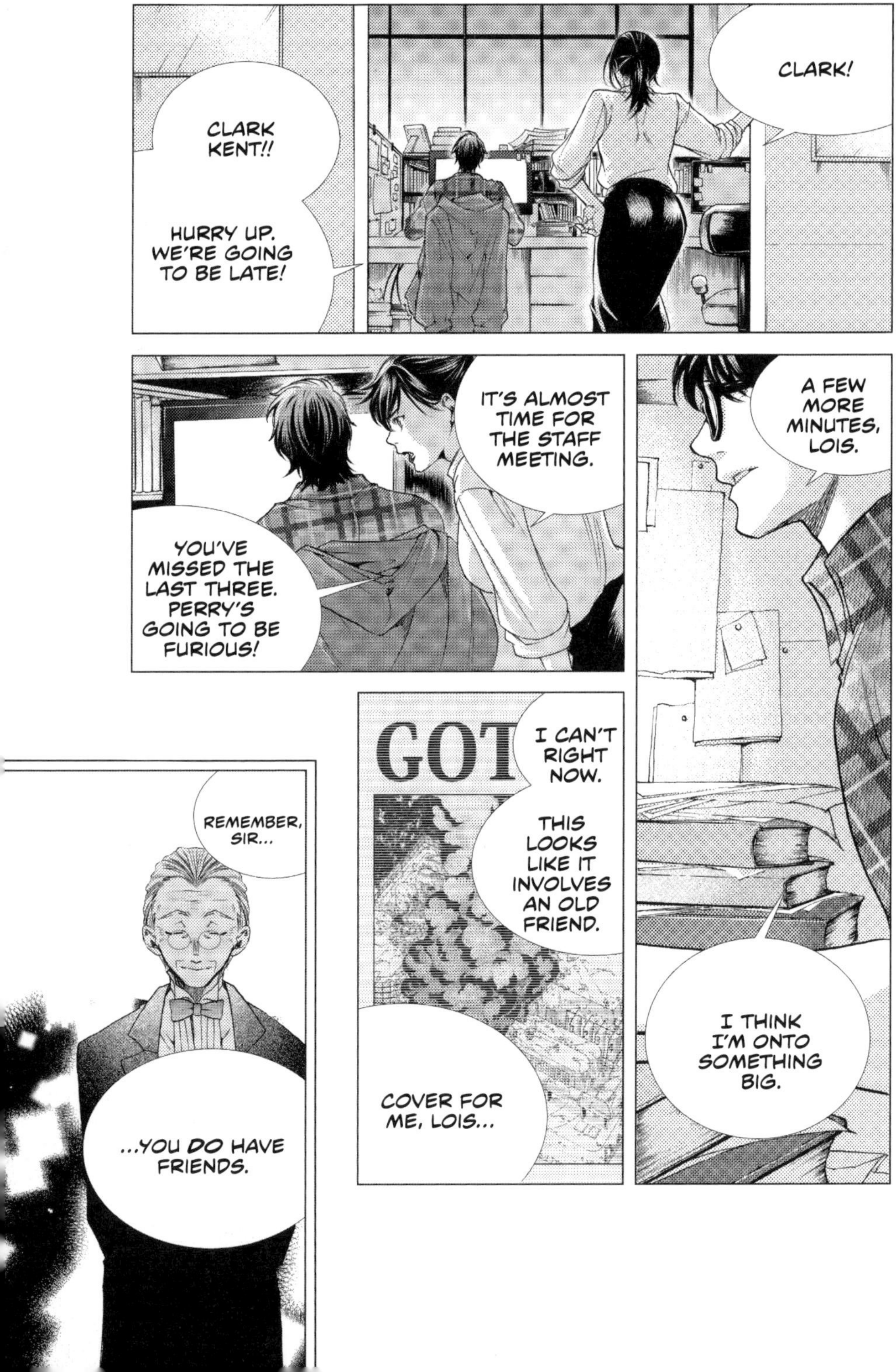
CLARK!
CLARK KENT!!
HURRY UP. WE'RE GOING TO BE LATE!
A FEW MORE MINUTES, LOIS.
I THINK I'M ONTO SOMETHING BIG.
IT'S ALMOST TIME FOR THE STAFF MEETING.
YOU'VE MISSED THE LAST THREE. PERRY'S GOING TO BE FURIOUS!
GOT
I CAN'T RIGHT NOW.
THIS LOOKS LIKE IT INVOLVES AN OLD FRIEND.
COVER FOR ME, LOIS...
REMEMBER, SIR...
...YOU DO HAVE FRIENDS.

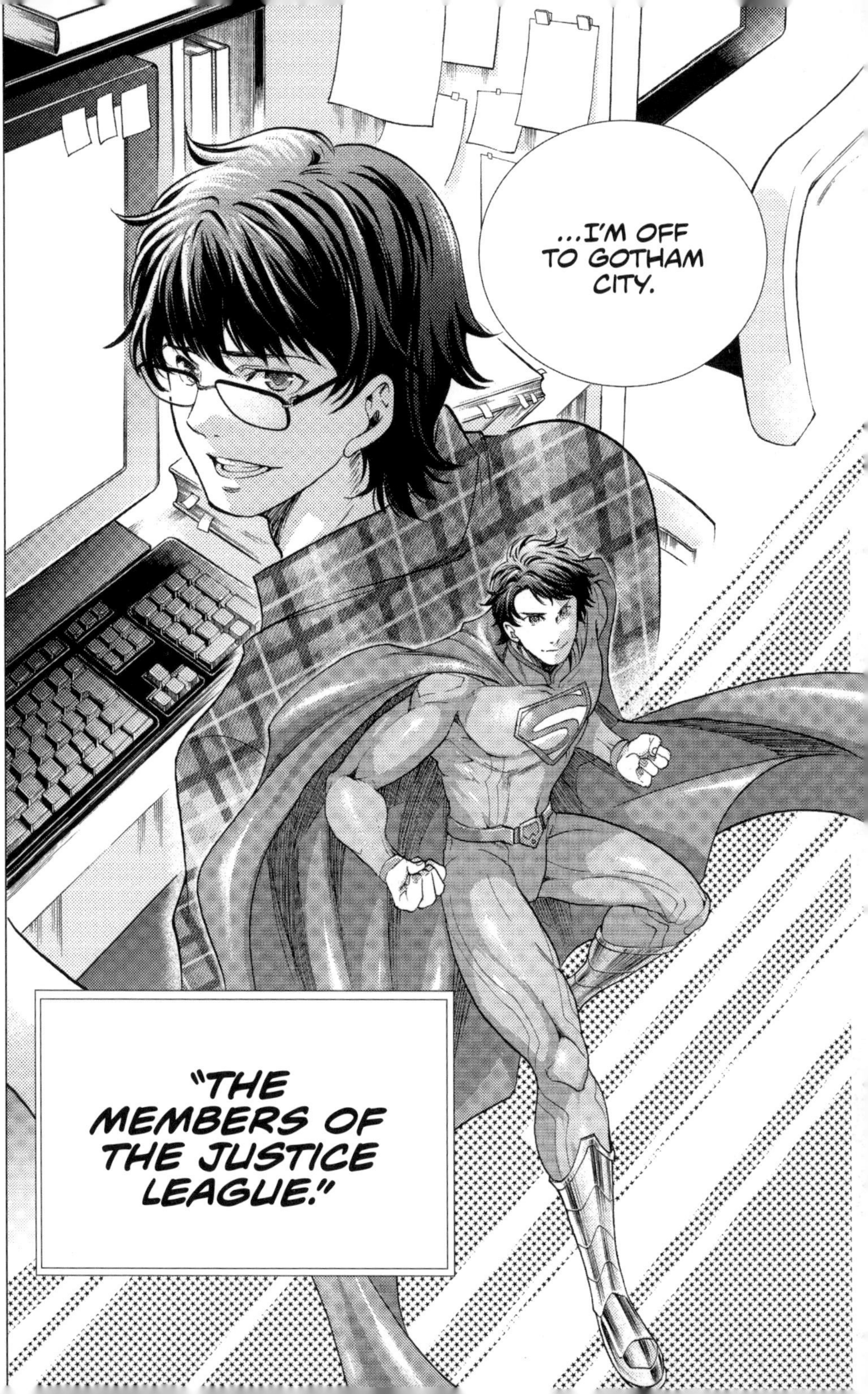
...I'M OFF TO GOTHAM CITY.
"THE MEMBERS OF THE JUSTICE LEAGUE."

# CHAPTER 3

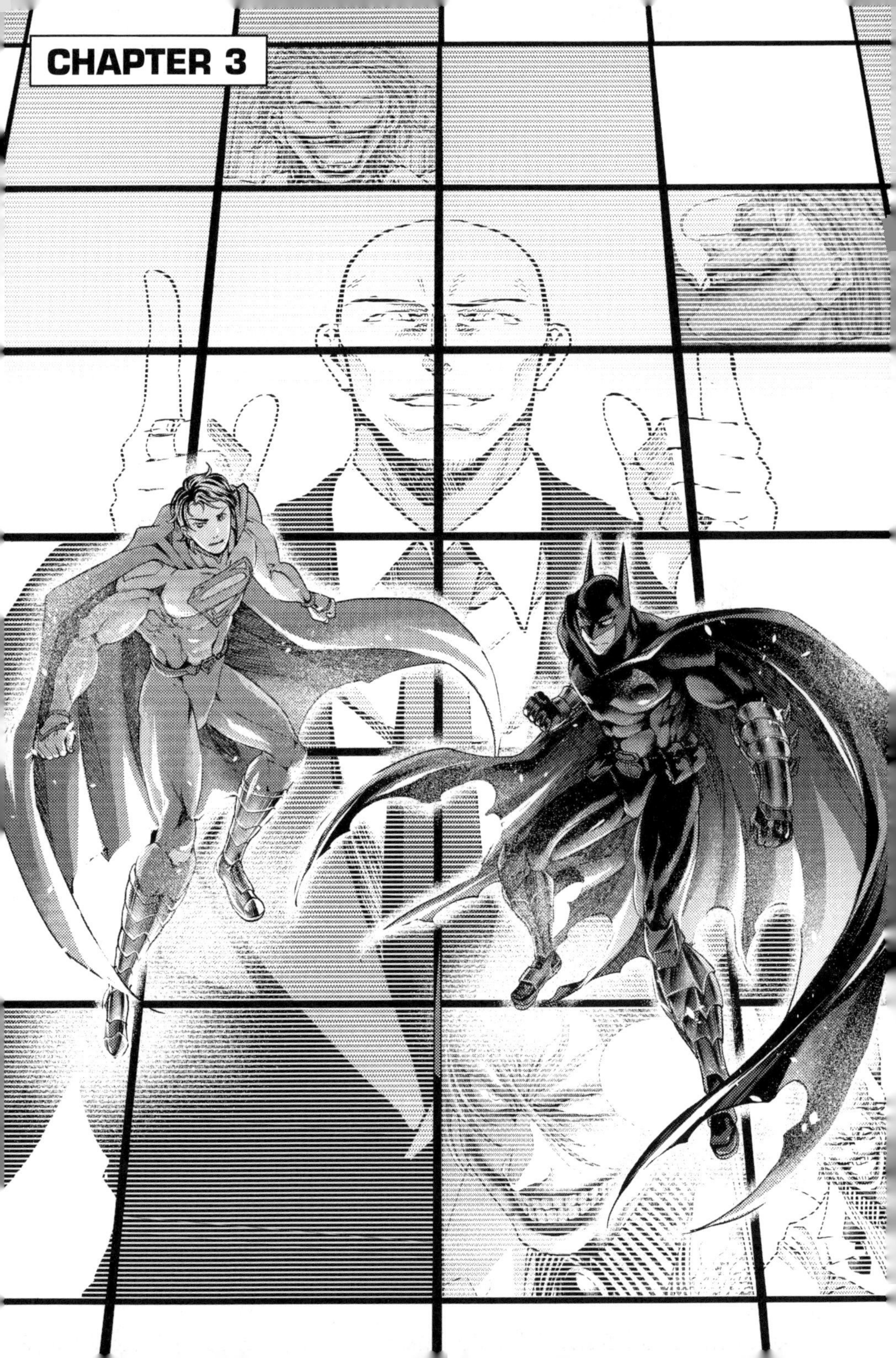

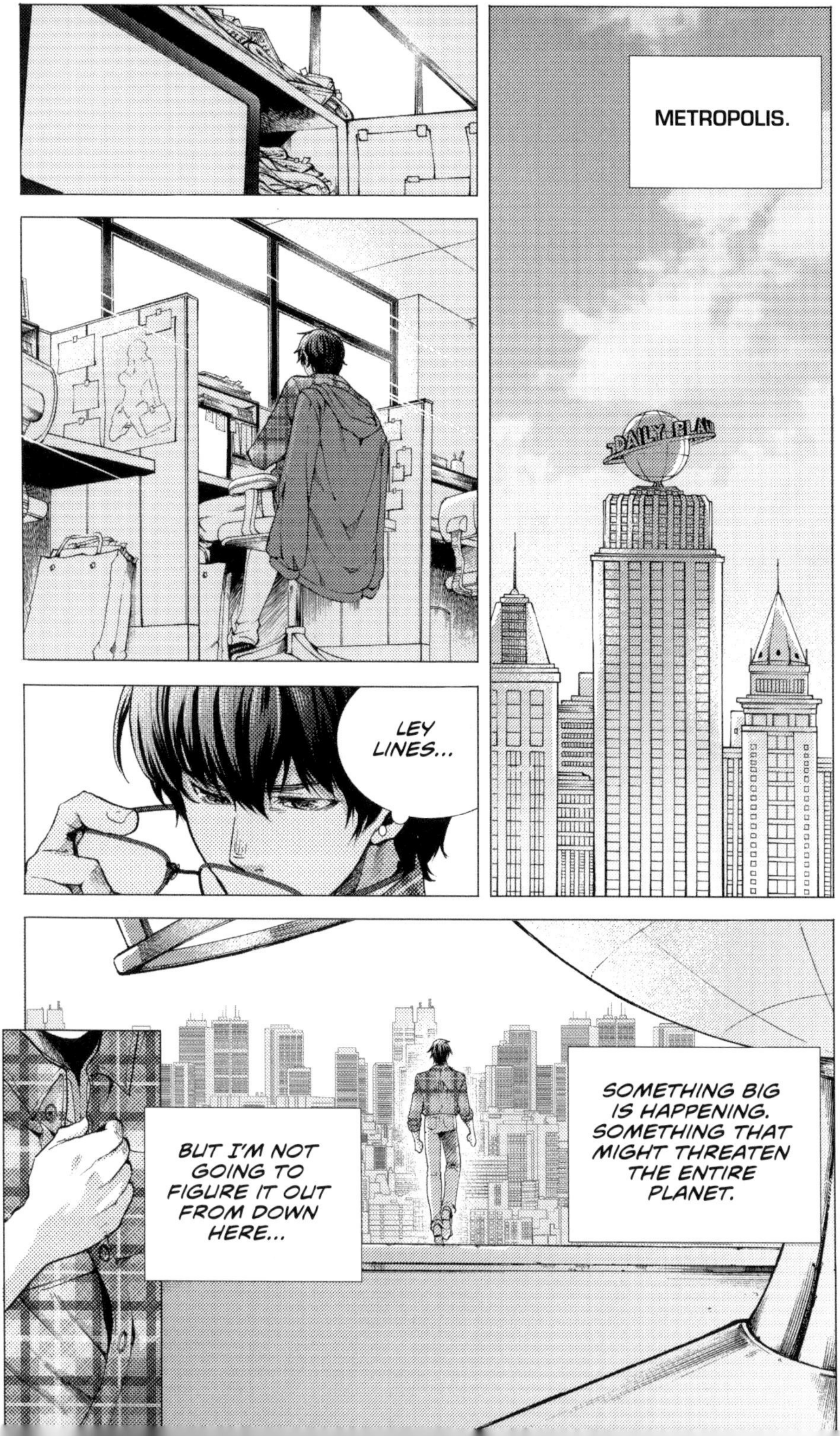
METROPOLIS.
LEY LINES...
SOMETHING BIG IS HAPPENING. SOMETHING THAT MIGHT THREATEN THE ENTIRE PLANET.
BUT I'M NOT GOING TO FIGURE IT OUT FROM DOWN HERE...

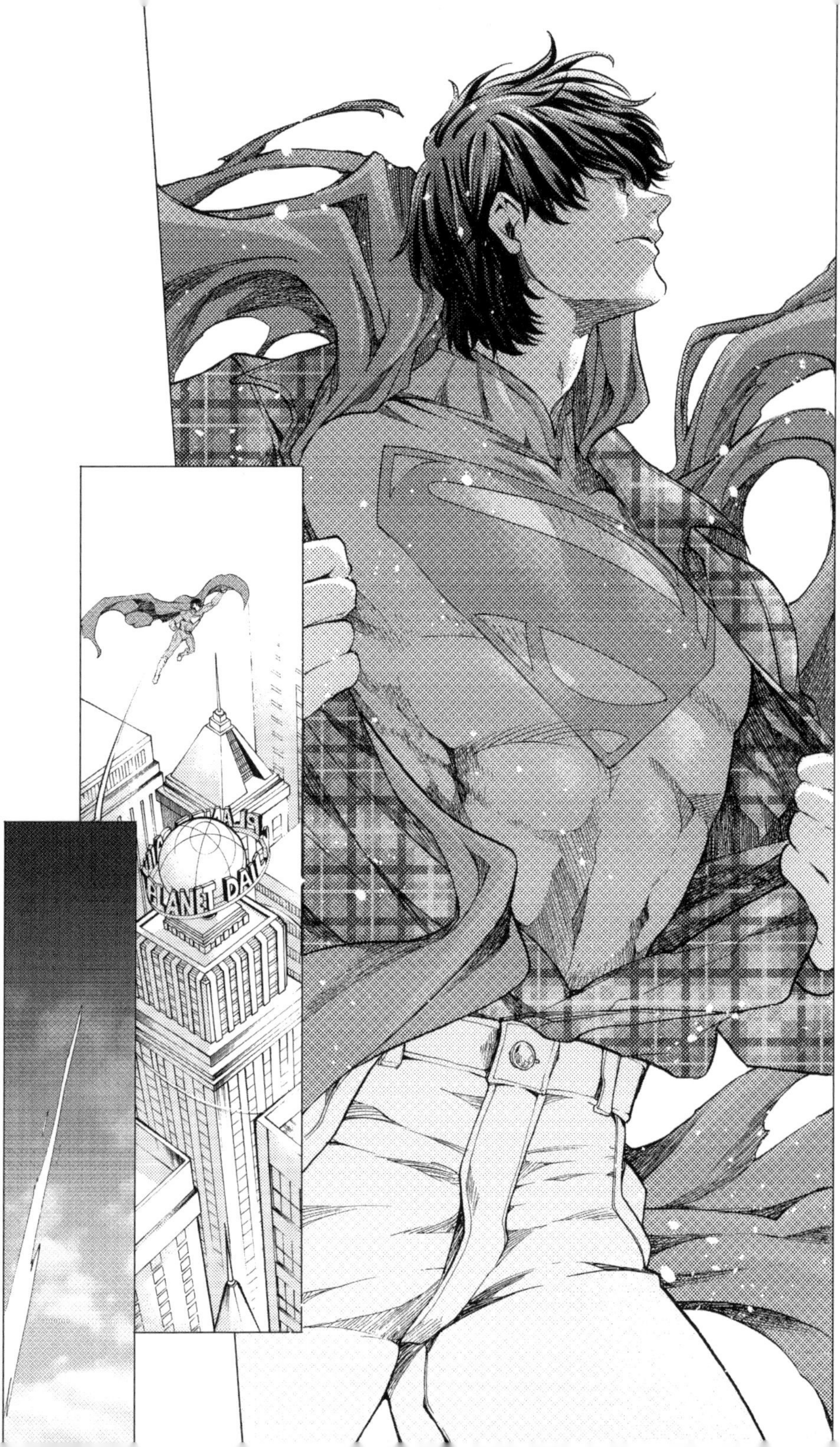
PLANET

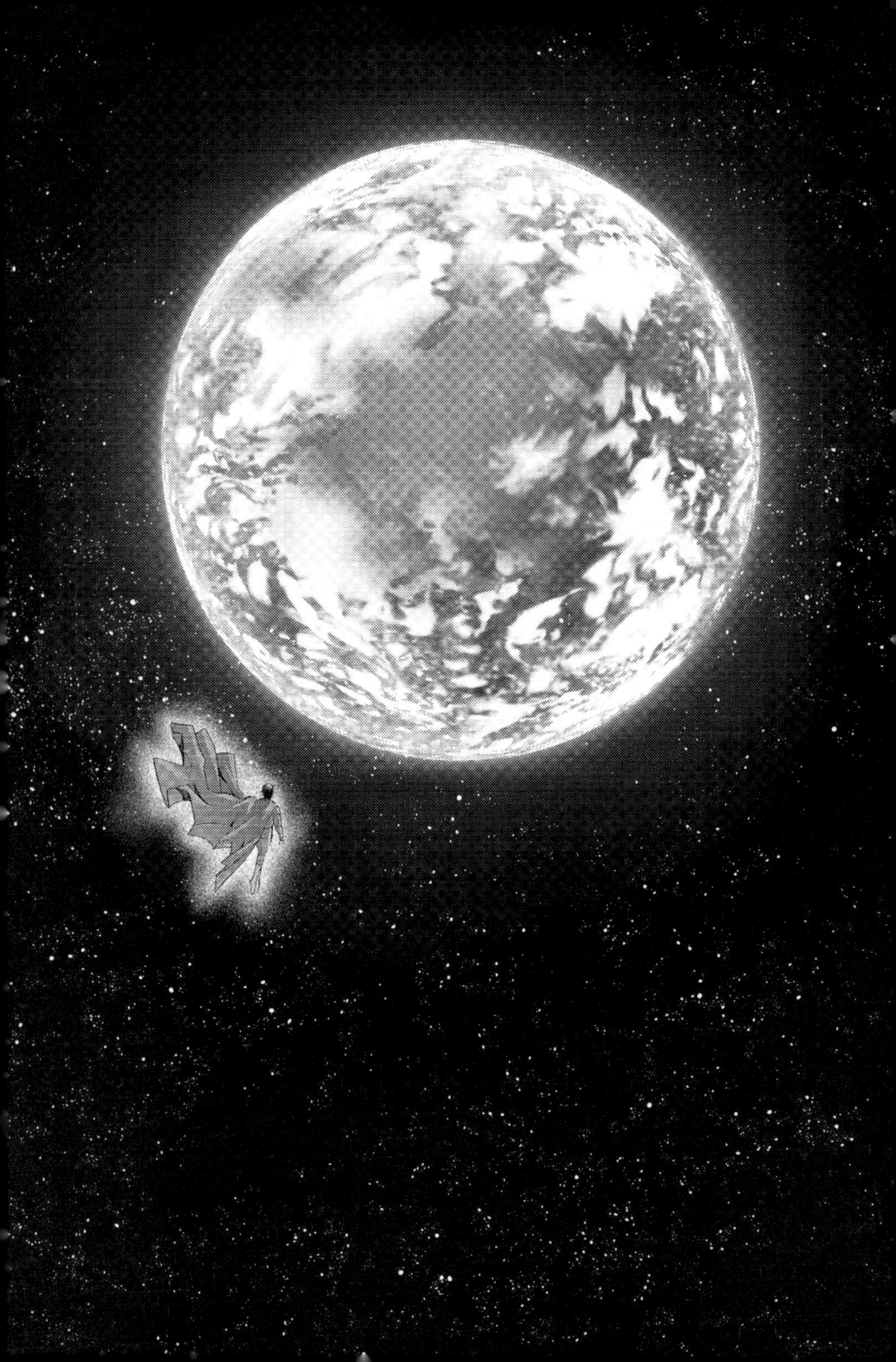

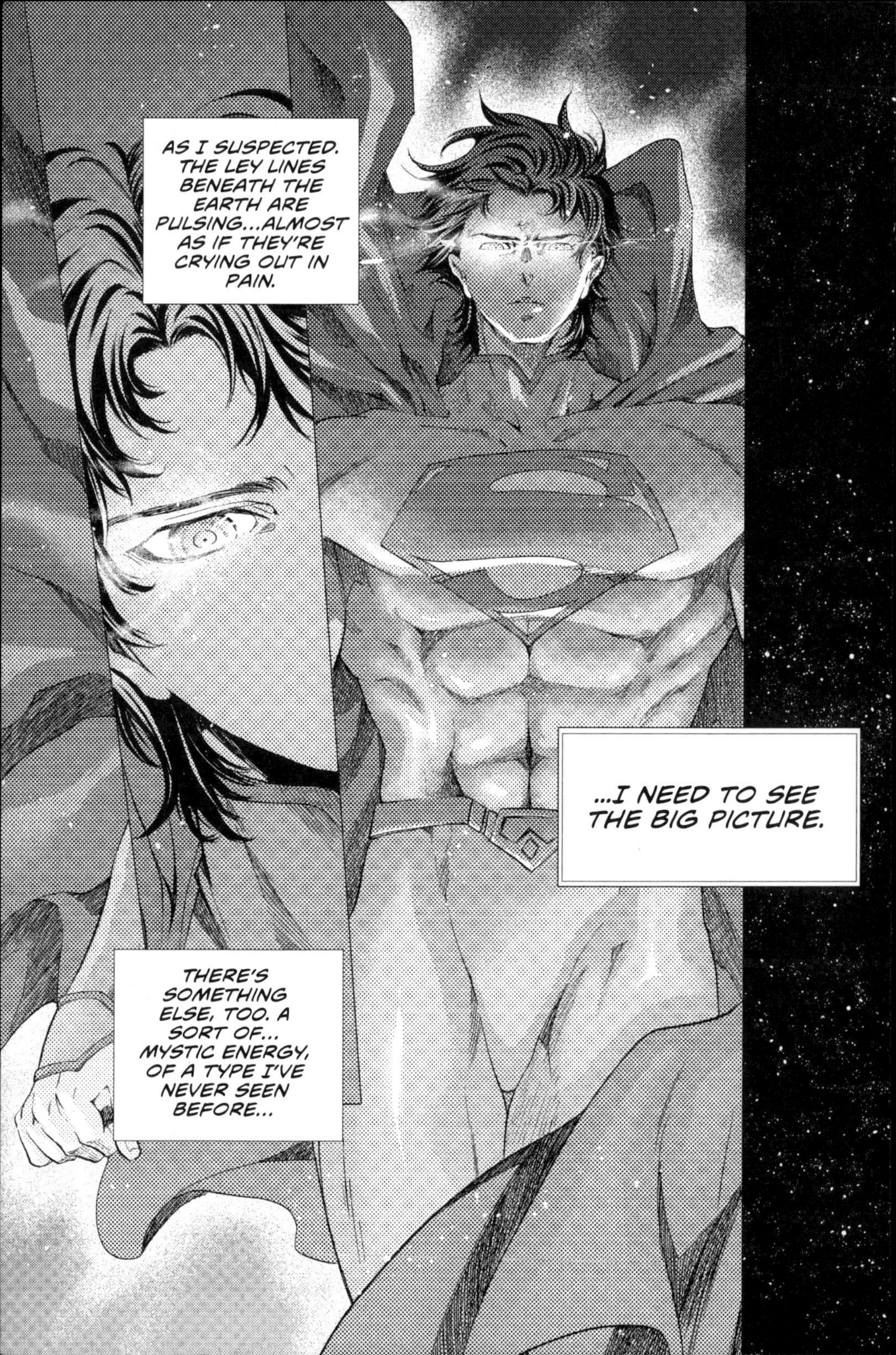
AS I SUSPECTED. THE LEY LINES BENEATH THE EARTH ARE PULSING...ALMOST AS IF THEY'RE CRYING OUT IN PAIN.
THERE'S SOMETHING ELSE, TOO. A SORT OF... MYSTIC ENERGY, OF A TYPE I'VE NEVER SEEN BEFORE...
...I NEED TO SEE THE BIG PICTURE.

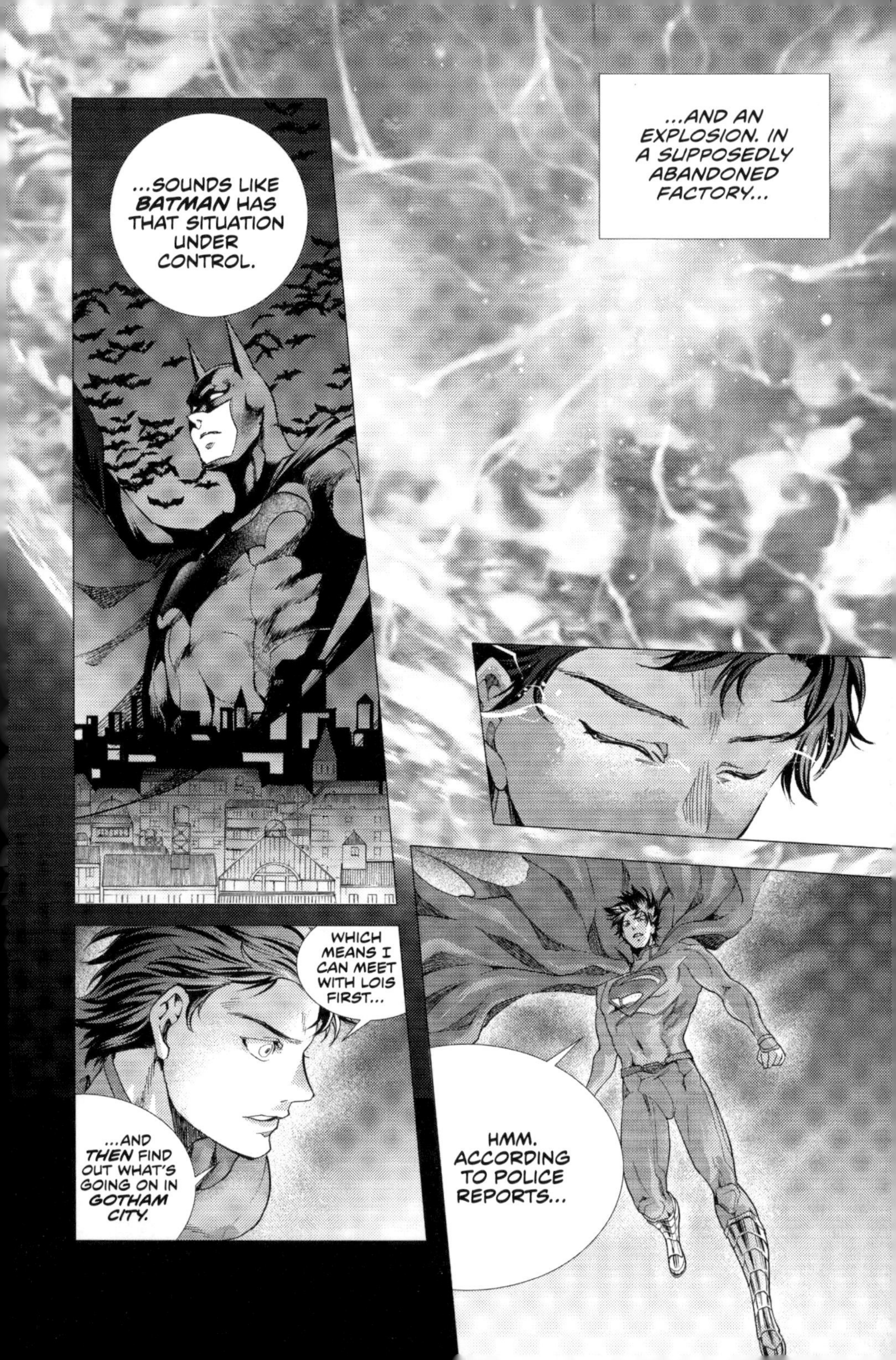
HMM. ACCORDING TO POLICE REPORTS...
...AND AN EXPLOSION. IN A SUPPOSEDLY ABANDONED FACTORY...
...SOUNDS LIKE *BATMAN* HAS THAT SITUATION UNDER CONTROL.
WHICH MEANS I CAN MEET WITH LOIS FIRST...
...AND *THEN* FIND OUT WHAT'S GOING ON IN *GOTHAM CITY.*

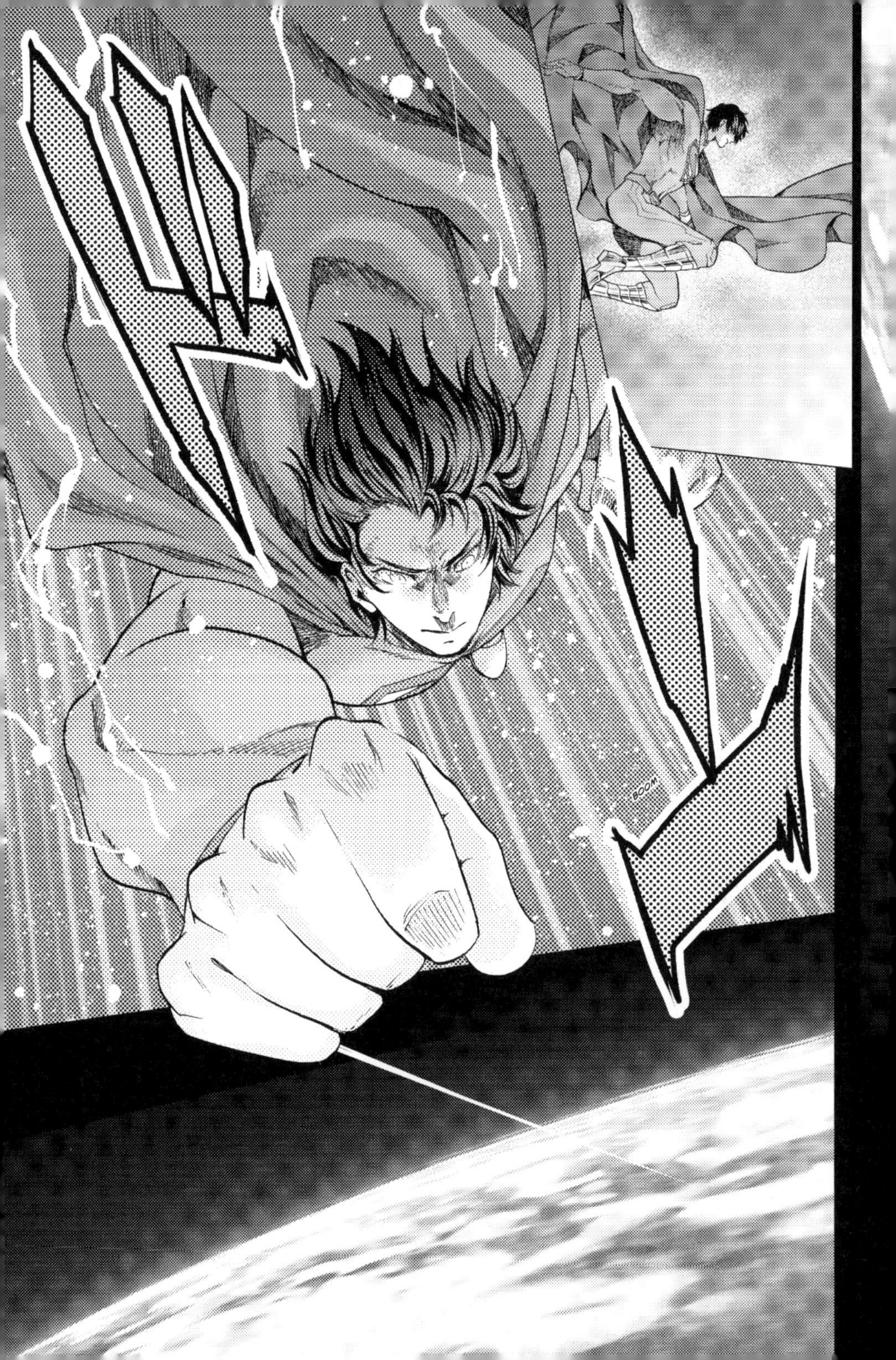
BOOM

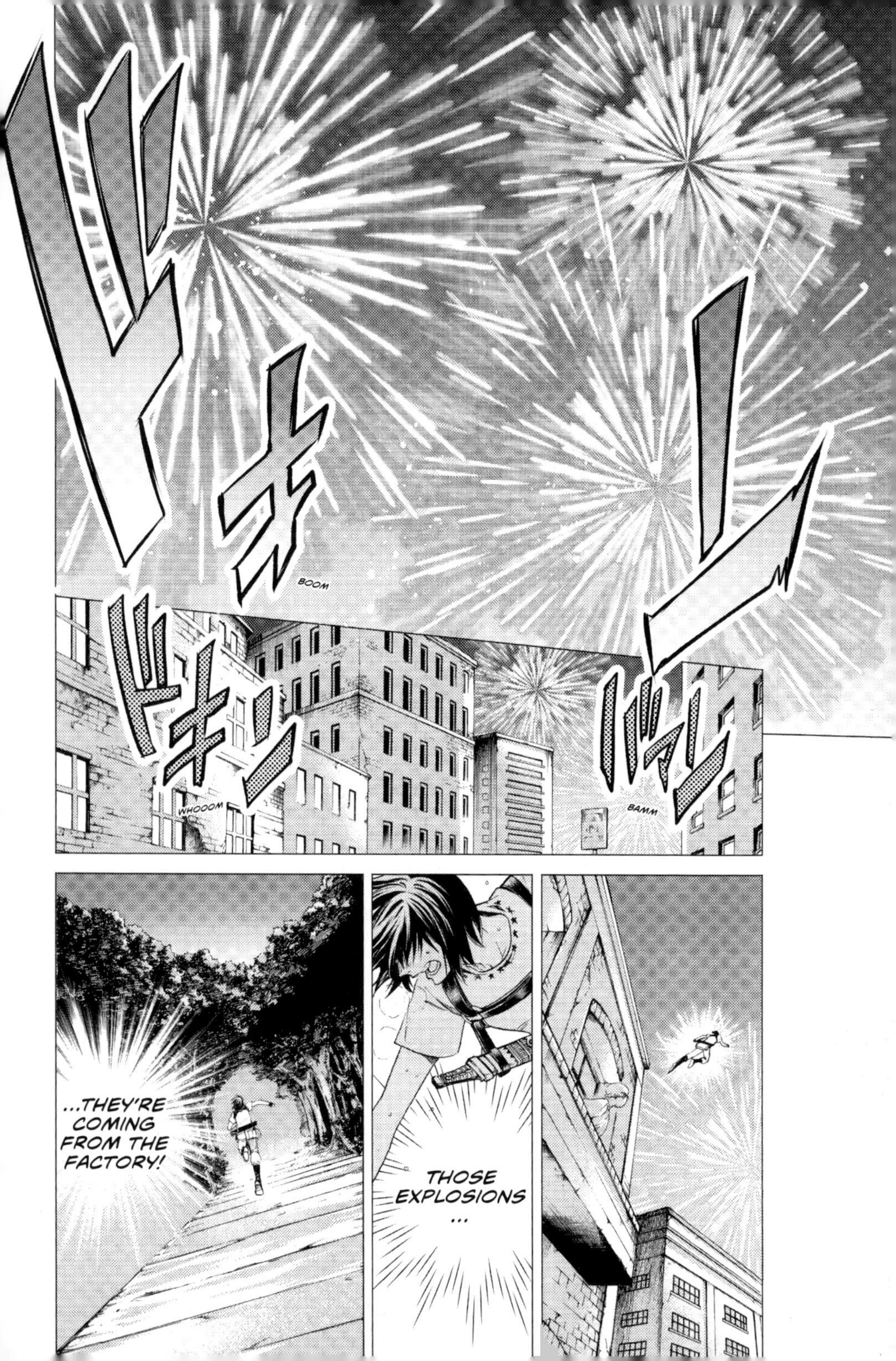
BOOM
BAMM
WHOOOM
THOSE EXPLOSIONS ...
...THEY'RE COMING FROM THE FACTORY!

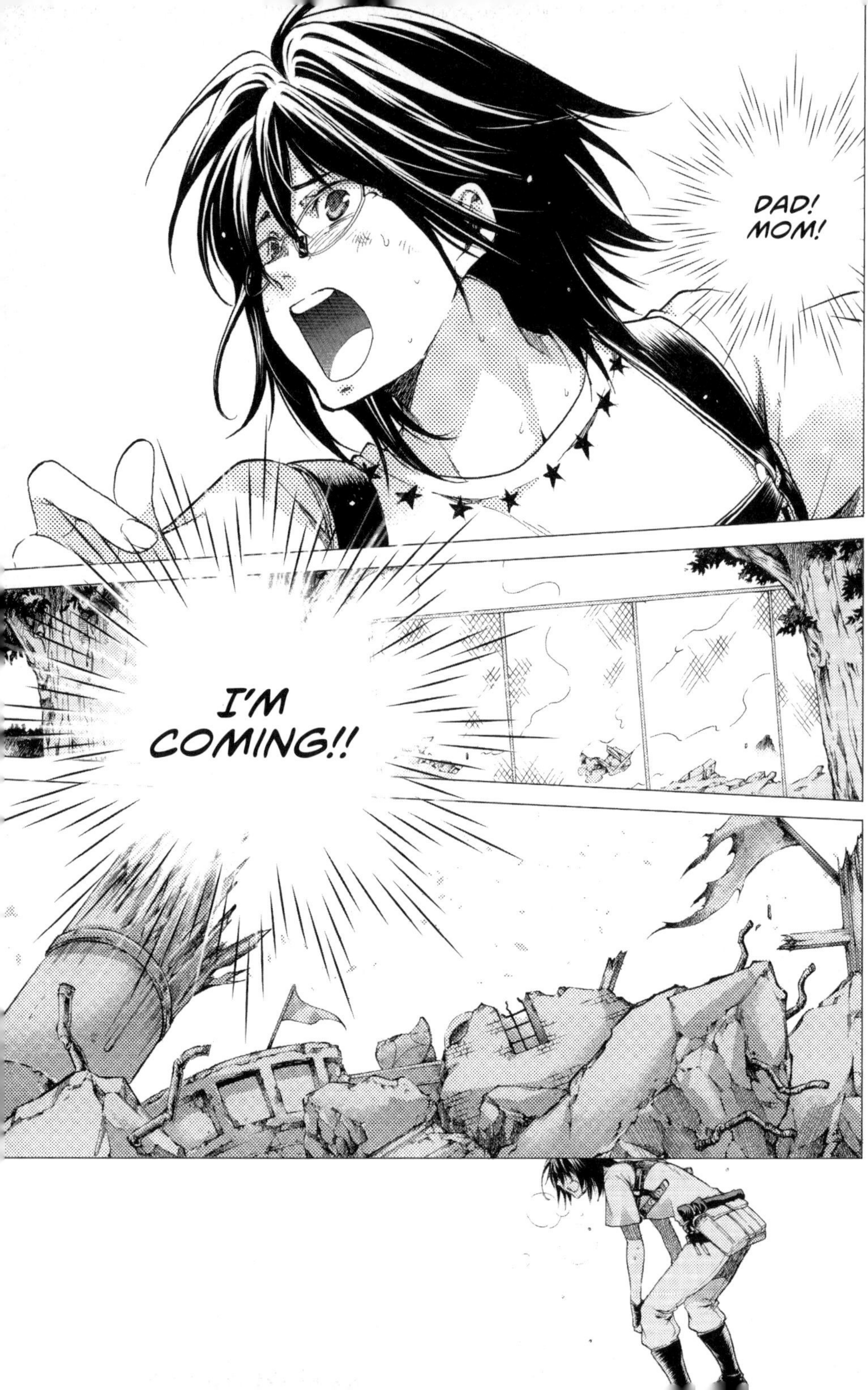
DAD! MOM!
I'M COMING!!

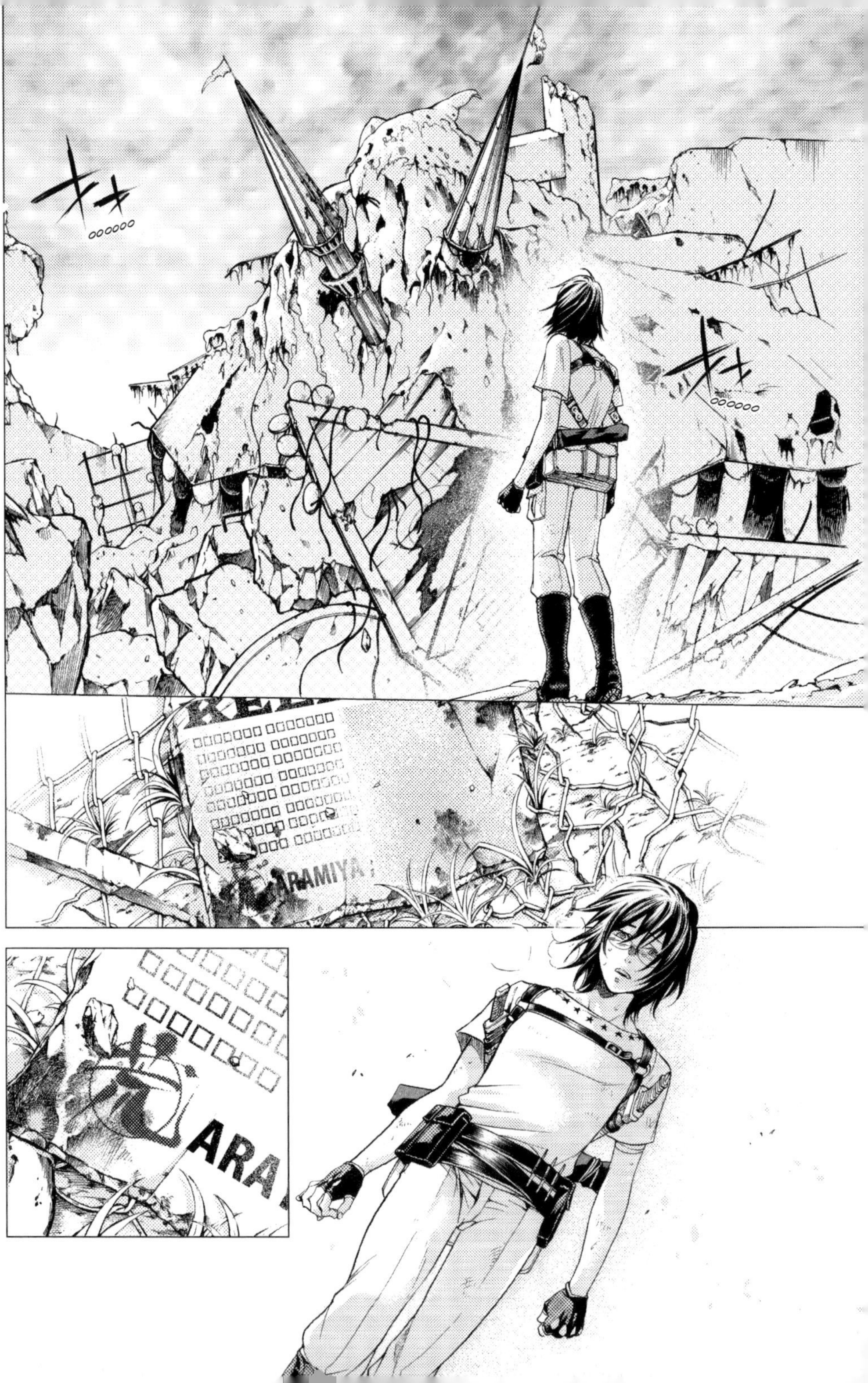
ARAMIYA
ARA

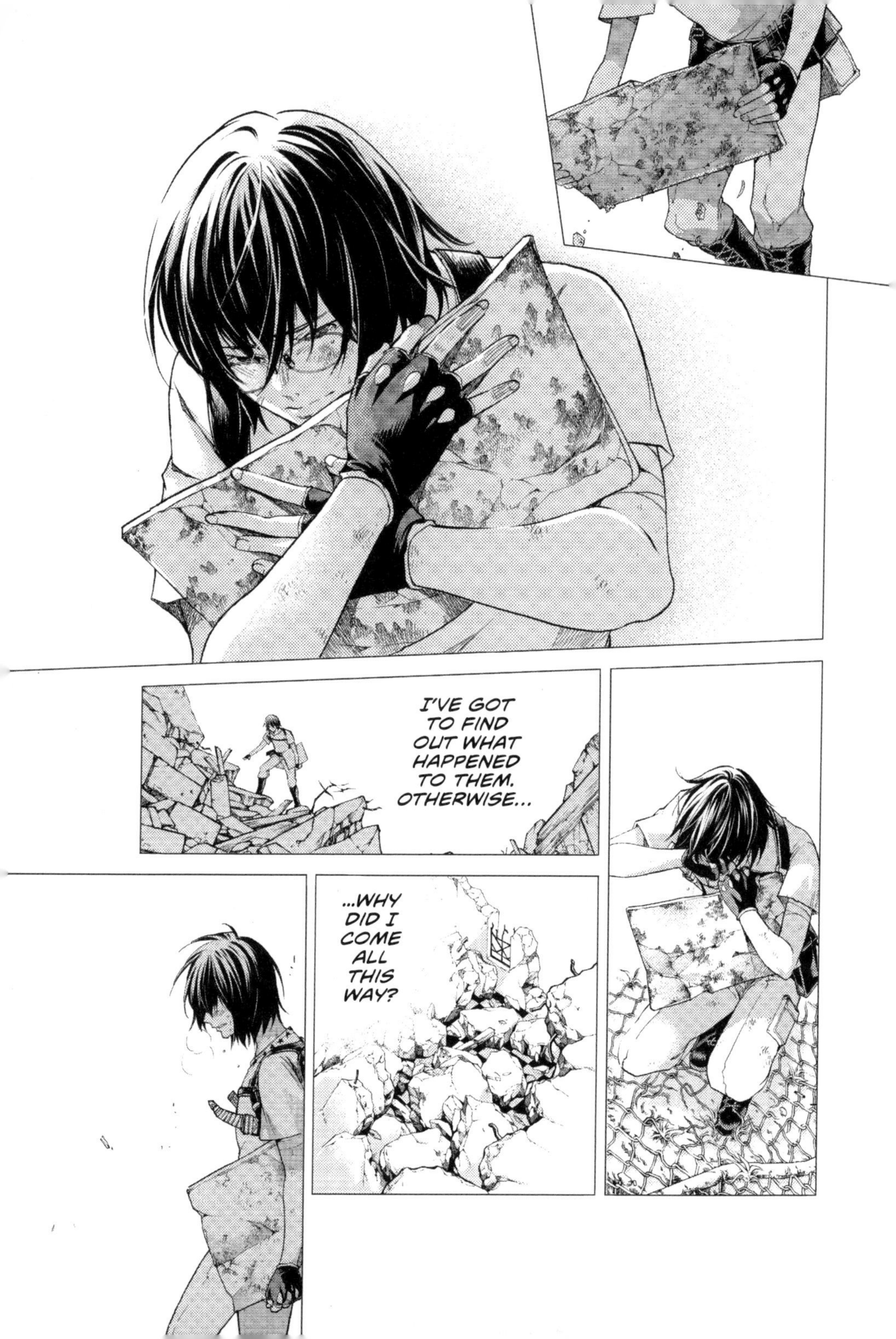
I'VE GOT TO FIND OUT WHAT HAPPENED TO THEM. OTHERWISE...
...WHY DID I COME ALL THIS WAY?

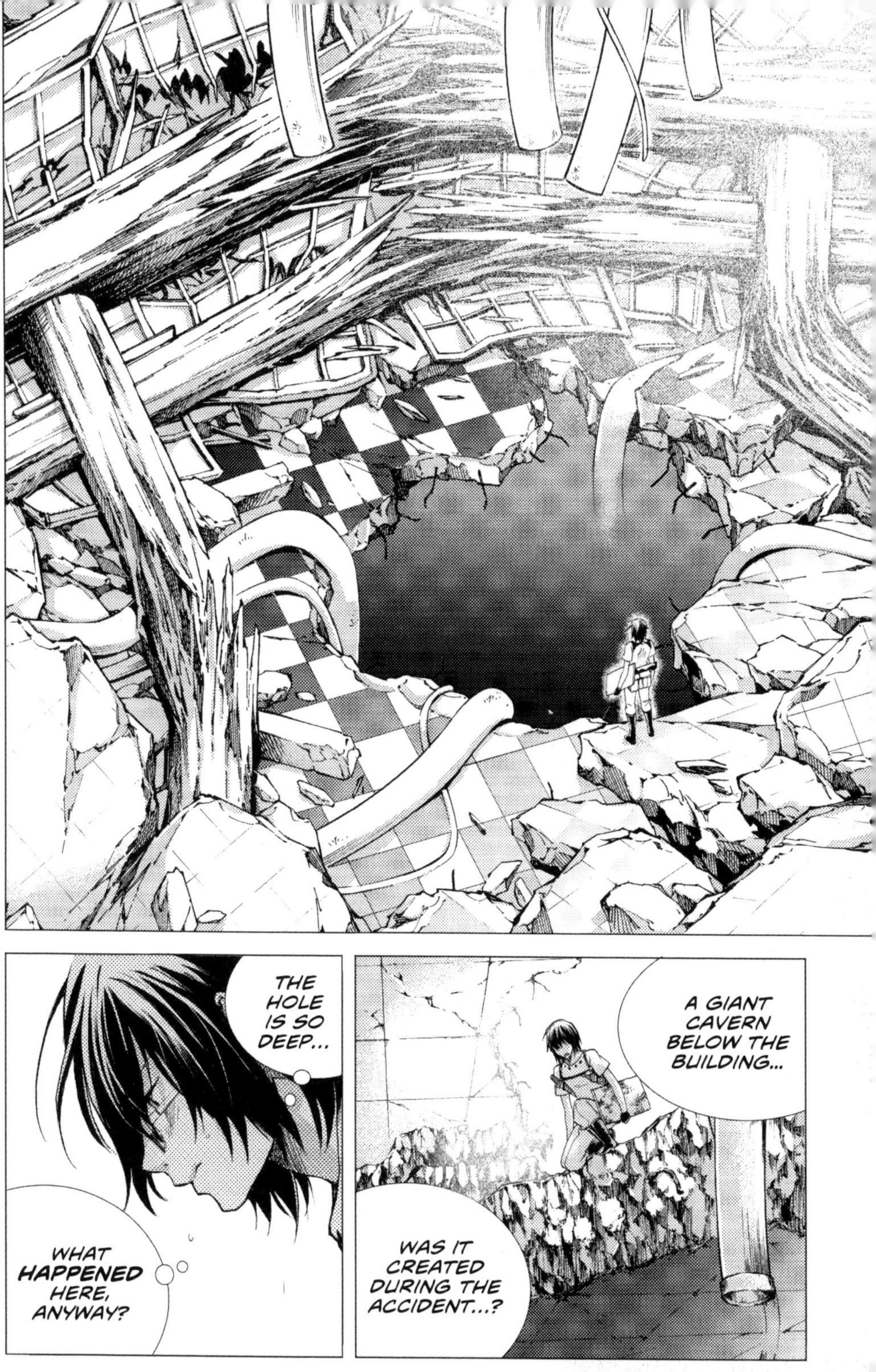
A GIANT CAVERN BELOW THE BUILDING...
WAS IT CREATED DURING THE ACCIDENT...?
THE HOLE IS SO DEEP...
WHAT **HAPPENED** HERE, ANYWAY?

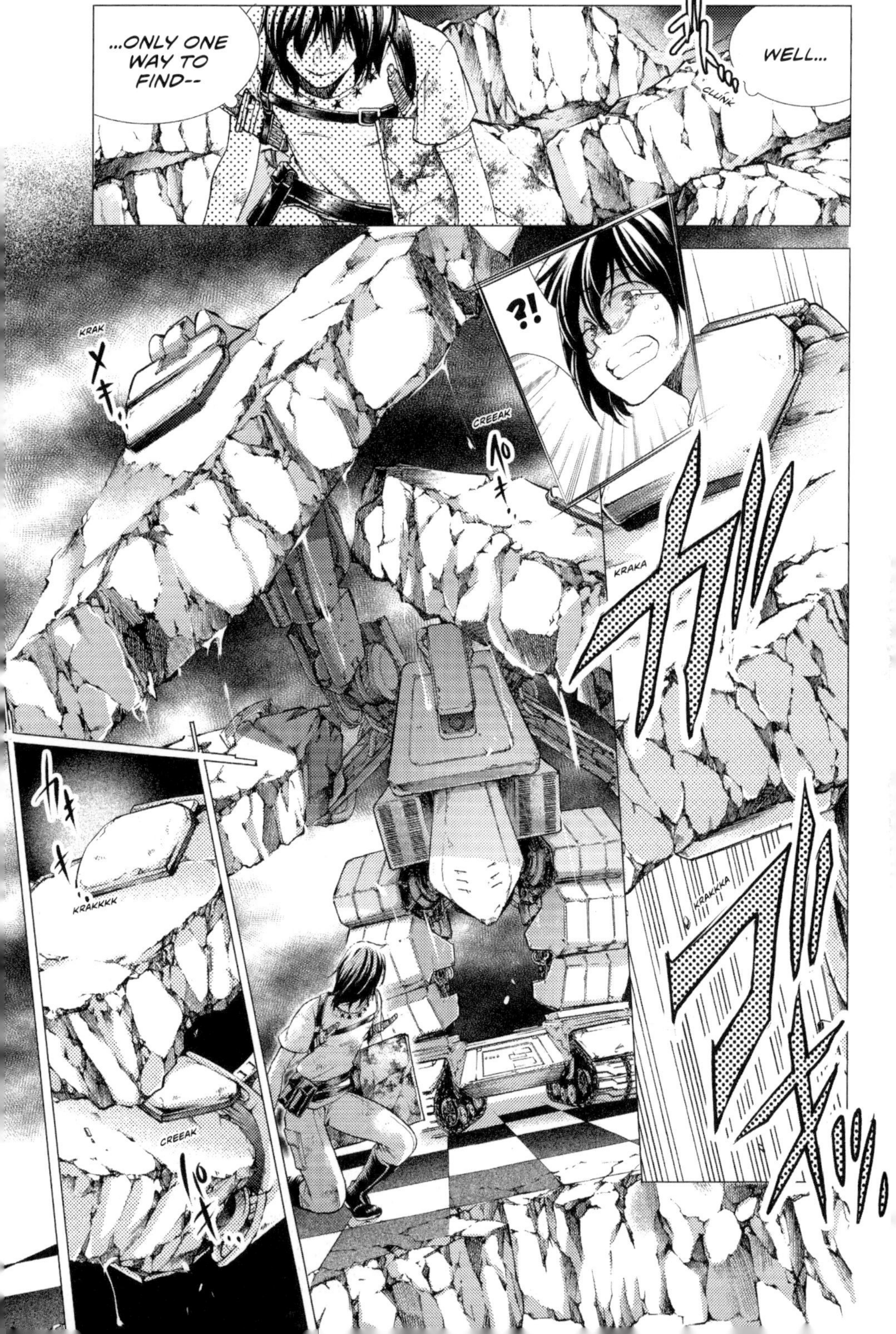
WELL...
CLUNK
...ONLY ONE WAY TO FIND--
?!
KRAKA
KRAKKKA
CREEAK
KRAK
KRAKKKK
CREEAK

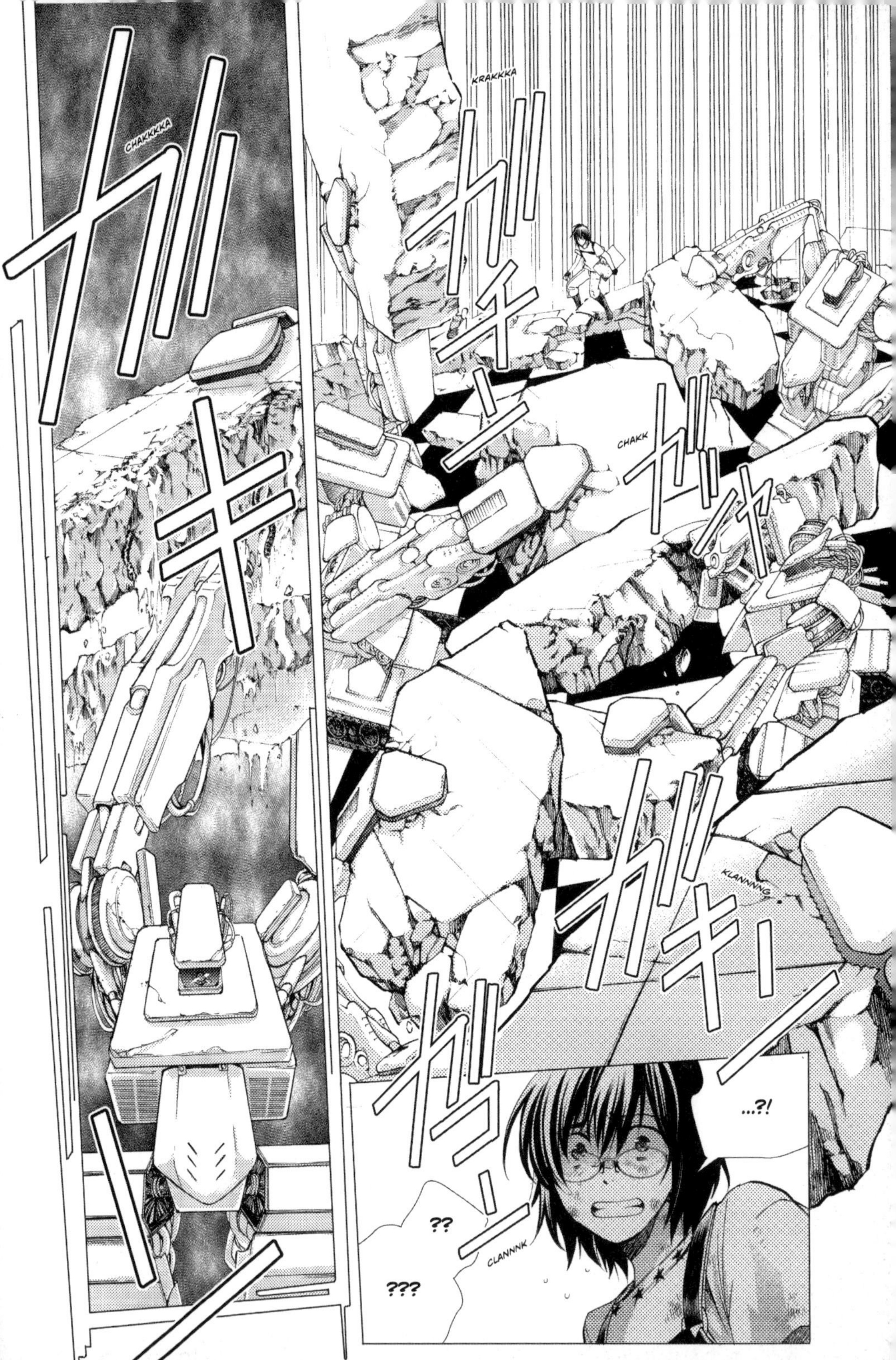
KRAKKKA
CHAKK
KLANNNNG
...?!
CLANNNK
??
???
CHAKKKKA

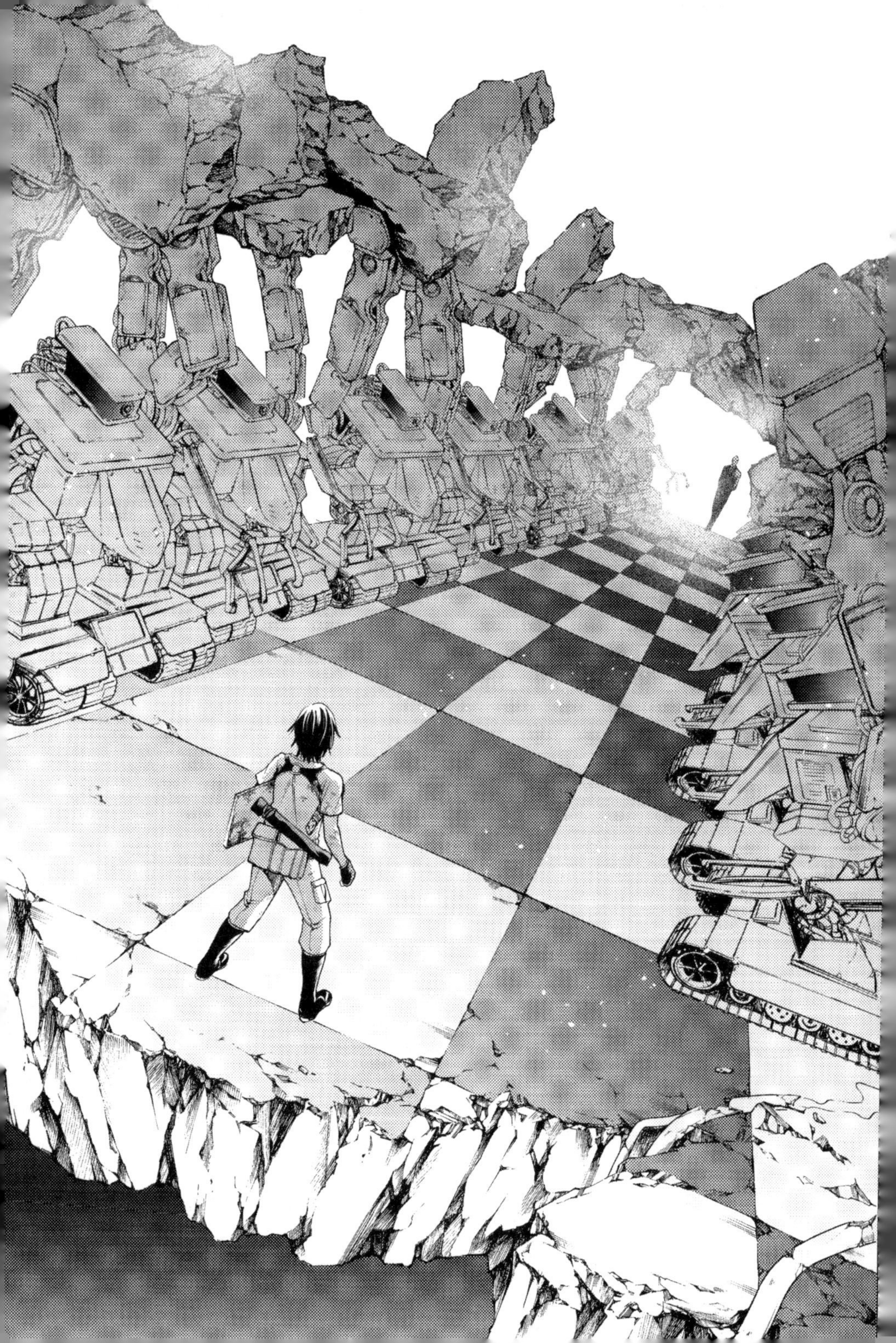

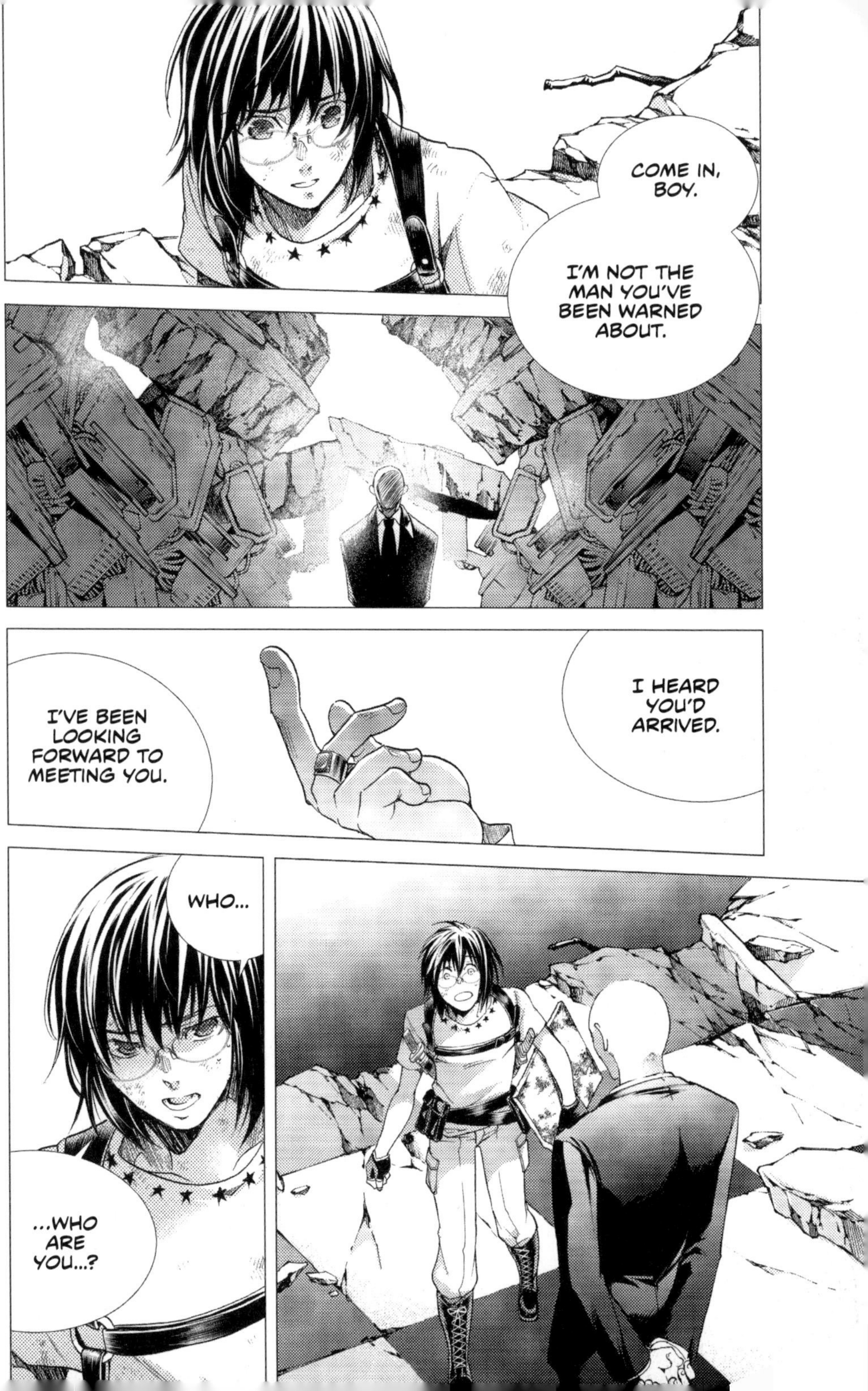
COME IN, BOY.
I'M NOT THE MAN YOU'VE BEEN WARNED ABOUT.
I HEARD YOU'D ARRIVED.
I'VE BEEN LOOKING FORWARD TO MEETING YOU.
WHO...
...WHO ARE YOU...?

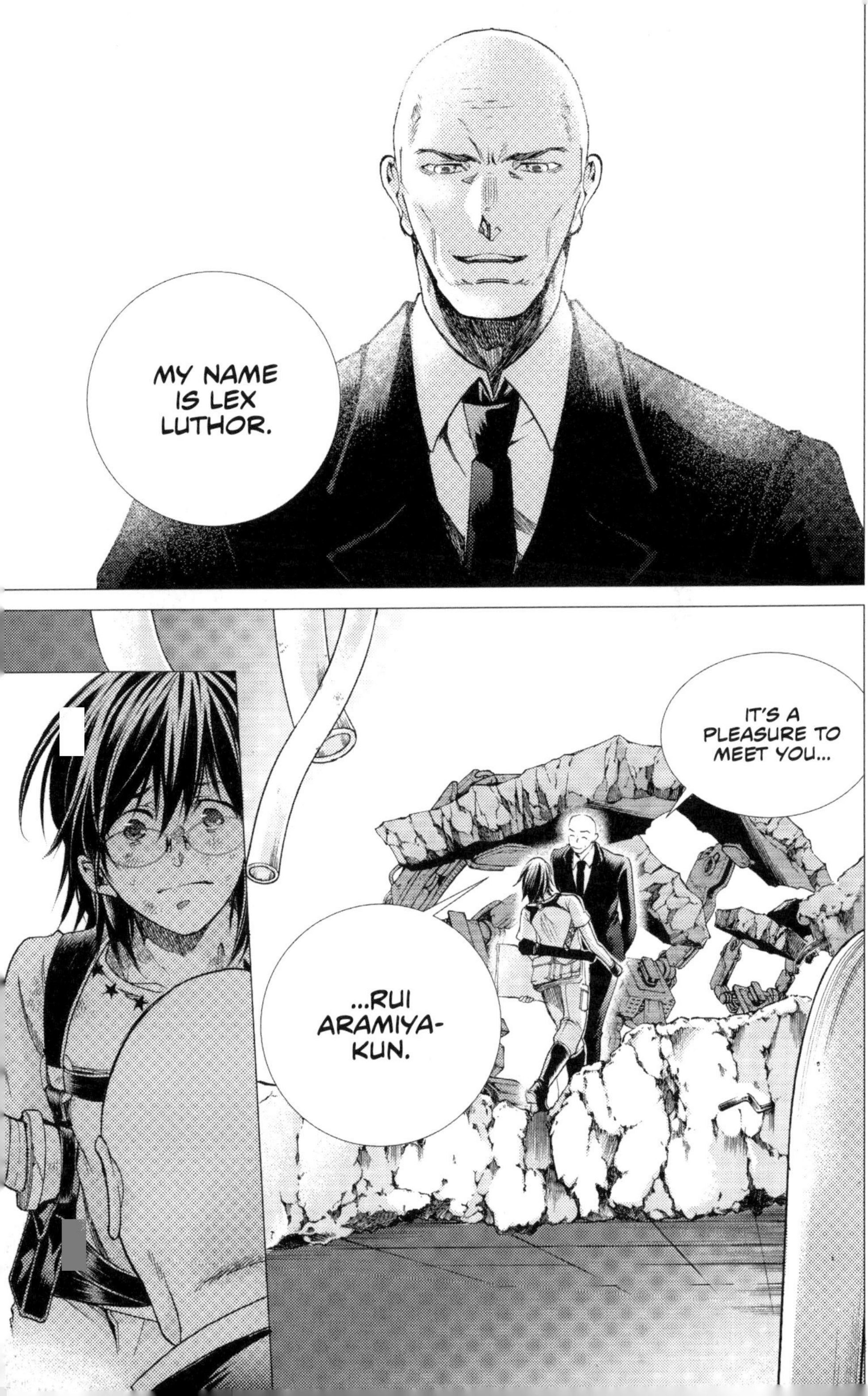
MY NAME IS LEX LUTHOR.
IT'S A PLEASURE TO MEET YOU...
...RUI ARAMIYA-KUN.

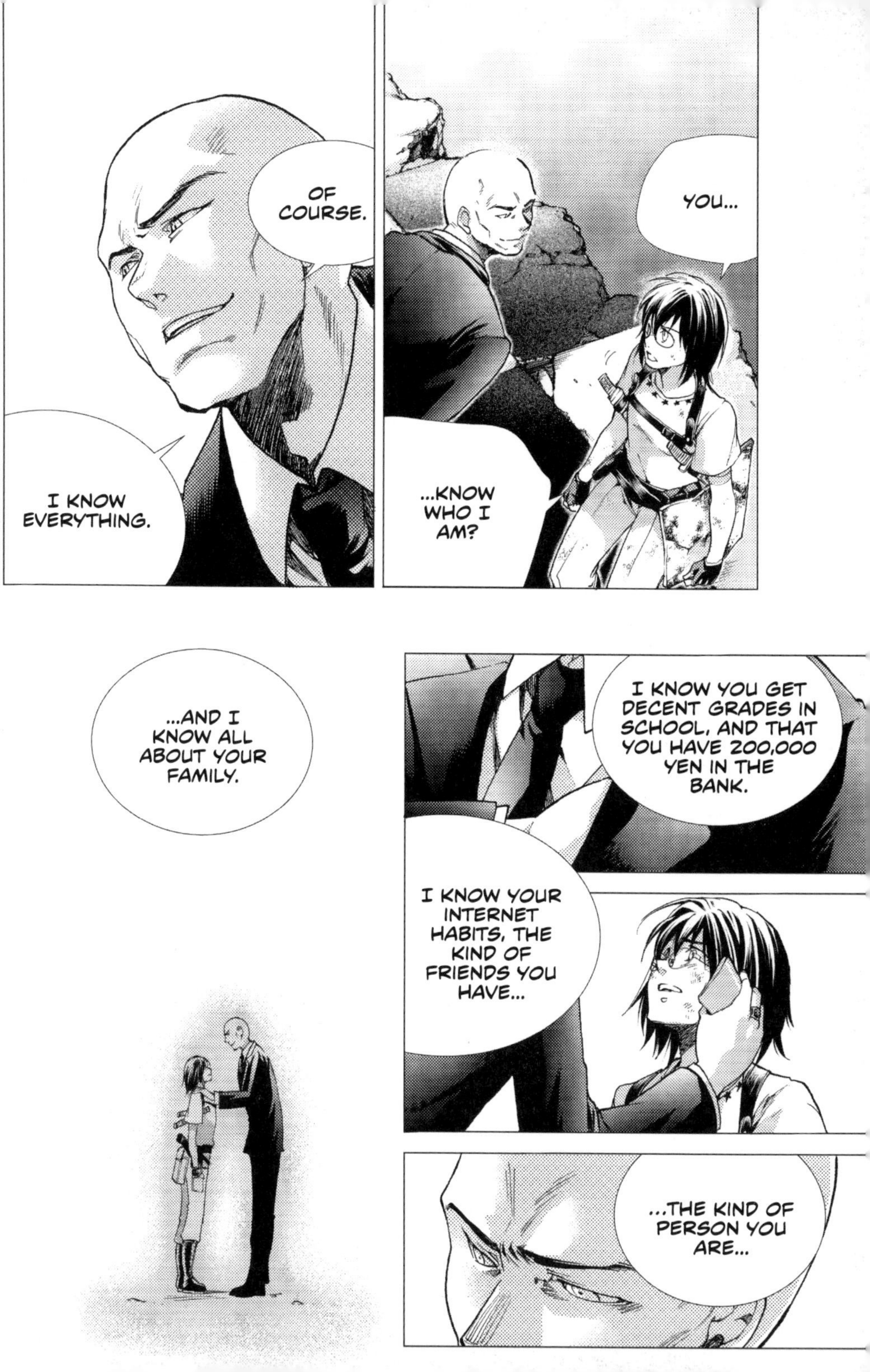
YOU...
...KNOW WHO I AM?
OF COURSE.
I KNOW EVERYTHING.
I KNOW YOU GET DECENT GRADES IN SCHOOL, AND THAT YOU HAVE 200,000 YEN IN THE BANK.
I KNOW YOUR INTERNET HABITS, THE KIND OF FRIENDS YOU HAVE...
...THE KIND OF PERSON YOU ARE...
...AND I KNOW ALL ABOUT YOUR FAMILY.

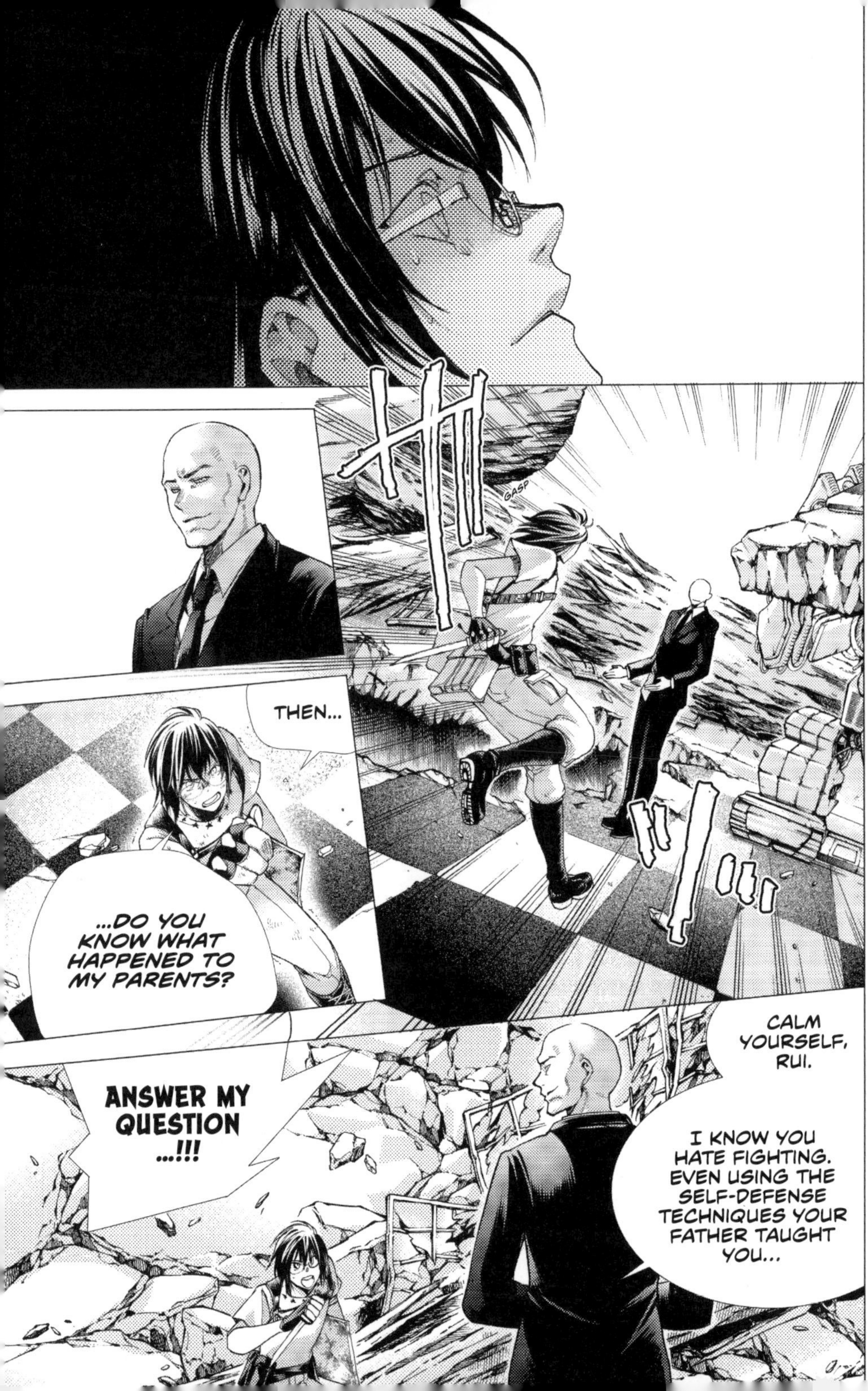

GASP
THEN...
...DO YOU KNOW WHAT HAPPENED TO MY PARENTS?
CALM YOURSELF, RUI.
ANSWER MY QUESTION ...!!!
I KNOW YOU HATE FIGHTING. EVEN USING THE SELF-DEFENSE TECHNIQUES YOUR FATHER TAUGHT YOU...

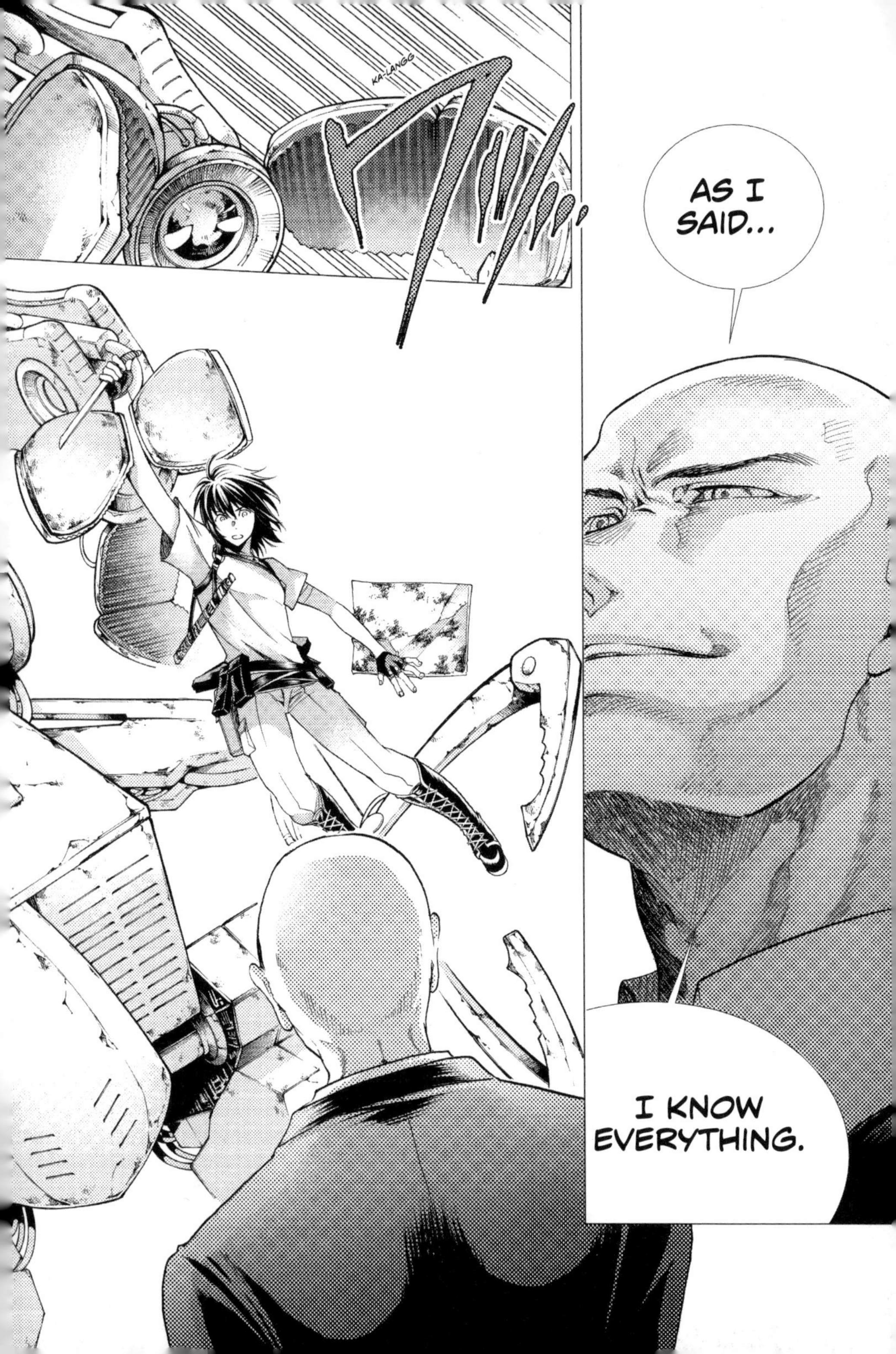
AS I SAID...
I KNOW EVERYTHING.
KA-LANGG

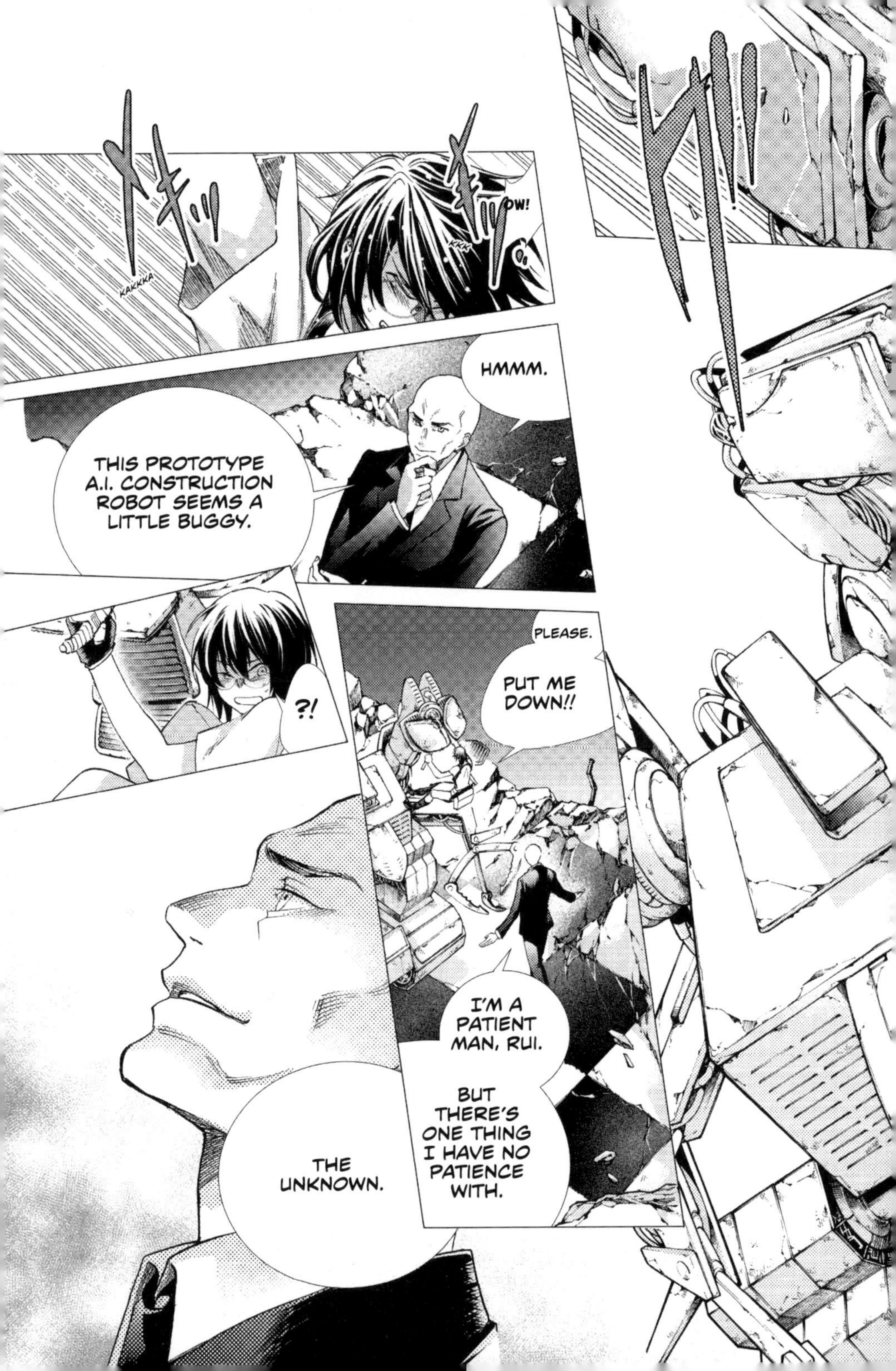
OW!
KKK
KAKKKA
HMMM.
THIS PROTOTYPE A.I. CONSTRUCTION ROBOT SEEMS A LITTLE BUGGY.
PLEASE.
PUT ME DOWN!!
?!
I'M A PATIENT MAN, RUI.
BUT THERE'S ONE THING I HAVE NO PATIENCE WITH.
THE UNKNOWN.

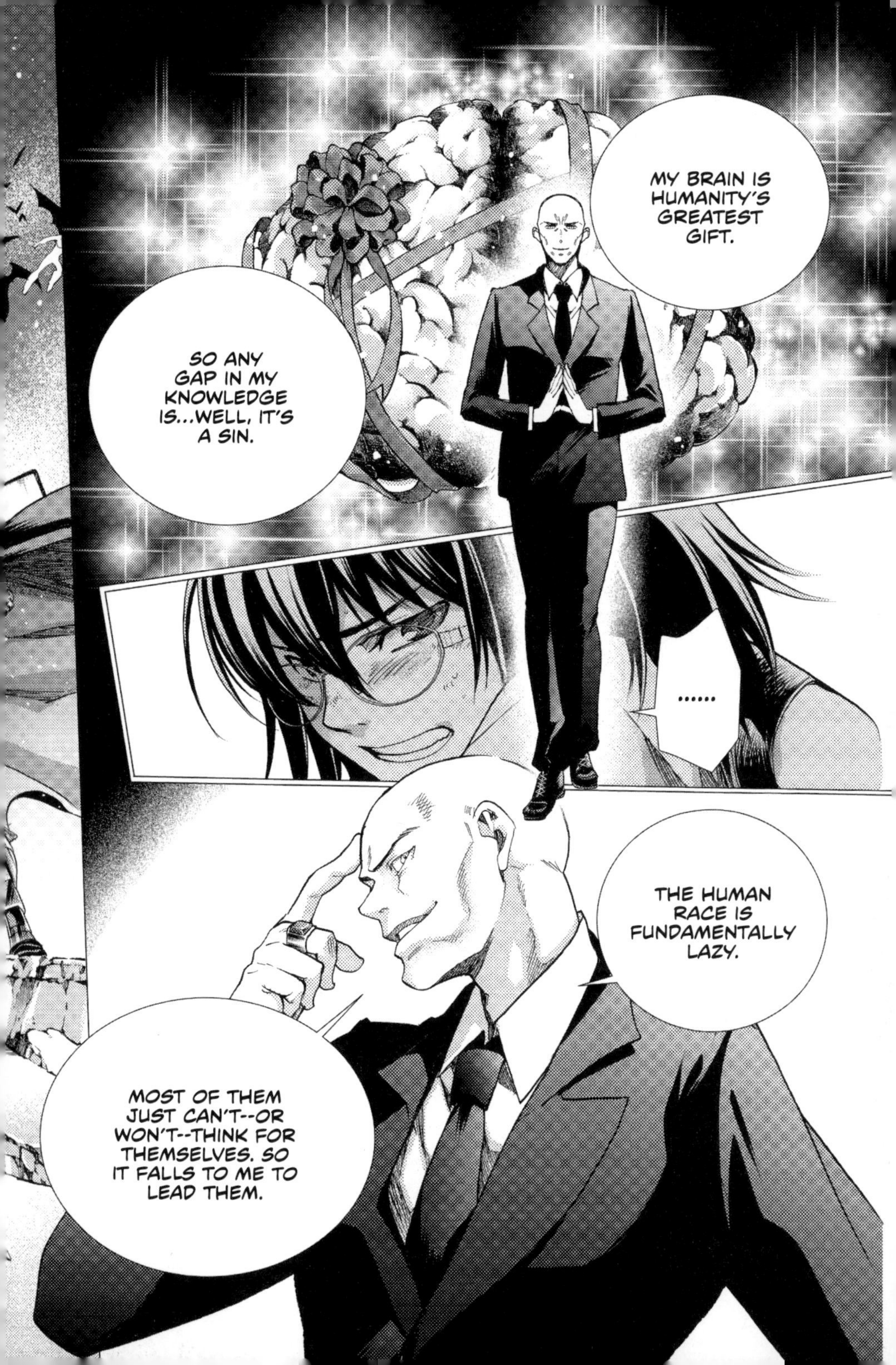
MY BRAIN IS HUMANITY'S GREATEST GIFT.
SO ANY GAP IN MY KNOWLEDGE IS...WELL, IT'S A SIN.
......
THE HUMAN RACE IS FUNDAMENTALLY LAZY.
MOST OF THEM JUST CAN'T--OR WON'T--THINK FOR THEMSELVES. SO IT FALLS TO ME TO LEAD THEM.

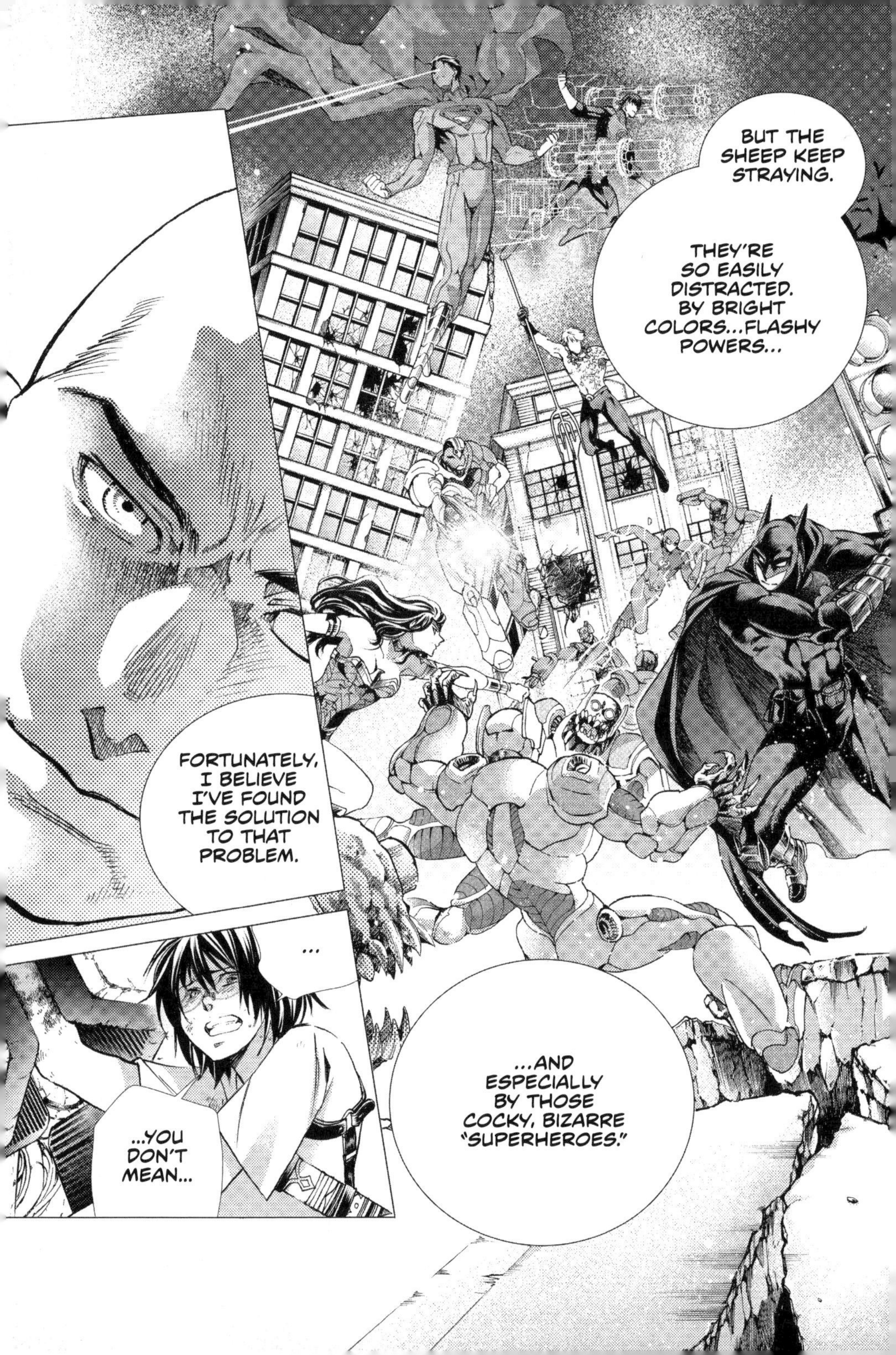
BUT THE SHEEP KEEP STRAYING.
THEY'RE SO EASILY DISTRACTED. BY BRIGHT COLORS...FLASHY POWERS...
...AND ESPECIALLY BY THOSE COCKY, BIZARRE "SUPERHEROES."
FORTUNATELY, I BELIEVE I'VE FOUND THE SOLUTION TO THAT PROBLEM.
...
...YOU DON'T MEAN...

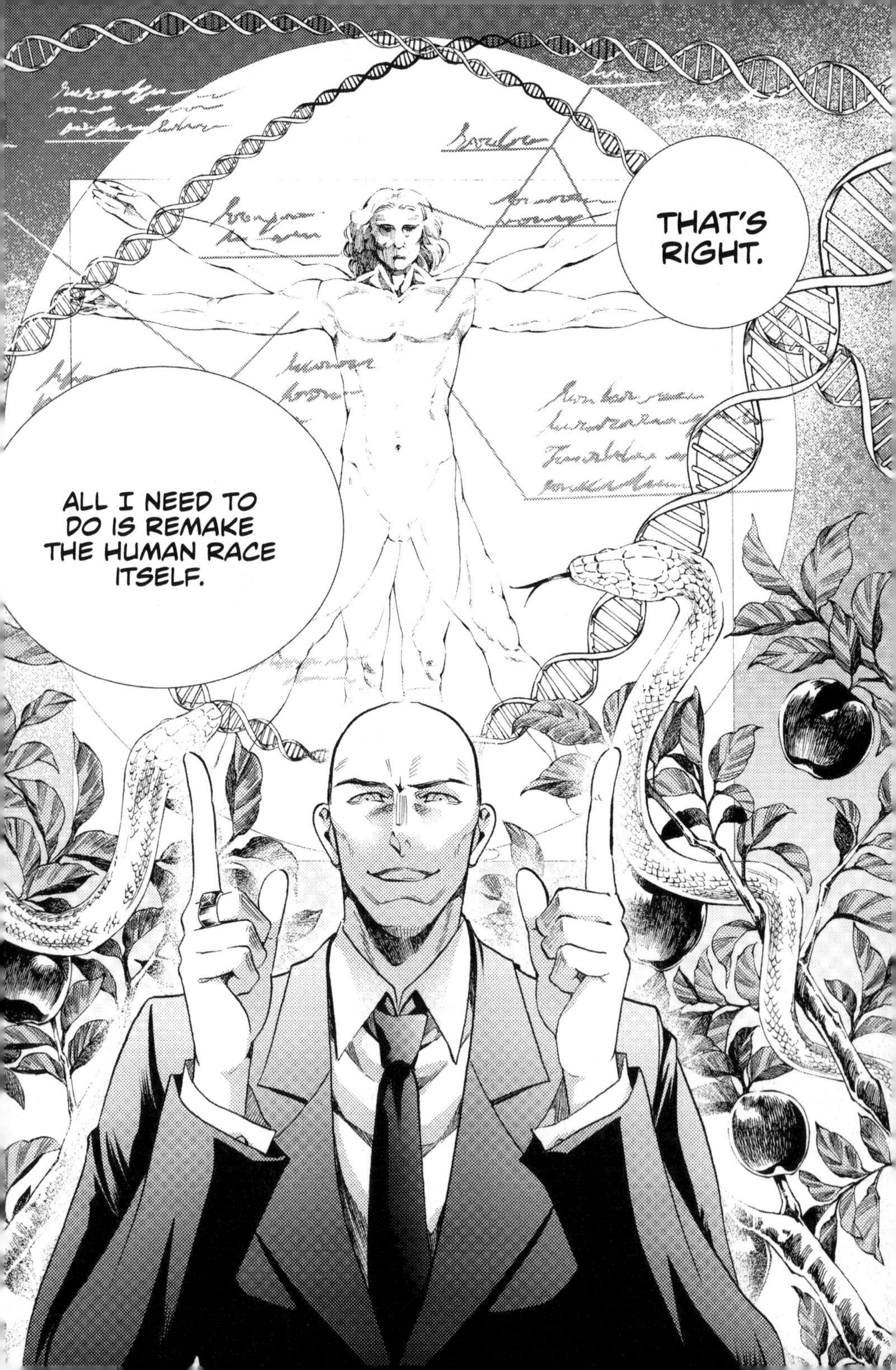
THAT'S RIGHT.
ALL I NEED TO DO IS REMAKE THE HUMAN RACE ITSELF.

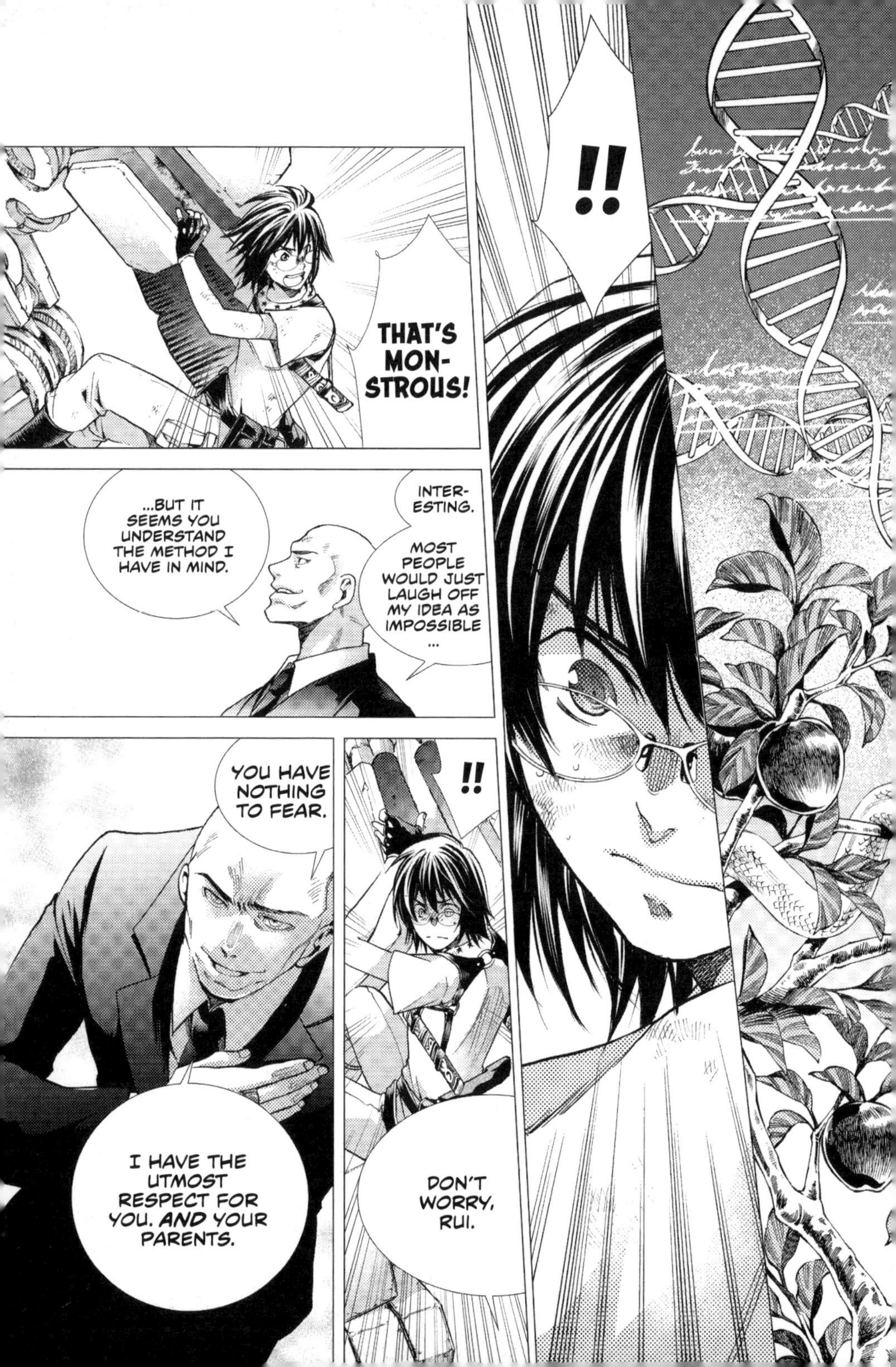
THAT'S MON-STROUS!
INTER-ESTING.
MOST PEOPLE WOULD JUST LAUGH OFF MY IDEA AS IMPOSSIBLE ...
...BUT IT SEEMS YOU UNDERSTAND THE METHOD I HAVE IN MIND.
YOU HAVE NOTHING TO FEAR.
I HAVE THE UTMOST RESPECT FOR YOU. *AND* YOUR PARENTS.
!!
DON'T WORRY, RUI.
!!

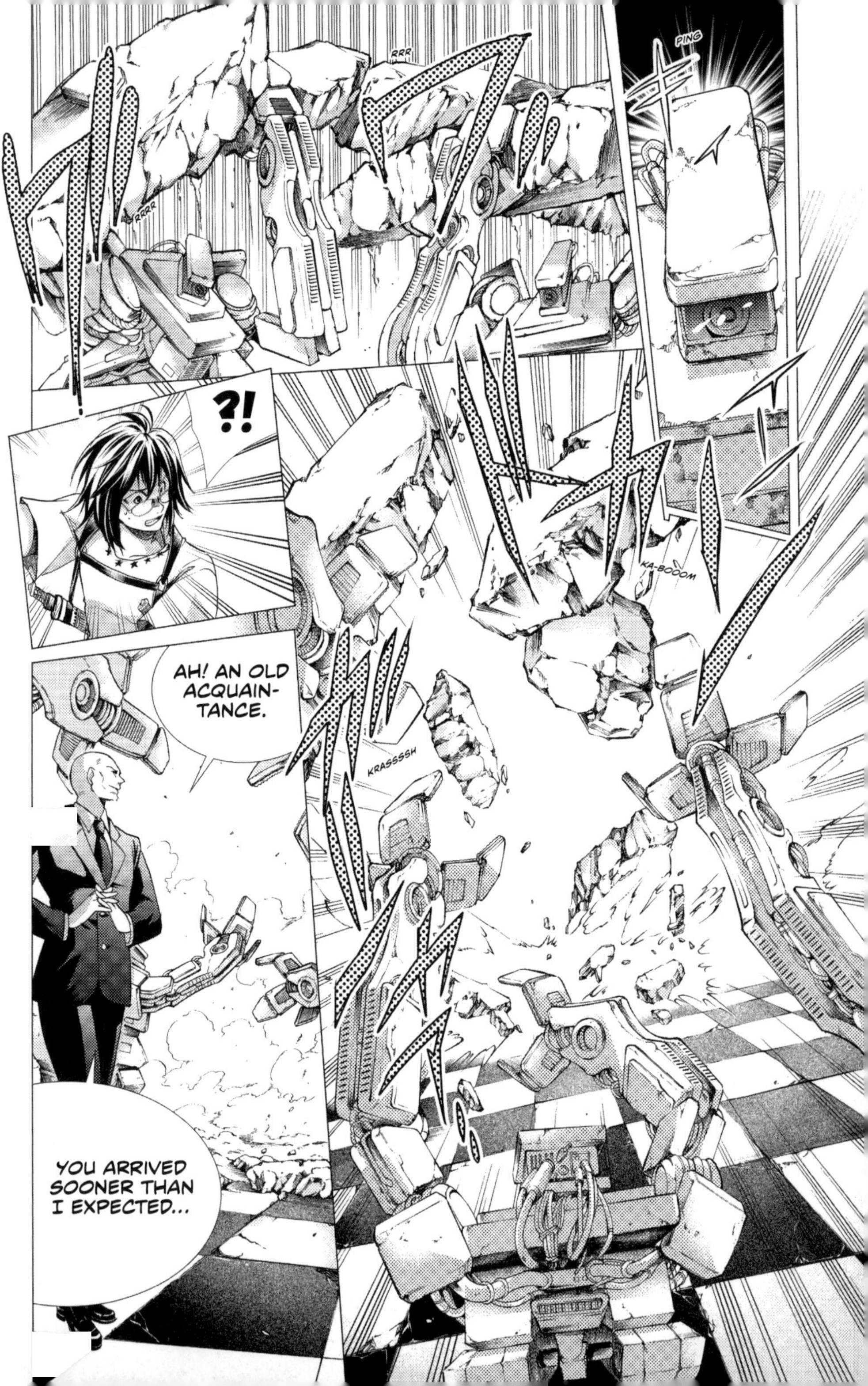
PING
RRR
RRRR
KA-BOOOM
KRASSSSH
?!
AH! AN OLD ACQUAIN-TANCE.
YOU ARRIVED SOONER THAN I EXPECTED...

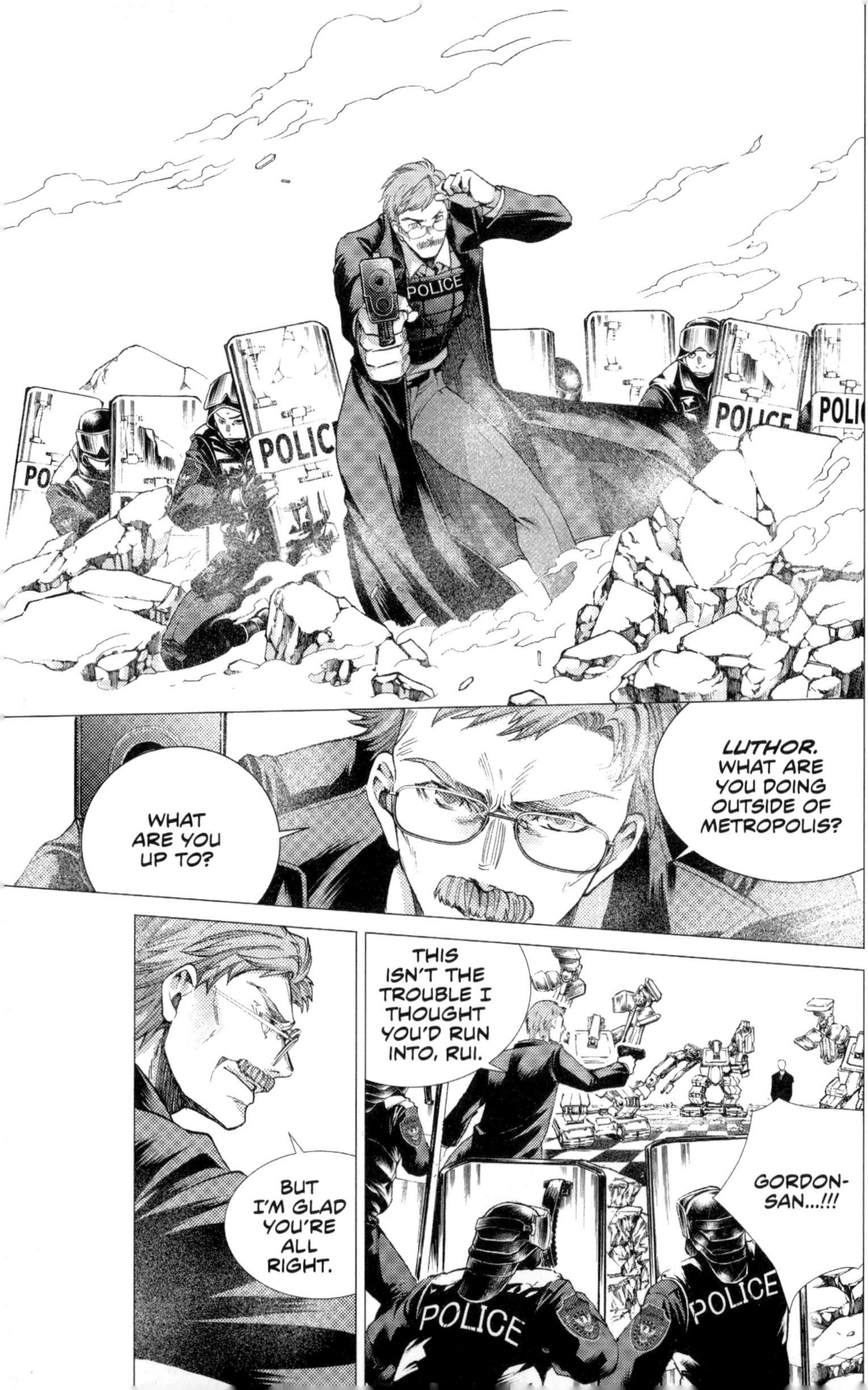
POLICE
LUTHOR. WHAT ARE YOU DOING OUTSIDE OF METROPOLIS?
WHAT ARE YOU UP TO?
THIS ISN'T THE TROUBLE I THOUGHT YOU'D RUN INTO, RUI.
GORDON-SAN...!!!
BUT I'M GLAD YOU'RE ALL RIGHT.

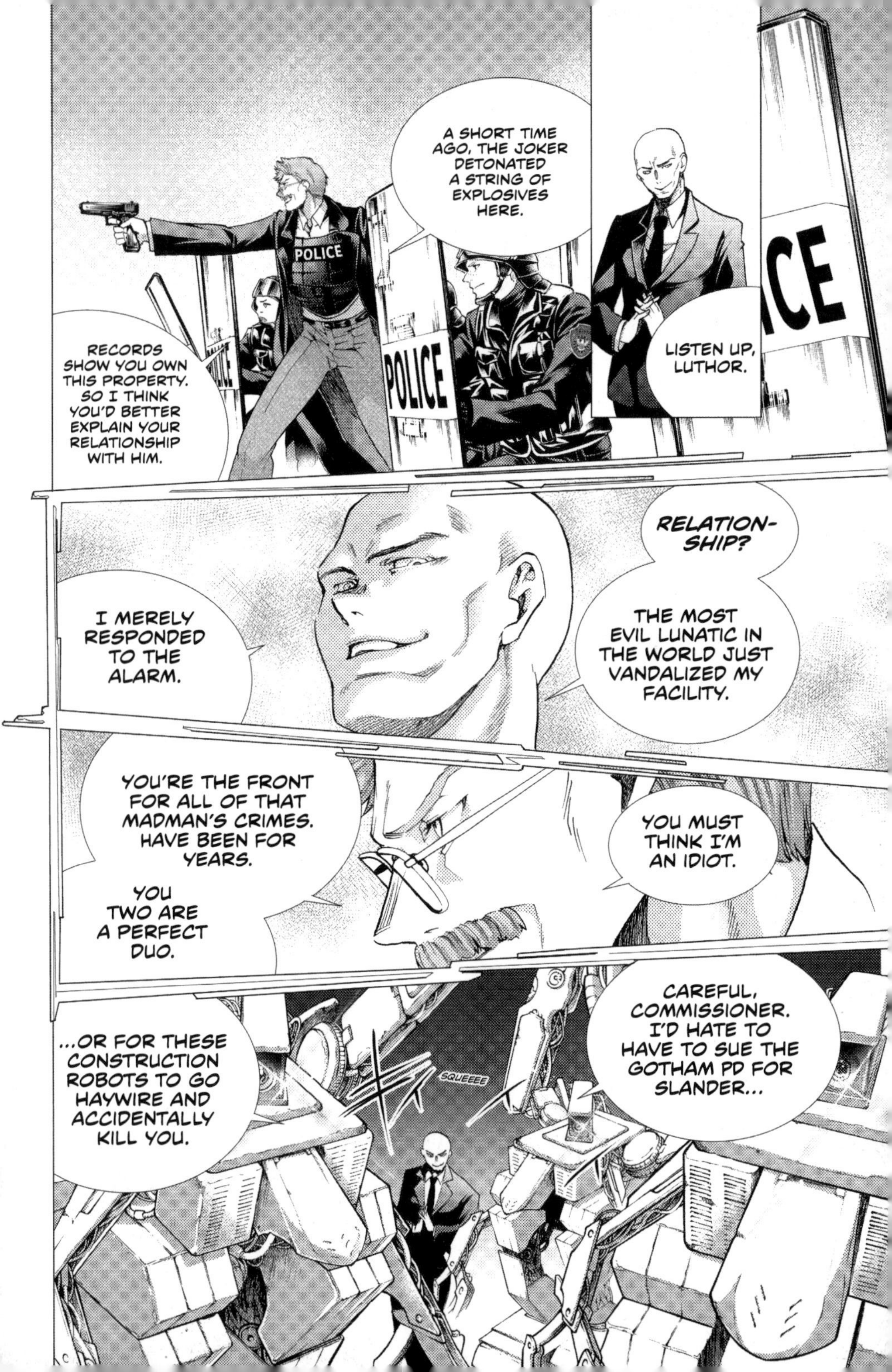
LISTEN UP, LUTHOR.
A SHORT TIME AGO, THE JOKER DETONATED A STRING OF EXPLOSIVES HERE.
RECORDS SHOW YOU OWN THIS PROPERTY. SO I THINK YOU'D BETTER EXPLAIN YOUR RELATIONSHIP WITH HIM.
POLICE
RELATION-SHIP?
THE MOST EVIL LUNATIC IN THE WORLD JUST VANDALIZED MY FACILITY.
I MERELY RESPONDED TO THE ALARM.
YOU MUST THINK I'M AN IDIOT.
YOU'RE THE FRONT FOR ALL OF THAT MADMAN'S CRIMES. HAVE BEEN FOR YEARS.
YOU TWO ARE A PERFECT DUO.
CAREFUL, COMMISSIONER. I'D HATE TO HAVE TO SUE THE GOTHAM PD FOR SLANDER...
SQUEEEE
...OR FOR THESE CONSTRUCTION ROBOTS TO GO HAYWIRE AND ACCIDENTALLY KILL YOU.

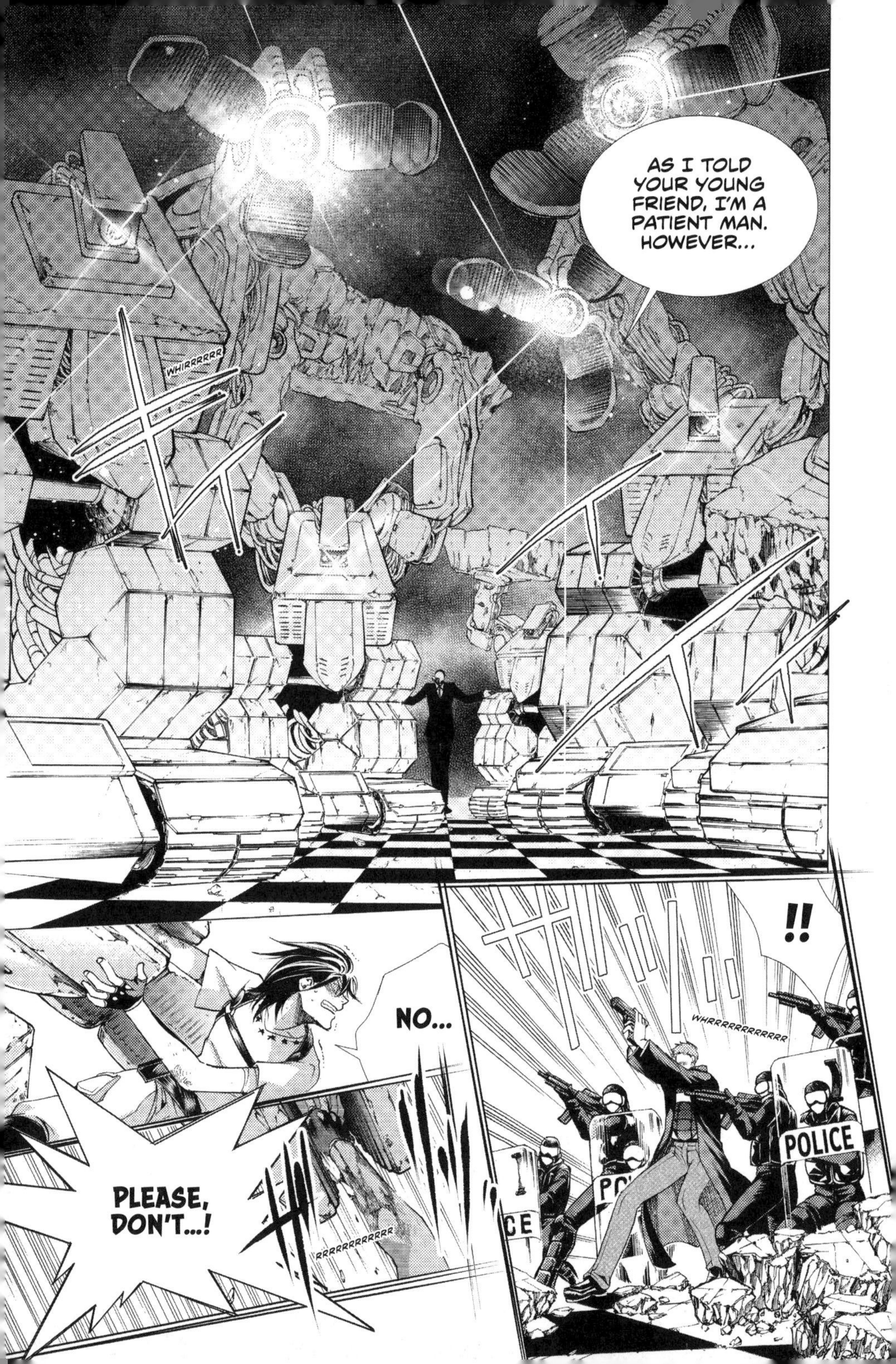
AS I TOLD YOUR YOUNG FRIEND, I'M A PATIENT MAN. HOWEVER...
WHIRRRRRR
!!
WHRRRRRRRRRRRR
POLICE
NO...
PLEASE, DON'T...!
RRRRRRRRRRRR

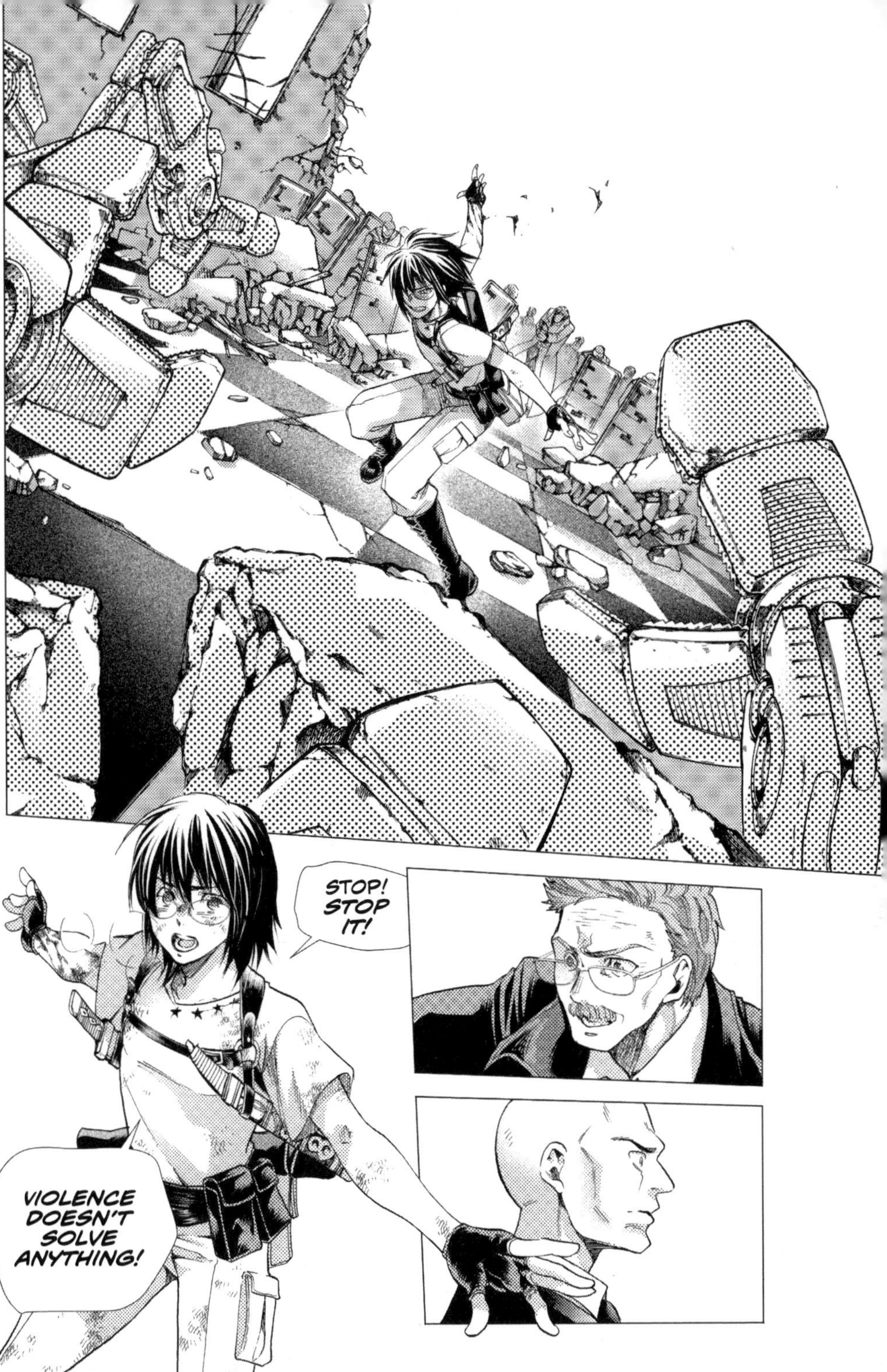
STOP! STOP IT!
VIOLENCE DOESN'T SOLVE ANYTHING!

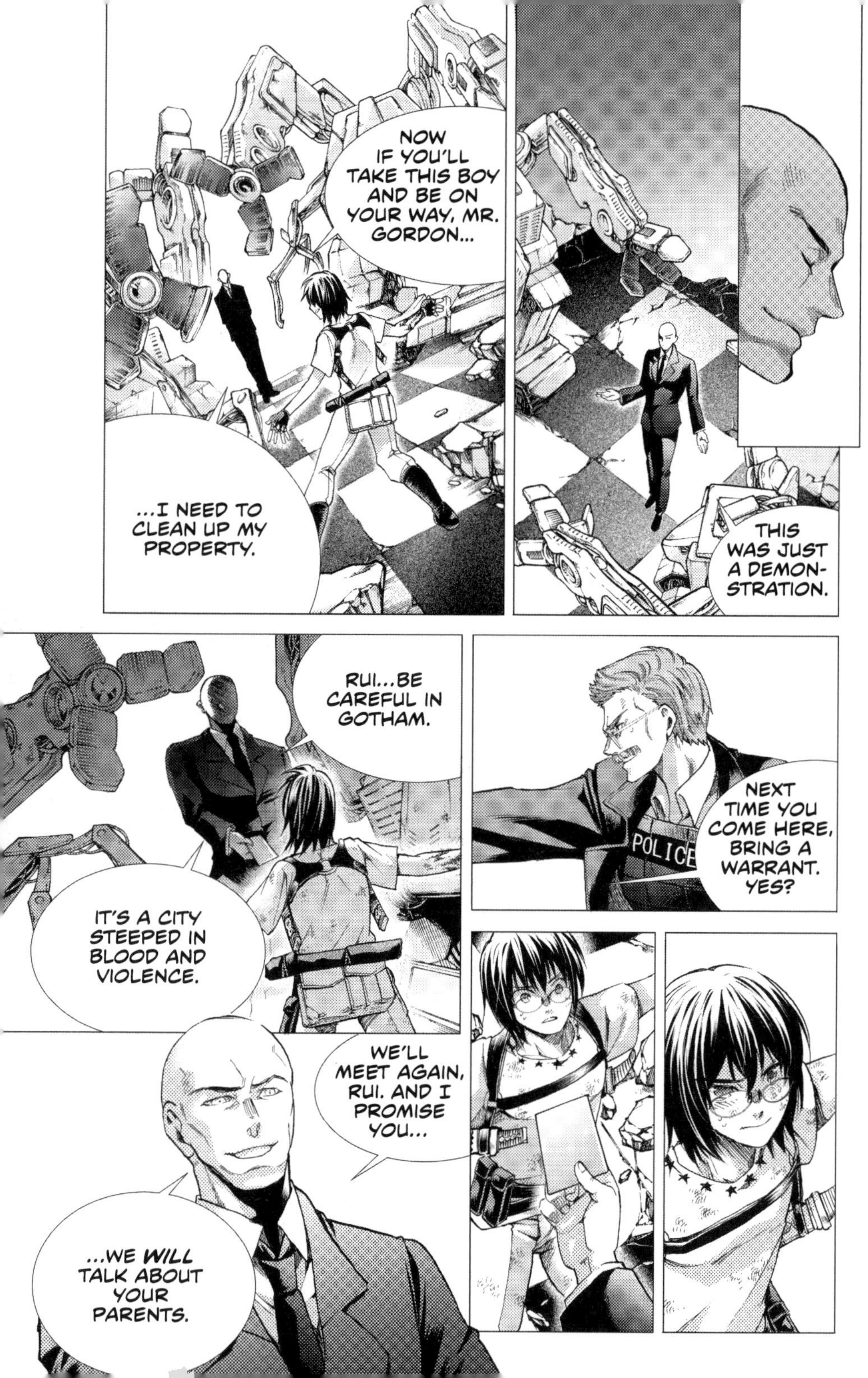
THIS WAS JUST A DEMON-STRATION.
NOW IF YOU'LL TAKE THIS BOY AND BE ON YOUR WAY, MR. GORDON...
...I NEED TO CLEAN UP MY PROPERTY.
NEXT TIME YOU COME HERE, BRING A WARRANT. YES?
POLICE
RUI...BE CAREFUL IN GOTHAM.
IT'S A CITY STEEPED IN BLOOD AND VIOLENCE.
WE'LL MEET AGAIN, RUI. AND I PROMISE YOU...
...WE *WILL* TALK ABOUT YOUR PARENTS.

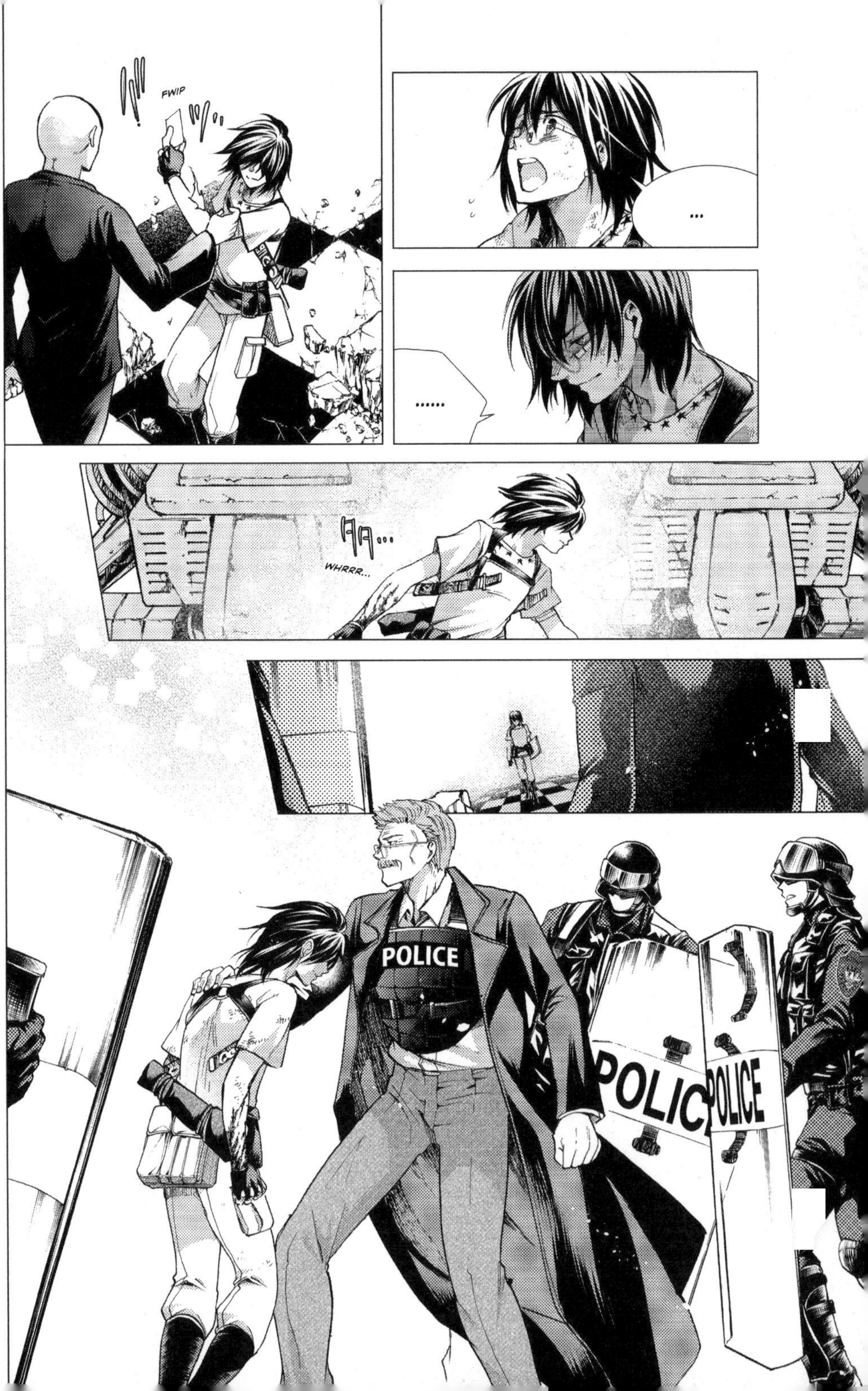

...
......
FWIP
WHRRR...
POLICE
POLICE
POLICE

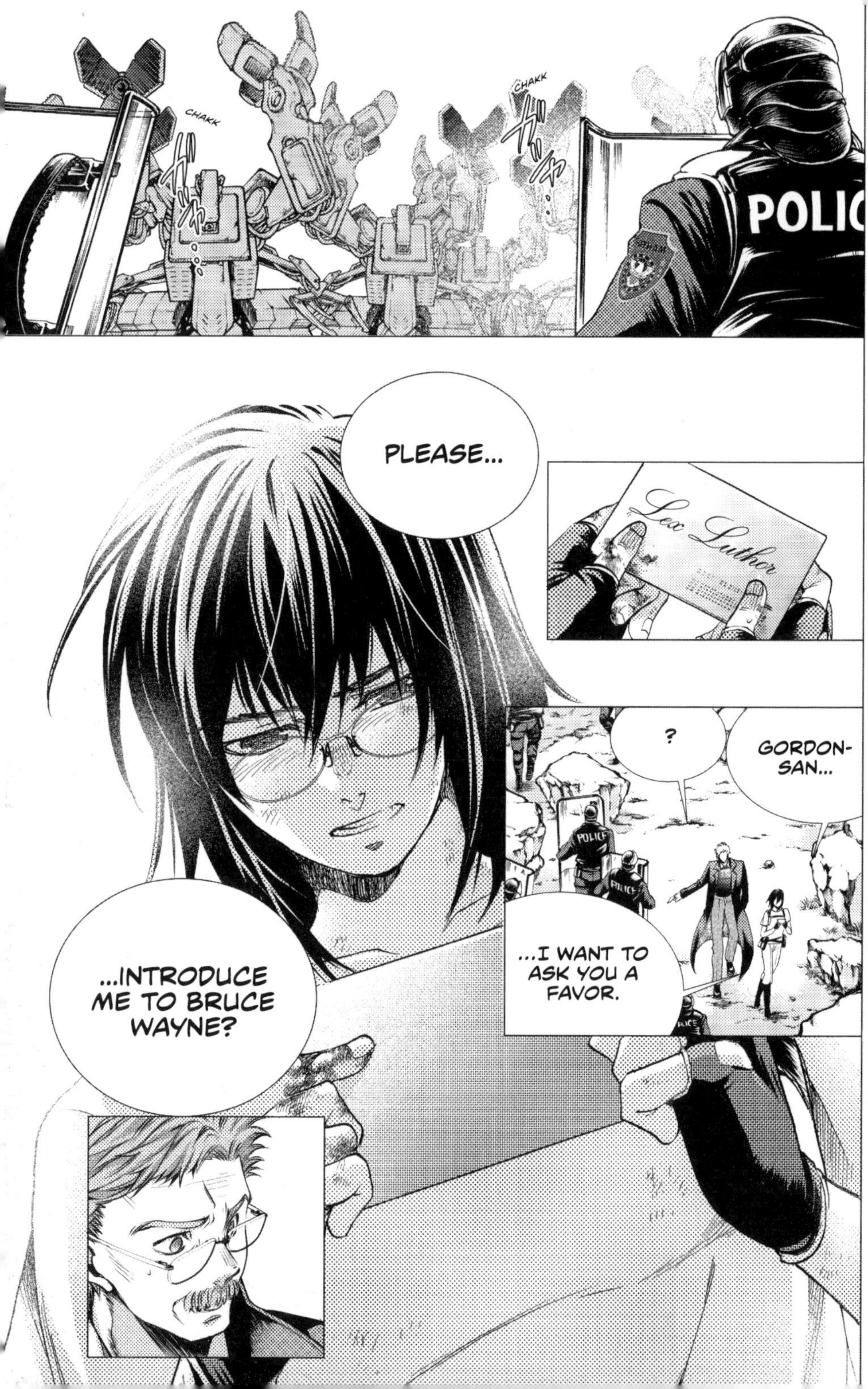

CHAKK
CHAKK
POLIC
Lex Luthor
GORDON-SAN...
?
POLICE
POLICE
...I WANT TO ASK YOU A FAVOR.
PLEASE...
...INTRODUCE ME TO BRUCE WAYNE?

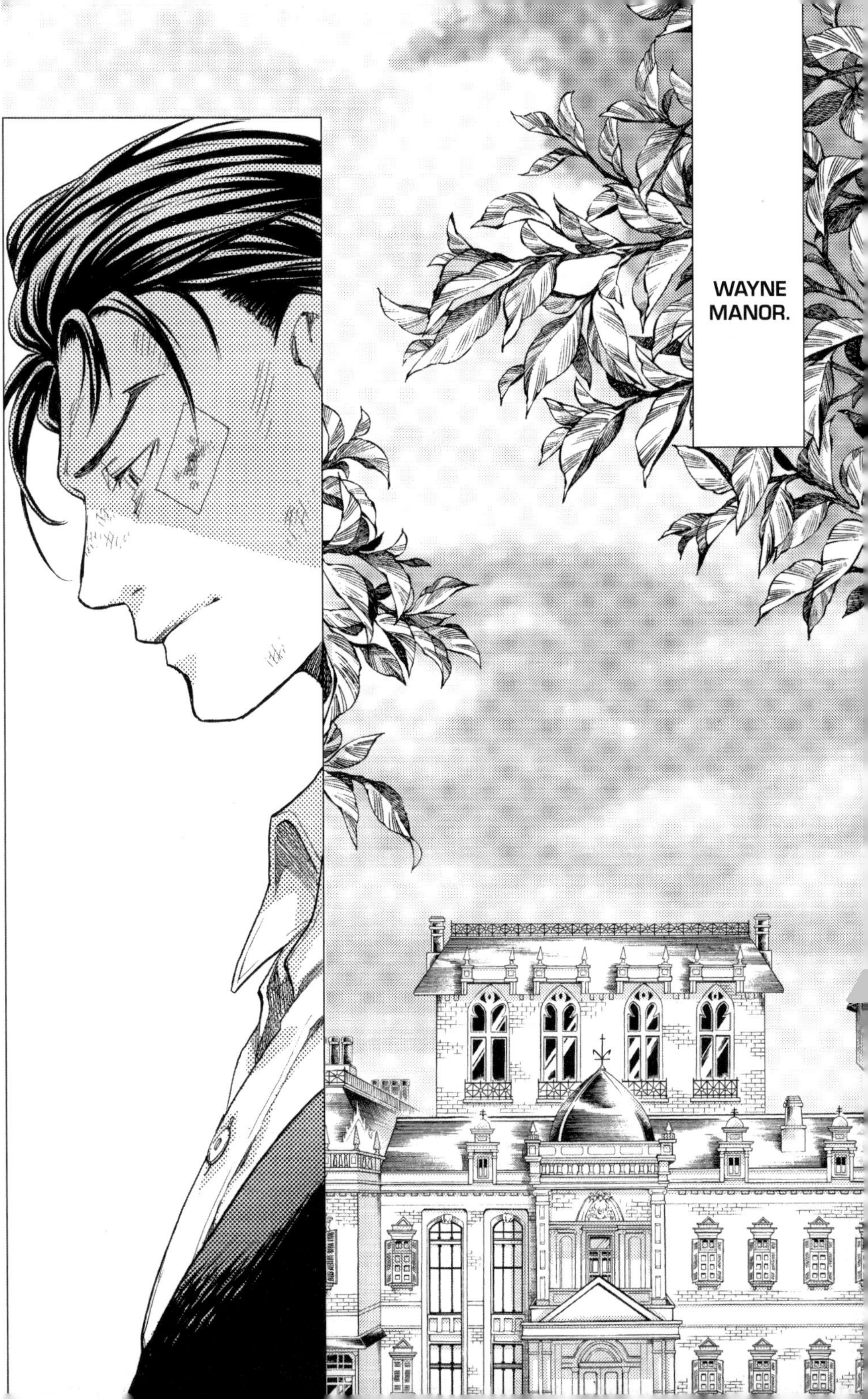
WAYNE MANOR.

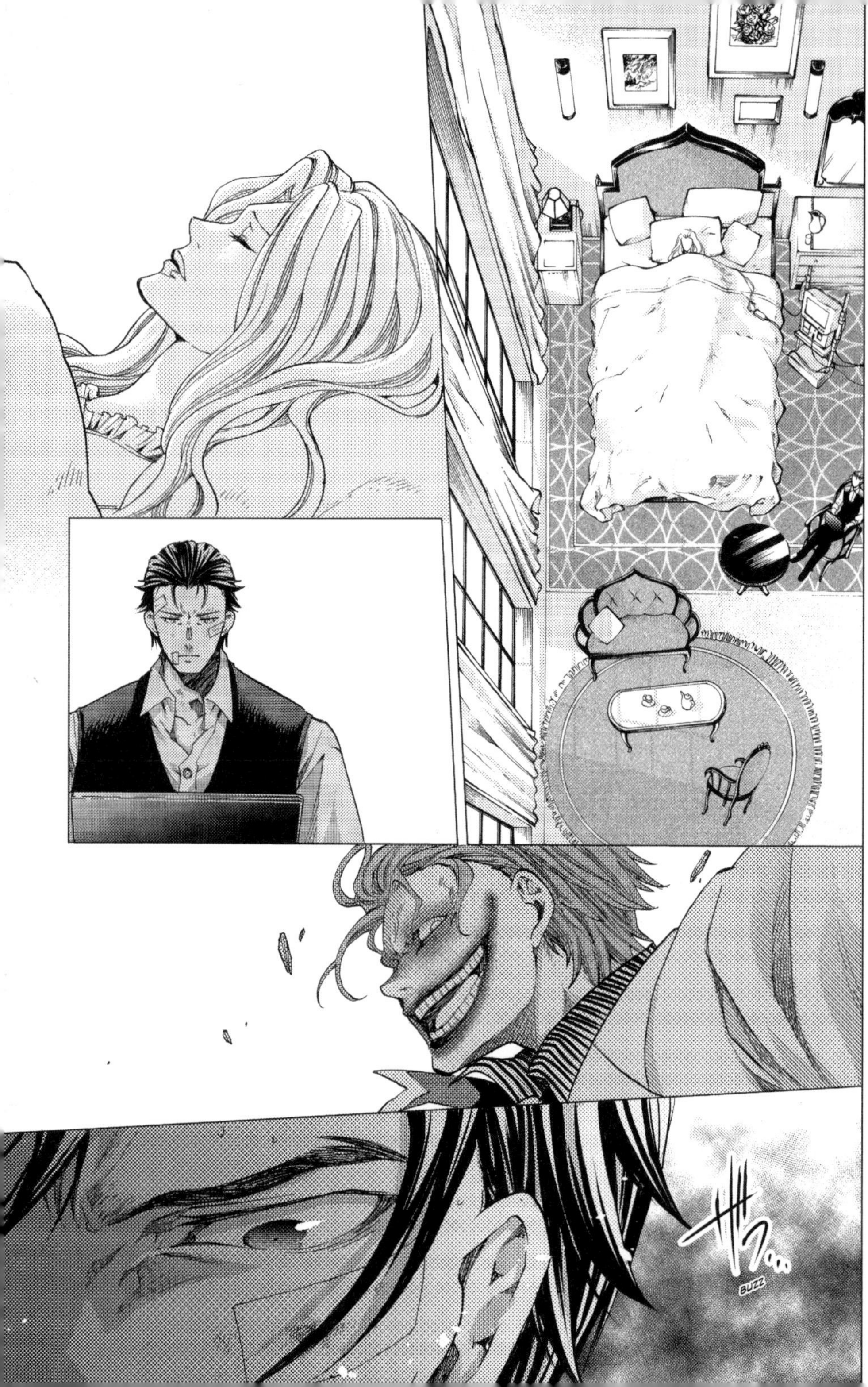
BUZZ

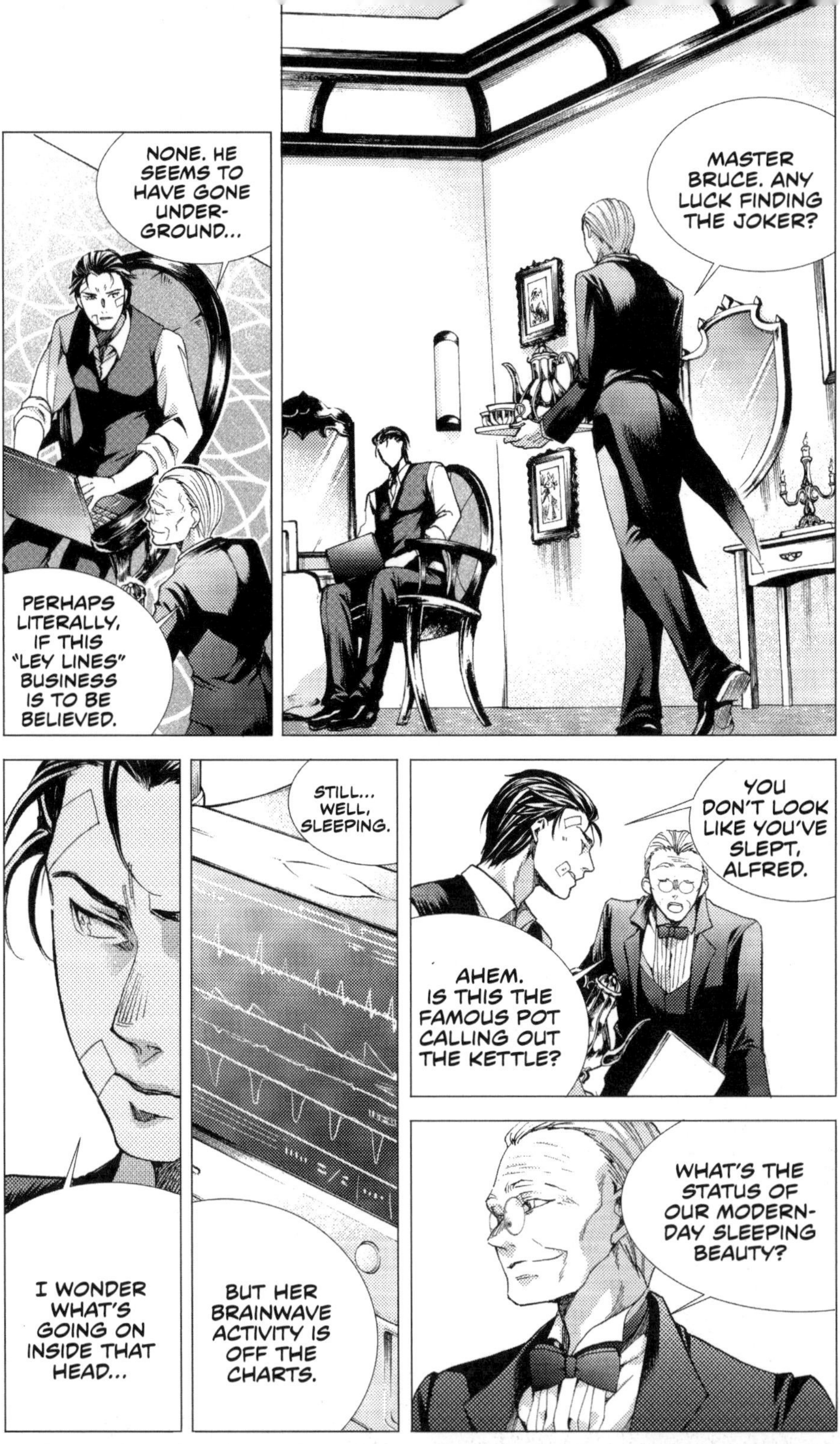
MASTER BRUCE. ANY LUCK FINDING THE JOKER?
NONE. HE SEEMS TO HAVE GONE UNDER-GROUND...
PERHAPS LITERALLY, IF THIS "LEY LINES" BUSINESS IS TO BE BELIEVED.
YOU DON'T LOOK LIKE YOU'VE SLEPT, ALFRED.
AHEM. IS THIS THE FAMOUS POT CALLING OUT THE KETTLE?
WHAT'S THE STATUS OF OUR MODERN-DAY SLEEPING BEAUTY?
STILL... WELL, SLEEPING.
BUT HER BRAINWAVE ACTIVITY IS OFF THE CHARTS.
I WONDER WHAT'S GOING ON INSIDE THAT HEAD...

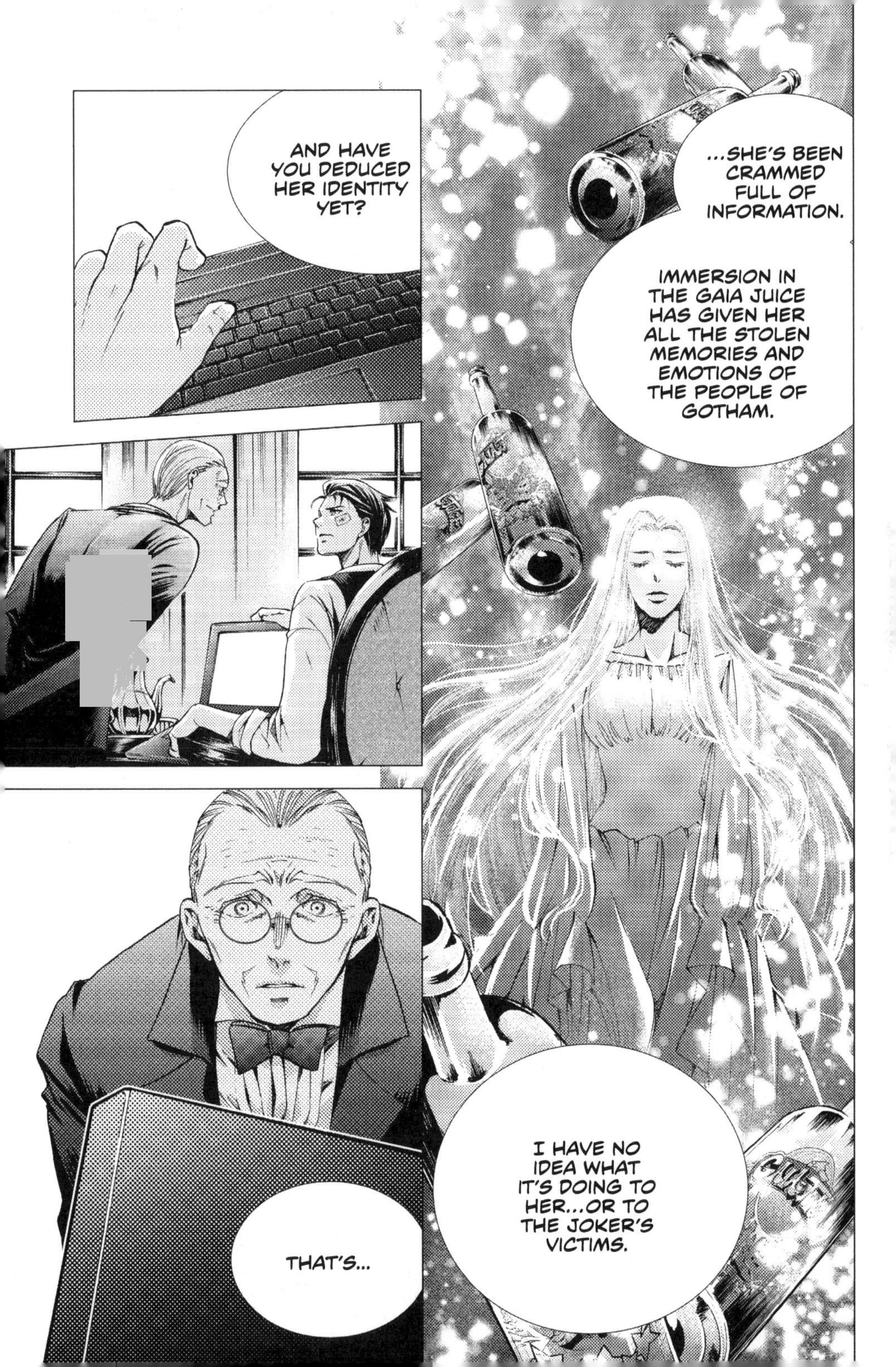
AND HAVE YOU DEDUCED HER IDENTITY YET?
THAT'S...
...SHE'S BEEN CRAMMED FULL OF INFORMATION.
IMMERSION IN THE GAIA JUICE HAS GIVEN HER ALL THE STOLEN MEMORIES AND EMOTIONS OF THE PEOPLE OF GOTHAM.
I HAVE NO IDEA WHAT IT'S DOING TO HER...OR TO THE JOKER'S VICTIMS.

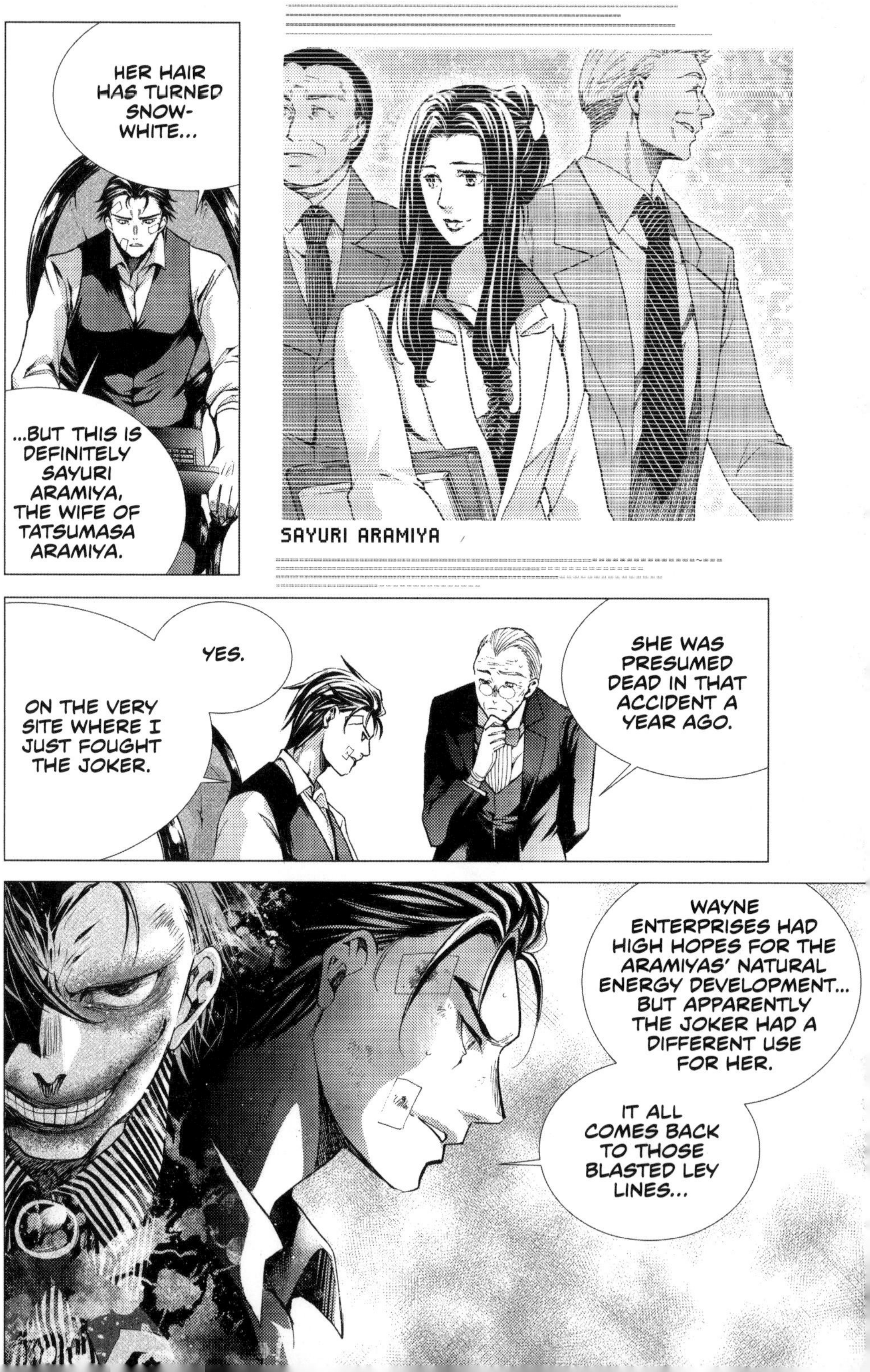
SAYURI ARAMIYA
HER HAIR HAS TURNED SNOW-WHITE...
...BUT THIS IS DEFINITELY SAYURI ARAMIYA, THE WIFE OF TATSUMASA ARAMIYA.
SHE WAS PRESUMED DEAD IN THAT ACCIDENT A YEAR AGO.
YES.
ON THE VERY SITE WHERE I JUST FOUGHT THE JOKER.
WAYNE ENTERPRISES HAD HIGH HOPES FOR THE ARAMIYAS' NATURAL ENERGY DEVELOPMENT... BUT APPARENTLY THE JOKER HAD A DIFFERENT USE FOR HER.
IT ALL COMES BACK TO THOSE BLASTED LEY LINES...

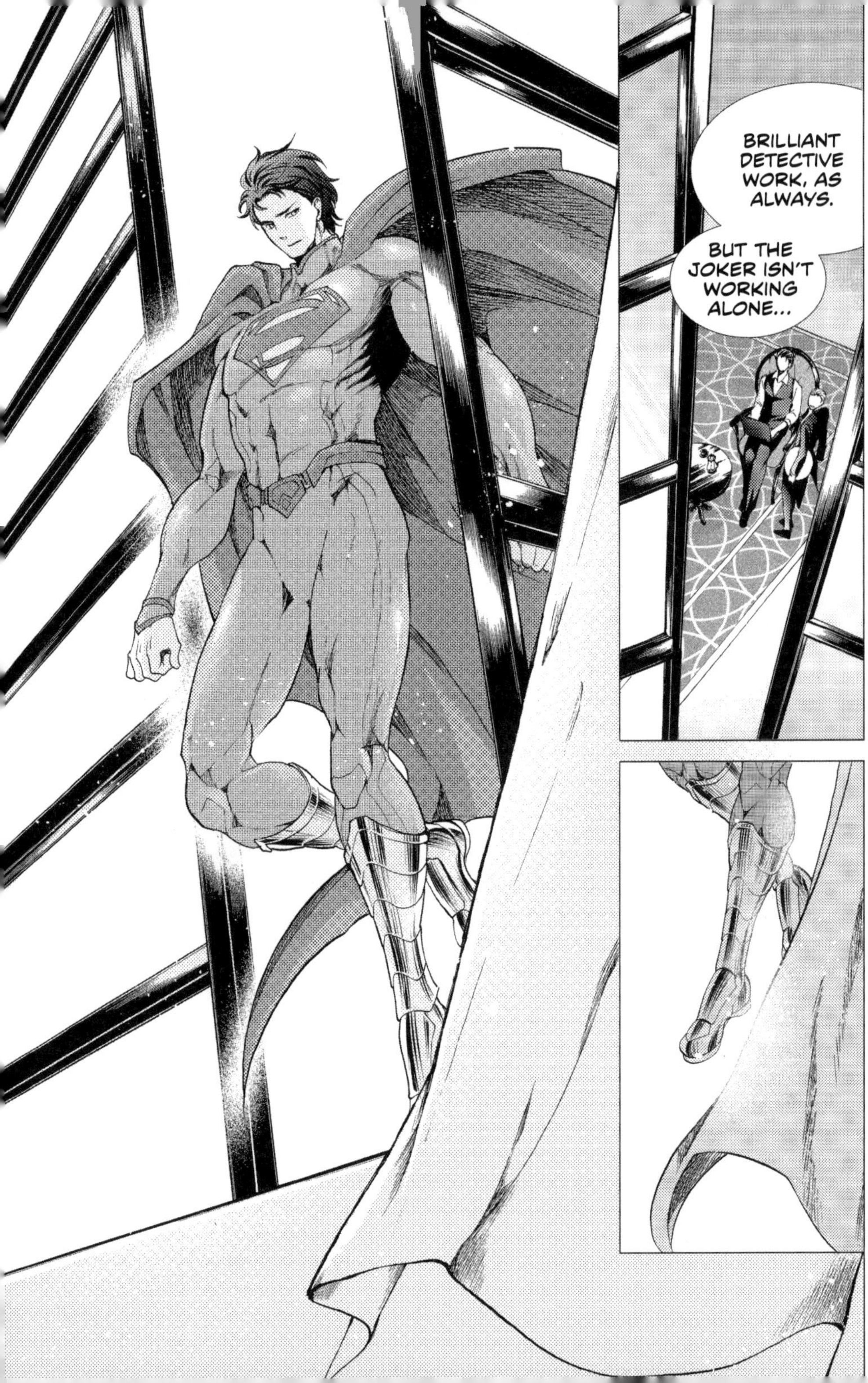
BRILLIANT DETECTIVE WORK, AS ALWAYS.
BUT THE JOKER ISN'T WORKING ALONE...

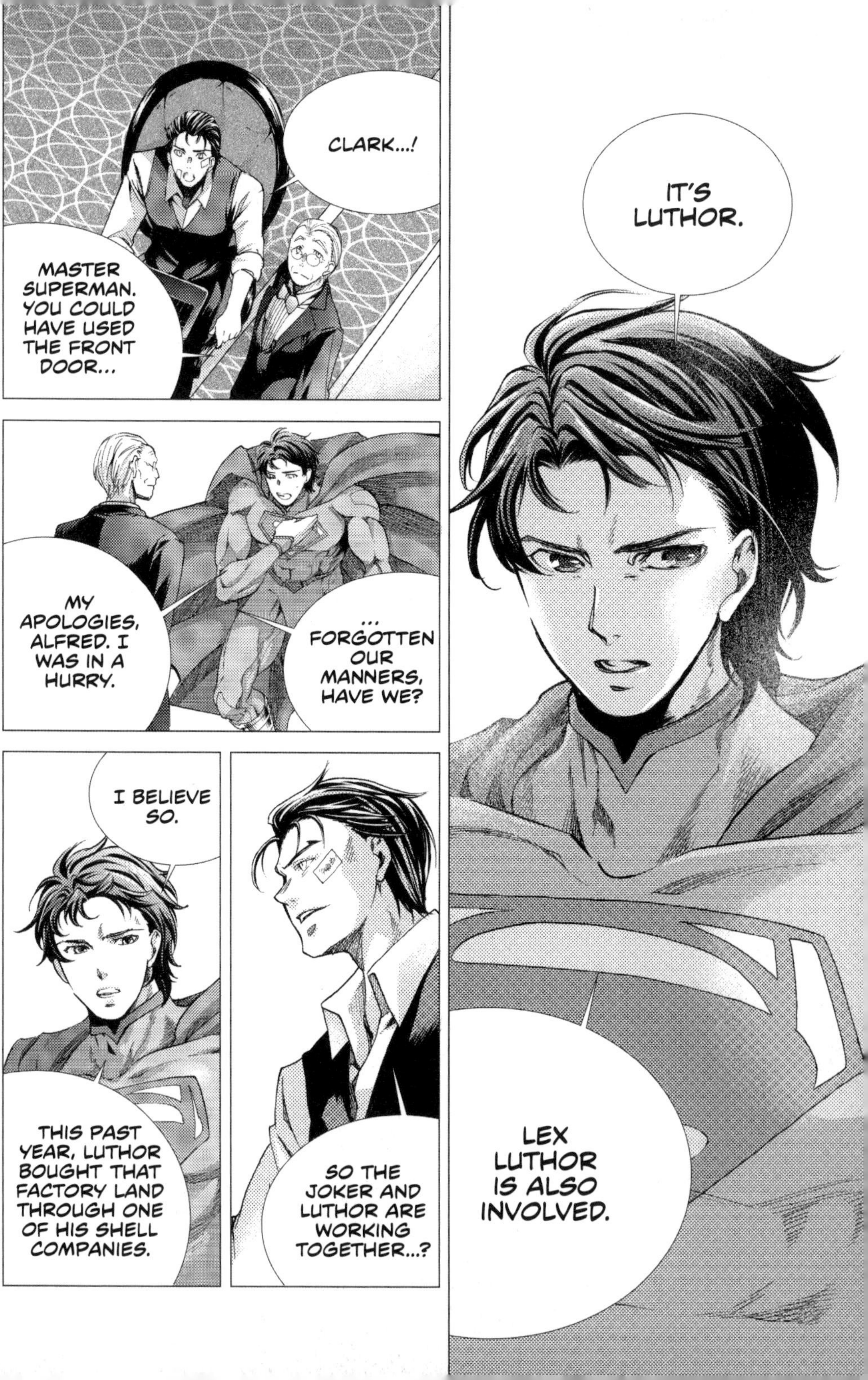
IT'S LUTHOR.
LEX LUTHOR IS ALSO INVOLVED.
CLARK...!
MASTER SUPERMAN. YOU COULD HAVE USED THE FRONT DOOR...
... FORGOTTEN OUR MANNERS, HAVE WE?
MY APOLOGIES, ALFRED. I WAS IN A HURRY.
SO THE JOKER AND LUTHOR ARE WORKING TOGETHER...?
I BELIEVE SO.
THIS PAST YEAR, LUTHOR BOUGHT THAT FACTORY LAND THROUGH ONE OF HIS SHELL COMPANIES.

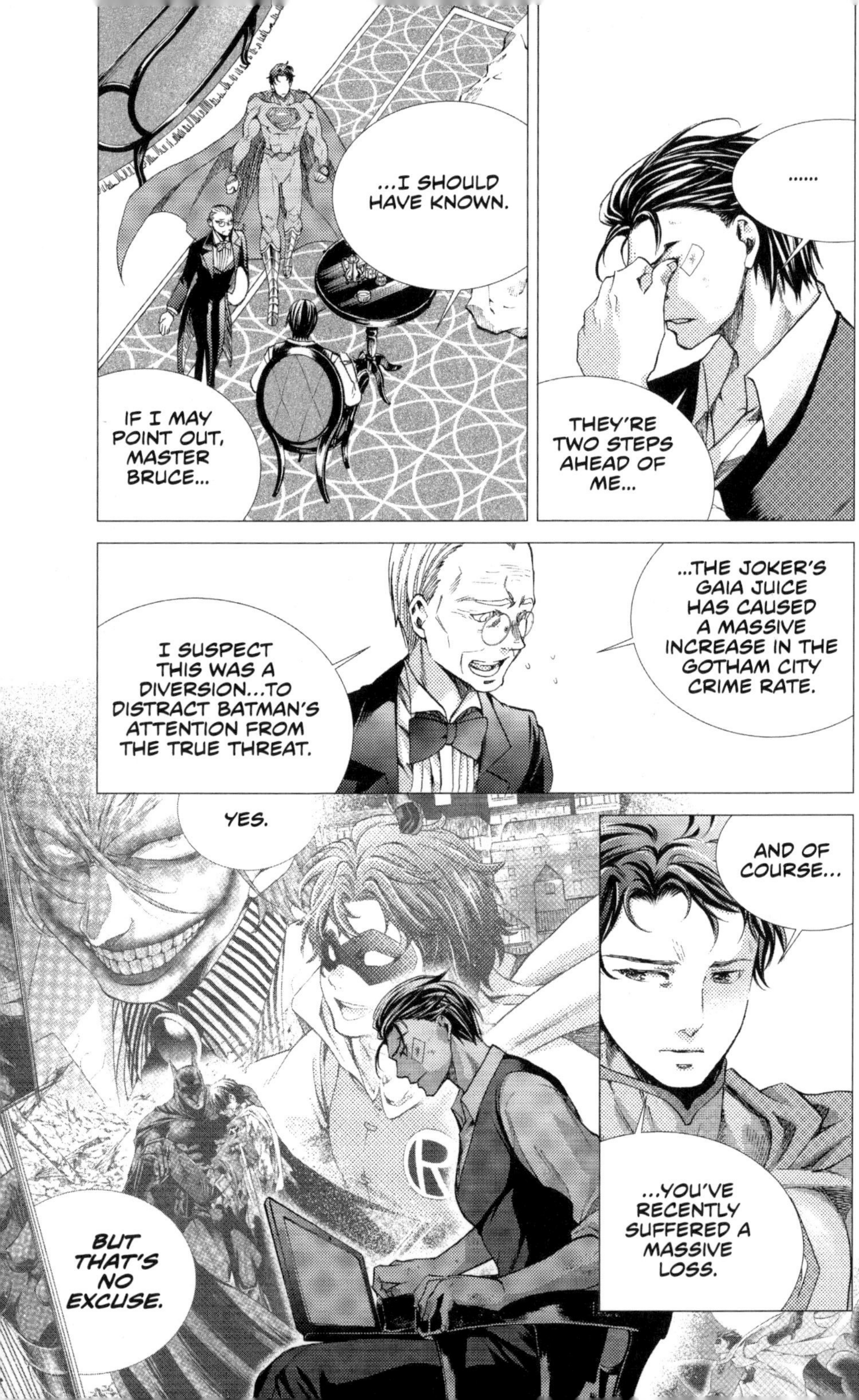
......
THEY'RE TWO STEPS AHEAD OF ME...
...I SHOULD HAVE KNOWN.
IF I MAY POINT OUT, MASTER BRUCE...
...THE JOKER'S GAIA JUICE HAS CAUSED A MASSIVE INCREASE IN THE GOTHAM CITY CRIME RATE.
I SUSPECT THIS WAS A DIVERSION...TO DISTRACT BATMAN'S ATTENTION FROM THE TRUE THREAT.
AND OF COURSE...
...YOU'VE RECENTLY SUFFERED A MASSIVE LOSS.
YES.
BUT THAT'S NO EXCUSE.

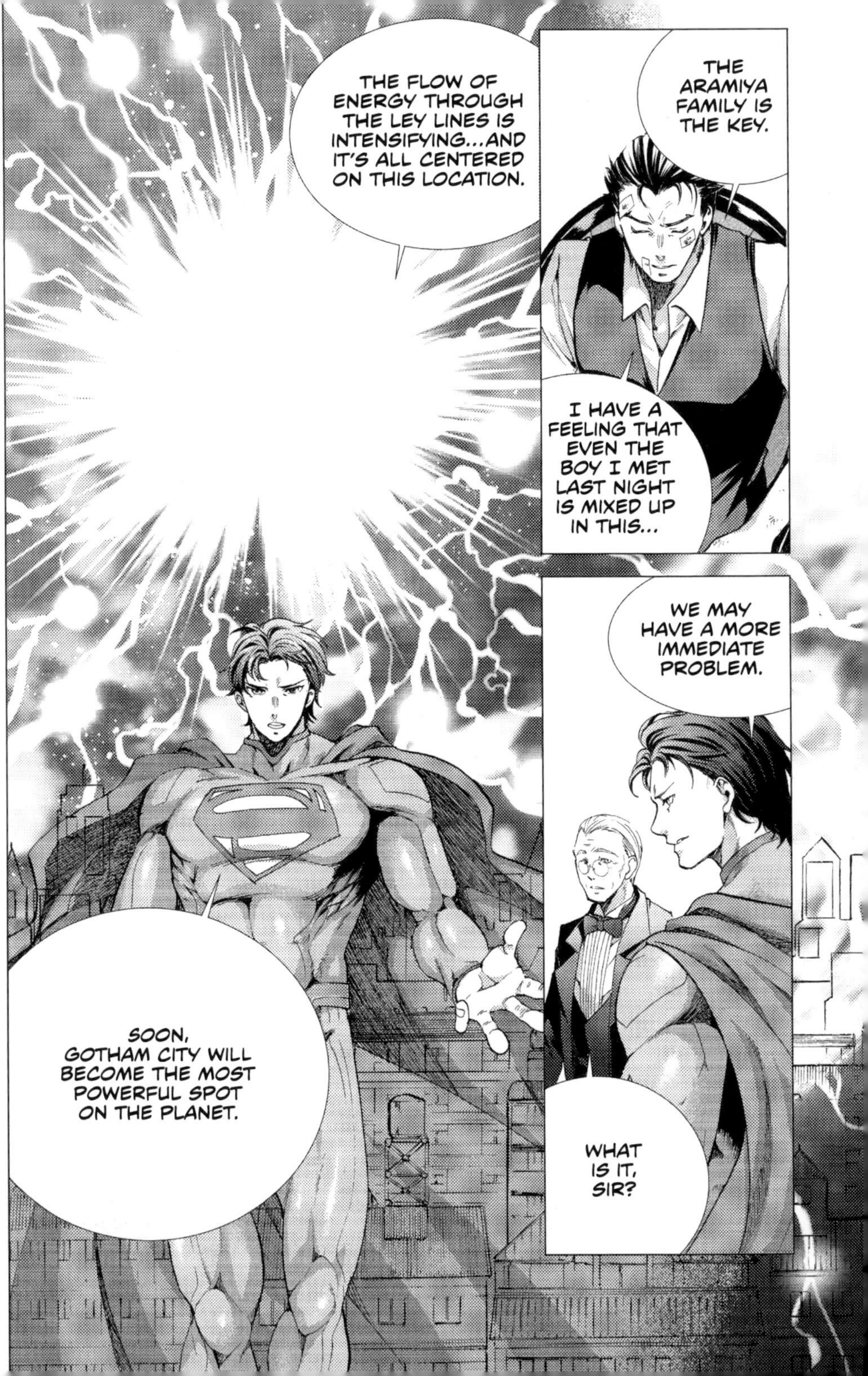
THE ARAMIYA FAMILY IS THE KEY.
I HAVE A FEELING THAT EVEN THE BOY I MET LAST NIGHT IS MIXED UP IN THIS...
WE MAY HAVE A MORE IMMEDIATE PROBLEM.
WHAT IS IT, SIR?
THE FLOW OF ENERGY THROUGH THE LEY LINES IS INTENSIFYING...AND IT'S ALL CENTERED ON THIS LOCATION.
SOON, GOTHAM CITY WILL BECOME THE MOST POWERFUL SPOT ON THE PLANET.

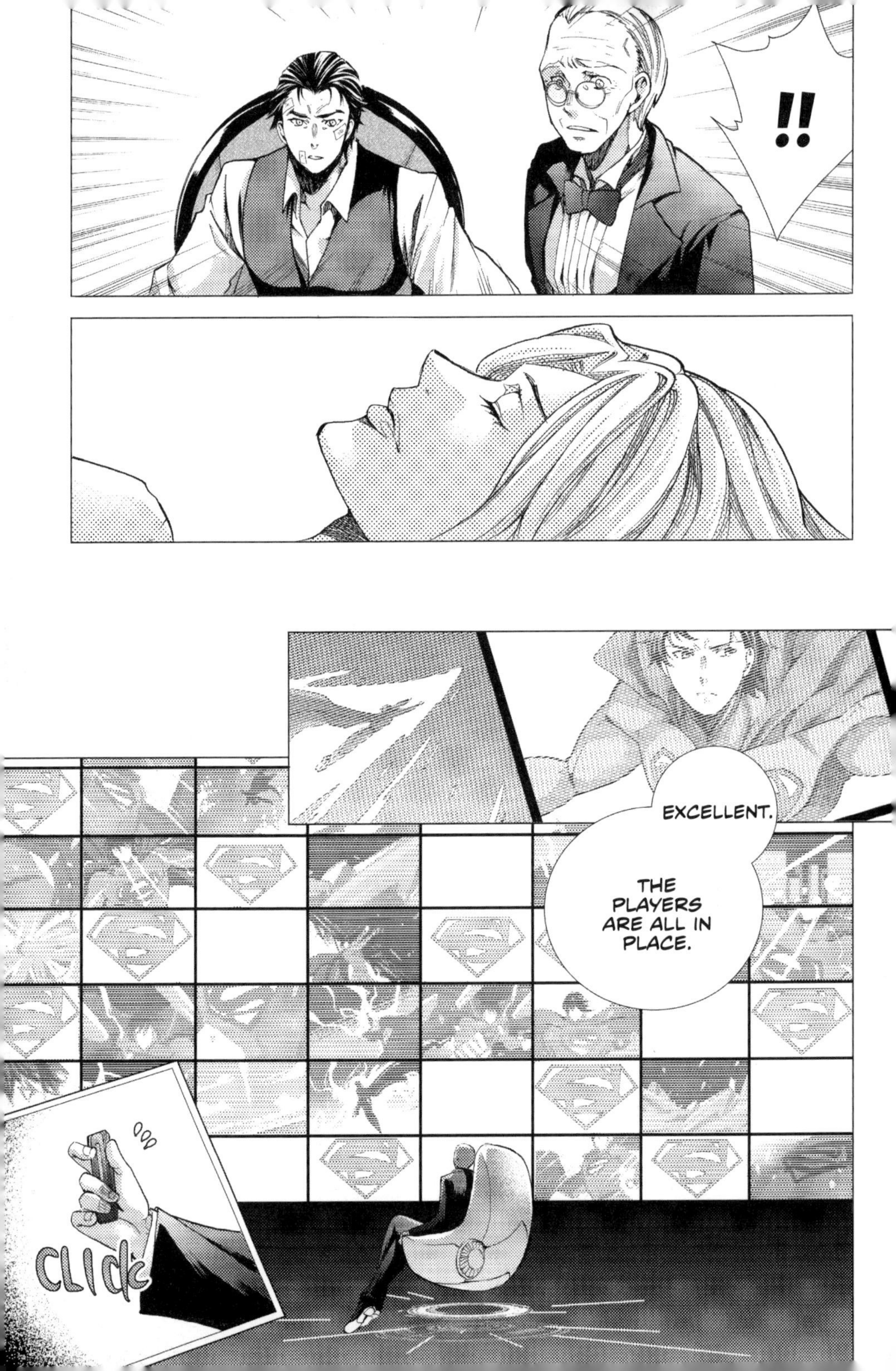
!!
EXCELLENT.
THE PLAYERS ARE ALL IN PLACE.
CLICK

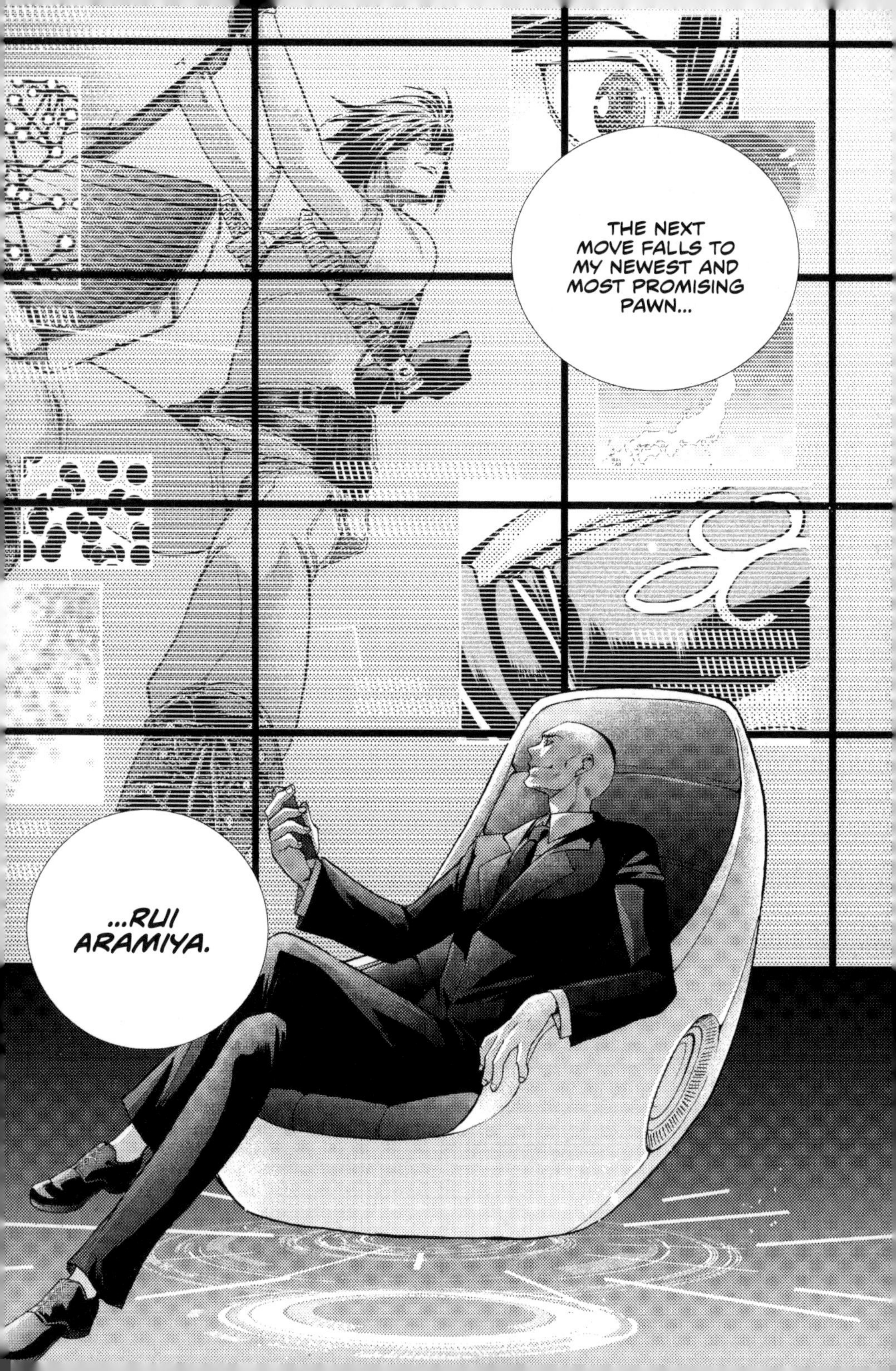
THE NEXT MOVE FALLS TO MY NEWEST AND MOST PROMISING PAWN...
...RUI ARAMIYA.

# CHAPTER 4

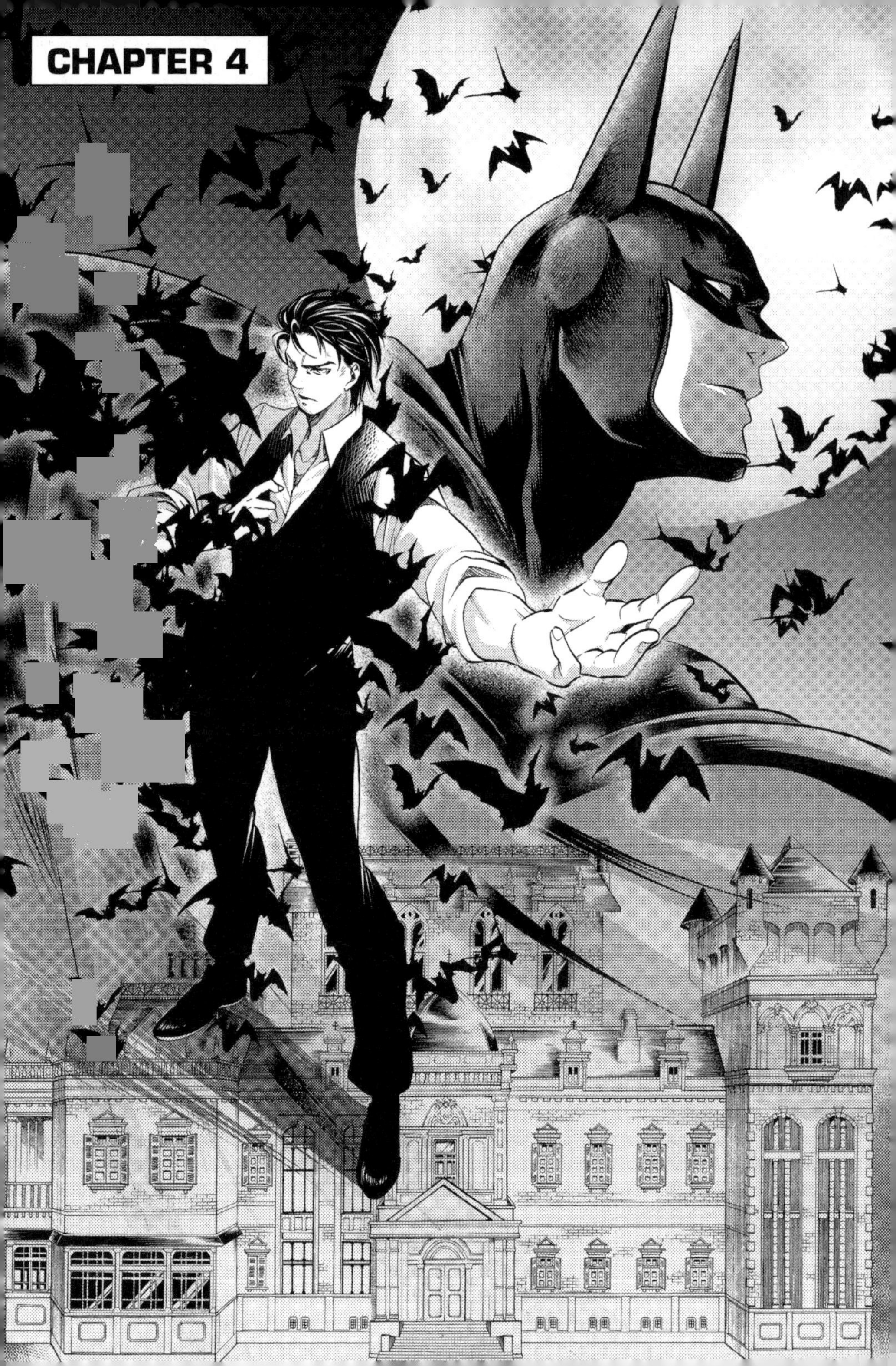

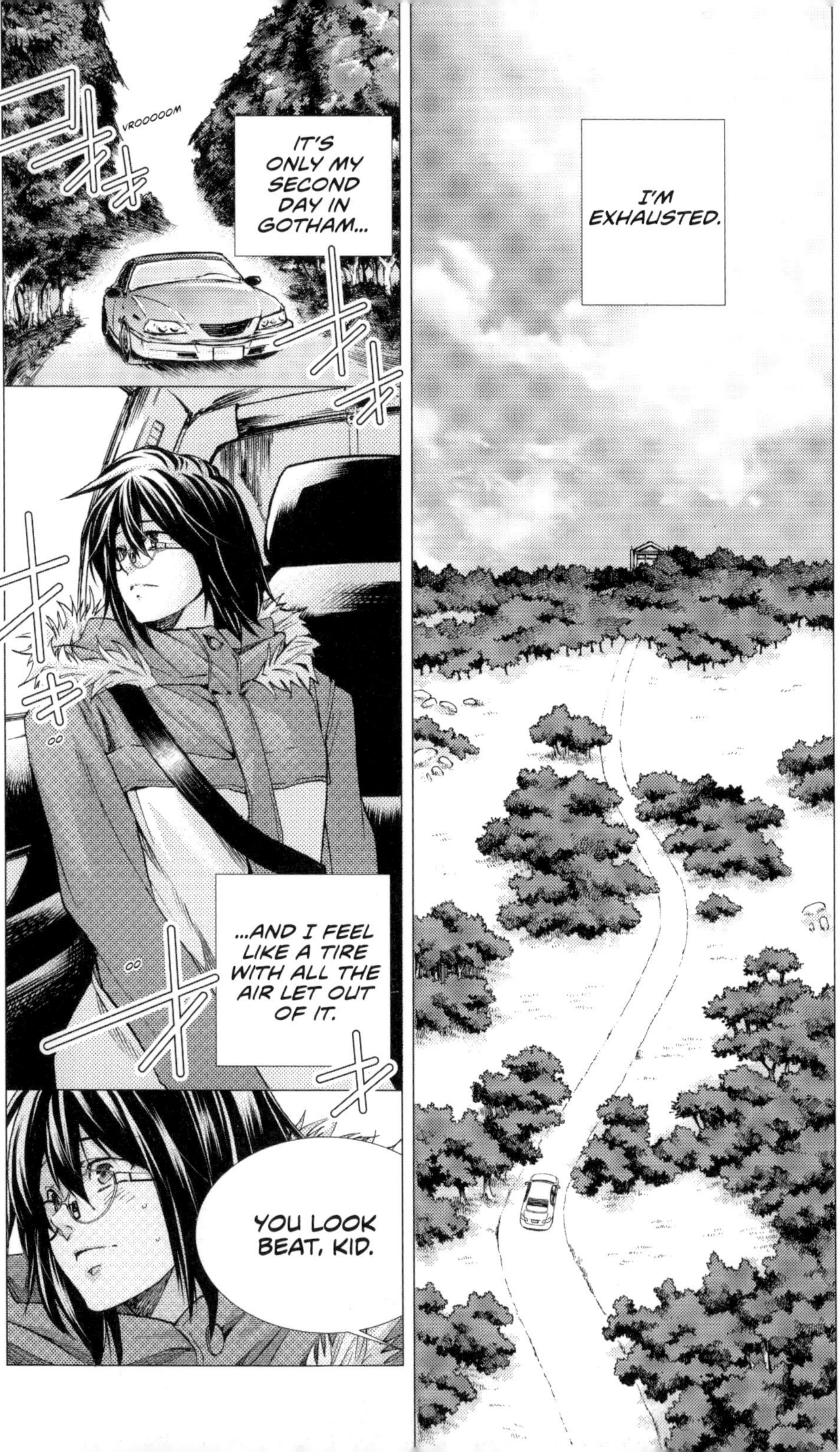
I'M EXHAUSTED.
IT'S ONLY MY SECOND DAY IN GOTHAM...
VROOOOOM
...AND I FEEL LIKE A TIRE WITH ALL THE AIR LET OUT OF IT.
YOU LOOK BEAT, KID.

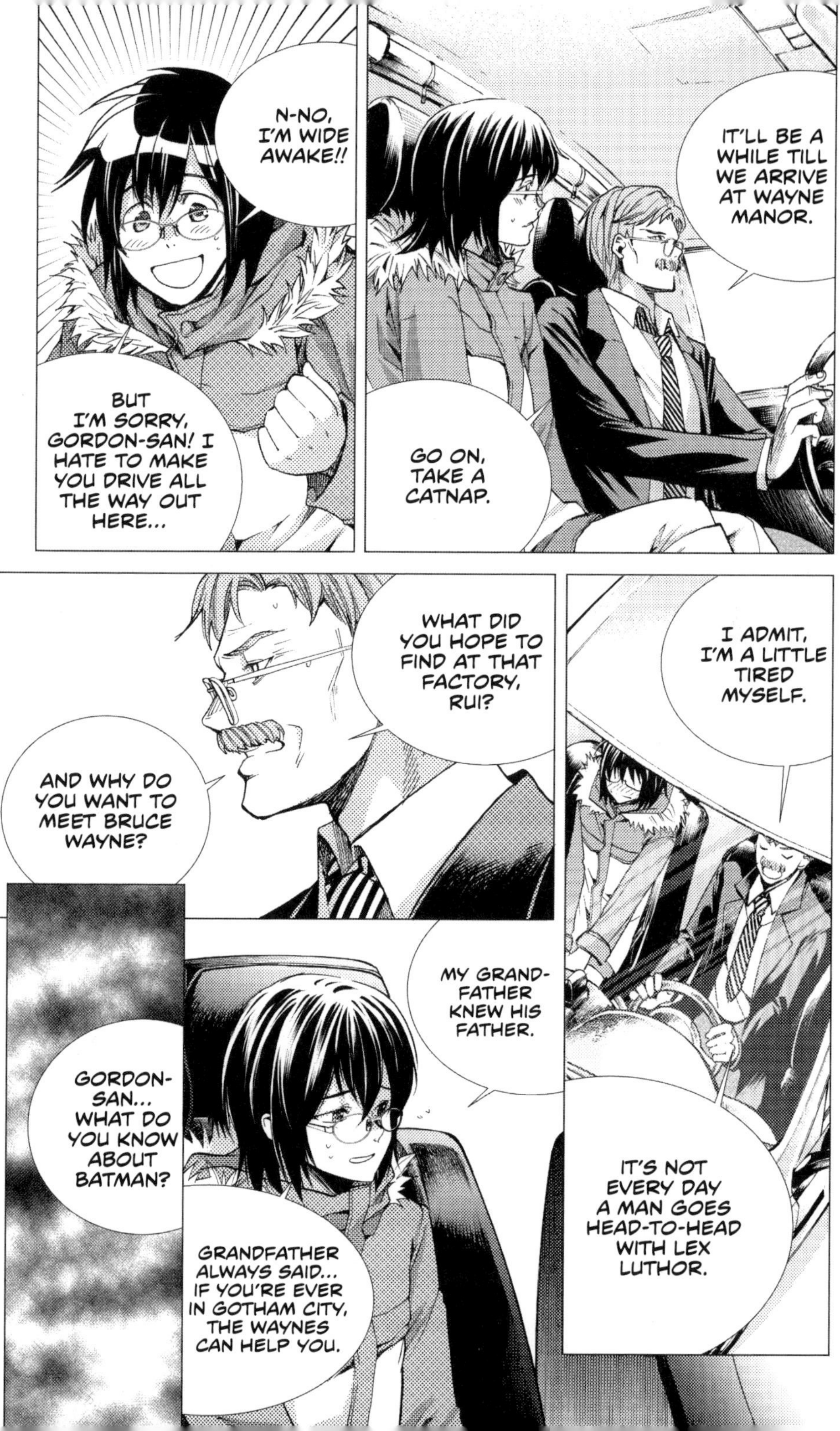
IT'LL BE A WHILE TILL WE ARRIVE AT WAYNE MANOR.
GO ON, TAKE A CATNAP.
N-NO, I'M WIDE AWAKE!!
BUT I'M SORRY, GORDON-SAN! I HATE TO MAKE YOU DRIVE ALL THE WAY OUT HERE...
I ADMIT, I'M A LITTLE TIRED MYSELF.
IT'S NOT EVERY DAY A MAN GOES HEAD-TO-HEAD WITH LEX LUTHOR.
WHAT DID YOU HOPE TO FIND AT THAT FACTORY, RUI?
AND WHY DO YOU WANT TO MEET BRUCE WAYNE?
MY GRAND-FATHER KNEW HIS FATHER.
GRANDFATHER ALWAYS SAID... IF YOU'RE EVER IN GOTHAM CITY, THE WAYNES CAN HELP YOU.
GORDON-SAN... WHAT DO YOU KNOW ABOUT BATMAN?

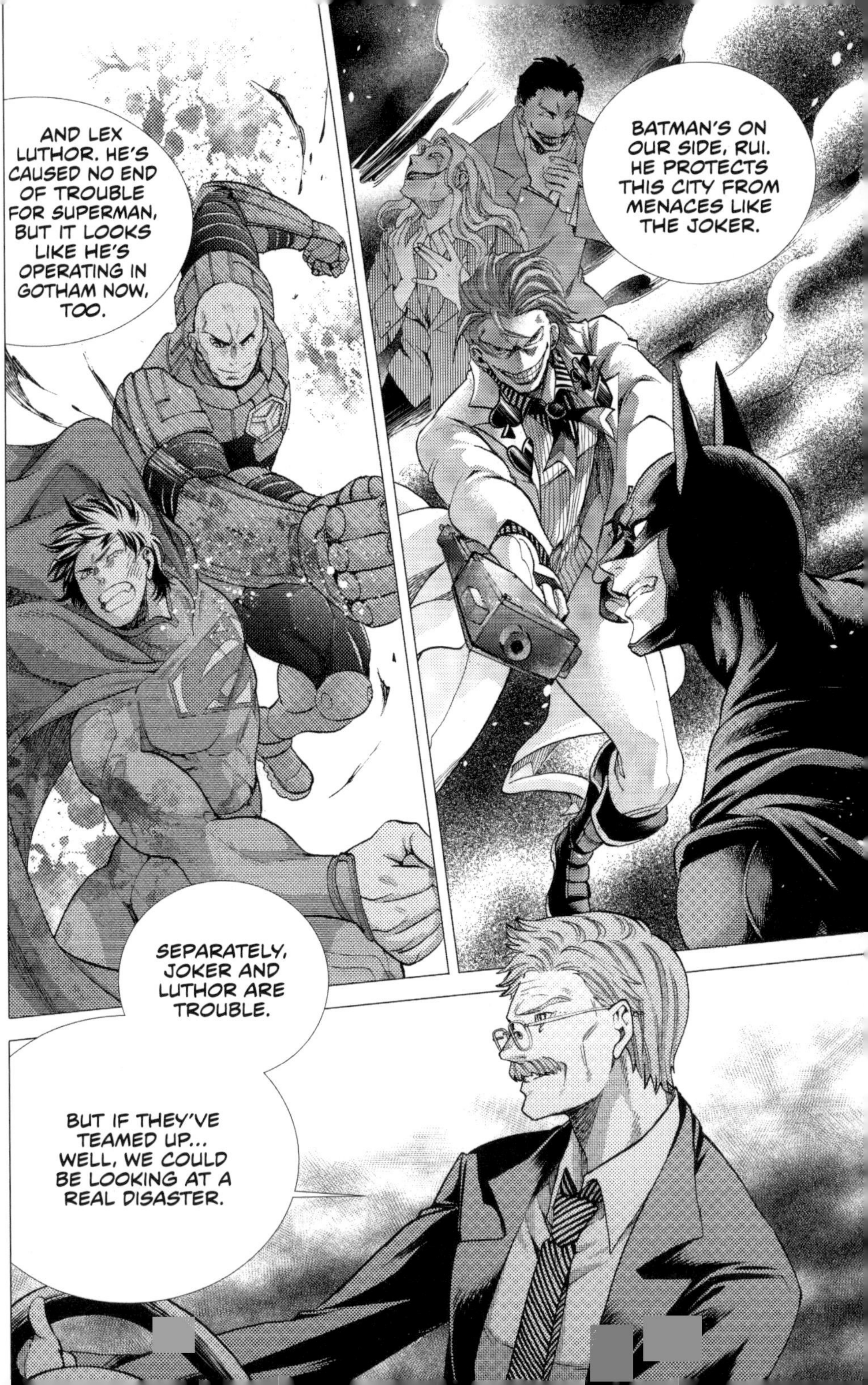
BATMAN'S ON OUR SIDE, RUI. HE PROTECTS THIS CITY FROM MENACES LIKE THE JOKER.
AND LEX LUTHOR. HE'S CAUSED NO END OF TROUBLE FOR SUPERMAN, BUT IT LOOKS LIKE HE'S OPERATING IN GOTHAM NOW, TOO.
SEPARATELY, JOKER AND LUTHOR ARE TROUBLE.
BUT IF THEY'VE TEAMED UP... WELL, WE COULD BE LOOKING AT A REAL DISASTER.

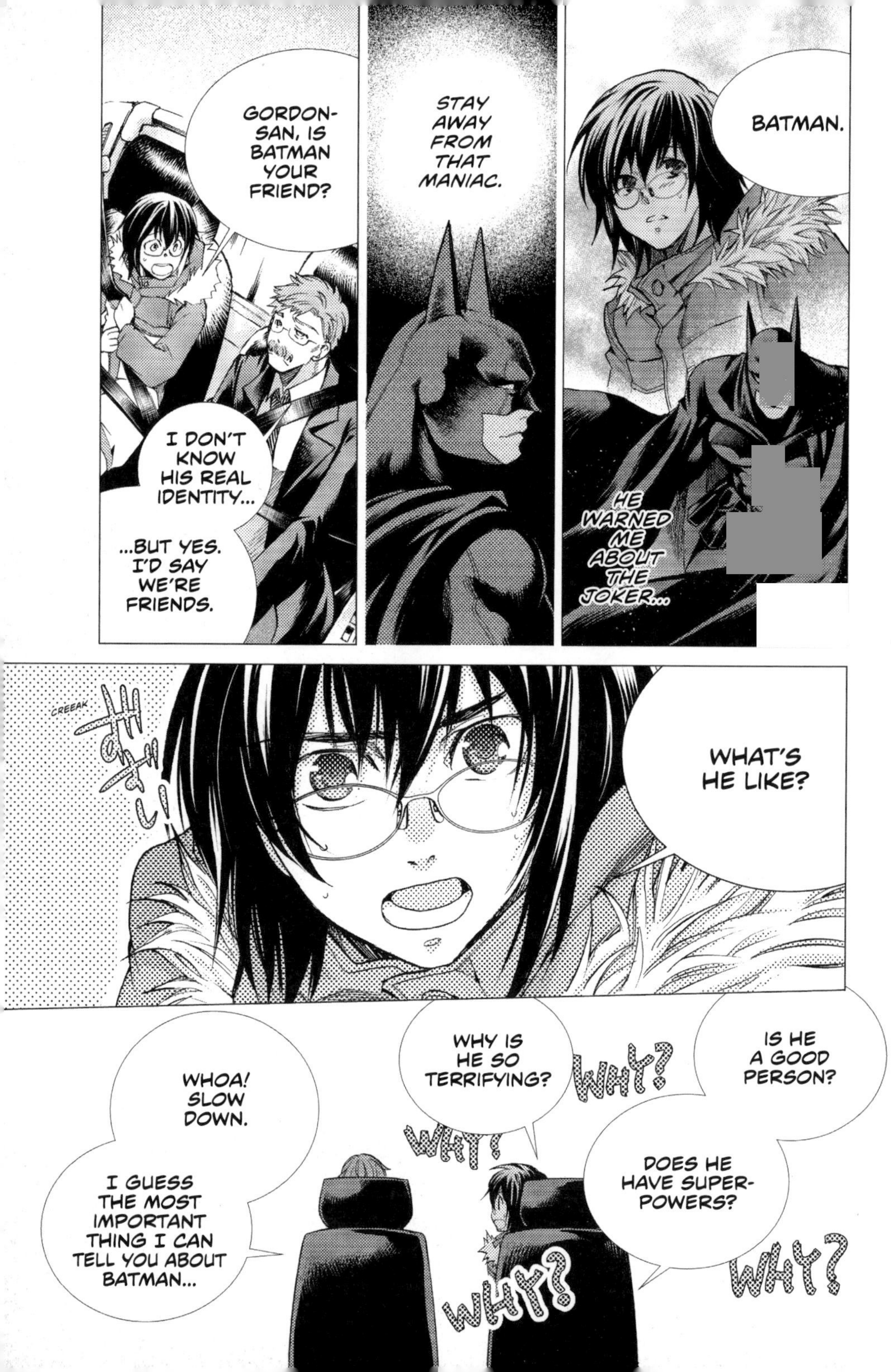
BATMAN.
HE WARNED ME ABOUT THE JOKER...
STAY AWAY FROM THAT MANIAC.
GORDON-SAN, IS BATMAN YOUR FRIEND?
I DON'T KNOW HIS REAL IDENTITY...
...BUT YES. I'D SAY WE'RE FRIENDS.
WHAT'S HE LIKE?
CREEAK
IS HE A GOOD PERSON?
WHY?
WHY IS HE SO TERRIFYING?
DOES HE HAVE SUPER-POWERS?
WHY?
WHY?
WHY?
WHOA! SLOW DOWN.
I GUESS THE MOST IMPORTANT THING I CAN TELL YOU ABOUT BATMAN...

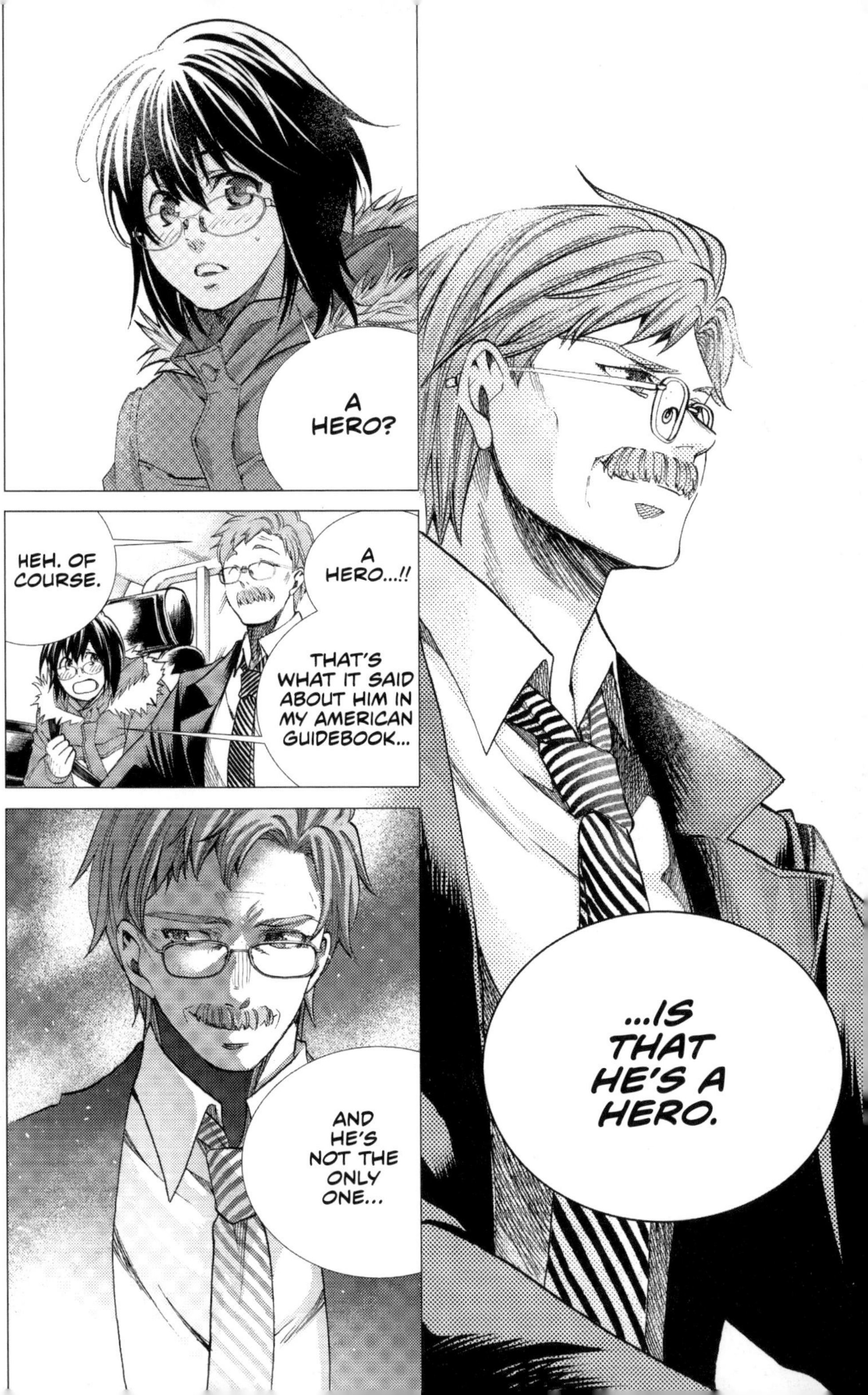
...IS THAT HE'S A HERO.
A HERO?
A HERO...!!
HEH. OF COURSE.
THAT'S WHAT IT SAID ABOUT HIM IN MY AMERICAN GUIDEBOOK...
AND HE'S NOT THE ONLY ONE...

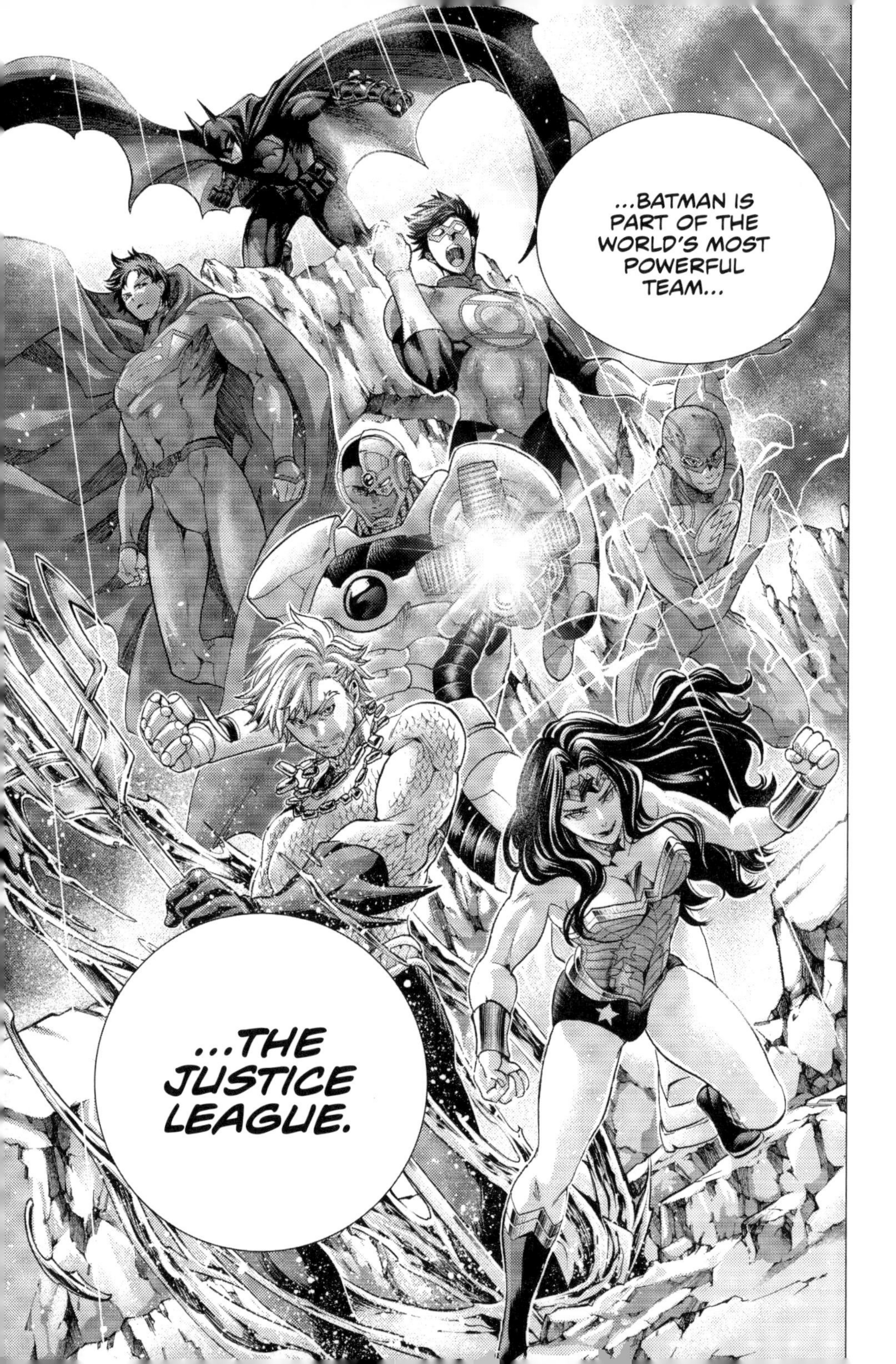
...BATMAN IS PART OF THE WORLD'S MOST POWERFUL TEAM...
...THE JUSTICE LEAGUE.

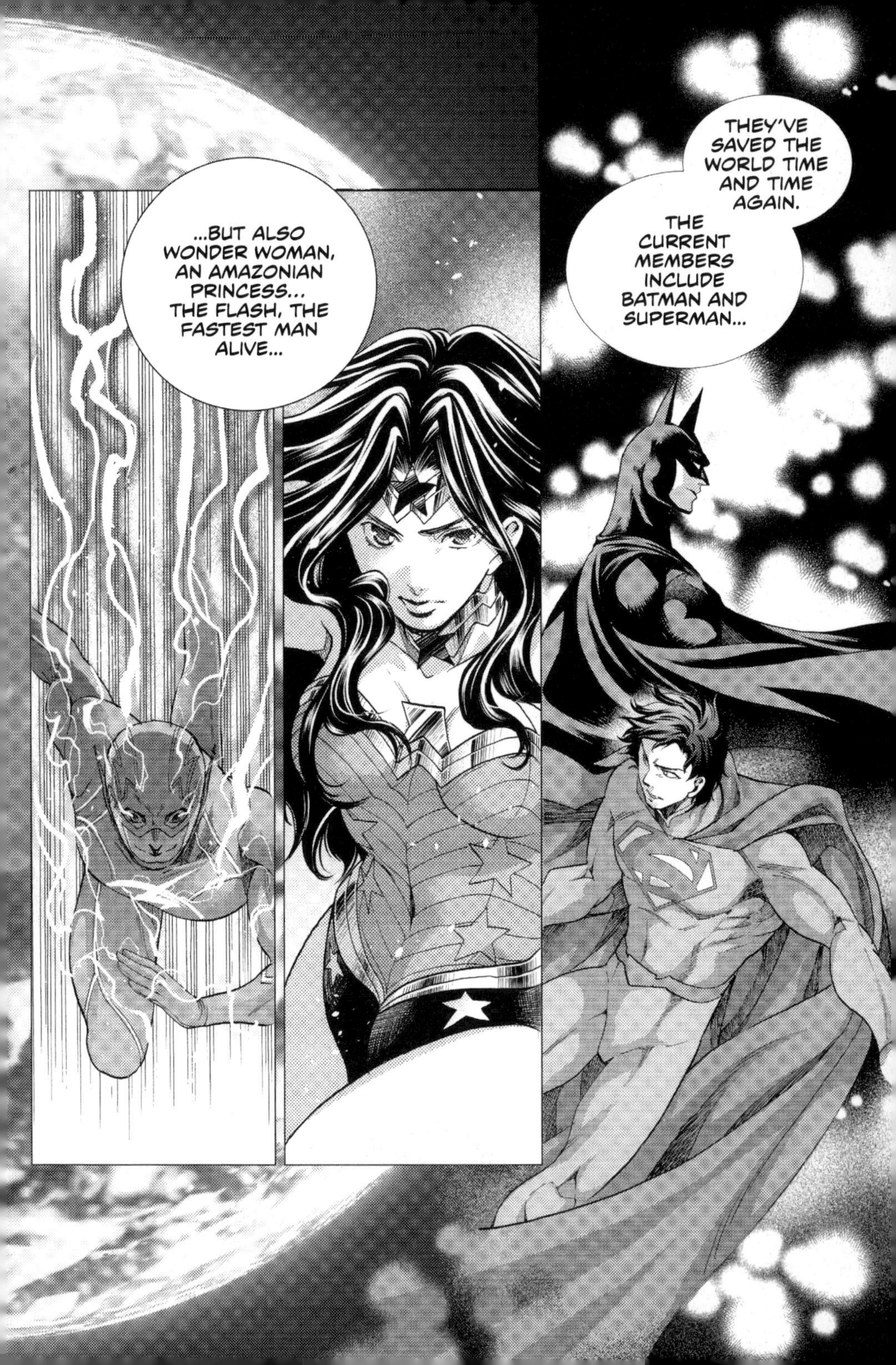
THEY'VE SAVED THE WORLD TIME AND TIME AGAIN.
THE CURRENT MEMBERS INCLUDE BATMAN AND SUPERMAN...
...BUT ALSO WONDER WOMAN, AN AMAZONIAN PRINCESS... THE FLASH, THE FASTEST MAN ALIVE...

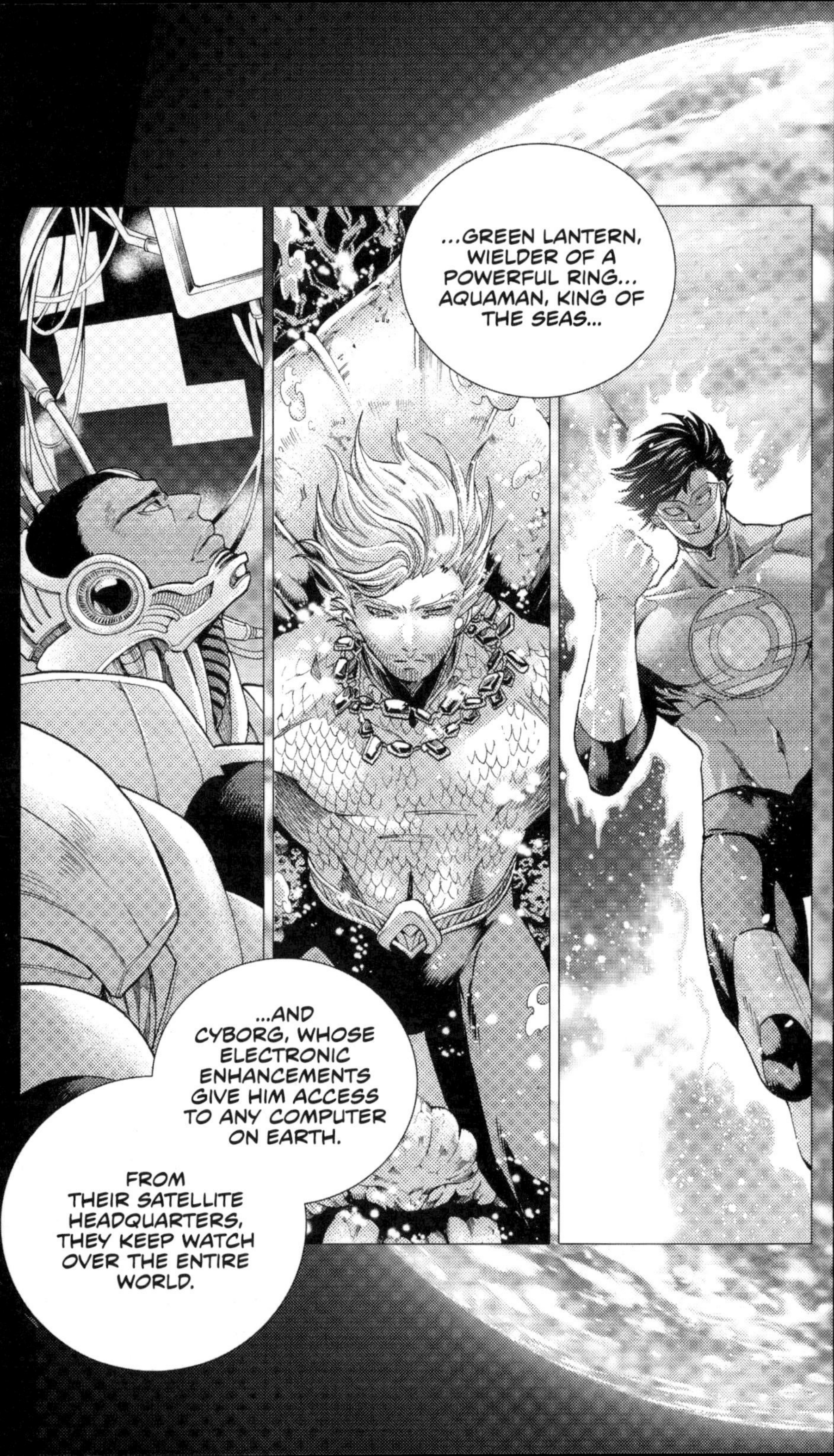
...GREEN LANTERN, WIELDER OF A POWERFUL RING... AQUAMAN, KING OF THE SEAS...
...AND CYBORG, WHOSE ELECTRONIC ENHANCEMENTS GIVE HIM ACCESS TO ANY COMPUTER ON EARTH.
FROM THEIR SATELLITE HEADQUARTERS, THEY KEEP WATCH OVER THE ENTIRE WORLD.

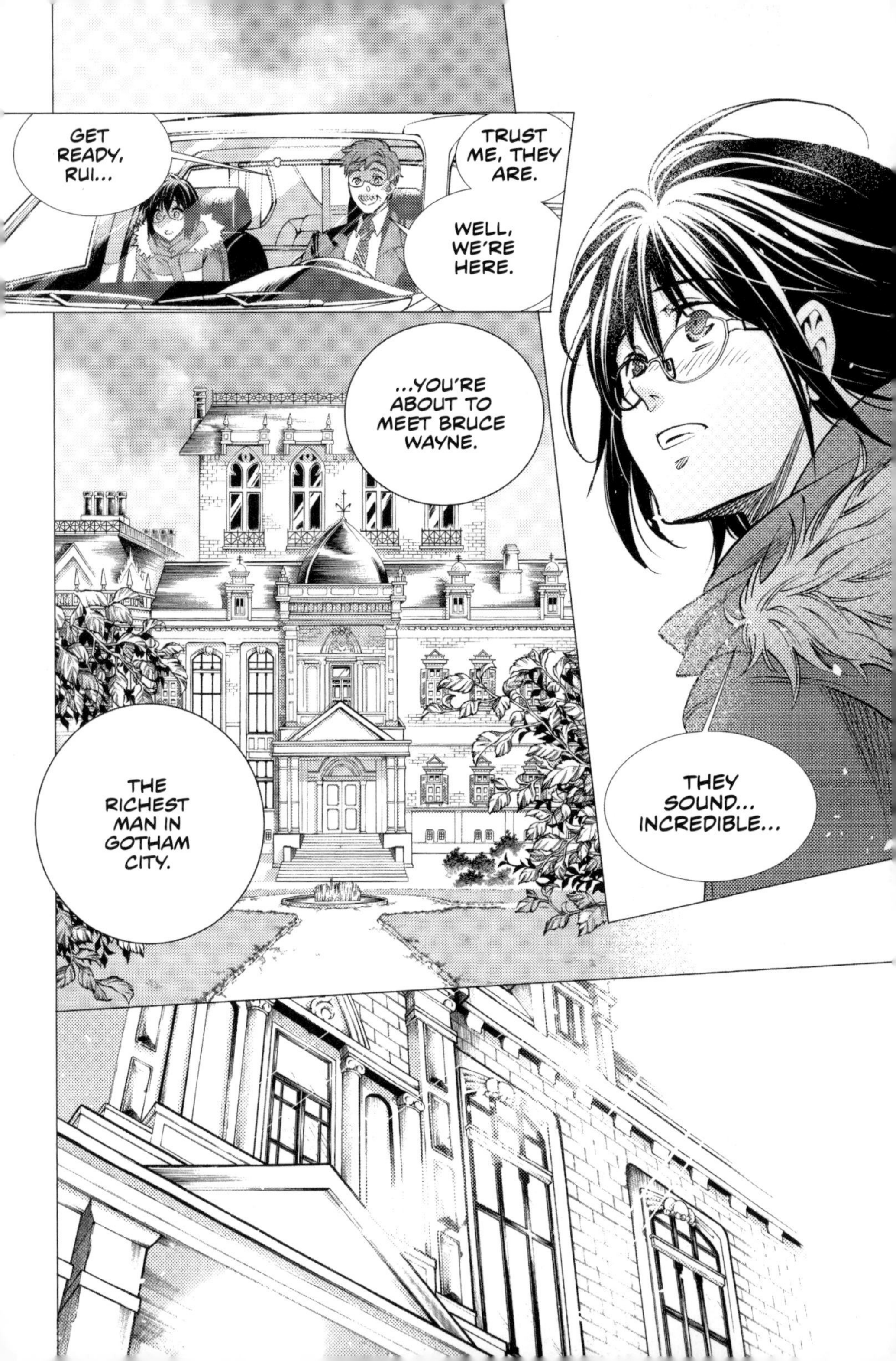
THEY SOUND... INCREDIBLE...
TRUST ME, THEY ARE.
WELL, WE'RE HERE.
GET READY, RUI...
...YOU'RE ABOUT TO MEET BRUCE WAYNE.
THE RICHEST MAN IN GOTHAM CITY.

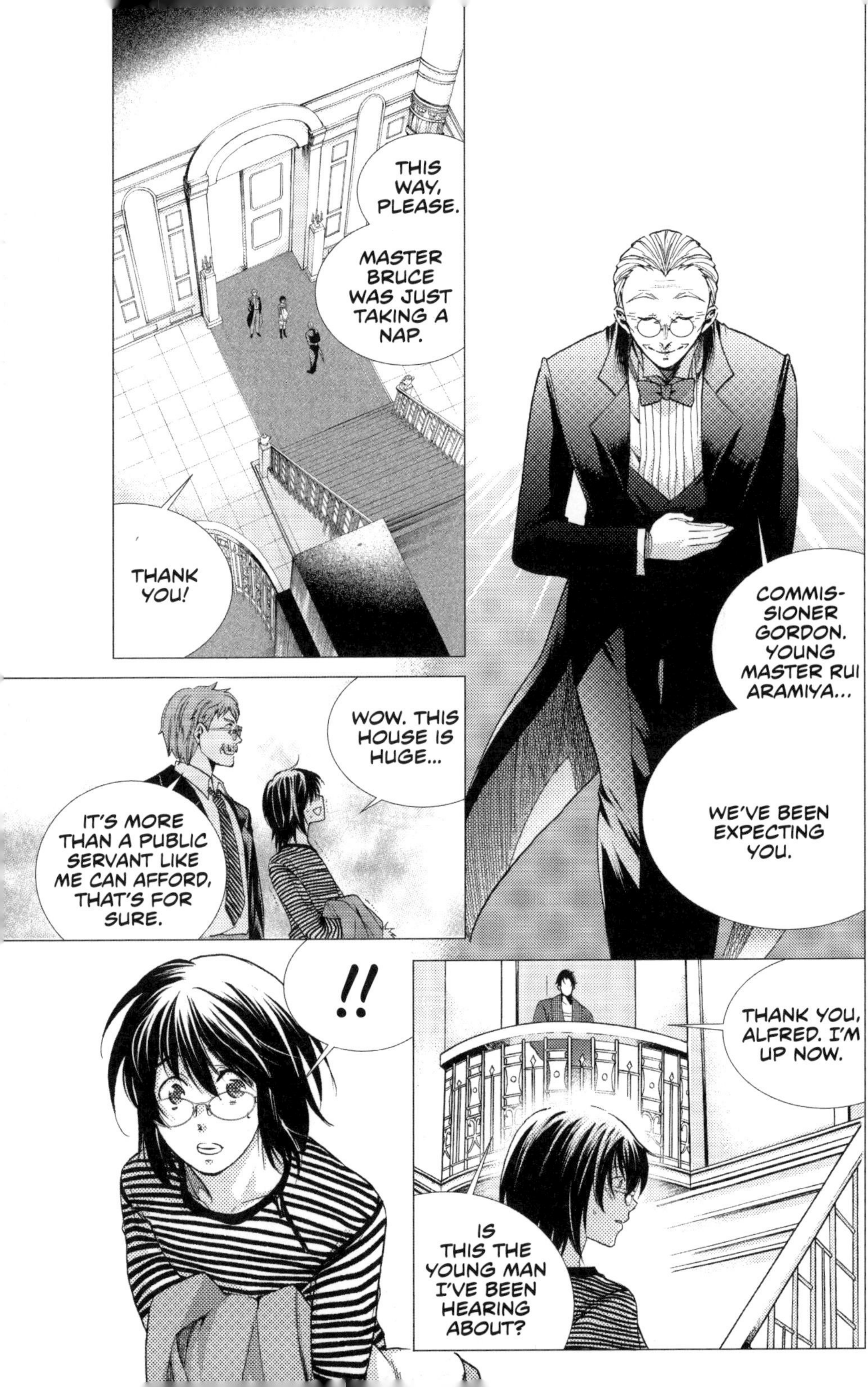
COMMIS-SIONER GORDON. YOUNG MASTER RUI ARAMIYA...
WE'VE BEEN EXPECTING YOU.
THIS WAY, PLEASE.
MASTER BRUCE WAS JUST TAKING A NAP.
THANK YOU!
WOW. THIS HOUSE IS HUGE...
IT'S MORE THAN A PUBLIC SERVANT LIKE ME CAN AFFORD, THAT'S FOR SURE.
THANK YOU, ALFRED. I'M UP NOW.
IS THIS THE YOUNG MAN I'VE BEEN HEARING ABOUT?
!!

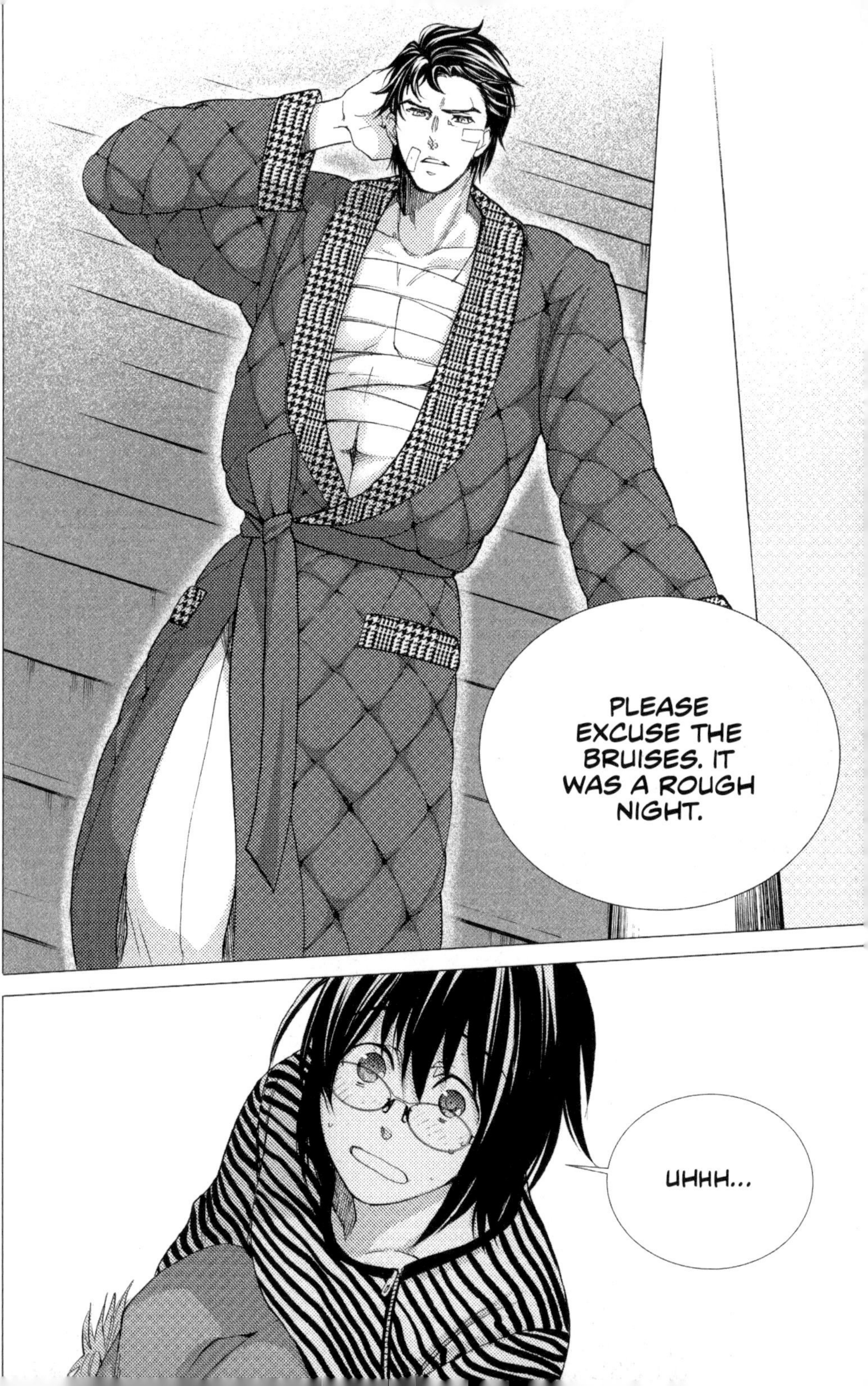
PLEASE EXCUSE THE BRUISES. IT WAS A ROUGH NIGHT.
UHHH...

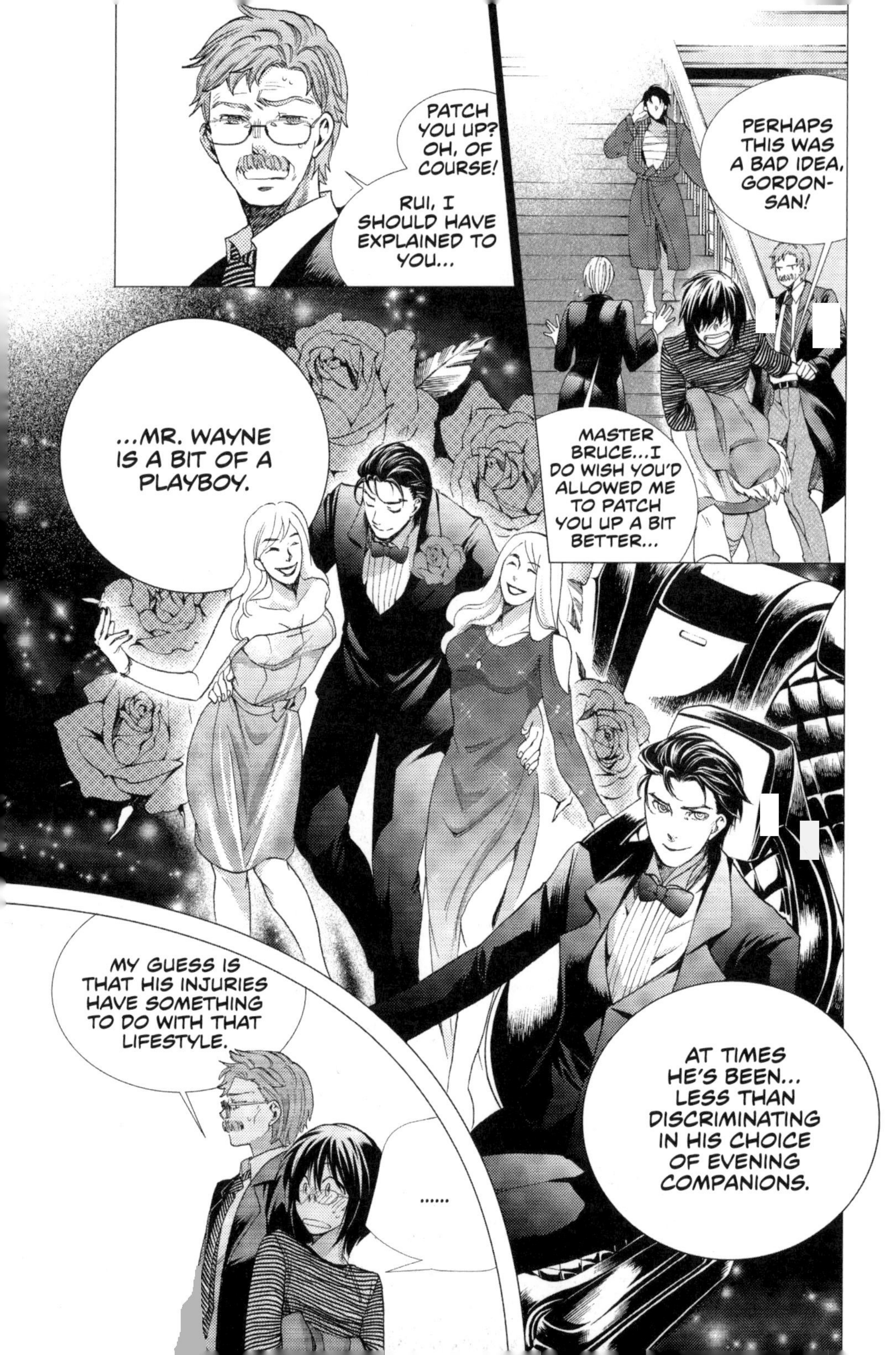
PERHAPS THIS WAS A BAD IDEA, GORDON-SAN!
MASTER BRUCE...I DO WISH YOU'D ALLOWED ME TO PATCH YOU UP A BIT BETTER...
PATCH YOU UP? OH, OF COURSE!
RUI, I SHOULD HAVE EXPLAINED TO YOU...
...MR. WAYNE IS A BIT OF A PLAYBOY.
AT TIMES HE'S BEEN... LESS THAN DISCRIMINATING IN HIS CHOICE OF EVENING COMPANIONS.
MY GUESS IS THAT HIS INJURIES HAVE SOMETHING TO DO WITH THAT LIFESTYLE.
......

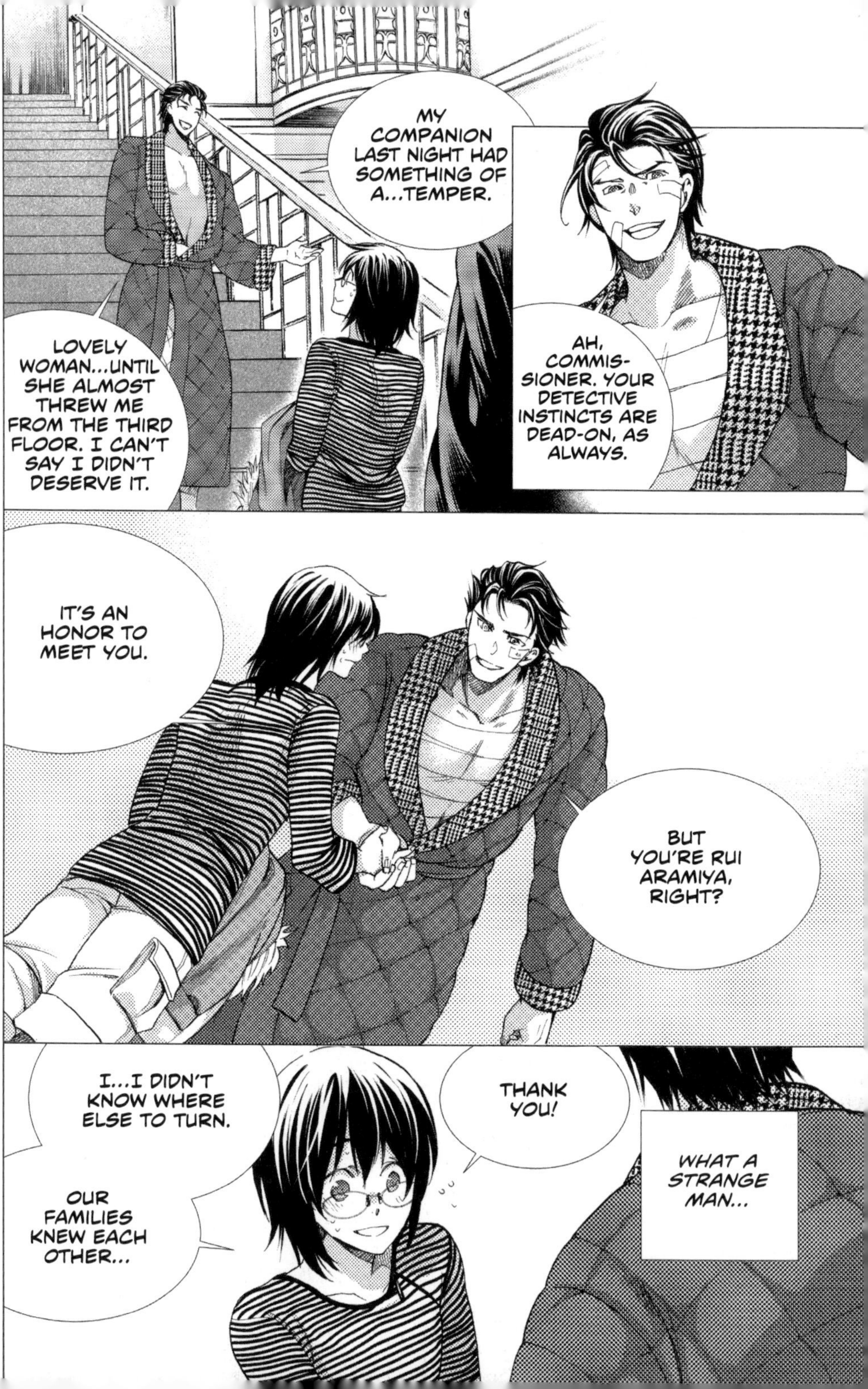
AH, COMMIS-SIONER. YOUR DETECTIVE INSTINCTS ARE DEAD-ON, AS ALWAYS.
MY COMPANION LAST NIGHT HAD SOMETHING OF A...TEMPER.
LOVELY WOMAN...UNTIL SHE ALMOST THREW ME FROM THE THIRD FLOOR. I CAN'T SAY I DIDN'T DESERVE IT.
BUT YOU'RE RUI ARAMIYA, RIGHT?
IT'S AN HONOR TO MEET YOU.
WHAT A STRANGE MAN...
THANK YOU!
I...I DIDN'T KNOW WHERE ELSE TO TURN.
OUR FAMILIES KNEW EACH OTHER...

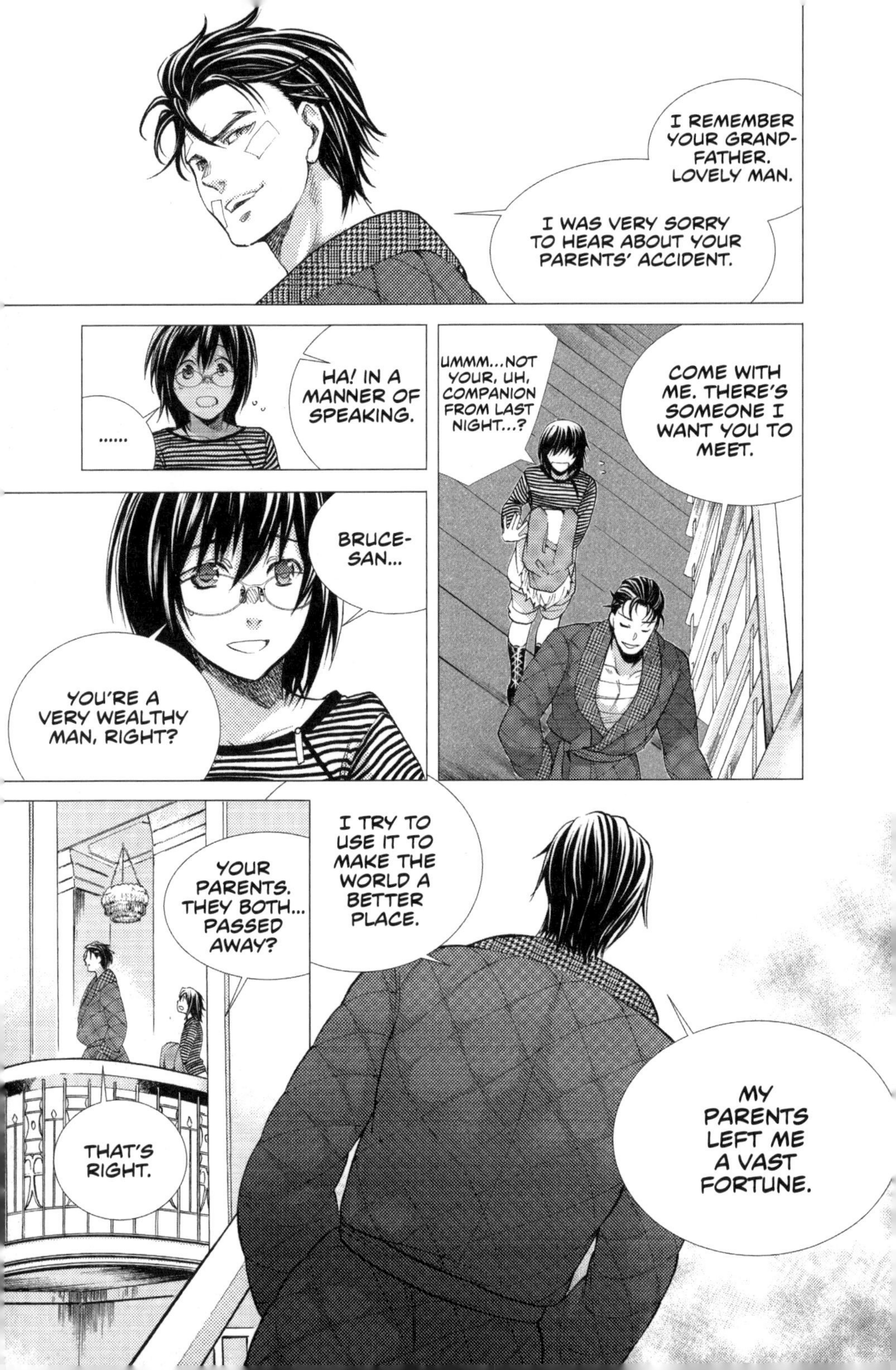
I REMEMBER YOUR GRAND-FATHER. LOVELY MAN.
I WAS VERY SORRY TO HEAR ABOUT YOUR PARENTS' ACCIDENT.
COME WITH ME. THERE'S SOMEONE I WANT YOU TO MEET.
UMMM...NOT YOUR, UH, COMPANION FROM LAST NIGHT...?
HA! IN A MANNER OF SPEAKING.
......
BRUCE-SAN...
YOU'RE A VERY WEALTHY MAN, RIGHT?
MY PARENTS LEFT ME A VAST FORTUNE.
I TRY TO USE IT TO MAKE THE WORLD A BETTER PLACE.
YOUR PARENTS. THEY BOTH... PASSED AWAY?
THAT'S RIGHT.

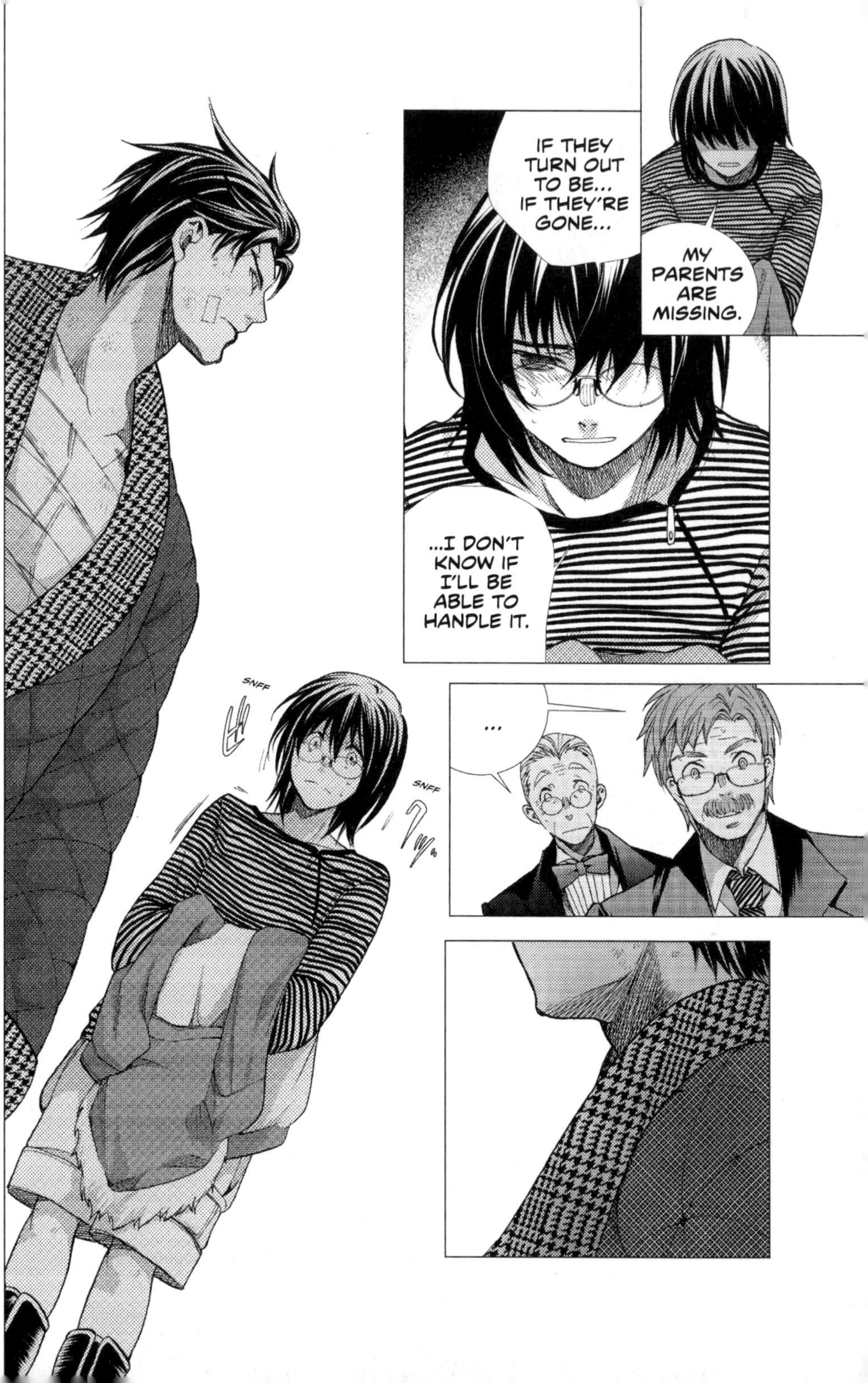
MY PARENTS ARE MISSING.
IF THEY TURN OUT TO BE... IF THEY'RE GONE...
...I DON'T KNOW IF I'LL BE ABLE TO HANDLE IT.
...
SNFF
SNFF

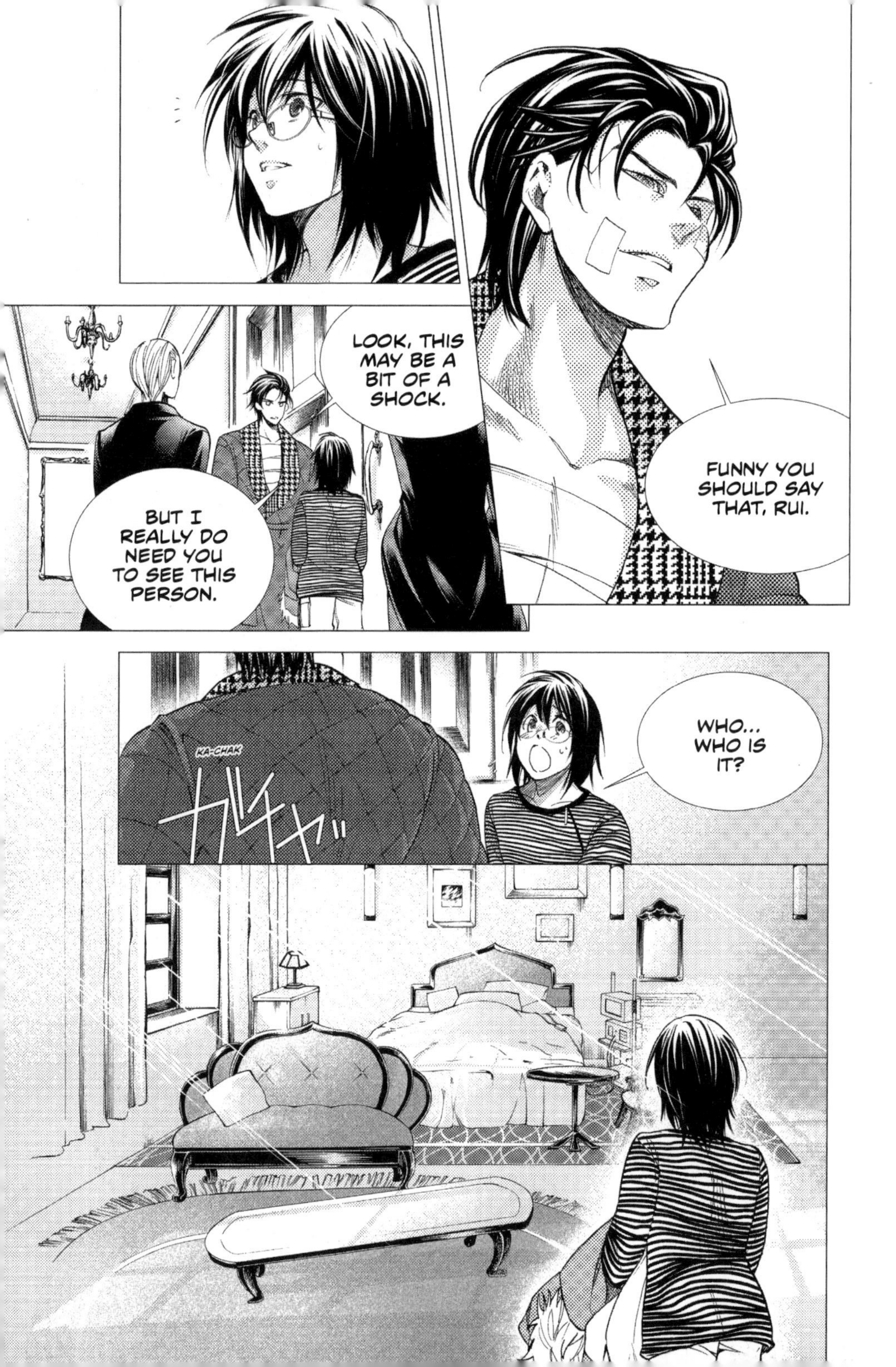
FUNNY YOU SHOULD SAY THAT, RUI.
LOOK, THIS MAY BE A BIT OF A SHOCK.
BUT I REALLY DO NEED YOU TO SEE THIS PERSON.
WHO... WHO IS IT?
KA-CHAK
ガチャ

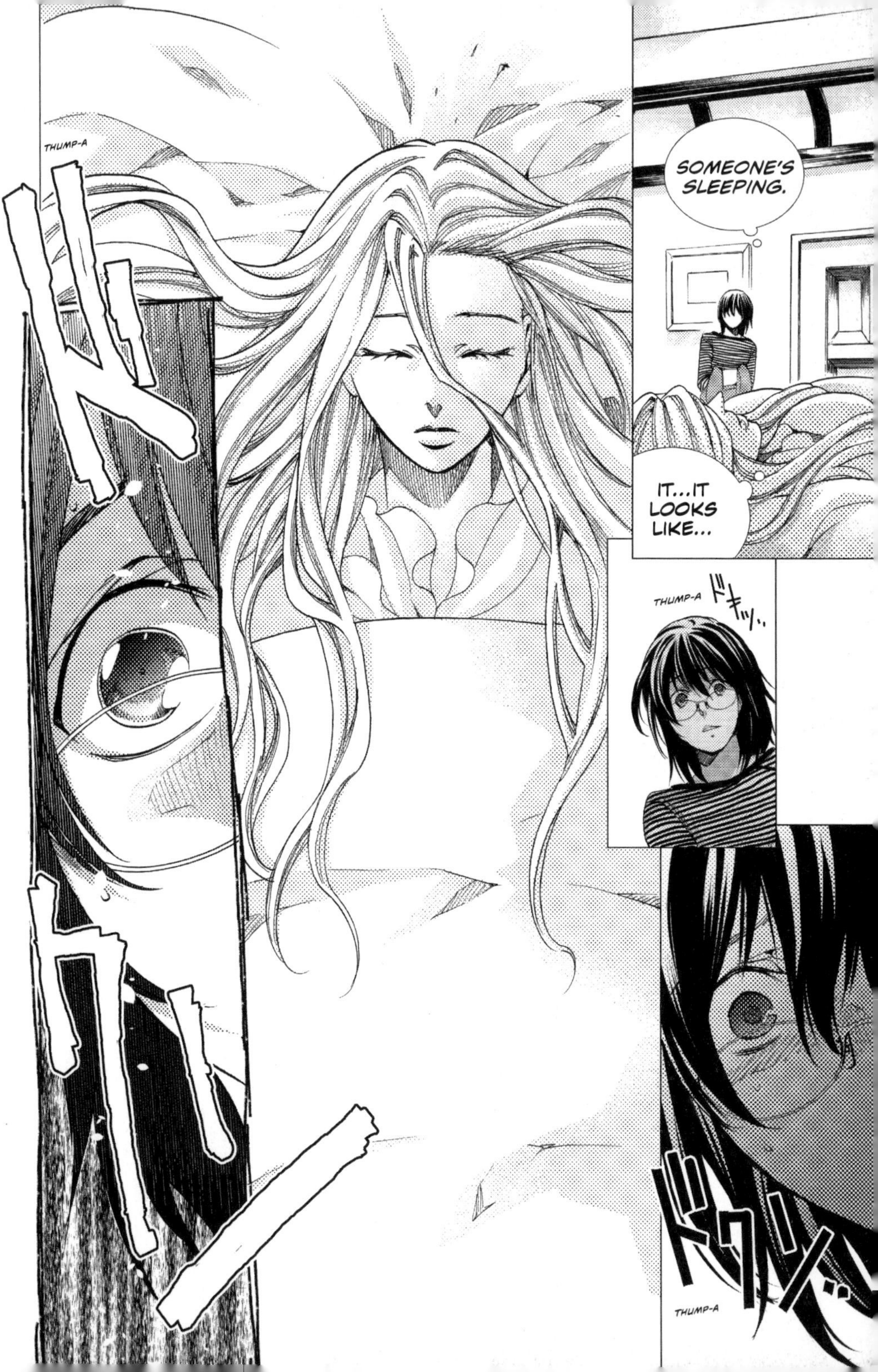
SOMEONE'S SLEEPING.
IT...IT LOOKS LIKE...
THUMP-A
ドキッ
THUMP-A
THUMP-A

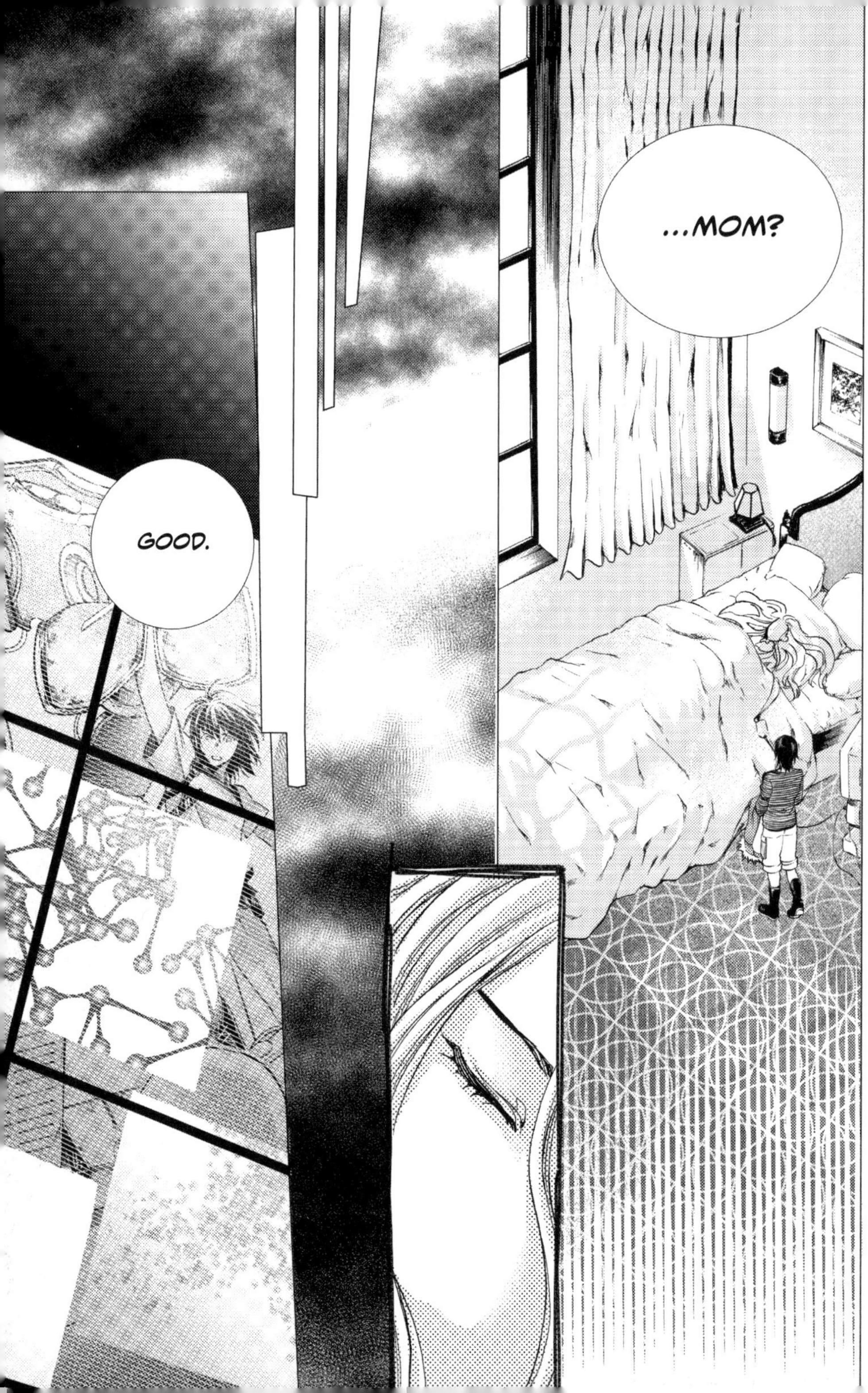
...MOM?
GOOD.

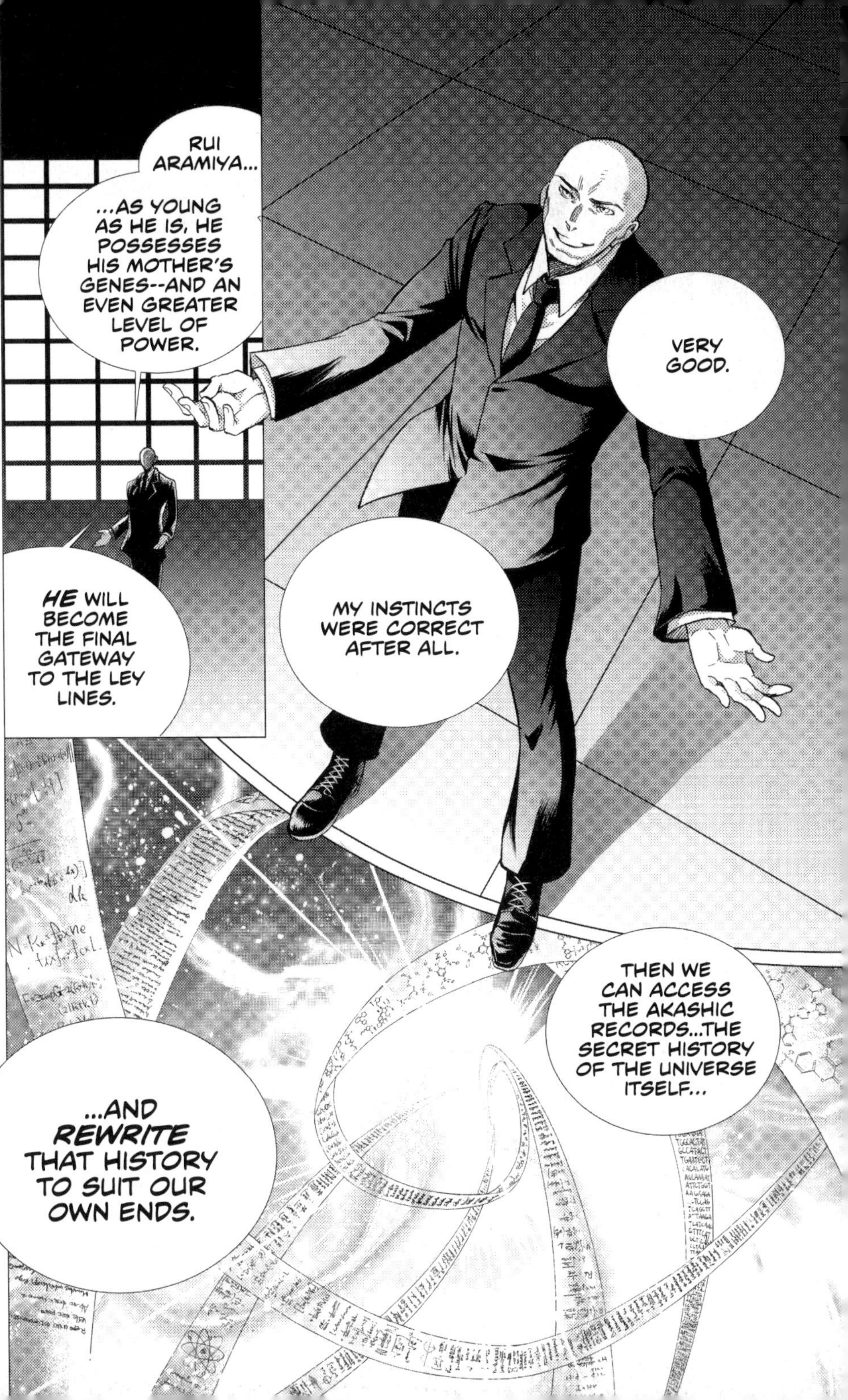
VERY GOOD.
MY INSTINCTS WERE CORRECT AFTER ALL.
RUI ARAMIYA...
...AS YOUNG AS HE IS, HE POSSESSES HIS MOTHER'S GENES--AND AN EVEN GREATER LEVEL OF POWER.
HE WILL BECOME THE FINAL GATEWAY TO THE LEY LINES.
THEN WE CAN ACCESS THE AKASHIC RECORDS...THE SECRET HISTORY OF THE UNIVERSE ITSELF...
...AND REWRITE THAT HISTORY TO SUIT OUR OWN ENDS.

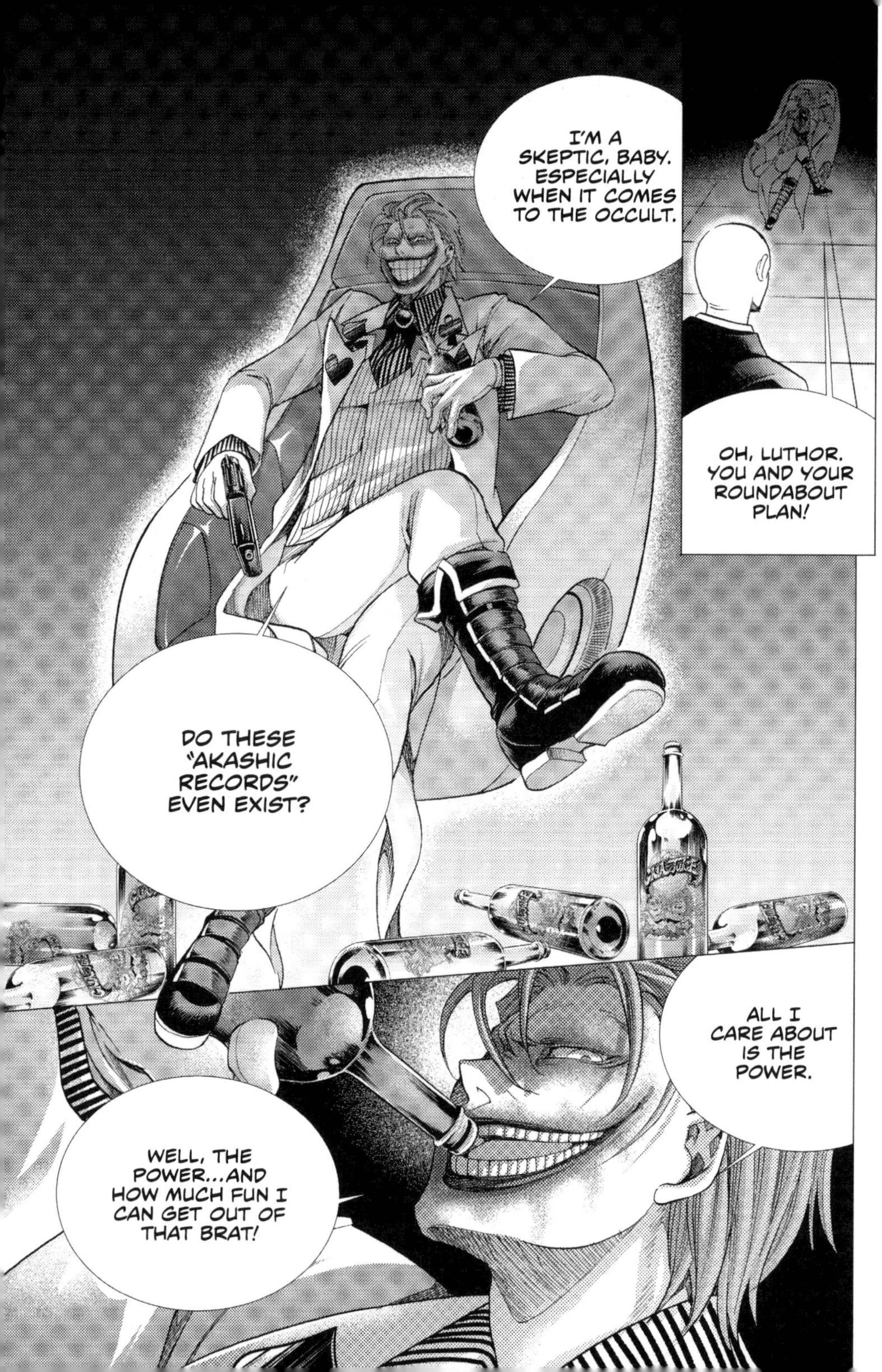
OH, LUTHOR. YOU AND YOUR ROUNDABOUT PLAN!
I'M A SKEPTIC, BABY. ESPECIALLY WHEN IT COMES TO THE OCCULT.
DO THESE "AKASHIC RECORDS" EVEN EXIST?
ALL I CARE ABOUT IS THE POWER.
WELL, THE POWER...AND HOW MUCH FUN I CAN GET OUT OF THAT BRAT!

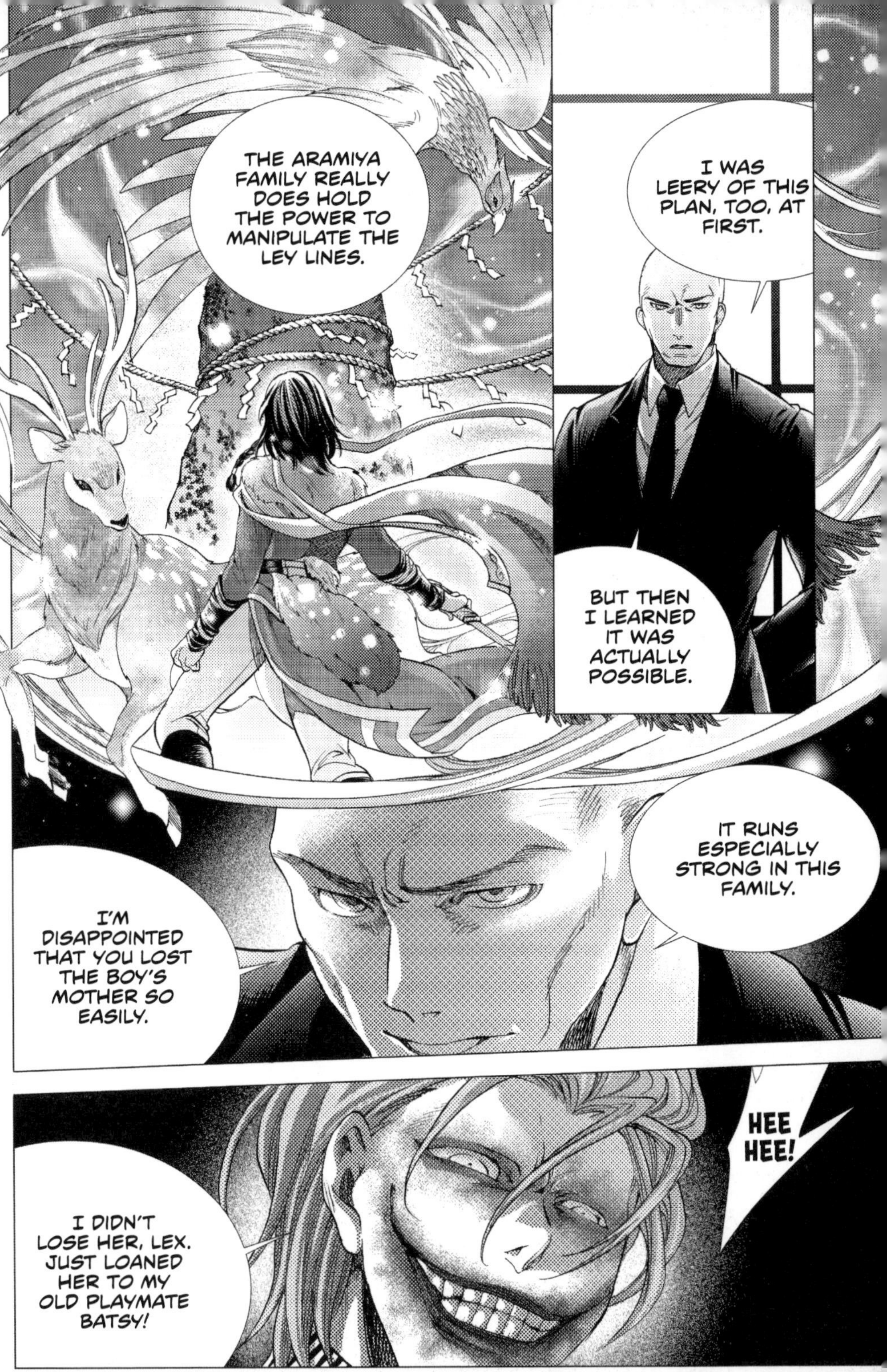
I WAS LEERY OF THIS PLAN, TOO, AT FIRST.
BUT THEN I LEARNED IT WAS ACTUALLY POSSIBLE.
THE ARAMIYA FAMILY REALLY DOES HOLD THE POWER TO MANIPULATE THE LEY LINES.
IT RUNS ESPECIALLY STRONG IN THIS FAMILY.
I'M DISAPPOINTED THAT YOU LOST THE BOY'S MOTHER SO EASILY.
HEE HEE!
I DIDN'T LOSE HER, LEX. JUST LOANED HER TO MY OLD PLAYMATE BATSY!

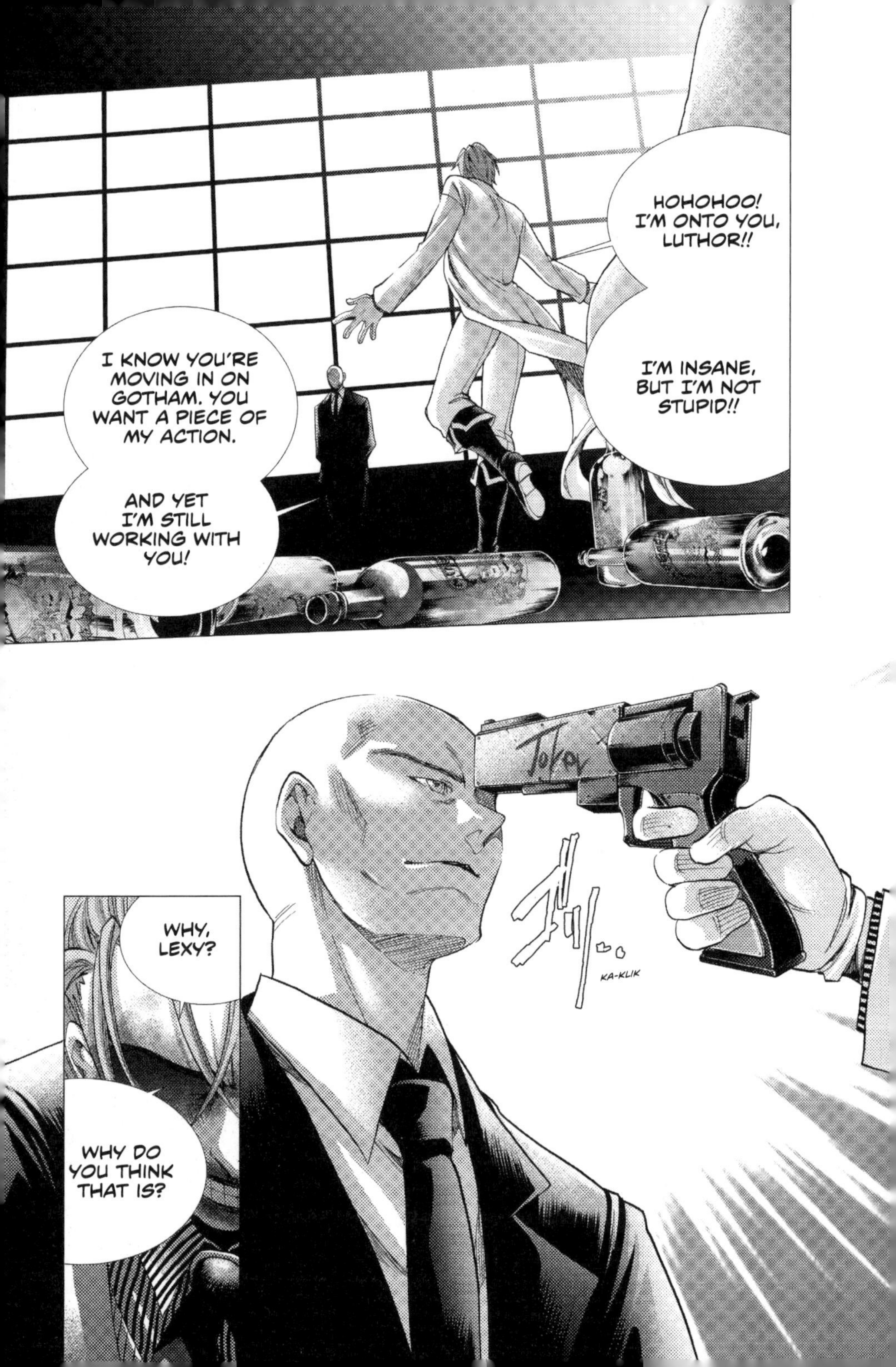
HOHOHOO! I'M ONTO YOU, LUTHOR!!
I'M INSANE, BUT I'M NOT STUPID!!
I KNOW YOU'RE MOVING IN ON GOTHAM. YOU WANT A PIECE OF MY ACTION.
AND YET I'M STILL WORKING WITH YOU!
KA-KLIK
WHY, LEXY?
WHY DO YOU THINK THAT IS?

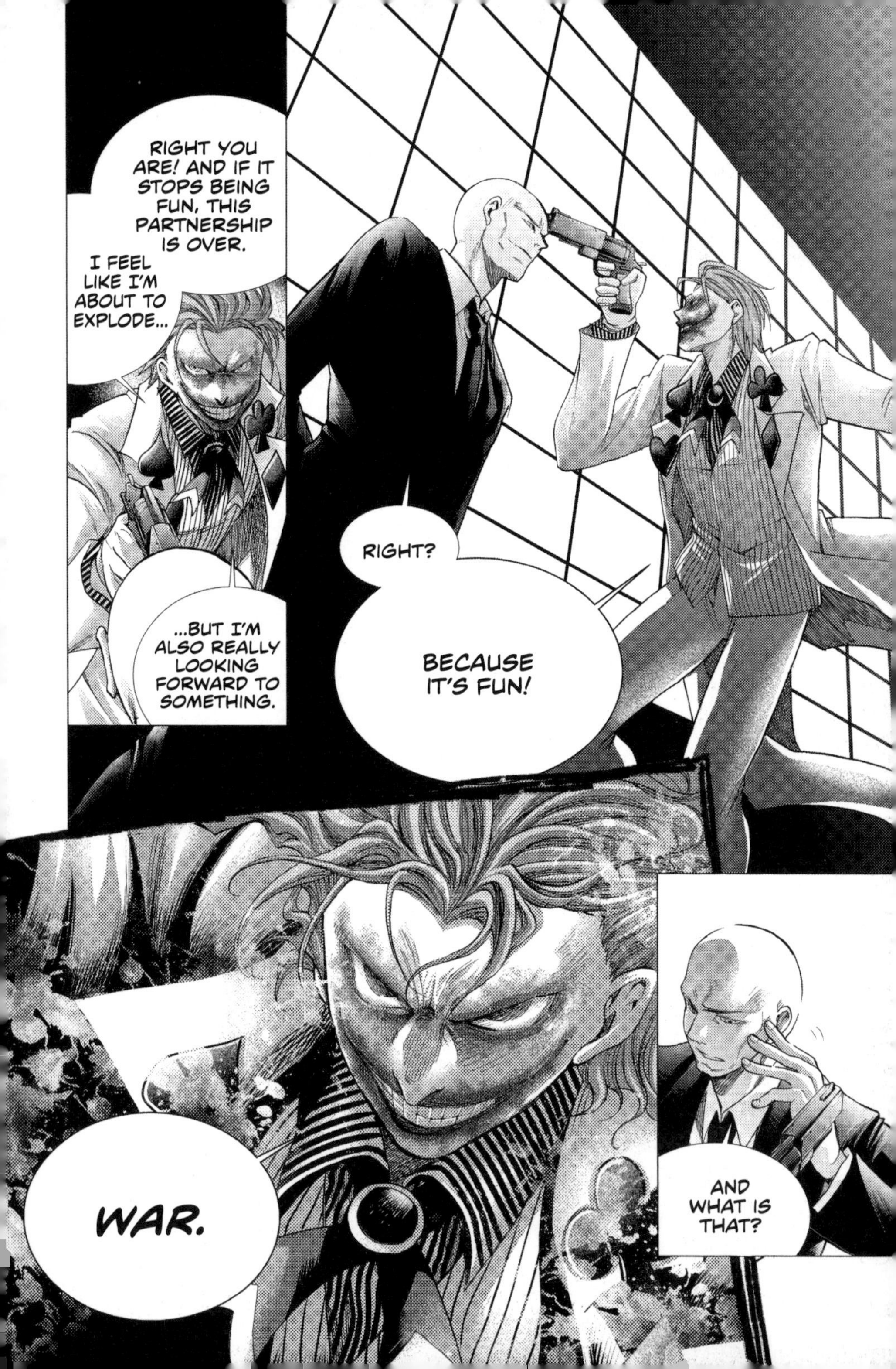
RIGHT?
BECAUSE IT'S FUN!
RIGHT YOU ARE! AND IF IT STOPS BEING FUN, THIS PARTNERSHIP IS OVER.
I FEEL LIKE I'M ABOUT TO EXPLODE...
...BUT I'M ALSO REALLY LOOKING FORWARD TO SOMETHING.
AND WHAT IS THAT?
WAR.

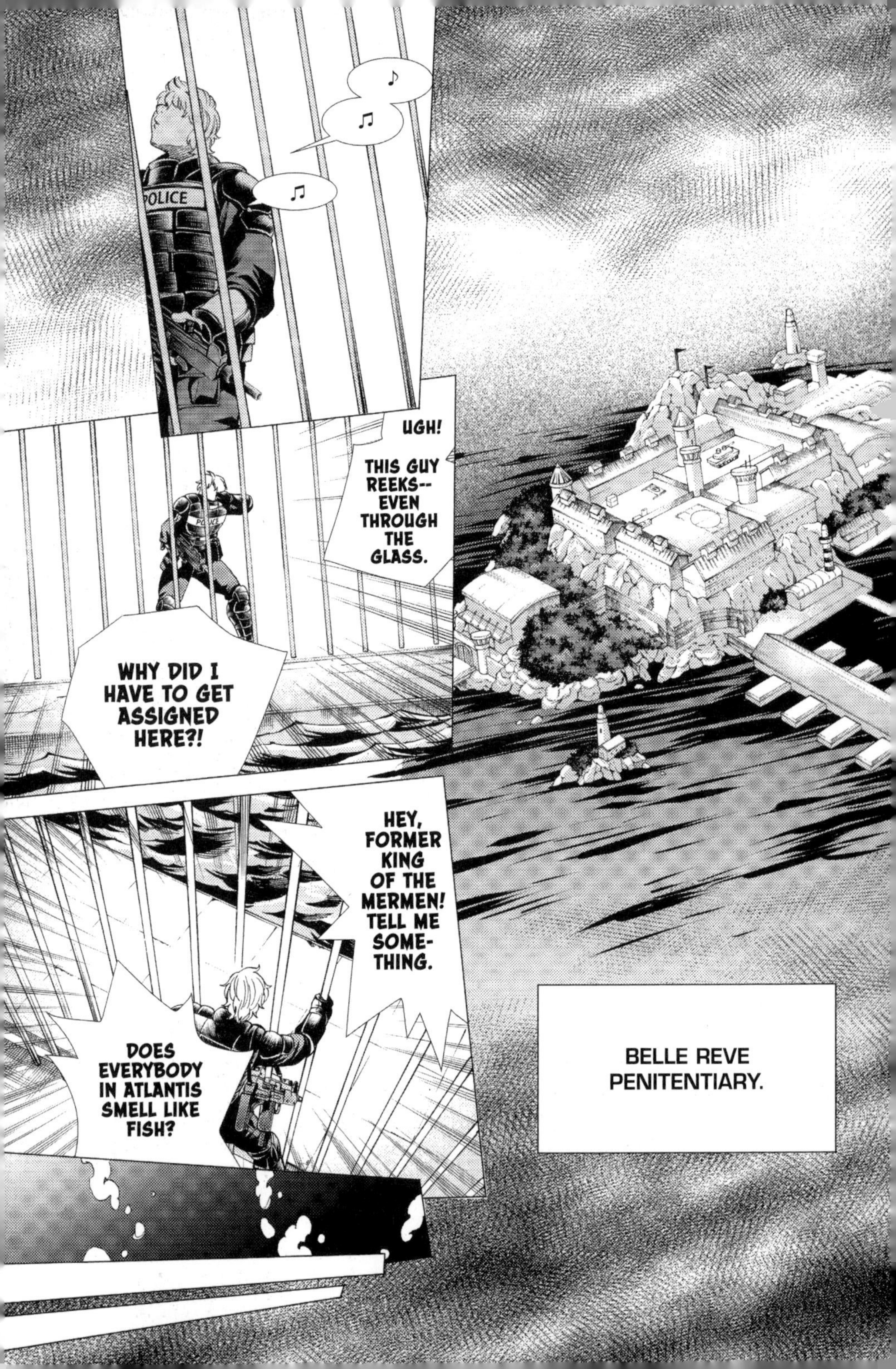
BELLE REVE PENITENTIARY.
♪
♫
♫
UGH!
THIS GUY REEKS--EVEN THROUGH THE GLASS.
WHY DID I HAVE TO GET ASSIGNED HERE?!
HEY, FORMER KING OF THE MERMEN! TELL ME SOME-THING.
DOES EVERYBODY IN ATLANTIS SMELL LIKE FISH?

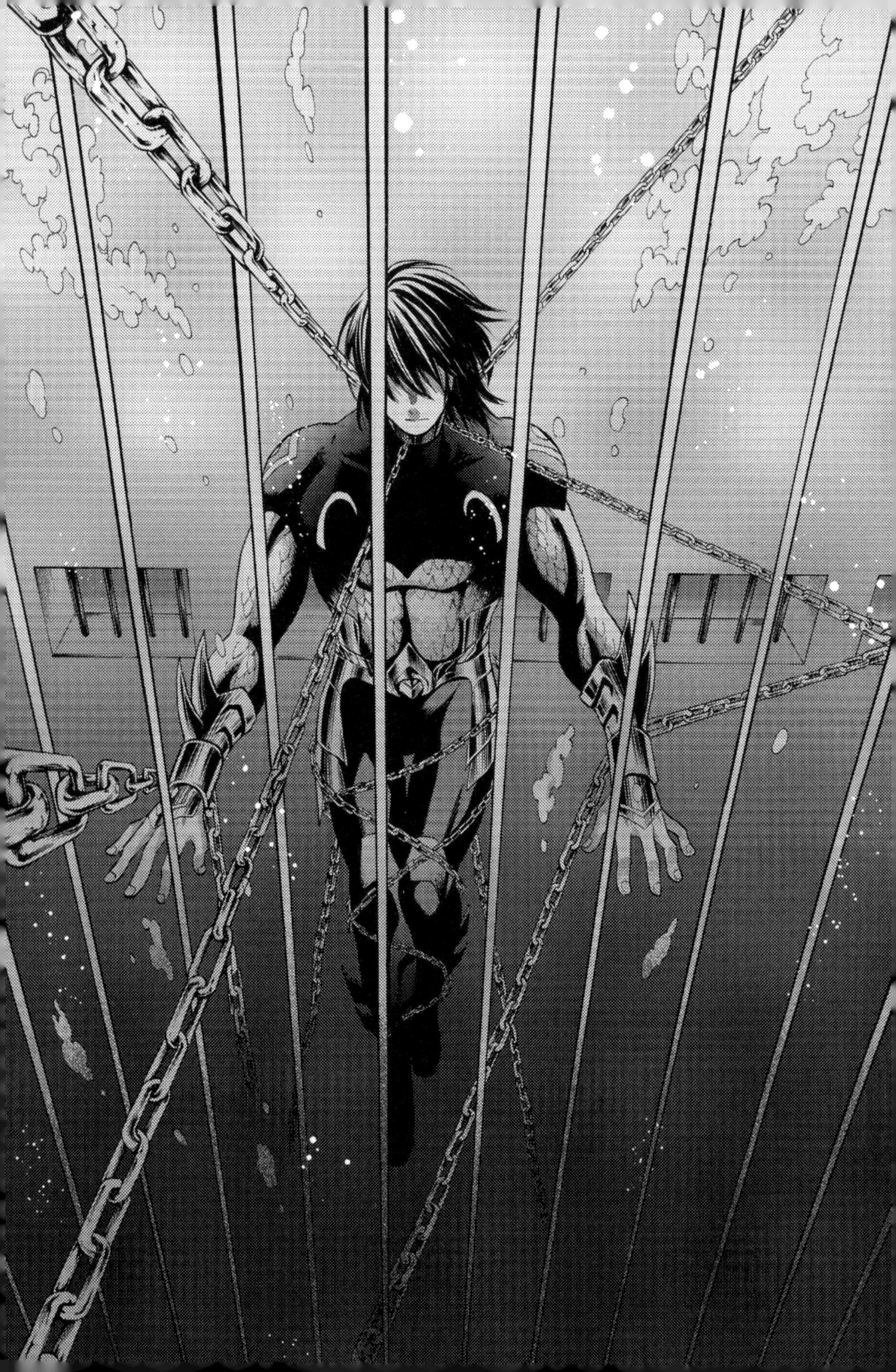

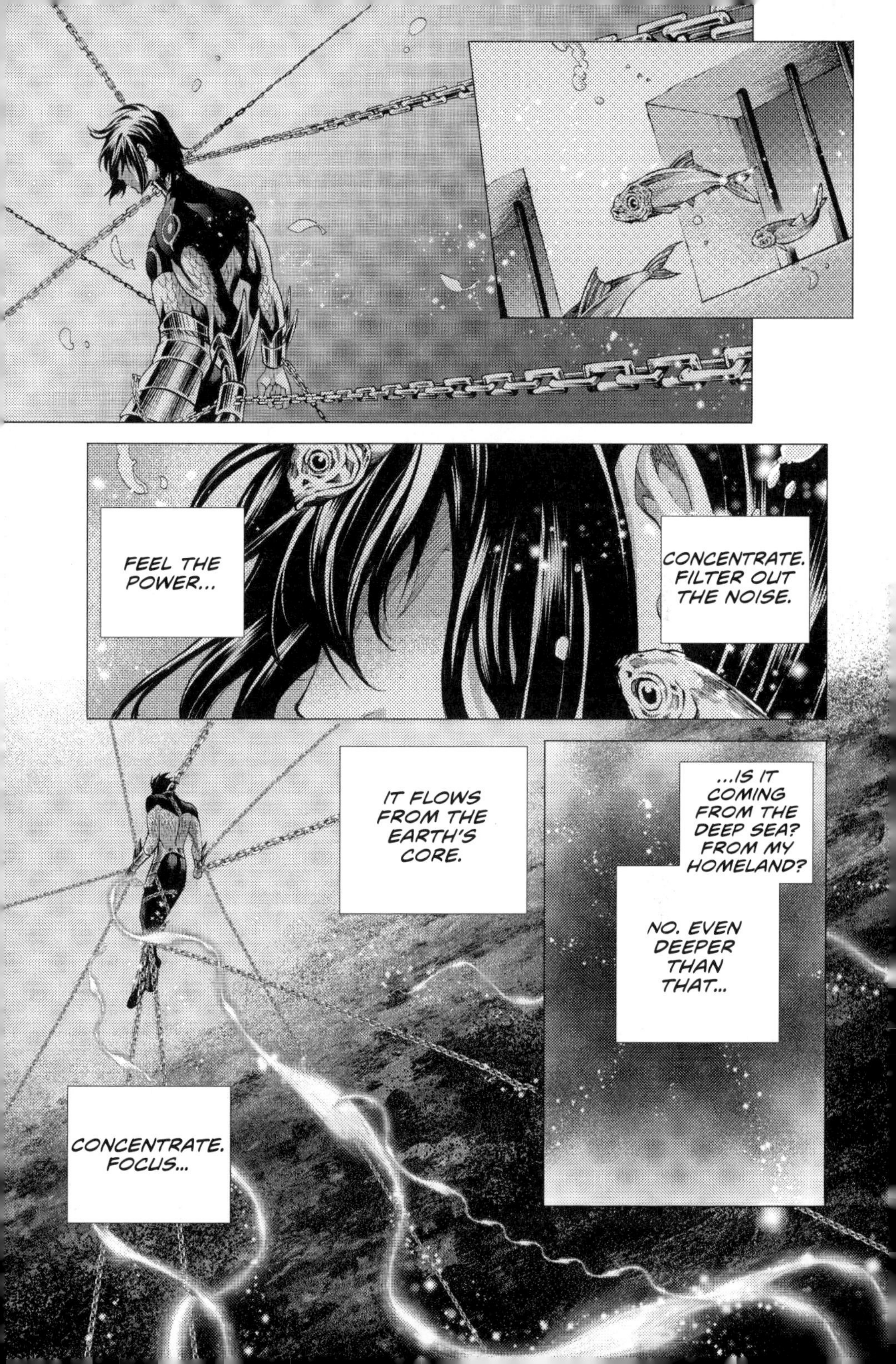
CONCENTRATE. FILTER OUT THE NOISE.
FEEL THE POWER...
...IS IT COMING FROM THE DEEP SEA? FROM MY HOMELAND?
NO. EVEN DEEPER THAN THAT...
IT FLOWS FROM THE EARTH'S CORE.
CONCENTRATE. FOCUS...

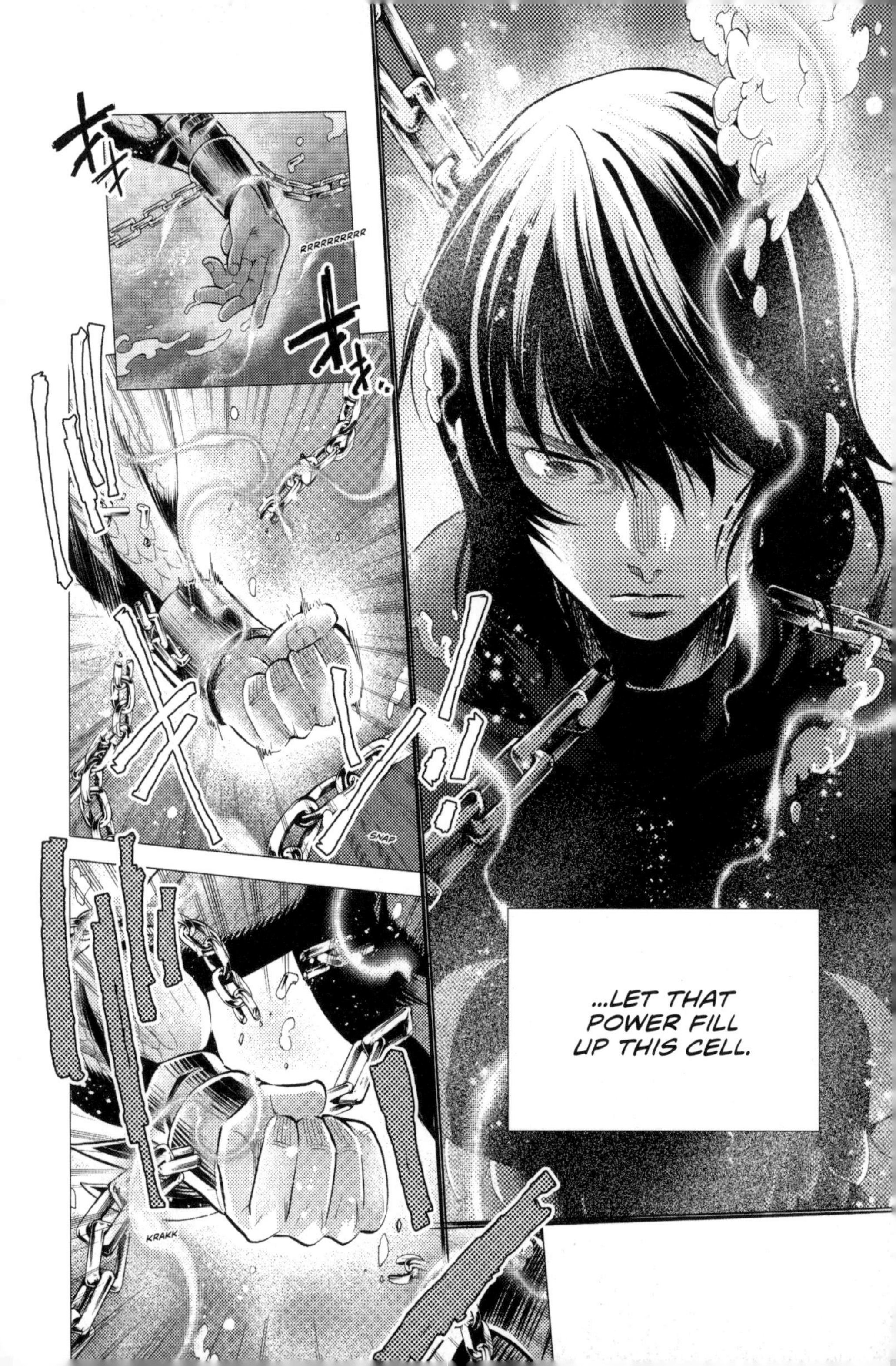
...LET THAT POWER FILL UP THIS CELL.
RRRRRRRRRR
SNAP
KRAKK

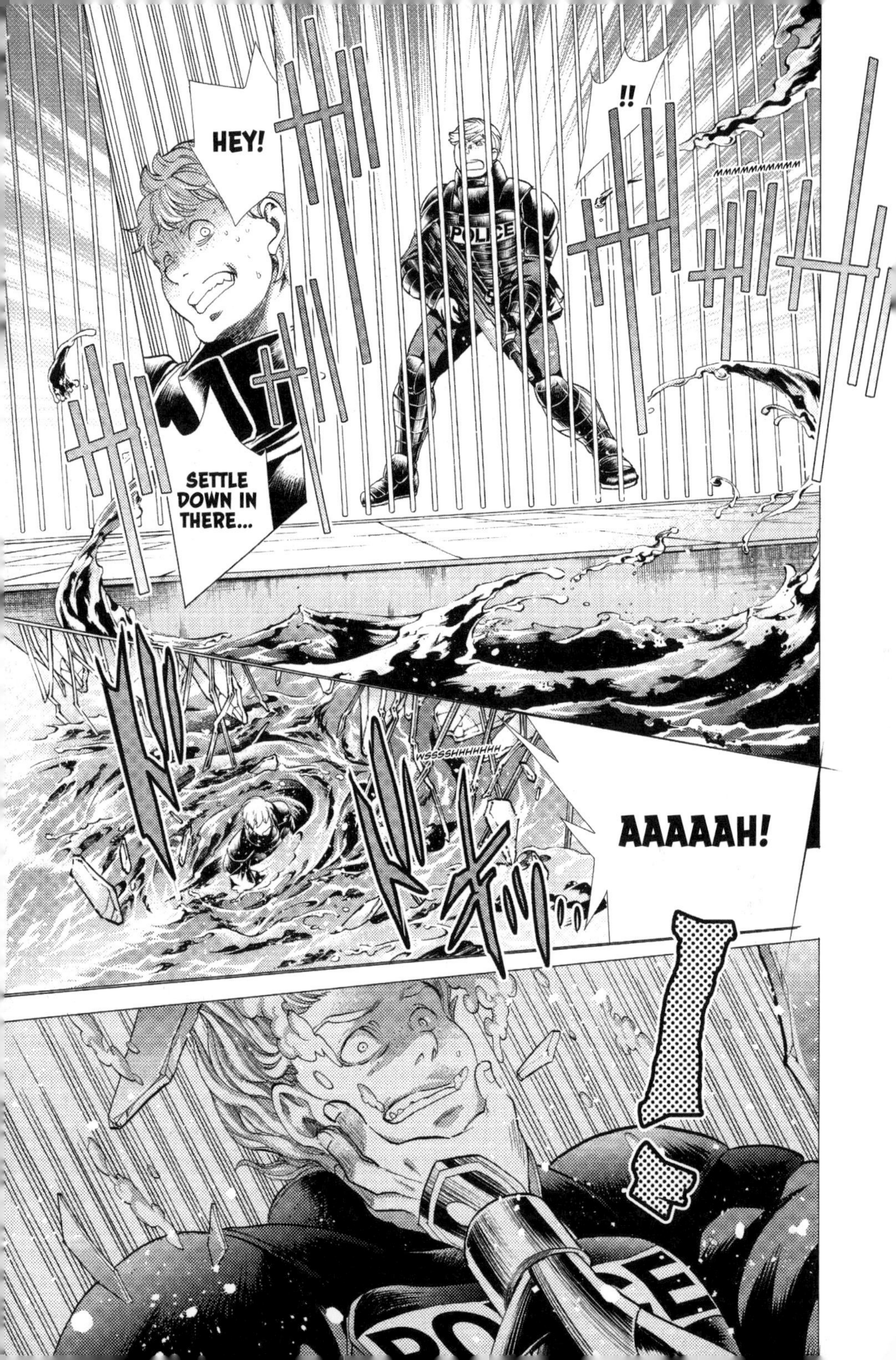
!!
HEY!
SETTLE DOWN IN THERE...
AAAAAH!

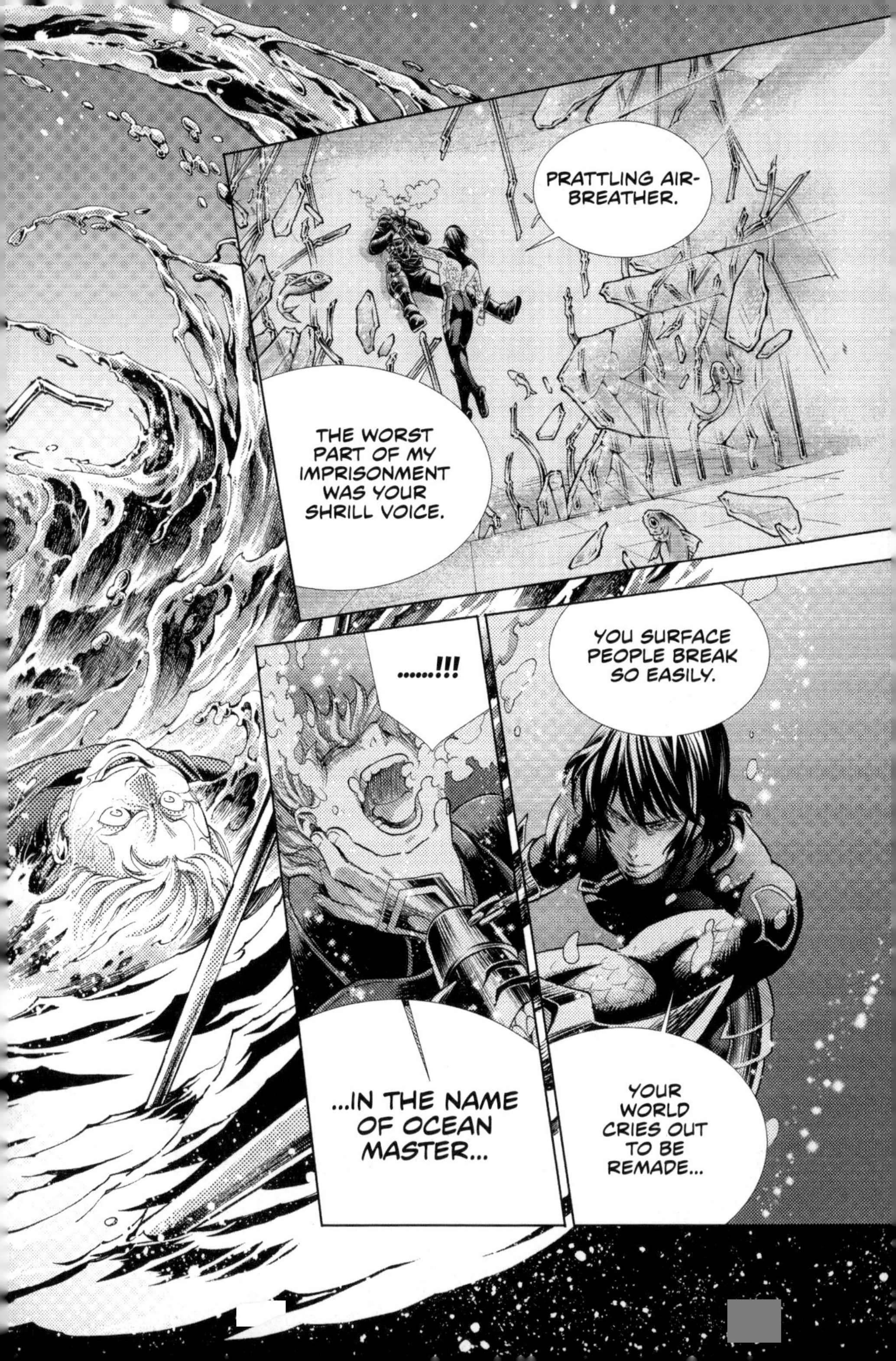
PRATTLING AIR-BREATHER.
THE WORST PART OF MY IMPRISONMENT WAS YOUR SHRILL VOICE.
YOU SURFACE PEOPLE BREAK SO EASILY.
YOUR WORLD CRIES OUT TO BE REMADE...
......!!!
...IN THE NAME OF OCEAN MASTER...

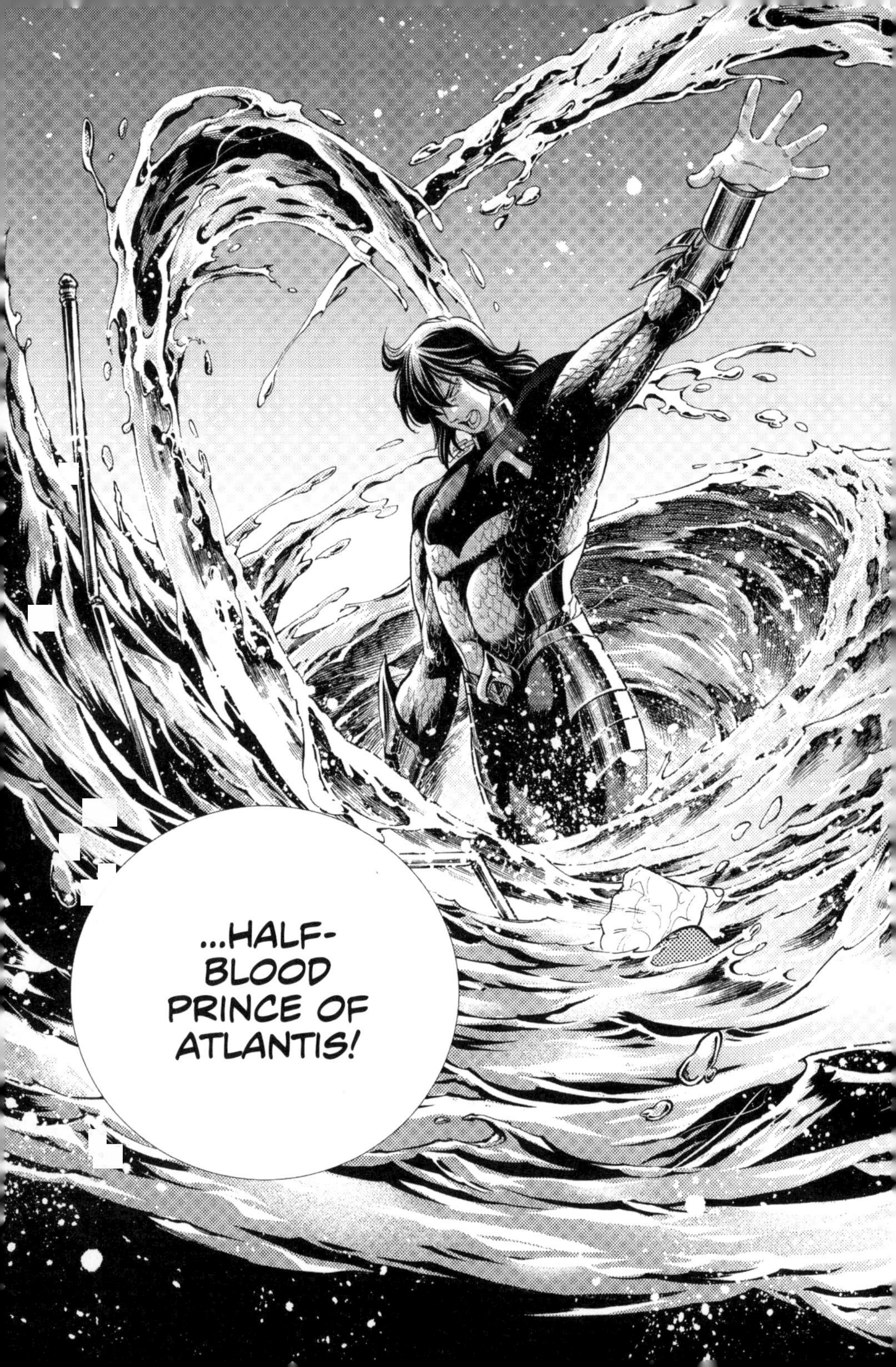
...HALF-BLOOD PRINCE OF ATLANTIS!

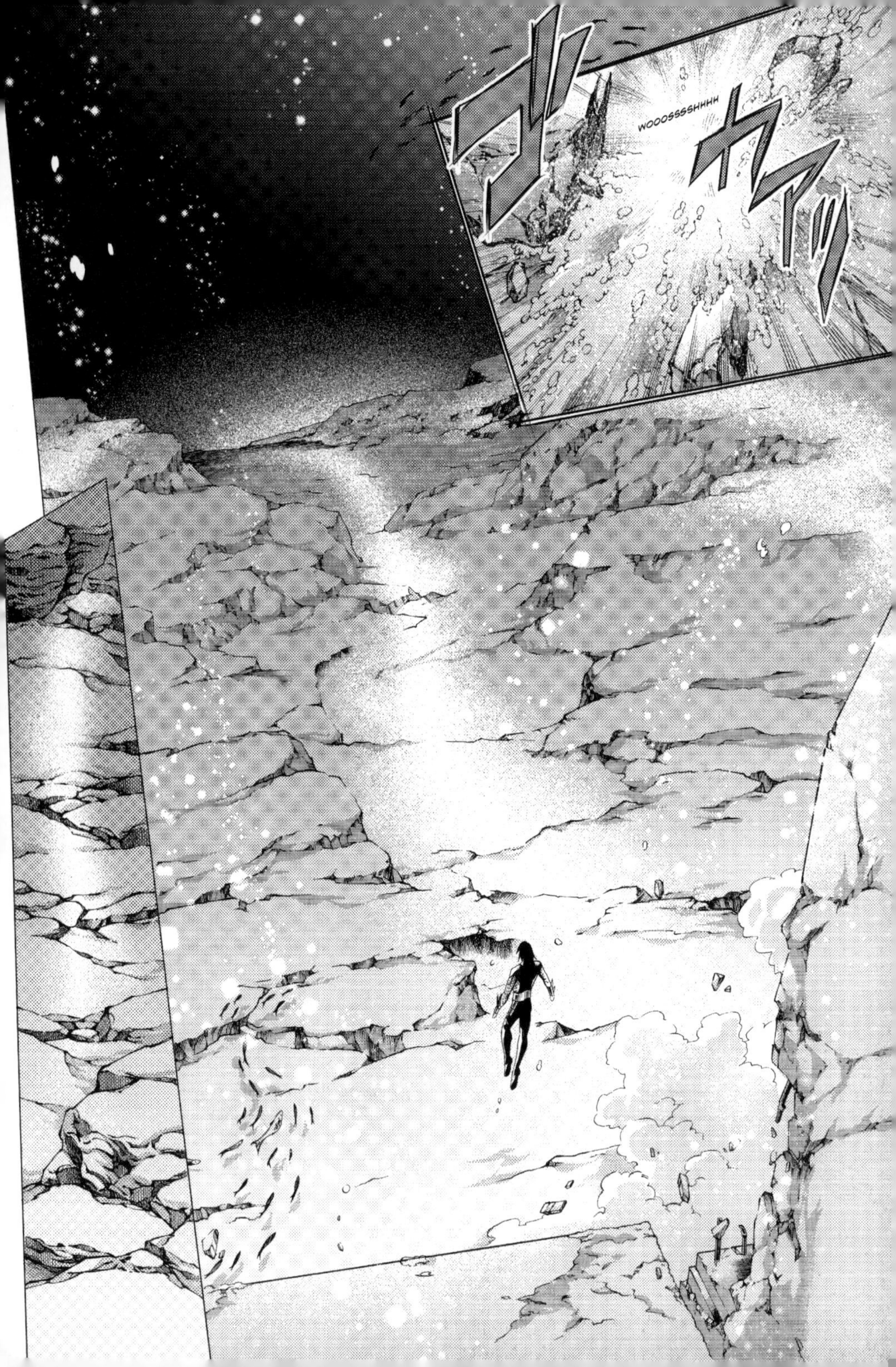
WOOOSSSSHHHH

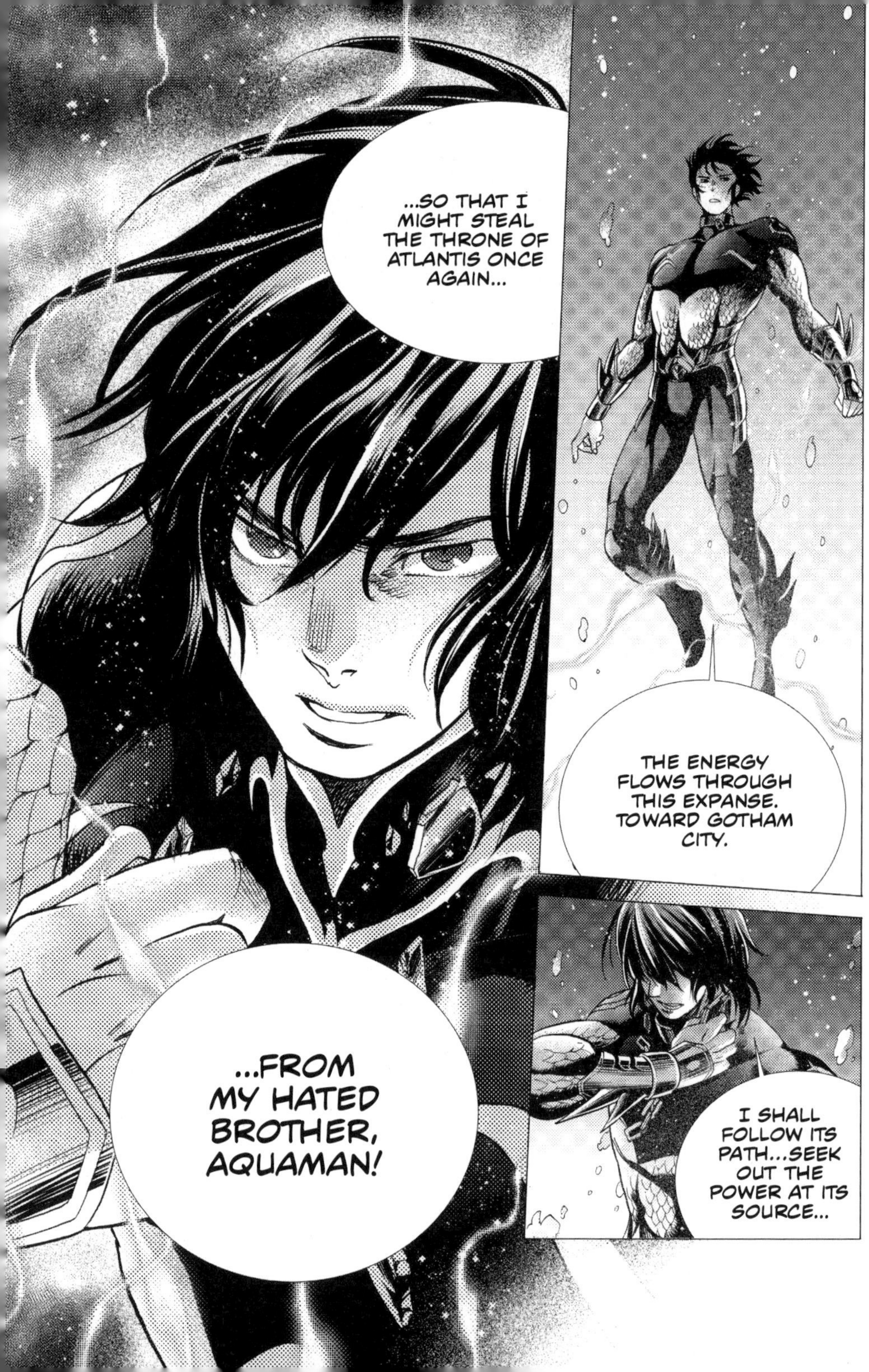
THE ENERGY FLOWS THROUGH THIS EXPANSE. TOWARD GOTHAM CITY.
I SHALL FOLLOW ITS PATH...SEEK OUT THE POWER AT ITS SOURCE...
...SO THAT I MIGHT STEAL THE THRONE OF ATLANTIS ONCE AGAIN...
...FROM MY HATED BROTHER, AQUAMAN!

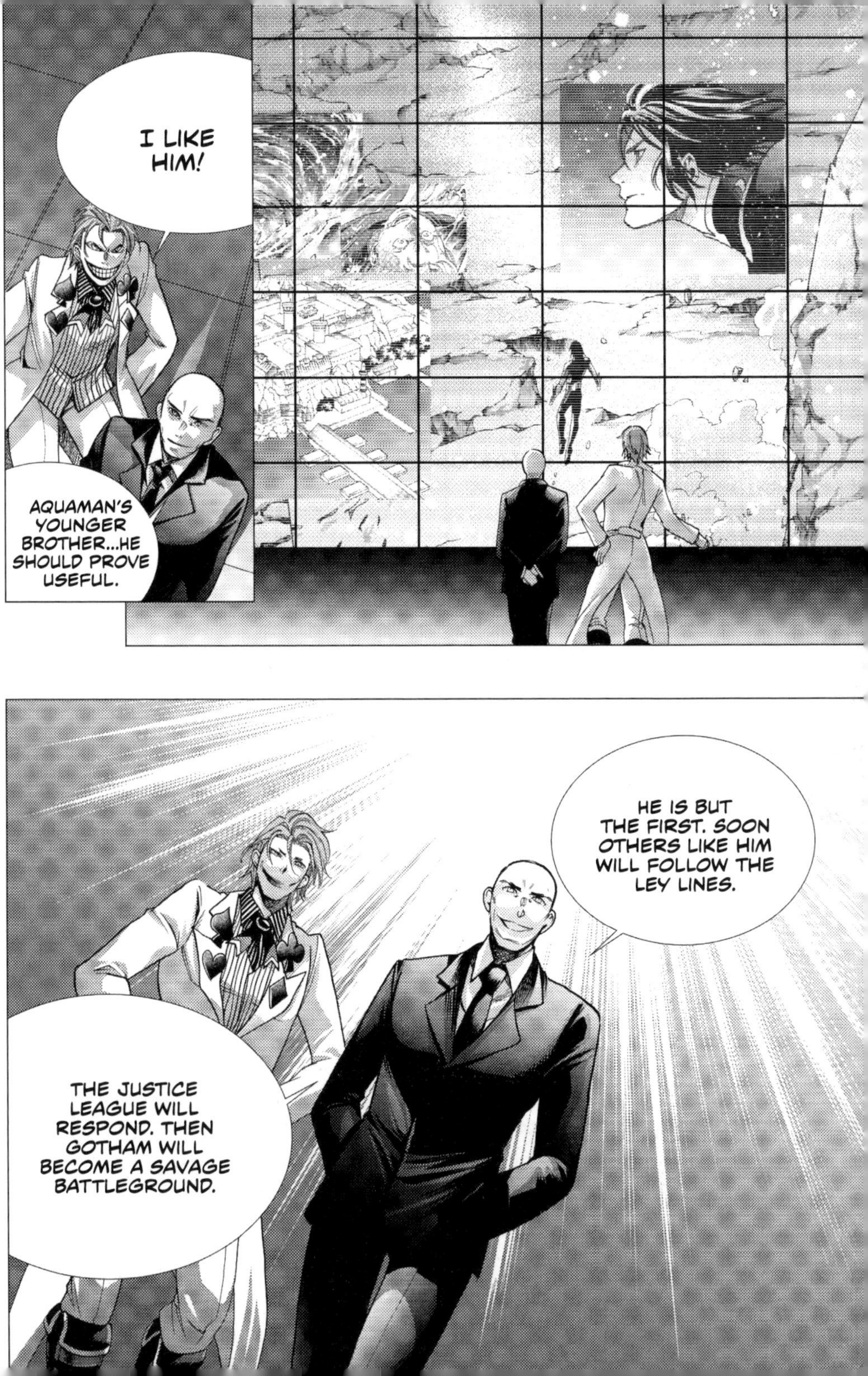
I LIKE HIM!
AQUAMAN'S YOUNGER BROTHER...HE SHOULD PROVE USEFUL.
HE IS BUT THE FIRST. SOON OTHERS LIKE HIM WILL FOLLOW THE LEY LINES.
THE JUSTICE LEAGUE WILL RESPOND. THEN GOTHAM WILL BECOME A SAVAGE BATTLEGROUND.

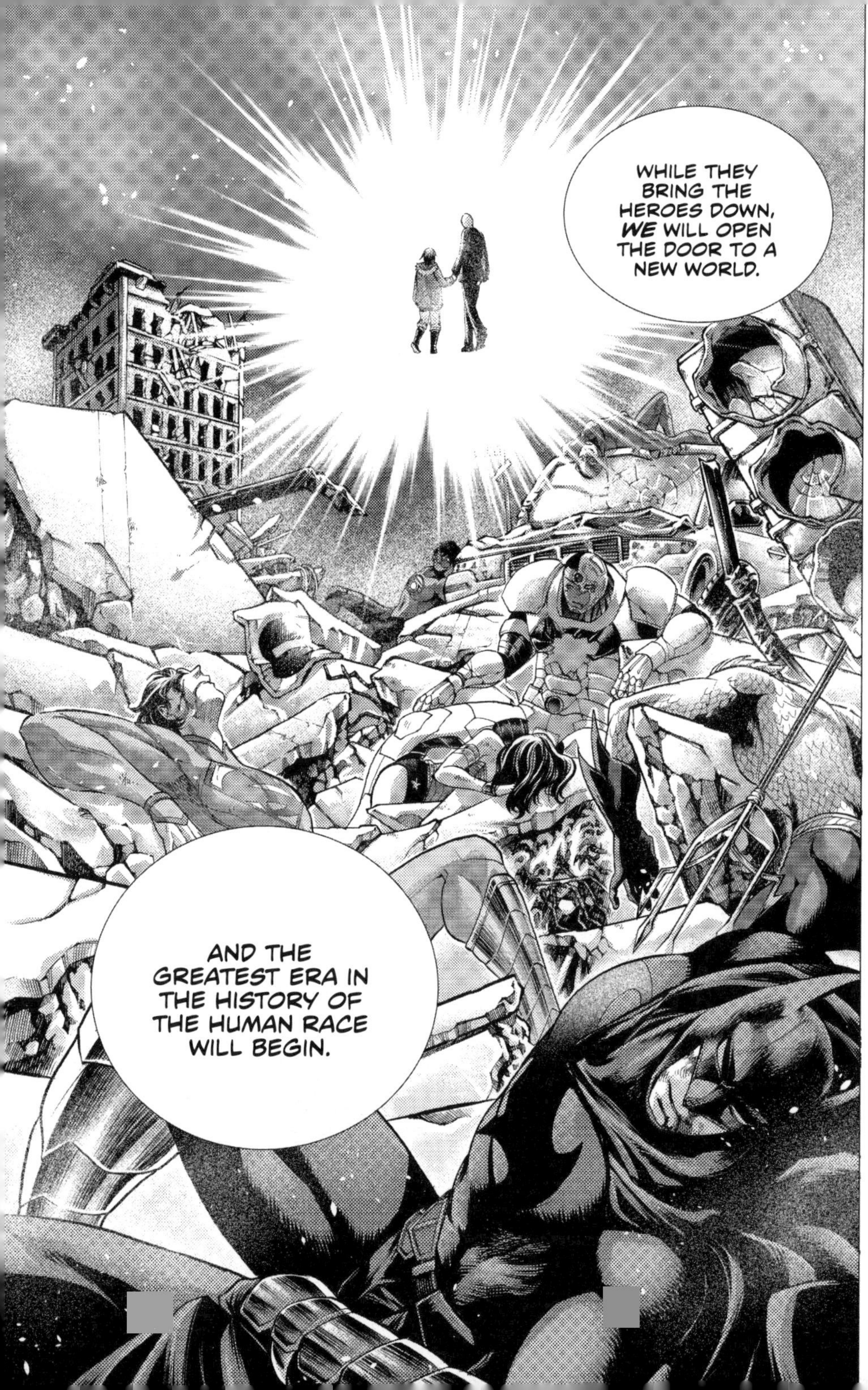
WHILE THEY BRING THE HEROES DOWN, ***WE*** WILL OPEN THE DOOR TO A NEW WORLD.
AND THE GREATEST ERA IN THE HISTORY OF THE HUMAN RACE WILL BEGIN.

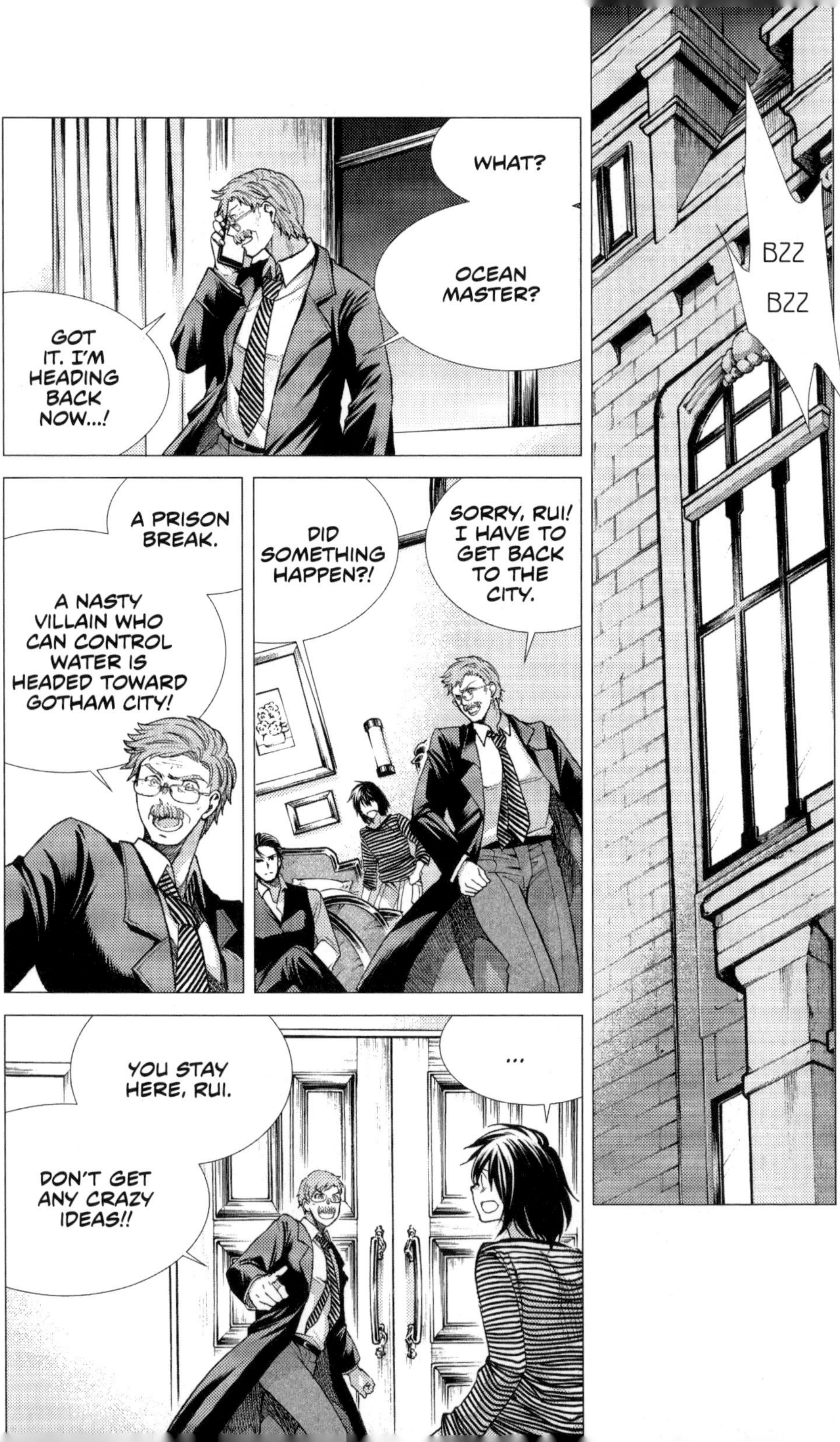
BZZ
BZZ
WHAT?
OCEAN MASTER?
GOT IT. I'M HEADING BACK NOW...!
SORRY, RUI! I HAVE TO GET BACK TO THE CITY.
DID SOMETHING HAPPEN?!
A PRISON BREAK.
A NASTY VILLAIN WHO CAN CONTROL WATER IS HEADED TOWARD GOTHAM CITY!
...
YOU STAY HERE, RUI.
DON'T GET ANY CRAZY IDEAS!!

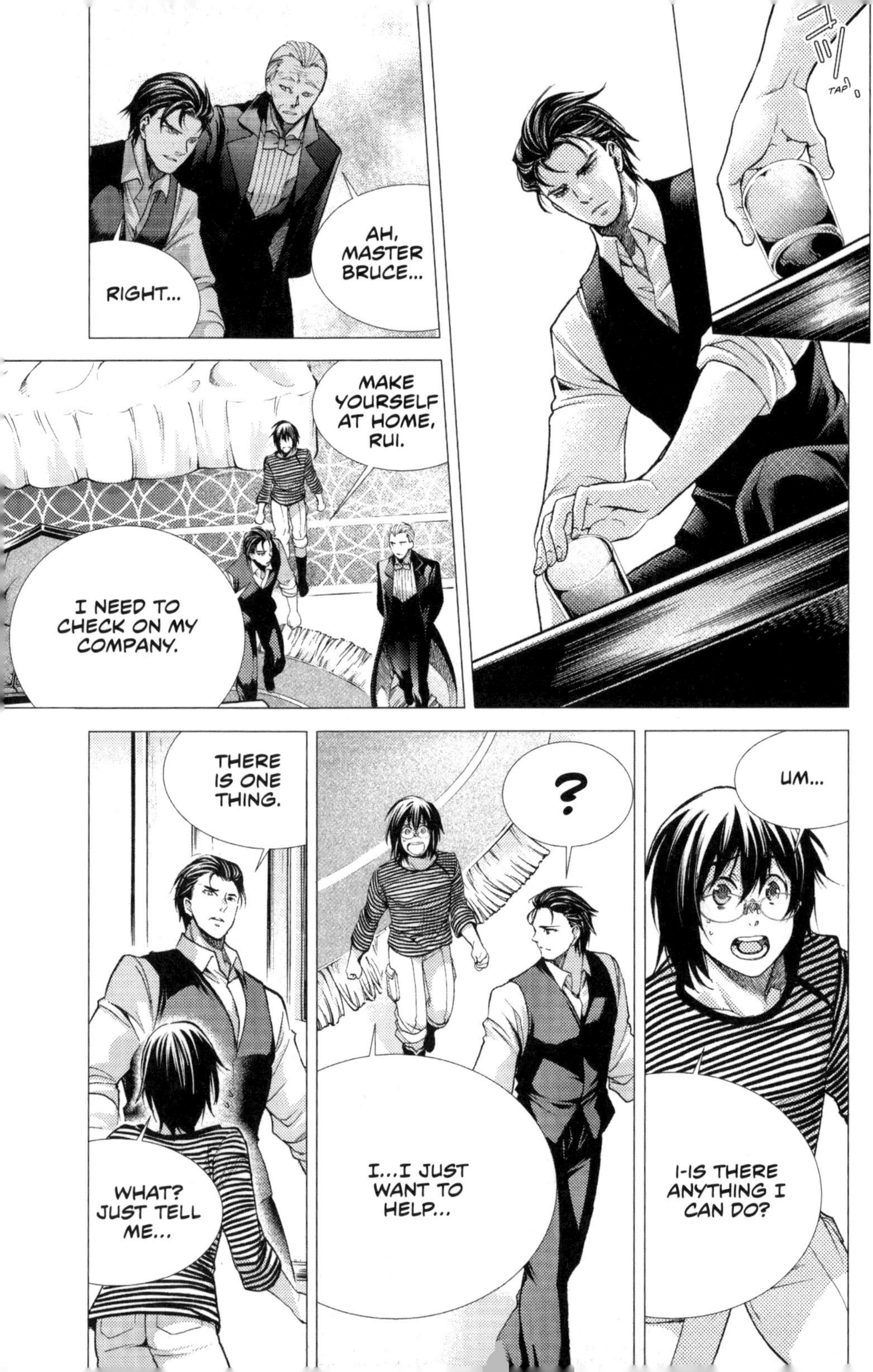
TAP
AH, MASTER BRUCE...
RIGHT...
MAKE YOURSELF AT HOME, RUI.
I NEED TO CHECK ON MY COMPANY.
UM...
I-IS THERE ANYTHING I CAN DO?
?
I...I JUST WANT TO HELP...
THERE IS ONE THING.
WHAT? JUST TELL ME...

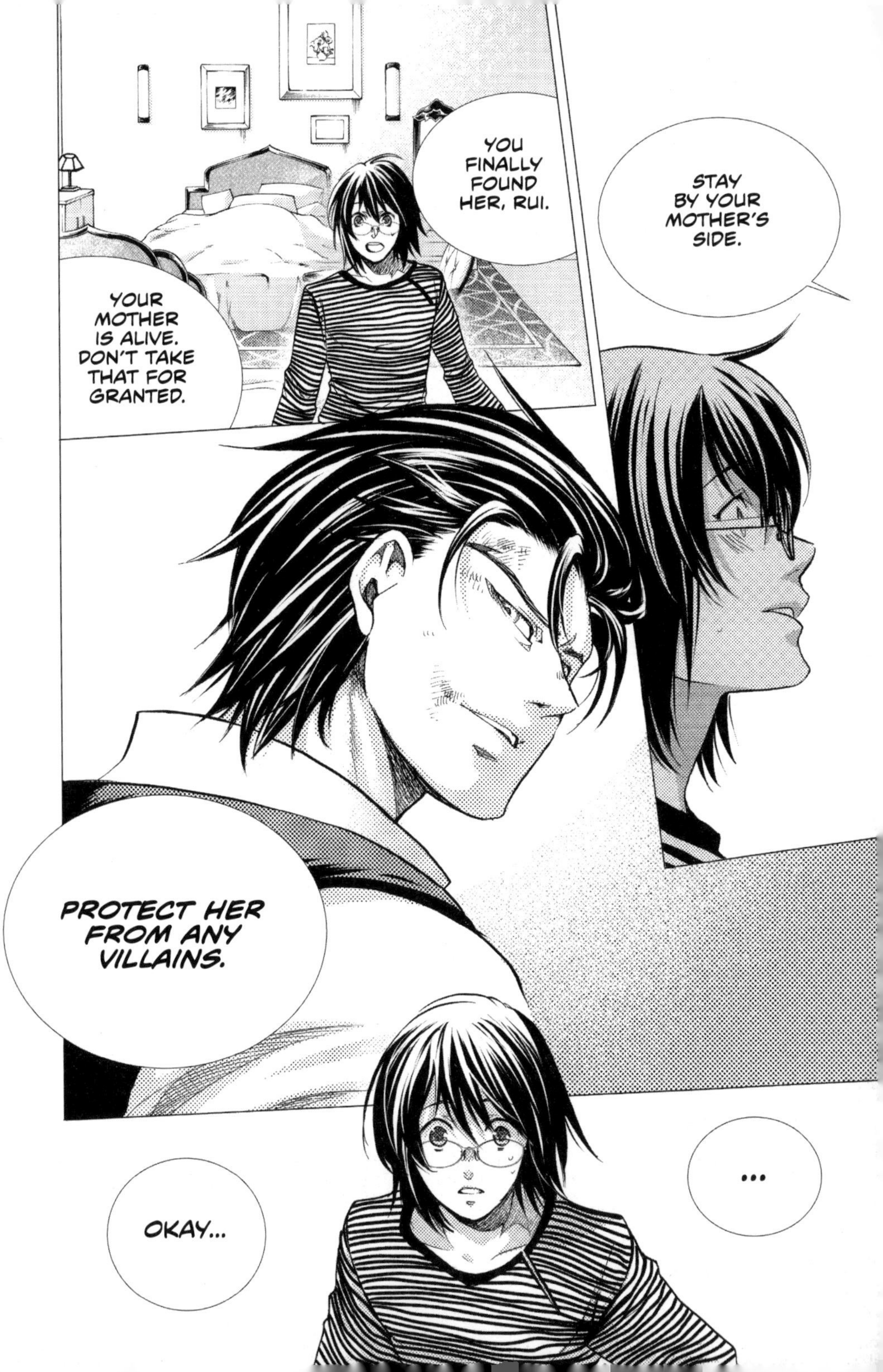
YOU FINALLY FOUND HER, RUI.
YOUR MOTHER IS ALIVE. DON'T TAKE THAT FOR GRANTED.
STAY BY YOUR MOTHER'S SIDE.
PROTECT HER FROM ANY VILLAINS.
...
OKAY...

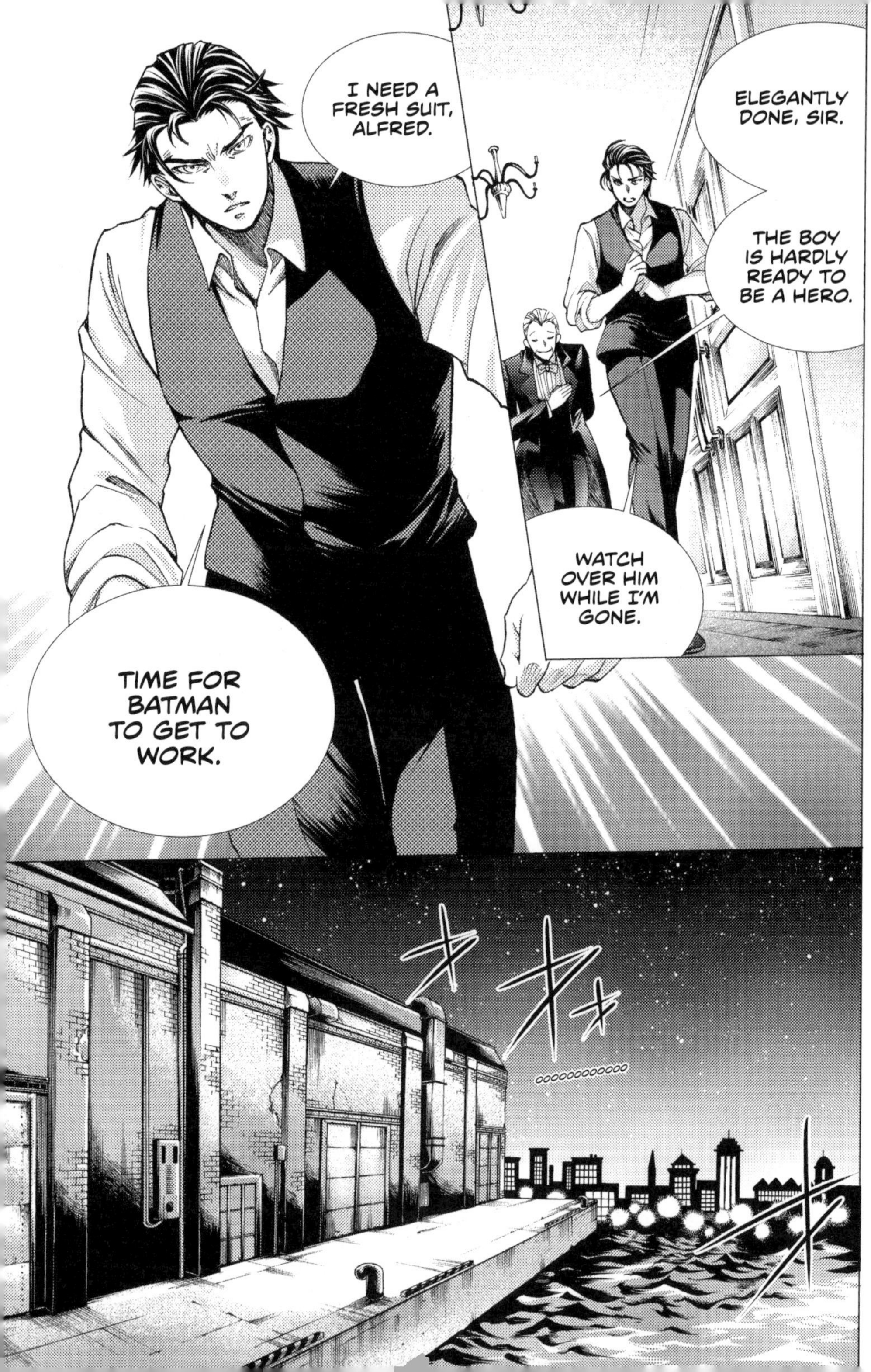
ELEGANTLY DONE, SIR.
THE BOY IS HARDLY READY TO BE A HERO.
WATCH OVER HIM WHILE I'M GONE.
I NEED A FRESH SUIT, ALFRED.
TIME FOR BATMAN TO GET TO WORK.
oooooooooooo

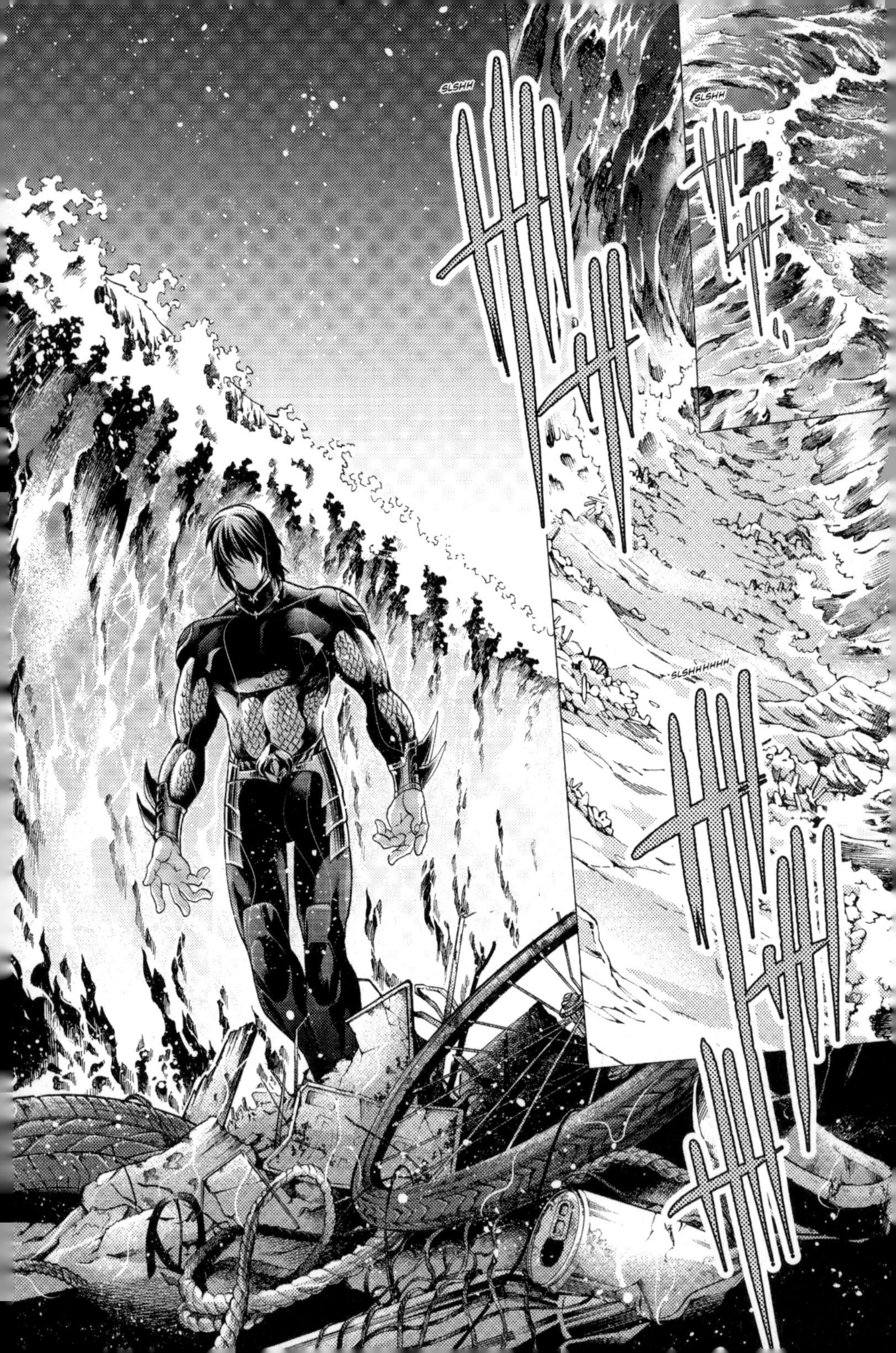
SLSHH
SLSHH
SLSHHHHHH

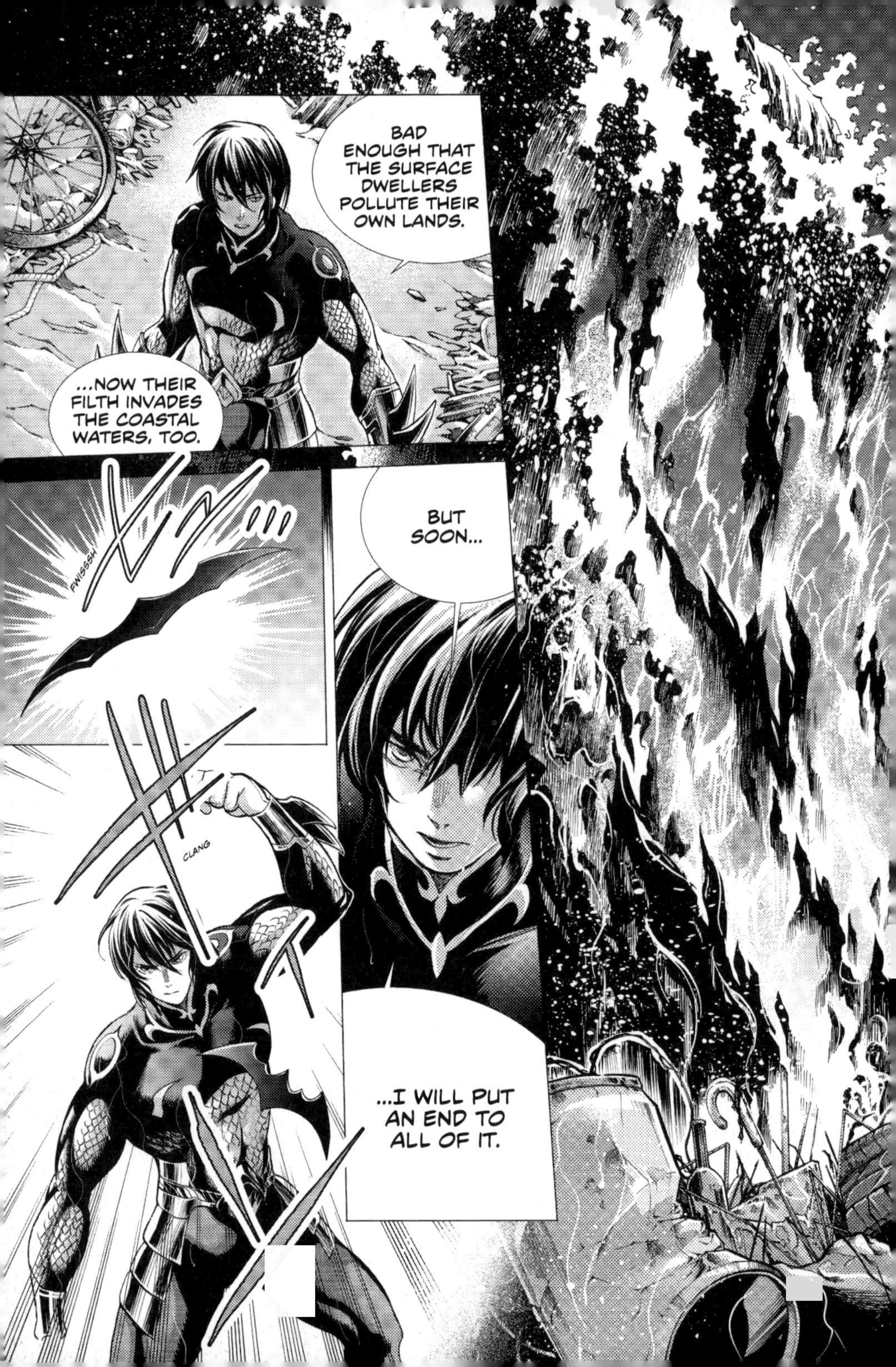
BAD ENOUGH THAT THE SURFACE DWELLERS POLLUTE THEIR OWN LANDS.
...NOW THEIR FILTH INVADES THE COASTAL WATERS, TOO.
BUT SOON...
...I WILL PUT AN END TO ALL OF IT.
FWISSSH
CLANG

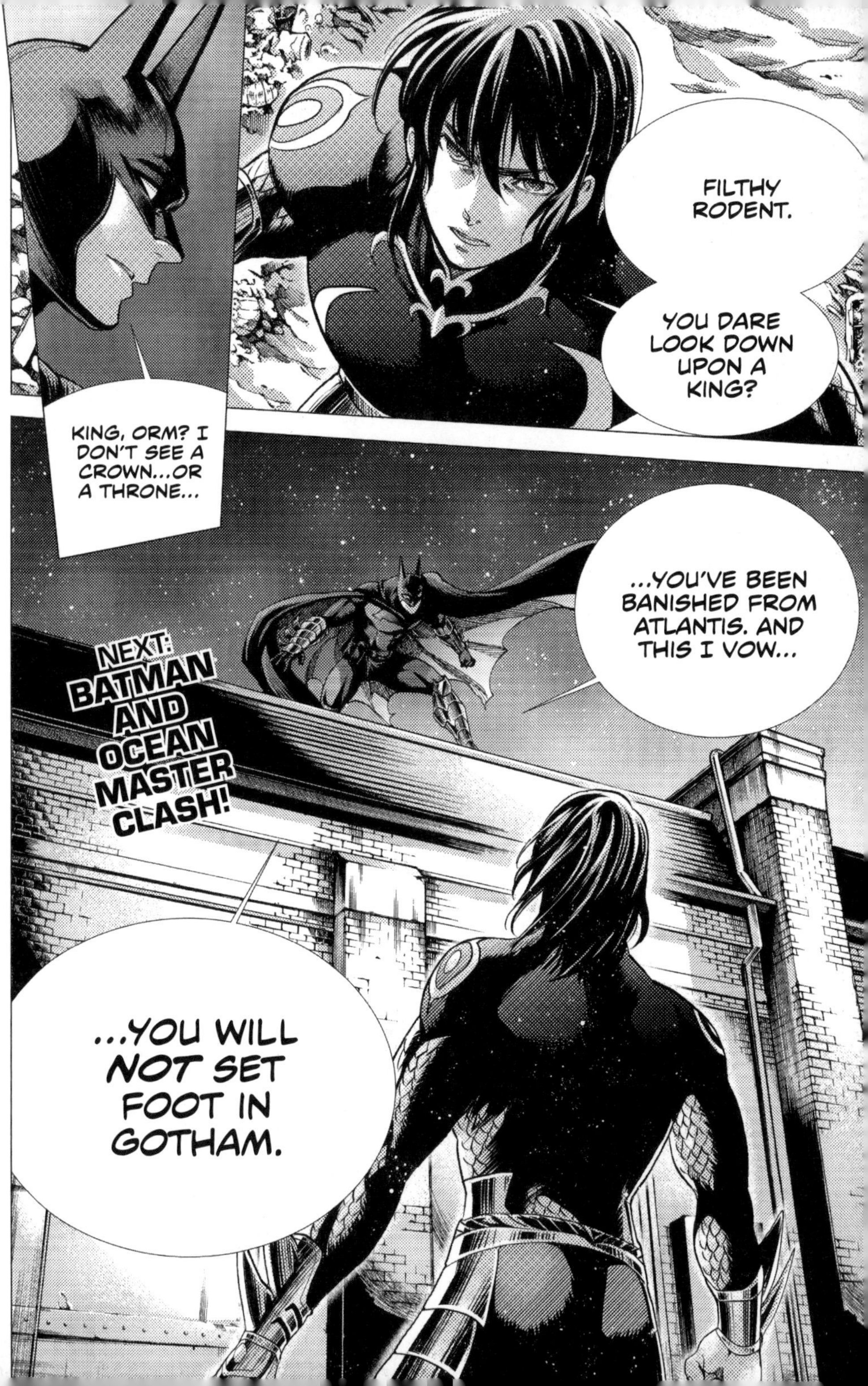
FILTHY RODENT.
YOU DARE LOOK DOWN UPON A KING?
KING, ORM? I DON'T SEE A CROWN...OR A THRONE...
...YOU'VE BEEN BANISHED FROM ATLANTIS. AND THIS I VOW...
...YOU WILL *NOT* SET FOOT IN GOTHAM.
NEXT: BATMAN AND OCEAN MASTER CLASH!

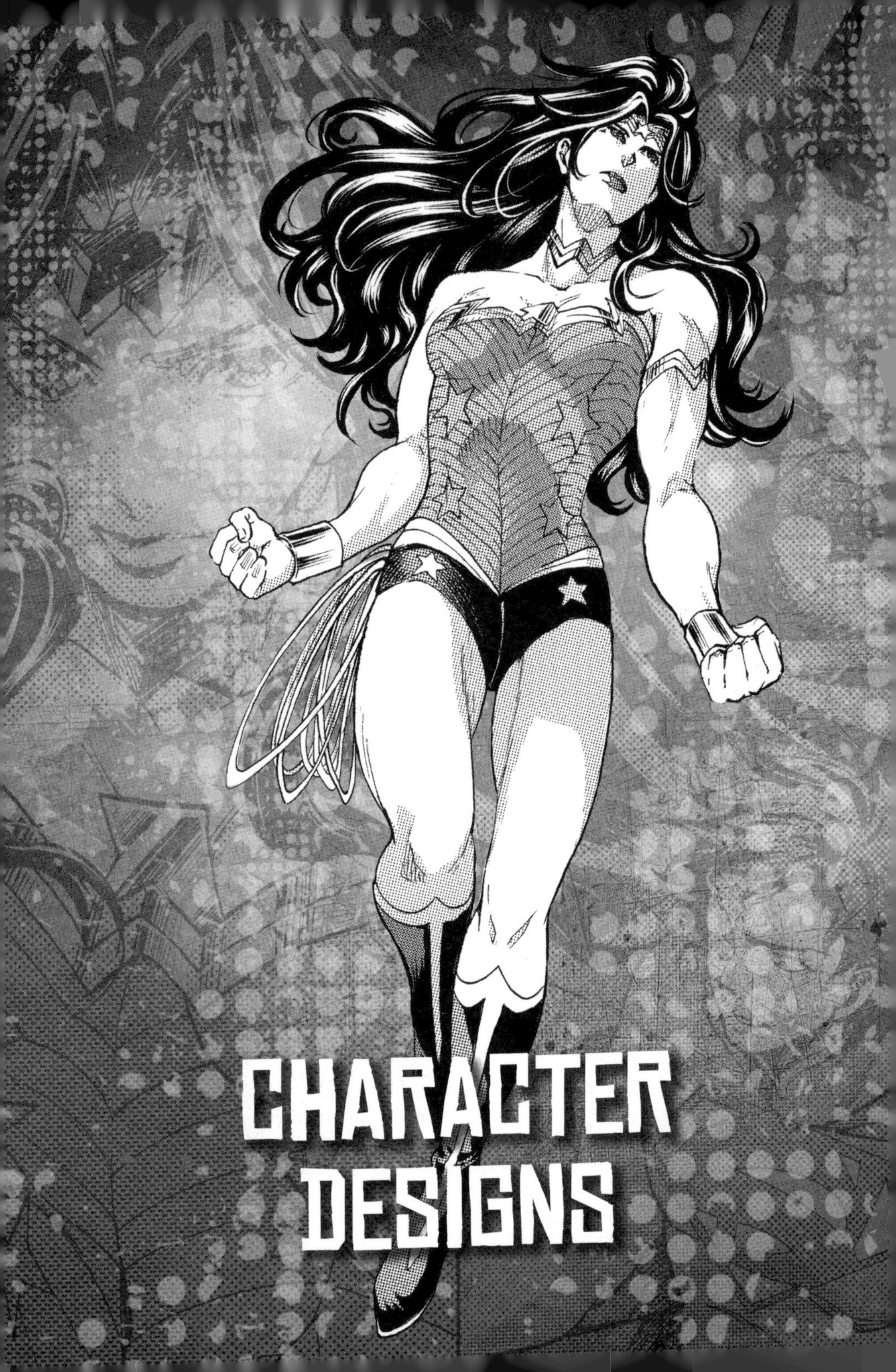

# CHARACTER DESIGNS

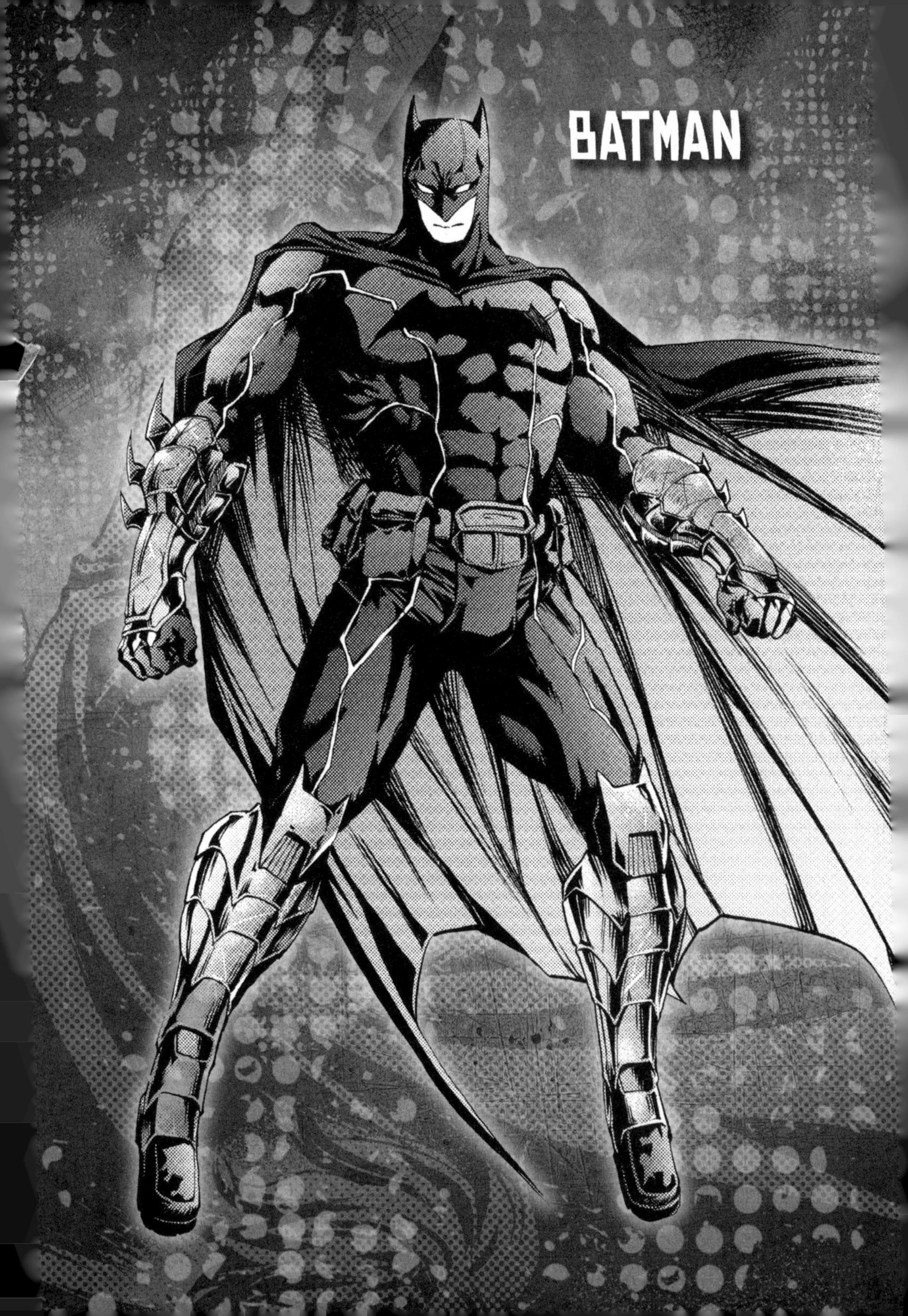
BATMAN

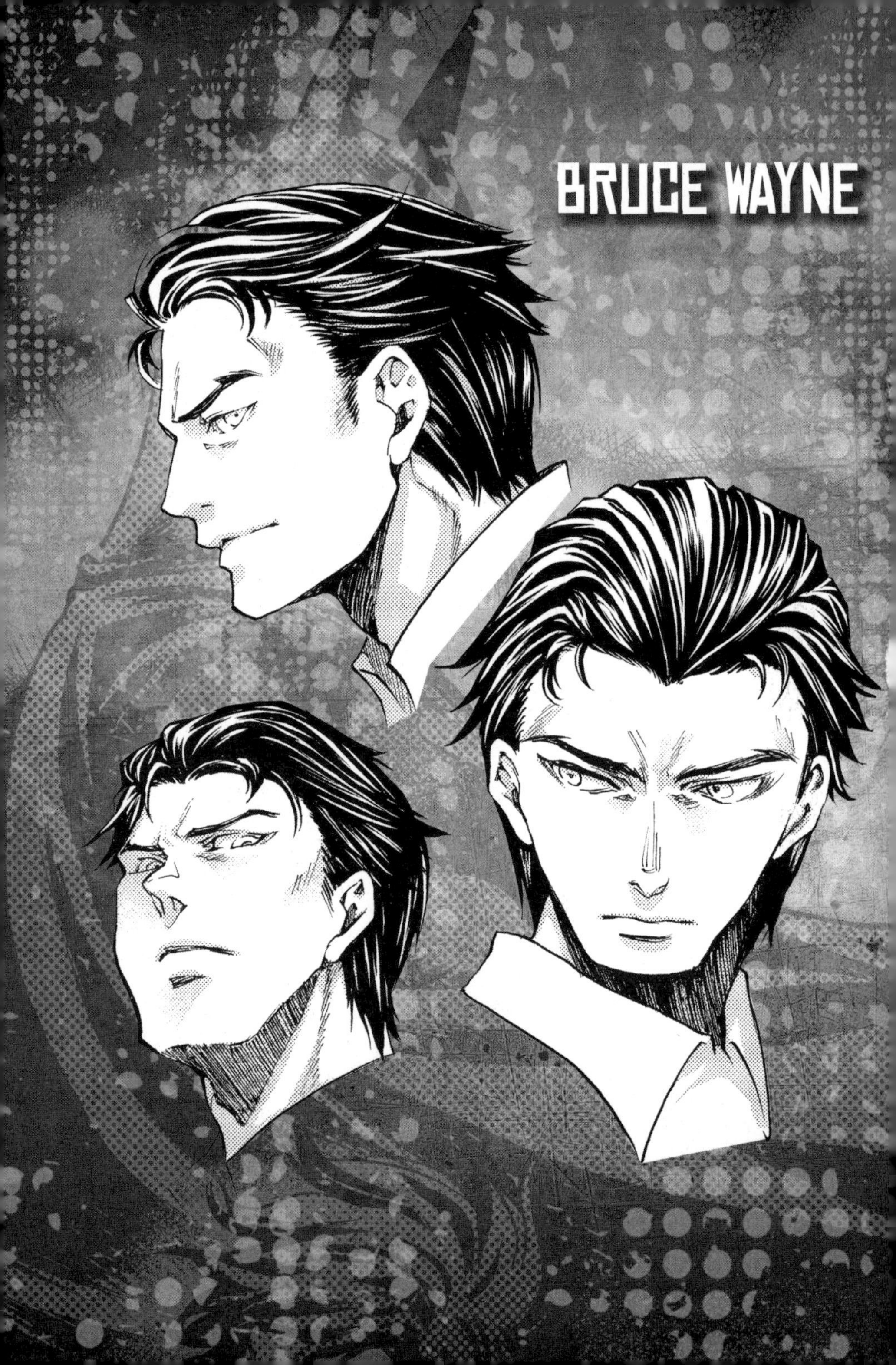
BRUCE WAYNE

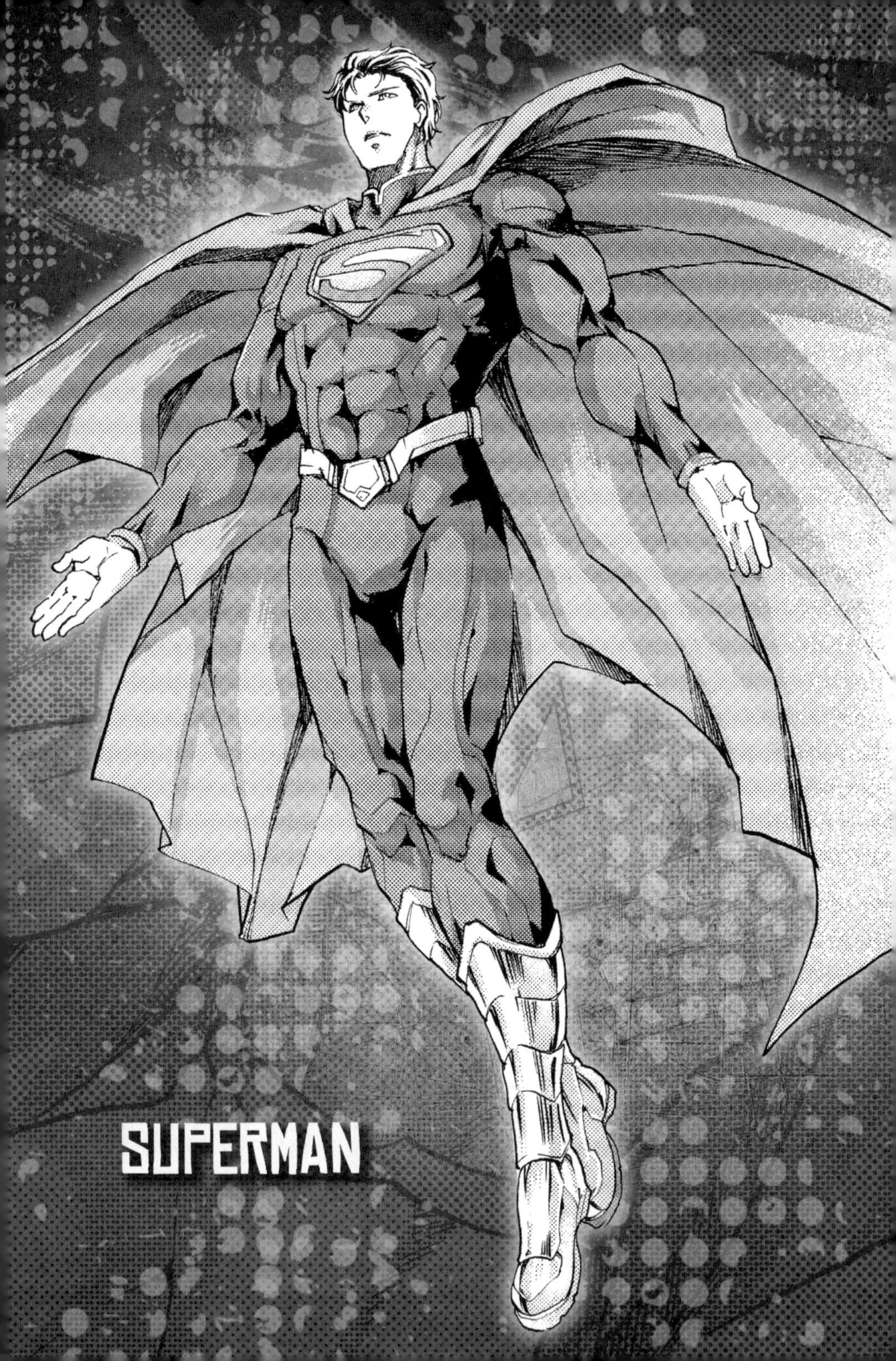
SUPERMAN

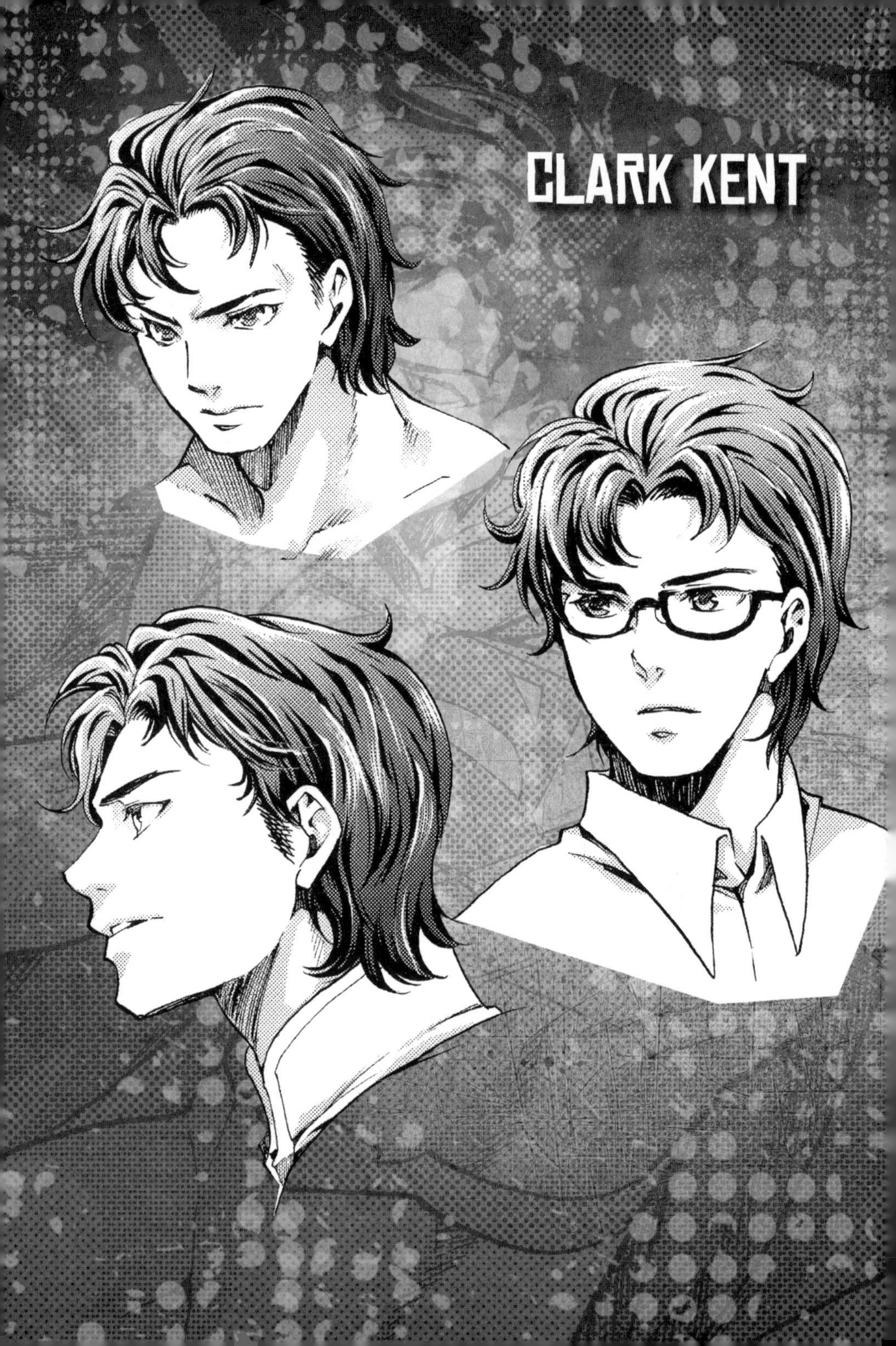
CLARK KENT

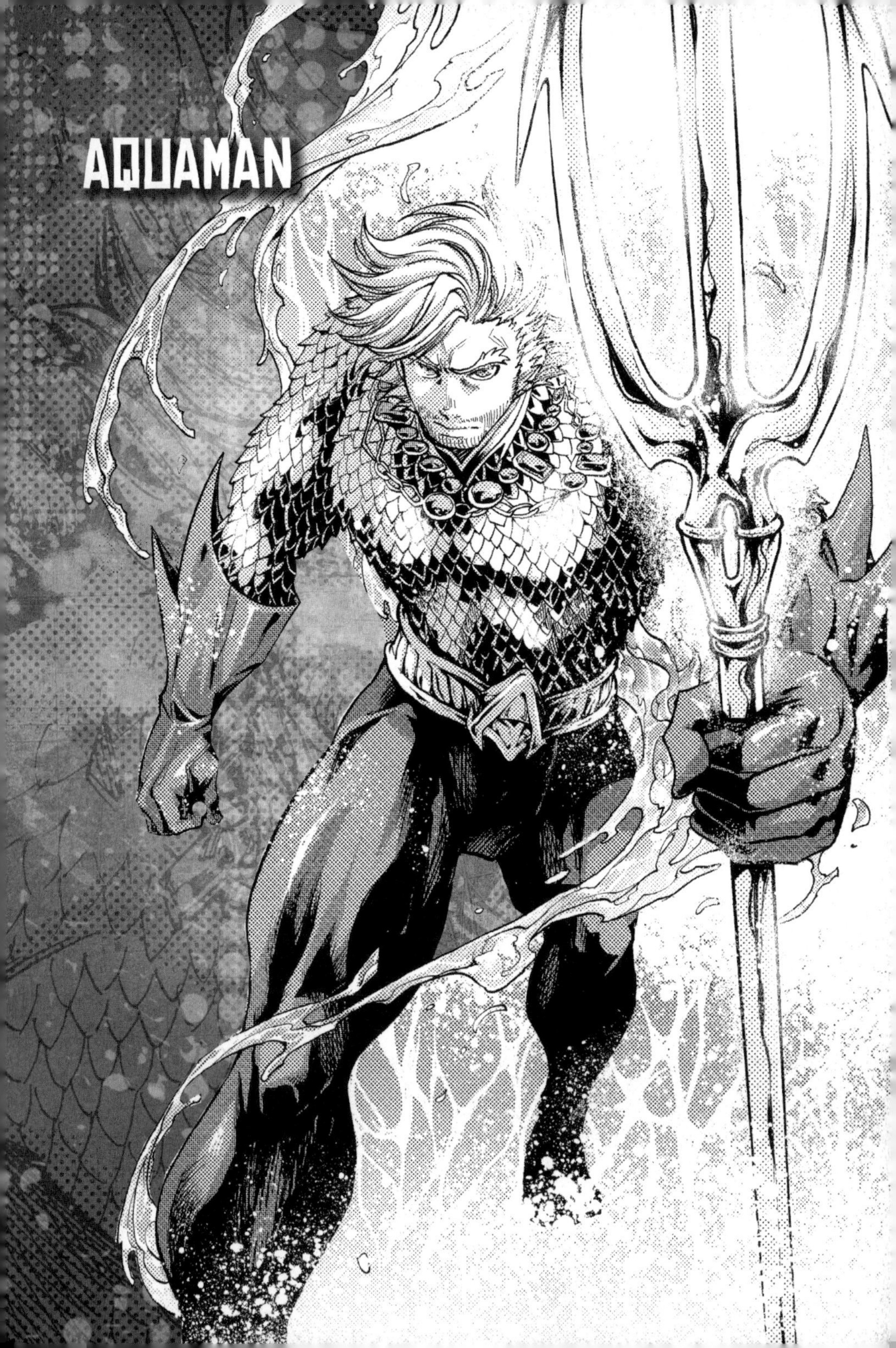
AQUAMAN

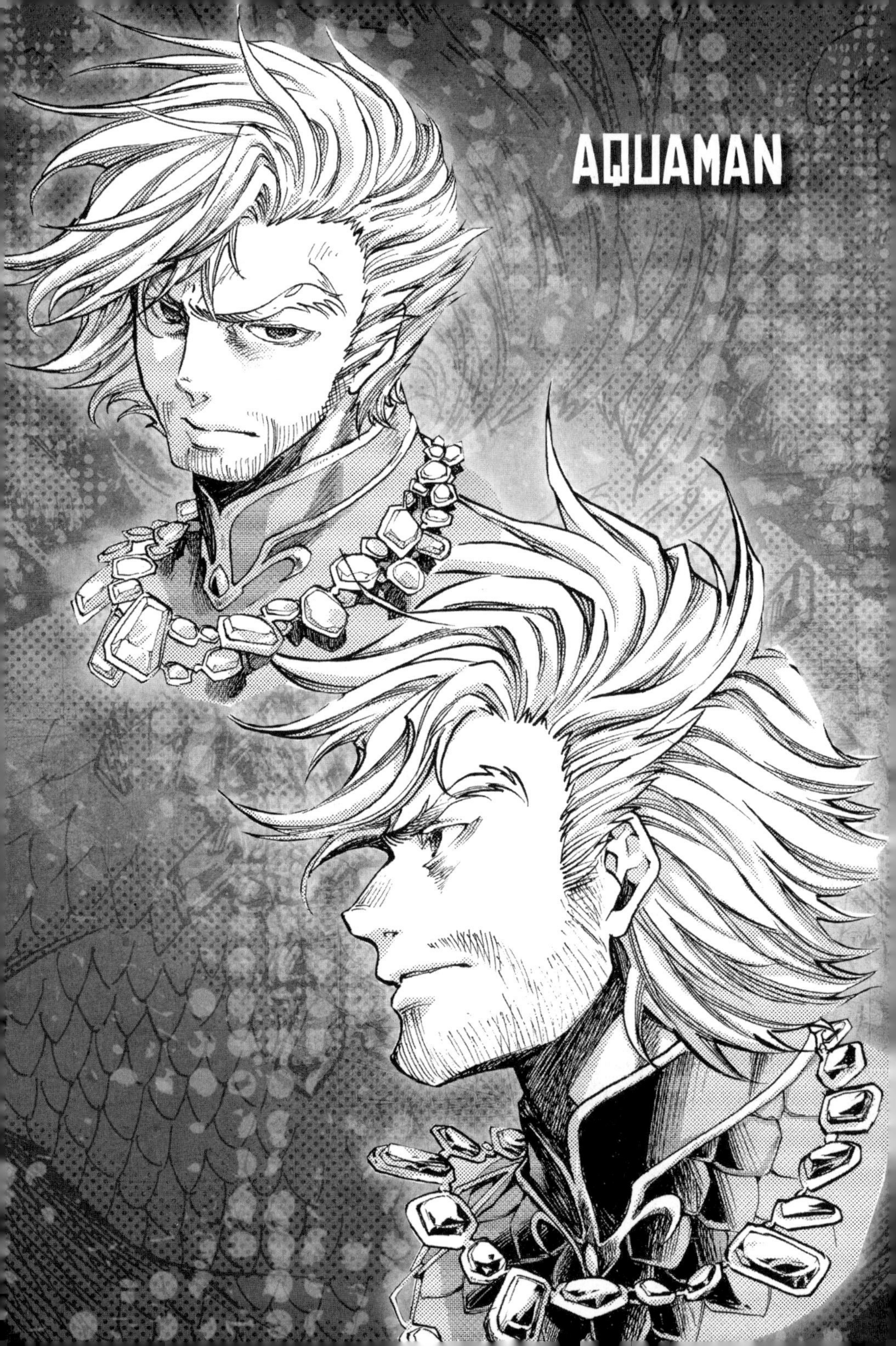
AQUAMAN

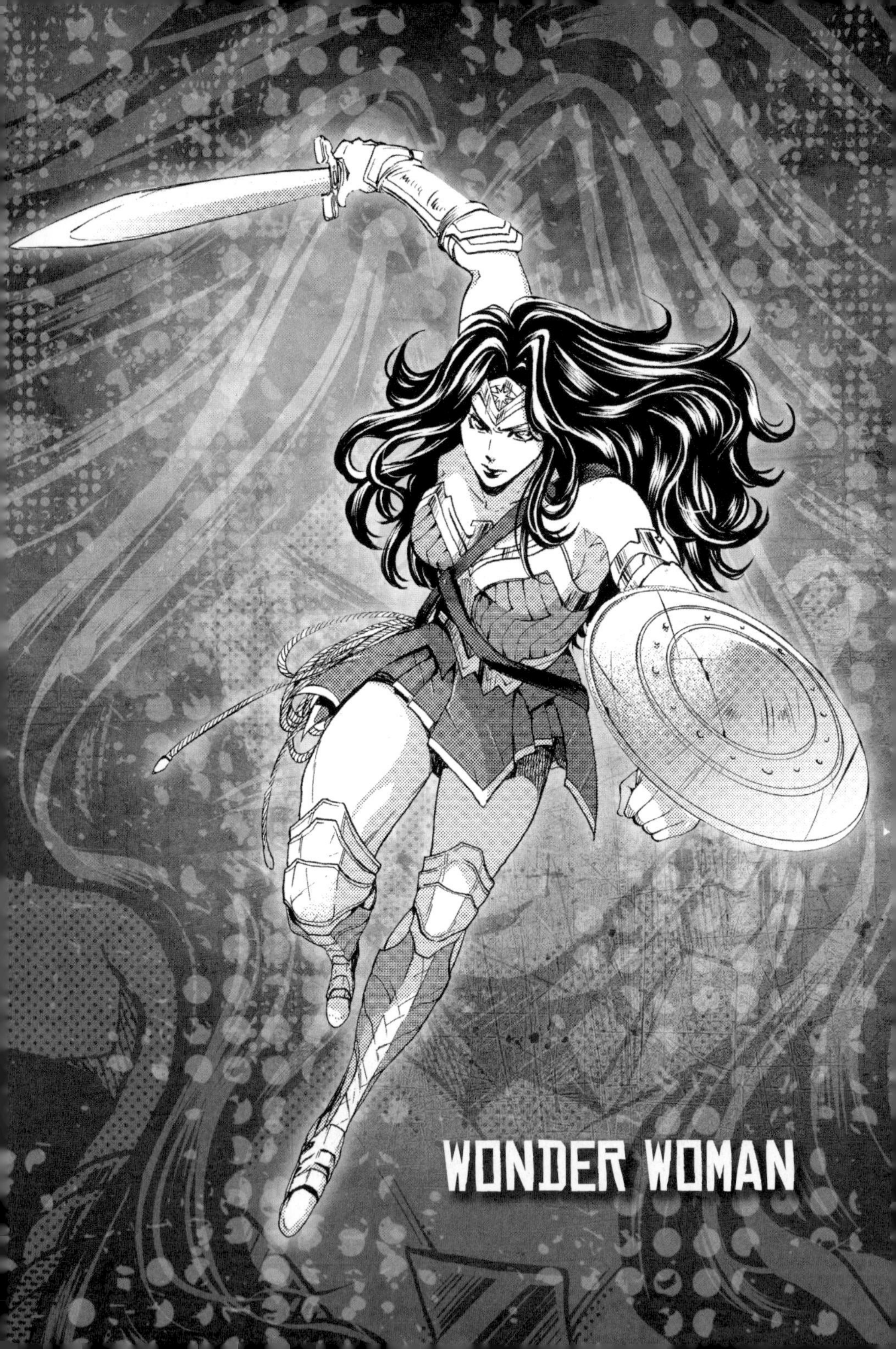
WONDER WOMAN

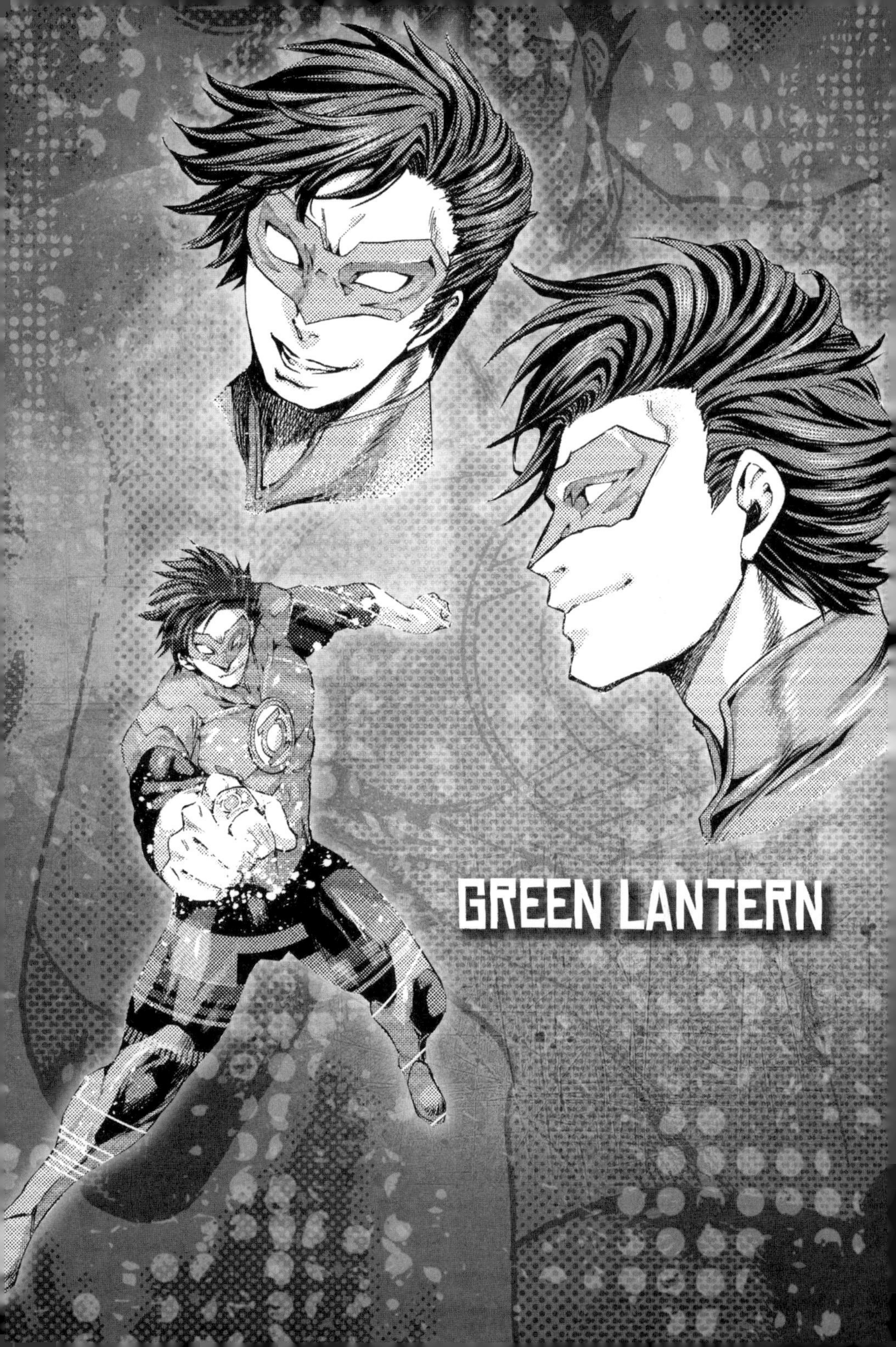
GREEN LANTERN

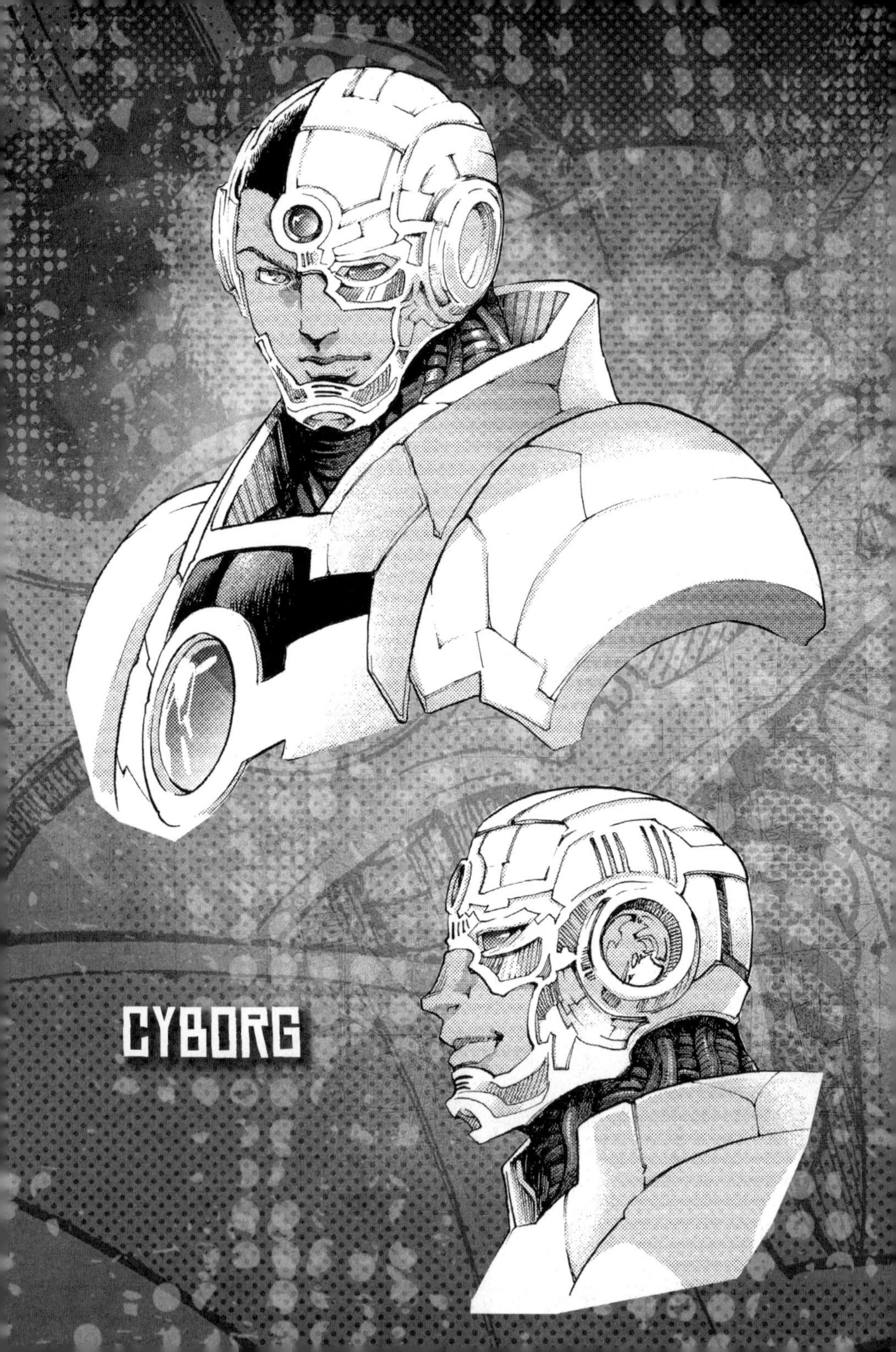
CYBORG

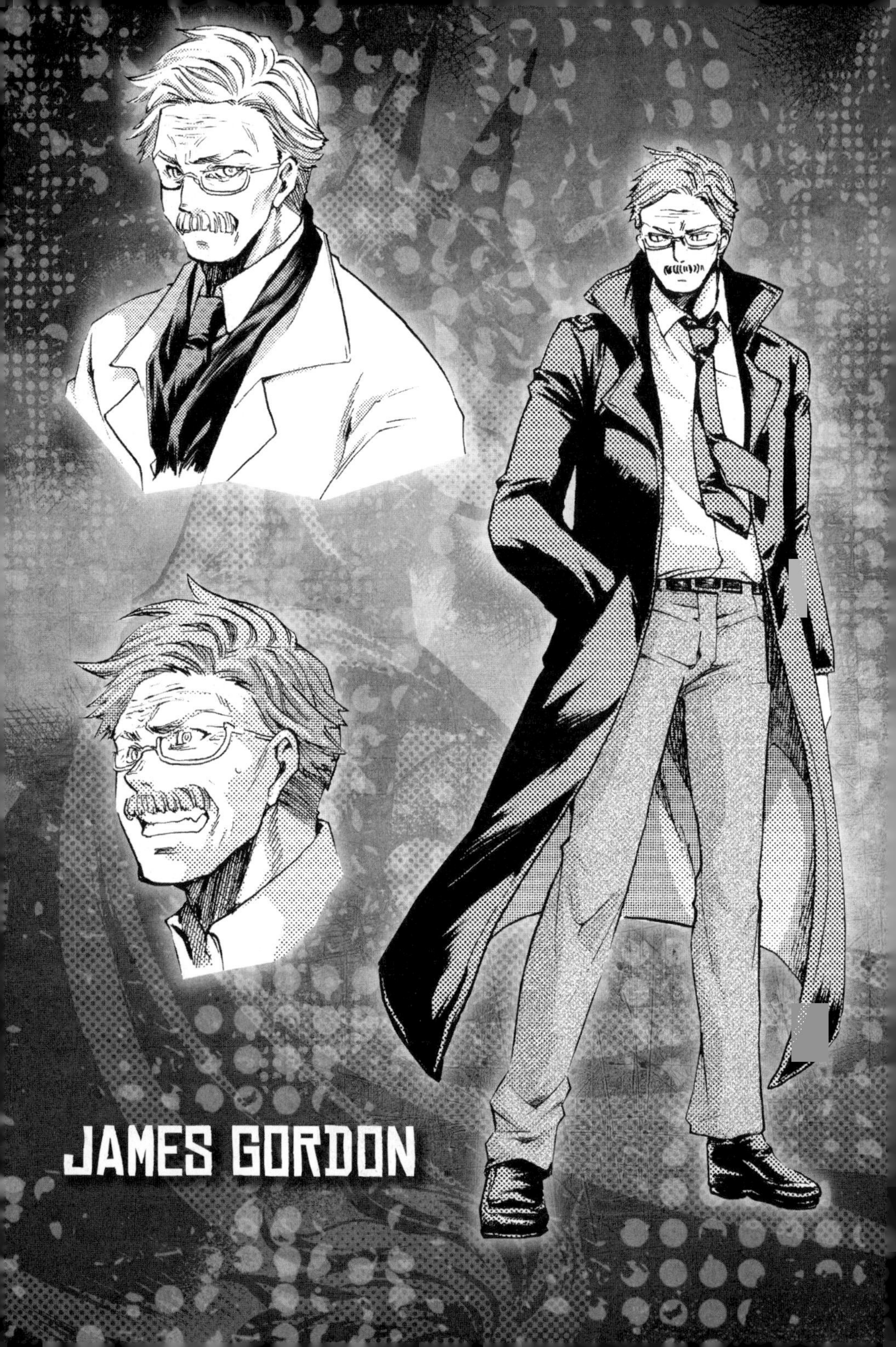
JAMES GORDON

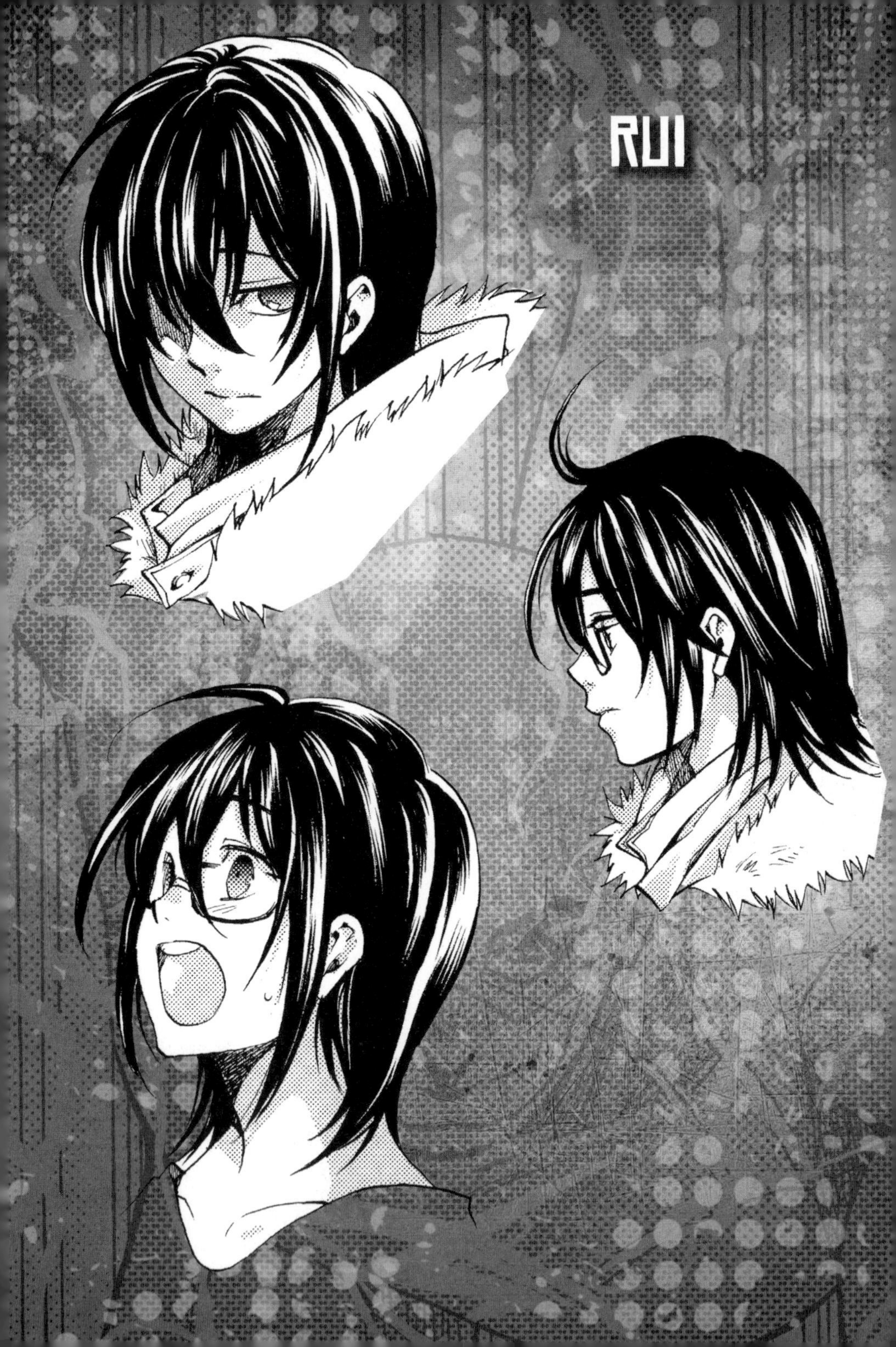
RUI

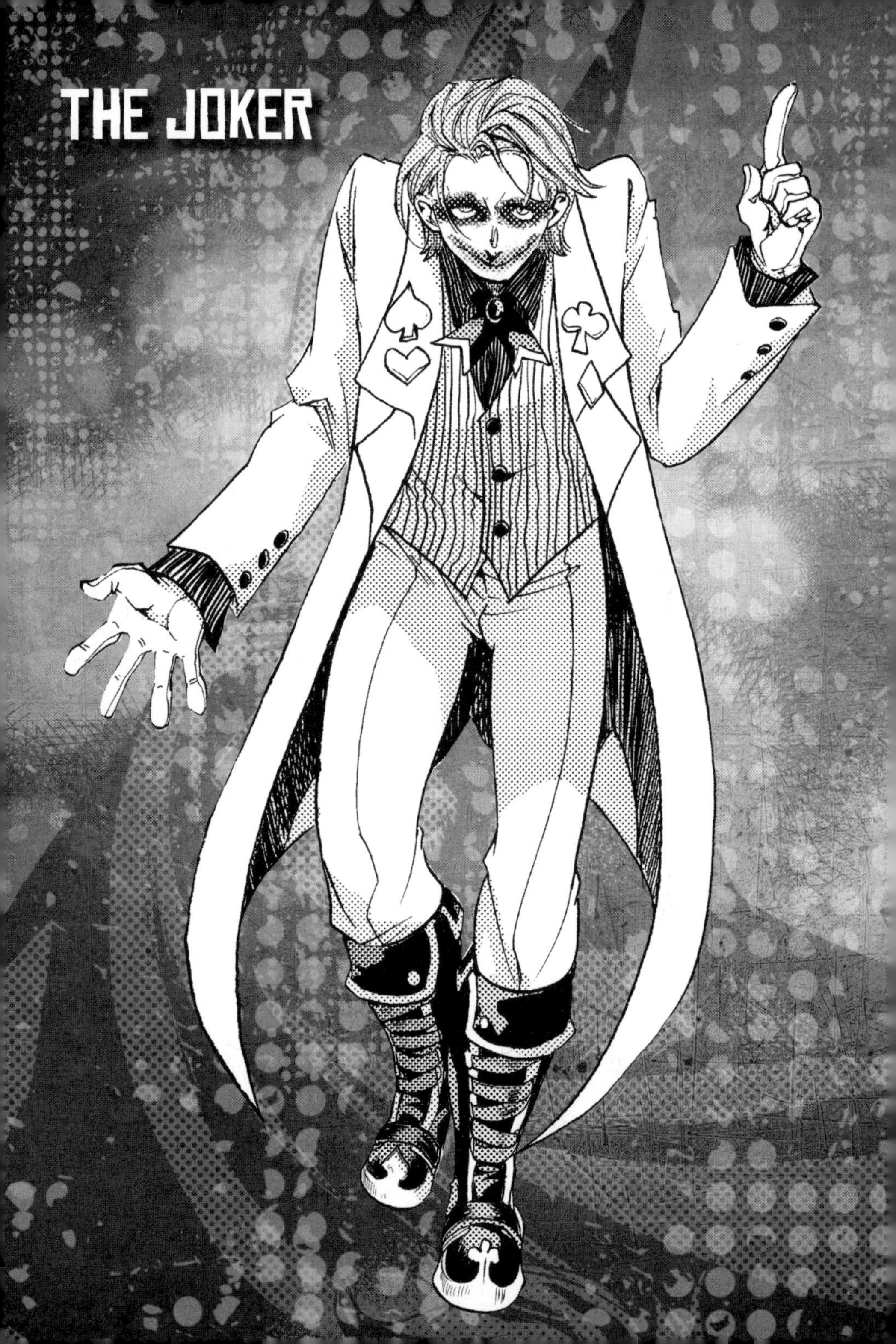
THE JOKER

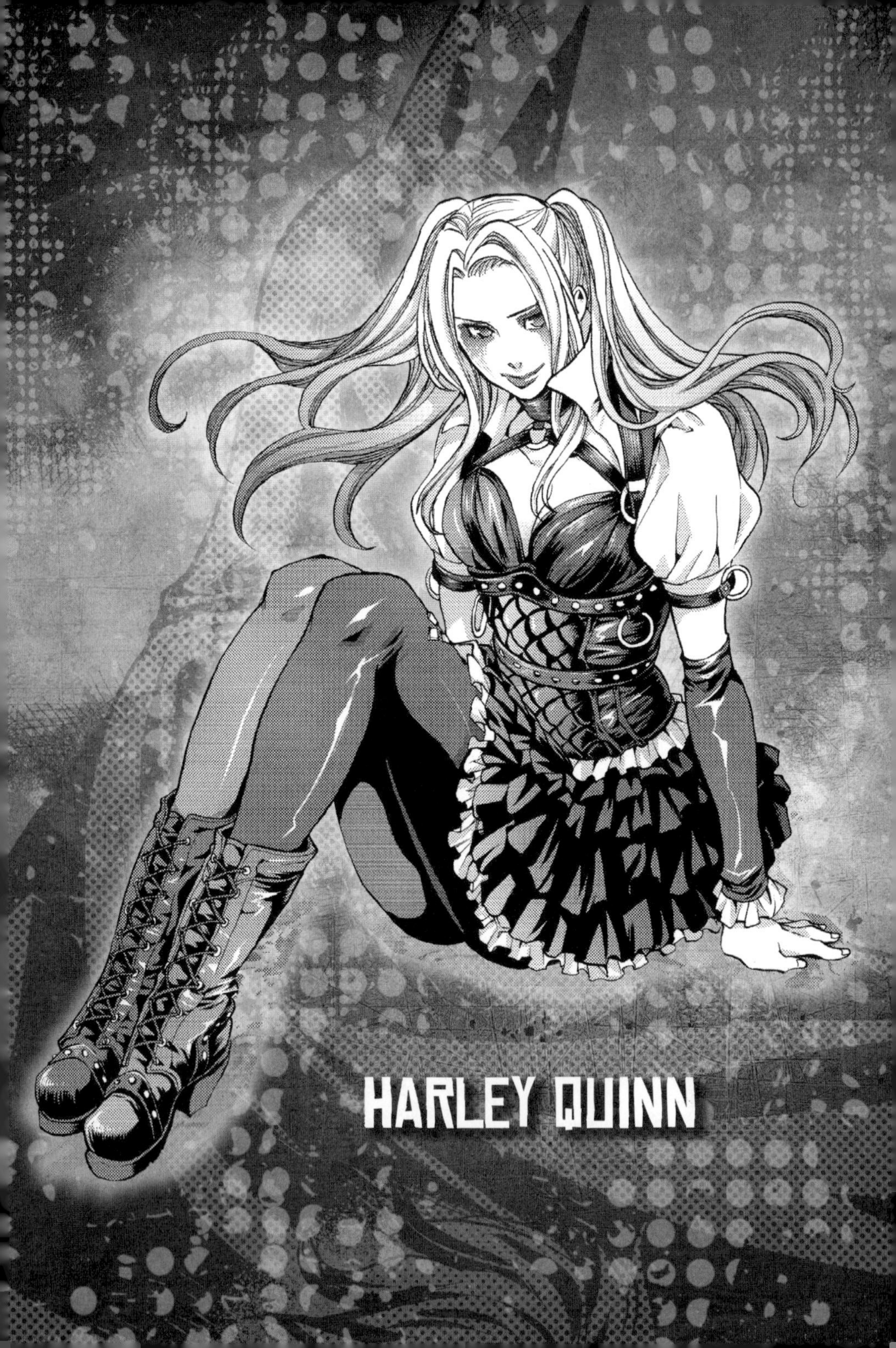
HARLEY QUINN

# AN INTERVIEW WITH SHIORI TESHIROGI

**▪Who is your favorite DC character?**

I might have to go with the Joker! After all, he's been played by a variety of actors in the movies (I especially like the Joker in *The Dark Knight*), and I also love his basic purple and green color scheme in the comics. But most of all, I'm attracted to how unfathomable he is, standing between the darkness and being comical.

**▪Did you have any difficulties drawing DC characters?**

It's a struggle every time, since these characters have such a deep history. I know only one side to the characters, and they all possess such massive levels of power that they can do anything, so it's a challenge to come up with ideas and scenes to depict their powers. Also, basically all American comics creators have great drawing abilities and artistic sense, so it might be tough to excite readers unless I up my own game.

**▪What do you think are the differences between American comics and manga?**

I feel they're alike in appearance but are quite different. With American comics, plenty of information is included in the panels and depicted powerfully, whereas with manga, there's more of an emphasis on creating stories and scenes that explore the characters' feelings, so there naturally tends to be more drawings of characters' expressions and close-ups of their faces.

That being said, American comics do have challenging panel layouts that manga doesn't have, and when they do focus on depicting emotions, it's often done in a poetic or novel way that surprises me.

**▪What has been challenging for you in making an American comic in manga form?**

I'm in the middle of a trial-and-error period, so it feels like many things have been challenging. When it comes to drawing even one American city, I'm constantly doing research, since I don't know cultural things or details. That, and if I only tried to pursue an "American comic feel," it would be awkward in Japan, so right now I'm striving to find a balance, applying a Japanese manga drawing style to an "American comic."

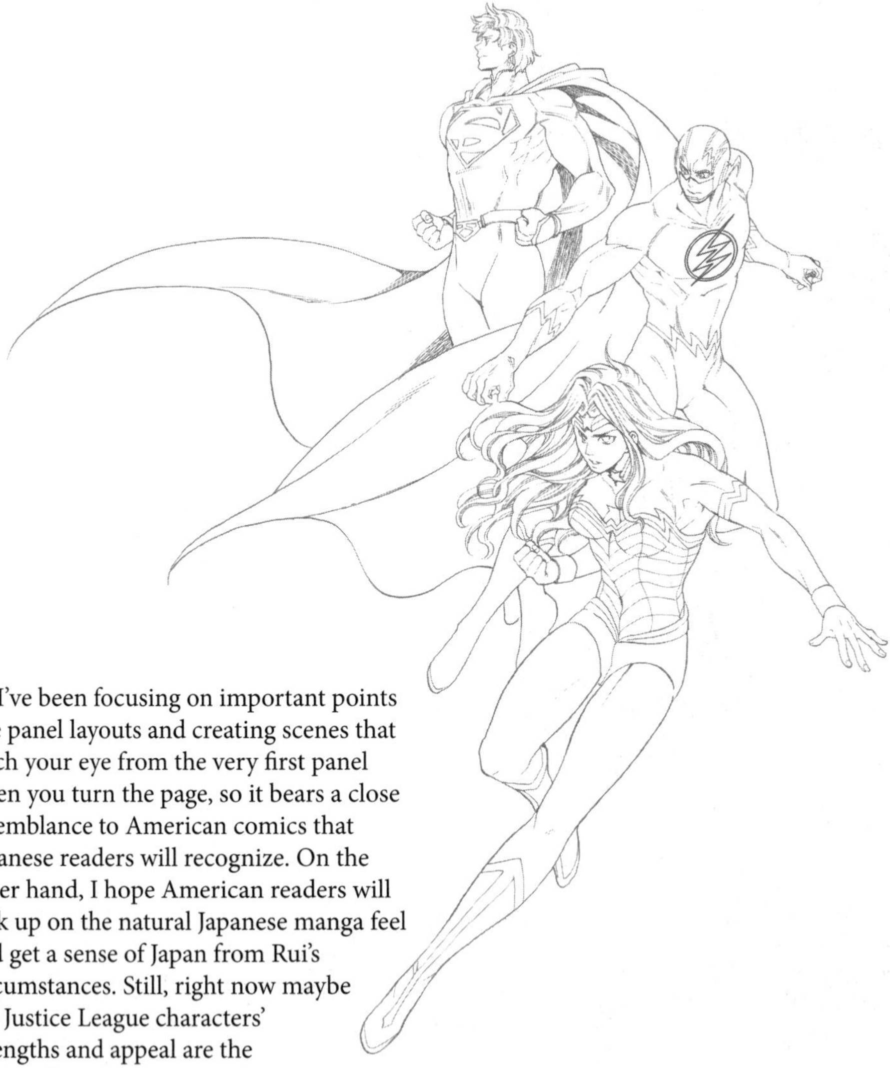

So I've been focusing on important points like panel layouts and creating scenes that catch your eye from the very first panel when you turn the page, so it bears a close resemblance to American comics that Japanese readers will recognize. On the other hand, I hope American readers will pick up on the natural Japanese manga feel and get a sense of Japan from Rui's circumstances. Still, right now maybe the Justice League characters' strengths and appeal are the biggest draw to this series.

**-END-**

# SHIORI TESHIROGI

Shiori Teshirogi is best known for writing and illustrating *Saint Seiya: The Lost Canvas – The Myth of Hades*, a spin-off of Masami Kurumada's Saint Seiya series. *The Lost Canvas* enjoyed such popularity that an anime adaptation was also produced.

Shiori lives for her pet cats, and has recently begun studying voice and practicing the Kaatsu fitness technique.

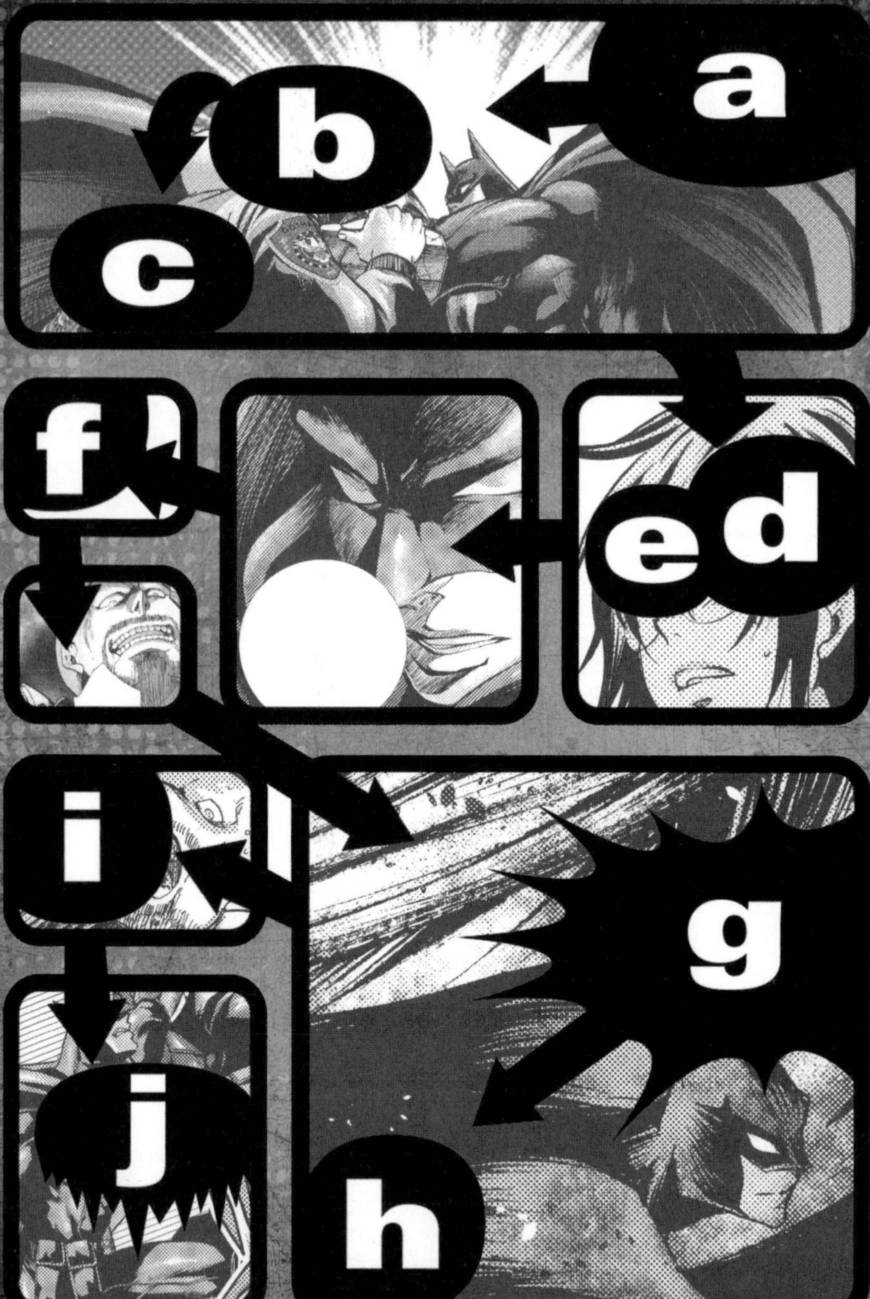
a
b
c
d
e
f
g
h
i
j

# STOP!

YOU'RE READING IN THE WRONG DIRECTION! THIS IS THE END OF THE GRAPHIC NOVEL.